Praise for *Th*

"A well-written and engaging t[...]ure on brain development, male-[...]:ors cause people to live happy lives . . . [...] will learn a great deal."
                                                —*The Washington Times*

"David Brooks is one of the most prominent public intellectuals of our time, known for, among other things, his playful dissections of the lifestyles of the American elite. Here he is chasing bigger game. *The Social Animal* is about the modern life of our species. It explores attachment, parenting, schooling, love, family, culture, achievement, marriage, politics, morality, aging, death and much more. . . . Brooks is a sharp, clear and often very funny writer."   —*The Washington Post*

"Brooks has done well to draw such vivid attention to the wide implications of the accumulated research on the mind and the triggers of human behaviour."   —*The Economist*

"Sensational . . . The book is appealing in many ways, not the least of which is Brooks' ability to synthesize vast amounts of research and present it in a fashion that calls to mind the hilarious social satire of Tom Wolfe. . . . His book aims to change our understanding of how we function and conduct our lives (we have a lot less control than we think). At the least, it will deepen your regard for the marvel that is the human brain."   —*The Philadelphia Inquirer*

"An uncommonly brilliant blend of sociology, intellect and allegory."
                                          —*Kirkus Reviews* (starred review)

"Truly the best road map for living one's life that I have ever read. . . . I can promise you that a slow careful reading of *The Social Animal* will change your life for the better. It should absolutely be on the required-reading list of every MBA program. . . . Trust me, this is a book of 'large ideas.'"   —*Kansas City Business Journal*

By David Brooks

ON PARADISE DRIVE:
HOW WE LIVE NOW (AND ALWAYS HAVE)
IN THE FUTURE TENSE

BOBOS IN PARADISE:
THE NEW UPPER CLASS AND
HOW THEY GOT THERE

THE SOCIAL ANIMAL:
THE HIDDEN SOURCES OF LOVE,
CHARACTER, AND ACHIEVEMENT

THE ROAD TO CHARACTER

THE SECOND MOUNTAIN:
THE QUEST FOR A MORAL LIFE

The

SOCIAL ANIMAL

—

The Hidden Sources of
Love, Character, and Achievement

DAVID BROOKS

Random House Trade Paperbacks
New York

2012 Random House Trade Paperback Edition

Copyright © 2011, 2012 by David Brooks

Published in the United States by Random House Trade Paperbacks,
an imprint of The Random House Publishing Group,
a division of Random House, Inc., New York.

RANDOM HOUSE TRADE PAPERBACKS and colophon
are trademarks of Random House, Inc.

Originally published in hardcover and in slightly different form
in the United States by Random House, an imprint of
The Random House Publishing Group, a division of
Random House, Inc., in 2011.

LIBRARY OF CONGRESS CATALOGING-IN-PUBLICATION DATA
Brooks, David
The social animal: the hidden sources of love, character, and
achievement / David Brooks.
p.   cm.
ISBN 978-0-8129-7937-4
eBook ISBN 978-0-679-60393-1
1. Man-woman relationships—United States.   2. Social mobility—
United States.   3. Social status—United States.   4. Elite
(Social sciences)—United States.   5. Character. I. Title.
HQ801.B76 2011   305.5'130973—dc22   2010045785

Printed in the United States of America

www.atrandom.com

Book design by Barbara M. Bachman

CONTENTS

INTRODUCTION

THIS IS THE HAPPIEST STORY YOU'VE EVER READ. IT'S ABOUT
two people who led wonderfully fulfilling lives. They had engrossing
careers, earned the respect of their friends, and made important contri-
butions to their neighborhood, their country, and their world.

And the odd thing was, they weren't born geniuses. They did okay
on the SAT and IQ tests and that sort of thing, but they had no extraordinary physical or mental gifts. They were fine-looking, but they
weren't beautiful. They played tennis and hiked, but even in high
school they weren't star athletes, and nobody would have picked them
out at that young age and said they were destined for greatness in any
sphere. Yet they achieved this success, and everyone who met them
sensed that they lived blessed lives.

How did they do it? They possessed what economists call noncognitive skills, which is the catchall category for hidden qualities that can't
be easily counted or measured, but which in real life lead to happiness
and fulfillment.

First, they had good character. They were energetic, honest, and dependable. They were persistent after setbacks and acknowledged their
mistakes. They possessed enough confidence to take risks and enough
integrity to live up to their commitments. They tried to recognize their
weaknesses, atone for their sins, and control their worst impulses.

Just as important, they had street smarts. They knew how to read
people, situations, and ideas. You could put them in front of a crowd, or
bury them with a bunch of reports, and they could develop an intuitive

feel for the landscape before them—what could go together and what would never go together, what course would be fruitful and what would never be fruitful. The skills a master seaman has to navigate the oceans, they had to navigate the world.

Over the centuries, zillions of books have been written about how to succeed. But these tales are usually told on the surface level of life. They describe the colleges people get into, the professional skills they acquire, the conscious decisions they make, and the tips and techniques they adopt to build connections and get ahead. These books often focus on an outer definition of success, having to do with IQ, wealth, prestige, and worldly accomplishments.

This story is told one level down. This success story emphasizes the role of the inner mind—the unconscious realm of emotions, intuitions, biases, longings, genetic predispositions, character traits, and social norms. This is the realm where character is formed and street smarts grow.

We are living in the middle of a revolution in consciousness. Over the past few years, geneticists, neuroscientists, psychologists, sociologists, economists, anthropologists, and others have made great strides in understanding the building blocks of human flourishing. And a core finding of their work is that we are not primarily the products of our conscious thinking. We are primarily the products of thinking that happens below the level of awareness.

The unconscious parts of the mind are not primitive vestiges that need to be conquered in order to make wise decisions. They are not dark caverns of repressed sexual urges. Instead, the unconscious parts of the mind are most of the mind—where most of the decisions and many of the most impressive acts of thinking take place. These submerged processes are the seedbeds of accomplishment.

In his book, *Strangers to Ourselves*, Timothy D. Wilson of the University of Virginia writes that the human mind can take in 11 million pieces of information at any given moment. The most generous estimate is that people can be consciously aware of forty of these. "Some researchers," Wilson notes, "have gone so far as to suggest that the unconscious mind does virtually all the work and that conscious will may be an illusion." The conscious mind merely confabulates stories that try to make sense of what the unconscious mind is doing of its own accord.

Wilson and most of the researchers I'll be talking about in this book do not go so far. But they do believe that mental processes that are inaccessible to consciousness organize our thinking, shape our judgments, form our characters, and provide us with the skills we need in order to thrive. John Bargh of Yale argues that just as Galileo "removed the earth from its privileged position at the center of the universe," so this intellectual revolution removes the conscious mind from its privileged place at the center of human behavior. This story removes it from the center of everyday life. It points to a deeper way of flourishing and a different definition of success.

The Empire of Emotion

This inner realm is illuminated by science, but it is not a dry, mechanistic place. It is an emotional and an enchanted place. If the study of the conscious mind highlights the importance of reason and analysis, study of the unconscious mind highlights the importance of passions and perception. If the outer mind highlights the power of the individual, the inner mind highlights the power of relationships and the invisible bonds between people. If the outer mind hungers for status, money, and applause, the inner mind hungers for harmony and connection—those moments when self-consciousness fades away and a person is lost in a challenge, a cause, the love of another or the love of God.

If the conscious mind is like a general atop a platform, who sees the world from a distance and analyzes things linearly and linguistically, the unconscious mind is like a million little scouts. The scouts career across the landscape, sending back a constant flow of signals and generating instant responses. They maintain no distance from the environment around them, but are immersed in it. They scurry about, interpenetrating other minds, landscapes, and ideas.

These scouts coat things with emotional significance. They come across an old friend and send back a surge of affection. They descend into a dark cave and send back a surge of fear. Contact with a beautiful landscape produces a feeling of sublime elevation. Contact with a brilliant insight produces delight, while contact with unfairness produces righteous anger. Each perception has its own flavor, texture, and force, and reactions loop around the mind in a stream of sensations, impulses, judgments, and desires.

These signals don't control our lives, but they shape our interpretation of the world and they guide us, like a spiritual GPS, as we chart our courses. If the general thinks in data and speaks in prose, the scouts crystallize with emotion, and their work is best expressed in stories, poetry, music, image, prayer, and myth.

I am not a touchy-feely person, as my wife has been known to observe. There is a great, though apocryphal, tale about an experiment in which middle-aged men were hooked up to a brain-scanning device and asked to watch a horror movie. Then they were hooked up and asked to describe their feelings for their wives. The brain scans were the same—sheer terror during both activities. I know how that feels. Nonetheless, if you ignore the surges of love and fear, loyalty and revulsion that course through us every second of every day, you are ignoring the most essential realm. You are ignoring the processes that determine what we want; how we perceive the world; what drives us forward; and what holds us back. And so I am going to tell you about these two happy people from the perspective of this enchanted inner life.

My Goals

I want to show you what this unconscious system looks like when it is flourishing, when the affections and aversions that guide us every day have been properly nurtured, the emotions properly educated. Through a thousand concrete examples, I am going to try to illustrate how the conscious and unconscious minds interact, how a wise general can train and listen to the scouts. To paraphrase Daniel Patrick Moynihan from another context, the central evolutionary truth is that the unconscious matters most. The central humanistic truth is that the conscious mind can influence the unconscious.

I'm writing this story, first, because while researchers in a wide variety of fields have shone their flashlights into different parts of the cave of the unconscious, illuminating different corners and openings, much of their work is done in academic silos. I'm going to try to synthesize their findings into one narrative.

Second, I'm going to try to describe how this research influences the way we understand human nature. Brain research rarely creates new philosophies, but it does vindicate some old ones. The research being done today reminds us of the relative importance of emotion over pure reason, social connections over individual choice, character over IQ, emergent, organic systems over linear, mechanistic ones, and the idea that we have multiple selves over the idea that we have a single self. If you want to put the philosophic implications in simple terms, the French Enlightenment, which emphasized reason, loses; the British Enlightenment, which emphasized sentiments, wins.

Third, I'm going to try to draw out the social, political, and moral implications of these findings. When Freud came up with his conception of the unconscious, it had a radical influence on literary criticism, social thinking, and even political analysis. We now have a more accurate conception of the unconscious. But these findings haven't yet had a broad impact on social thought.

Finally, I'm going to try to help counteract a bias in our culture. The conscious mind writes the autobiography of our species. Unaware of what is going on deep down inside, the conscious mind assigns itself the starring role. It gives itself credit for performing all sorts of tasks it doesn't really control. It creates views of the world that highlight those elements it can understand and ignores the rest.

As a result, we have become accustomed to a certain constricted way of describing our lives. Plato believed that reason was the civilized part of the brain, and we would be happy so long as reason subdued the primitive passions. Rationalist thinkers believed that logic was the acme of intelligence, and mankind was liberated as reason conquered habit and superstition. In the nineteenth century, the conscious mind was represented by the scientific Dr. Jekyll while the unconscious was the barbaric Mr. Hyde.

Many of these doctrines have faded, but people are still blind to the way unconscious affections and aversions shape daily life. We still have admissions committees that judge people by IQ measures and not by practical literacy. We still have academic fields that often treat human beings as rational utility-maximizing individuals. Modern society has created a giant apparatus for the cultivation of the hard skills, while failing to develop the moral and emotional faculties down below. Children are coached on how to jump through a thousand scholastic hoops. Yet by far the most important decisions they will make are about whom to marry and whom to befriend, what to love and what to despise, and how to control impulses. On these matters, they are almost entirely on their own. We are good at talking about material incentives, but bad about talking about emotions and intuitions. We are good at teaching technical skills, but when it comes to the most important things, like character, we have almost nothing to say.

My Other Purpose

The new research gives us a fuller picture of who we are. But I confess I got pulled into this subject in hopes of answering more limited and practical questions. In my day job I write about policy and politics. And over the past generations we have seen big policies yield disappointing results. Since 1983 we've reformed the education system again and again, yet more than a quarter of high-school students drop out, even though all rational incentives tell them not to. We've tried to close the gap between white and black achievement, but have failed. We've spent a generation enrolling more young people in college without understanding why so many don't graduate.

One could go on: We've tried feebly to reduce widening inequality. We've tried to boost economic mobility. We've tried to stem the tide of children raised in single-parent homes. We've tried to reduce the polarization that marks our politics. We've tried to ameliorate the boom-and-bust cycle of our economies. In recent decades, the world has tried to export capitalism to Russia, plant democracy in the Middle East, and boost development in Africa. And the results of these efforts are mostly disappointing.

The failures have been marked by a single feature: Reliance on an overly simplistic view of human nature. Many of these policies were based on the shallow social-science model of human behavior. Many of the policies were proposed by wonks who are comfortable only with traits and correlations that can be measured and quantified. They were passed through legislative committees that are as capable of speaking about the deep wellsprings of human action as they are of speaking in ancient Aramaic. They were executed by officials that have only the most superficial grasp of what is immovable and bent about human beings. So of course they failed. And they will continue to fail unless the new knowledge about our true makeup is integrated more fully into the world of public policy, unless the enchanted story is told along with the prosaic one.

The Plan

To illustrate how unconscious abilities really work and how, under the right circumstances, they lead to human flourishing, I'm going to walk, stylistically, in the footsteps of Jean-Jacques Rousseau. In 1760 Rousseau completed a book called *Emile*, which was about how human beings could be educated. Rather than just confine himself to an abstract description of human nature, he created a character named Emile and gave him a tutor, using their relationship to show how happiness looks in concrete terms. Rousseau's innovative model allowed him to do many things. It allowed him to write in a way that was fun to read. It allowed him to illustrate how general tendencies could actually play out in individual lives. It drew Rousseau away from the abstract and toward the concrete.

Without hoping to rival Rousseau's genius, I'm borrowing his method. To illustrate how the recent scientific findings play out in real life, I've created two major characters—Harold and Erica. I use these characters to show how life actually develops. The story takes place perpetually in the current moment, the early twenty-first century, because I want to describe different features of the way we live now, but I trace their paths from birth to learning, friendship to love, work to wisdom, and then to old age. I use them to describe how genes shape individual lives, how brain chemistry works in particular cases, how family structure and cultural patterns can influence development in specific terms. In short, I use these characters to bridge the gap between the sort of general patterns researchers describe and the individual experiences that are the stuff of real life.

Fellowship

Harold and Erica matured and deepened themselves during the course of their lives. That's one reason why this story is such a happy one. It is a tale of human progress and a defense of progress. It is about people who learn from their parents and their parents' parents, and who, after trials and tribulations, wind up committed to each other.

Finally, this is a story of fellowship. Because when you look deeper into the unconscious, the separations between individuals begin to get a little fuzzy. It becomes ever more obvious that the swirls that make up our own minds are shared swirls. We become who we are in conjunction with other people becoming who they are.

We have inherited an image of ourselves as Homo sapiens, as thinking individuals separated from the other animals because of our superior power of reason. This is mankind as Rodin's thinker—chin on fist, cogitating alone and deeply. In fact, we are separated from the other animals because we have phenomenal social skills that enable us to teach, learn, sympathize, emote, and build cultures, institutions, and the complex mental scaffolding of civilizations. Who are we? We are like spiritual Grand Central stations. We are junctions where millions of sensations, emotions, and signals interpenetrate every second. We are communications centers, and through some process we are not close to understanding, we have the ability to partially govern this traffic—to shift attention from one thing to another, to choose and commit. We become fully ourselves only through the ever-richening interplay of our networks. We seek, more than anything else, to establish deeper and more complete connections.

And so before I begin the story of Harold and Erica, I want to introduce you to another couple, a real couple, Douglas and Carol Hofstadter. Douglas is a professor at Indiana University, and he and Carol were very much in love. They'd throw dinner parties and then afterward, they would wash the dishes together and relive and examine the conversations they had just had.

Then Carol died of a brain tumor, when their kids were five and two. A few weeks later, Hofstadter came upon a photograph of Carol. Here's what he wrote in his book, *I Am a Strange Loop*:

> I looked at her face and looked so deeply that I felt I was behind her eyes and all at once I found myself saying, as tears flowed, "That's me! That's me!" And those simple words brought back many thoughts that I had had before, about the fusion of our souls into one higher-level entity, about the fact that at the core of both our souls lay our identical hopes and dreams for our children, about the notion that those hopes were not separate or distinct hopes but were just one hope, one clear thing that defined us both, that welded us into a unit, the kind of unit I had but dimly imagined before being married and having children. I realized that though Carol had died, that core piece of her had not died at all, but that it had lived on very determinedly in my brain.

The Greeks used to say we suffer our way to wisdom. After his wife's death, Hofstadter suffered his way toward an understanding, which as a scientist he confirms every day. The essence of that wisdom is that below our awareness there are viewpoints and emotions that help guide us as we wander through our lives. These viewpoints and emotions can leap from friend to friend and lover to lover. The unconscious is not merely a dark, primitive zone of fear and pain. It is also a place where spiritual states arise and dance from soul to soul. It collects the wisdom of the ages. It contains the soul of the species. This book will not try to discern God's role in all this. But if there is a divine creativity, surely it is active in this inner soulsphere, where brain matter produces emotion, where love rewires the neurons.

The unconscious is impulsive, emotional, sensitive, and unpredictable. It has its shortcomings. It needs supervision. But it can be brilliant. It's capable of processing blizzards of data and making daring creative leaps. Most of all, it is also wonderfully gregarious. Your unconscious, that inner extrovert, wants you to reach outward and connect. It wants you to achieve communion with work, friend, family, nation, and cause. Your unconscious wants to entangle you in the thick web of relations that are the essence of human flourishing. It longs and pushes for love, for the kind of fusion Douglas and Carol Hofstadter shared. Of all the blessings that come with being alive, it is the most awesome gift.

The Social Animal

CHAPTER I

DECISION MAKING

AFTER THE BOOM AND BUST, AFTER THE GO-GO FRENZY and the Wall Street meltdown, the Composure Class rose once again to the fore. The people in this group hadn't made their money through hedge-fund wizardry or by some big financial score. They'd earned it by climbing the meritocratic ladder of success. They'd made good grades in school, established solid social connections, joined quality companies, medical practices, and firms. Wealth had just settled down upon them gradually like a gentle snow.

You'd see a paragon of the Composure Class lunching al fresco at some shaded bistro in Aspen or Jackson Hole. He's just back from China and stopping by for a corporate board meeting on his way to a five-hundred-mile bike-a-thon to support the fight against lactose intolerance. He is asexually handsome, with a little less body fat than Michelangelo's *David*, and hair so lush and luxuriously wavy that, if you saw him in L.A., you'd ask, "Who's that handsome guy with George Clooney?" As he crosses his legs you observe that they are immeasurably long and slender. He doesn't really have thighs. Each leg is just one elegant calf on top of another.

His voice is like someone walking in socks on a Persian carpet—so calm and composed, he makes Barack Obama sound like Lenny Bruce. He met his wife at the Clinton Global Initiative. They happened to be wearing the same Doctors Without Borders support bracelets and

quickly discovered they had the same yoga instructor and their Ful-
bright Scholarships came only two years apart. They are a wonderfully
matched pair, with the only real tension between them involving their
workout routines. For some reason, today's high-prestige men do a lot
of running and biking and only work on the muscles in the lower half of
their bodies. High-status women, on the other hand, pay ferocious attention to their torsos, biceps, and forearms so they can wear sleeveless
dresses all summer and crush rocks into pebbles with their bare hands.

So Mr. Casual Elegance married Ms. Sculpted Beauty in a ceremony
officiated by Bill and Melinda Gates, and they produced three wonderful children: Effortless Brilliance, Global Compassion, and Artistically
Gifted. Like most upper- and upper-middle-class children, these kids
are really good at obscure sports. Centuries ago, members of the educated class discovered that they could no longer compete in football,
baseball, and basketball, so they stole lacrosse from the American Indians to give them something to dominate.

The kids all excelled at homogenous and proudly progressive private
high schools, carefully spending their summers interning at German
science labs. Junior year, their parents sat them down and solemnly informed them that they were now old enough to start reading *The Economist*. They went off to selective colleges with good sports teams, like
Duke and Stanford, and then they launched careers that would reflect
well on their parents—for example by becoming chief economist at the
World Bank after a satisfying few years with the Joffrey Ballet.

Members of the Composure Class spend much of their adult lives
going into rooms and making everybody else feel inferior. This effect is
only magnified by the fact that they are sincere, modest, and nice.
Nothing gives them greater pleasure than inviting you out to their
weekend place. This involves meeting them Friday afternoon at some
private airport. They arrive with their belongings in a tote bag because
when you have your own plane you don't need luggage that actually
closes.

It's best to tuck away a few granola bars if you go on one of these
jaunts because the sumptuary code of this new gentry means that they
will semi-starve you all weekend. This code involves lavish spending on

durables and spartan spending on consumables. They'll give you a ride on a multimillion-dollar Gulfstream 5, and serve a naked turkey slice sandwich on stale bread from the Safeway. They will have a nine-bedroom weekend mansion, but they brag that the furniture is from Ikea, and on Saturday they'll offer you one of those Hunger Strike Lunches—four lettuce shards and three grams of tuna salad—because they think everybody eats as healthily as they do.

It has become fashionable in these circles to have dogs a third as tall as the ceiling heights, so members of the Composure Class have these gigantic bearlike hounds named after Jane Austen characters. The dogs are crossbreeds between Saint Bernards and velociraptors, and they will gently lay their giant muzzles on tabletops or Range Rover roofs, whichever is higher. The weekend itself will consist of long bouts of strenuous activity interrupted by short surveys of the global economic situation and bright stories about their closest friends—Rupert, Warren, Colin, Sergey, Bono, and the Dalai Lama. In the evenings they will traipse down to a resort community for ice cream and a stroll. Spontaneous applause may erupt on the sidewalks as they parade their immaculate selves down the avenues, licking their interesting gelatos. People will actually choose to vacation in these places just to bathe in the aura of human perfection.

The Meeting

It was in one of those precincts that, one summer's day, a man and a woman met for the first time. These young people, in their late twenties, would go on to be the parents of Harold, one of the heroes of this story. And the first thing you should know about these soon-to-be parents is that they were both good-hearted, but sort of shallow—even though their son would go on to be intellectually ambitious and sort of profound. They had been drawn to this resort community by the gravitational pull of Composure Class success, which they someday hoped to join. They were staying in group homes with other aspiring young professionals, and a blind lunch date had been arranged by a mutual friend.

Their names were Rob and Julia, and they got their first glimpse of each other in front of a Barnes & Noble. Rob and Julia smiled broadly at each other as they approached, and a deep, primeval process kicked in. Each saw different things. Rob, being a certain sort of man, took in most of what he wanted to know through his eyes. His male Pleistocene ancestors were confronted with the puzzling fact that human females do not exhibit any physical signals when they're ovulating, unlike many other animals. So the early hunters made do with the closest markers of fertility available.

And so Rob looked for the traits almost all heterosexual men look for in a woman. David Buss surveyed over ten thousand people in thirty-seven different societies and found that standards of female beauty are pretty much the same around the globe. Men everywhere value clear skin, full lips, long lustrous hair, symmetrical features, shorter distances between the mouth and chin and between the nose and chin, and a waist-to-hip ratio of about 0.7. A study of painting going back thousands of years found that most of the women depicted had this ratio. *Playboy* bunnies tend to have this ratio, though their over-all fleshiness can change with the fashions. Even the famously thin su-permodel Twiggy had exactly a 0.73 percent waist-to-hip ratio.

Rob liked what he saw. He was struck by a vague and alluring sense that Julia carried herself well, for there is nothing that so enhances beauty as self-confidence. He enjoyed the smile that spread across her face, and unconsciously noted that the end of her eyebrows dipped down. The orbicularis oculi muscle, which controls this part of the eyebrow, cannot be consciously controlled, so when the tip of the eyebrow dips, that means the smile is genuine not fake.

Rob registered her overall level of attractiveness, subliminally aware that attractive people generally earn significantly higher incomes.

Rob also liked the curve he instantly discerned under her blouse, and followed its line with an appreciation that went to the core of his being. Somewhere in the back of his brain, he knew that a breast is merely an organ, a mass of skin and fat. And yet, he was incapable of thinking in that way. He went through his days constantly noting their presence around him. The line of a breast on a piece of paper was enough to arrest his attention. The use of the word "boob" was a source of subliminal annoyance to him, because that undignified word did not deserve to be used in connection with so holy a form, and he sensed it was used, mostly by women, to mock his deep fixation.

And of course breasts exist in the form they do precisely to arouse this reaction. There is no other reason human breasts should be so much larger than the breasts of other primates. Apes are flat-chested. Larger human breasts do not produce more milk than smaller ones. They serve no nutritional purpose, but they do serve as signaling devices and set off primitive light shows in the male brain. Men consistently rate women with attractive bodies and unattractive faces more highly than women with attractive faces and unattractive bodies. Nature does not go in for art for art's sake, but it does produce art.

Julia had a much more muted reaction upon seeing her eventual life mate. This is not because she was unimpressed by the indisputable hotness of the man in front of her. Women are sexually attracted to men with larger pupils. Women everywhere prefer men who have symmetrical features and are slightly older, taller, and stronger than they are. By these and other measures, Harold's future father passed the test.

It's just that she was, by nature and upbringing, guarded and slow to trust. She, like 89 percent of all people, did not believe in love at first sight. Moreover, she was compelled to care less about looks than her future husband was. Women, in general, are less visually aroused than men, a trait that has nearly cut the market for pornography in half.

That's because while Pleistocene men could pick their mates on the basis of fertility cues they could discern at a glance, Pleistocene women faced a more vexing problem. Human babies require years to become self-sufficient, and a single woman in a prehistoric environment could not gather enough calories to provide for a family. She was compelled to choose a man not only for insemination, but for companionship and continued support. And to this day, when a woman sets her eyes upon a potential mate, her time frame is different from his.

That's why men will leap into bed more quickly than women. Various research teams have conducted a simple study. They pay an attractive woman to go up to college men and ask them to sleep with her.

Seventy-five percent of men say yes to this proposition, in study after study. Then they have an attractive man approach college women with the same offer. Zero percent say yes.

Women have good reasons to be careful. While most men are fertile, there is wide variation among the hairier sex when it comes to stability. Men are much more likely to have drug and alcohol addictions. They are much more likely to murder than women, and much, much more likely to abandon their children. There are more lemons in the male population than in the female population, and women have found that it pays to trade off a few points in the first-impression department in exchange for reliability and social intelligence down the road.

So while Rob was looking at cleavage, Julia was looking for signs of trustworthiness. She didn't need to do this consciously—thousands of years of genetics and culture had honed her trusting sensor.

Marion Eals and Irwin Silverman of York University have conducted studies that suggest women are on average 60 to 70 percent more proficient than men at remembering details from a scene and the locations of objects placed in a room. Over the past few years, Julia had used her powers of observation to discard entire categories of men as potential partners, and some of her choices were idiosyncratic. She rejected men who wore Burberry, because she couldn't see herself looking at the same damn pattern on scarves and raincoats for the rest of her life. Somehow she was able to discern poor spellers just by looking at them, and they made her heart wither. She viewed fragranced men the way Churchill viewed the Germans—they were either at your feet or at your throat. She would have nothing to do with men who wore sports-related jewelry because her boyfriend should not love Derek Jeter more than her. And though there had recently been a fad for men who can cook, she was unwilling to have a serious relationship with anybody who could dice better than she could or who would surprise her with smugly unpretentious Gruyère grilled cheese sandwiches as a makeup present after a fight. It was simply too manipulative.

She looked furtively at Rob as he approached across the sidewalk. Janine Willis and Alexander Todorov of Princeton have found that people can make snap judgments about a person's trustworthiness, competence, aggressiveness and likability within the first tenth of a second. These sorts of first glimpses are astonishingly accurate in predicting how people will feel about each other months later. People rarely revise their first impression, they just become more confident that they are right. In other research, Todorov gave his subjects microsecond glimpses of the faces of competing politicians. His research subjects could predict, with 70 percent accuracy, who would win the election between the two candidates.

Using her own powers of instant evaluation, Julia noticed Rob was good-looking, but he was not one of those men who are so good-looking that they don't need to be interesting. While Rob was mentally undressing her, she was mentally dressing him. At the moment, he was wearing brown corduroy slacks, which did credit to Western civilization, and a deep purplish/maroonish pullover, so that altogether he looked like an elegant eggplant. He had firm but not ferretlike cheeks, suggesting he would age well and some day become the most handsome man in his continuing-care retirement facility.

He was tall, and since one study estimated that each inch of height corresponds to $6,000 of annual salary in contemporary America, that matters. He also radiated a sort of inner calm, which would make him infuriating to argue with. He seemed, to her quick judging eye, to be one of those creatures blessed by fate, who has no deep calluses running through his psyche, no wounds to cover or be wary of.

But just as the positive judgments began to pile up, Julia's frame of mind flipped. Julia knew that one of her least-attractive features was that she had a hypercritical inner smart-ass. She'd be enjoying the company of some normal guy, and suddenly she would begin with the scrutiny. Before it was over, she was Dorothy Parker and the guy was a pool of metaphorical blood on the floor.

Julia's inner smart-ass noticed that Rob was one of those guys who believes nobody really cares if your shoes are shined. His fingernails were uneven. Moreover, he was a bachelor. Julia distrusted bachelors as somehow unserious, and since she would never date a married man, this cut down the pool of men she could uncritically fall in love with.

John Tierney of *The New York Times* has argued that many single people are afflicted with a "Flaw-O-Matic," an internal device that instantly spots shortcomings in a potential mate. A man might be handsome and brilliant, Tierney observes, but he gets cast in the discard pile because he has dirty elbows. A woman may be partner in a big law firm, but she's vetoed as a long-term mate because she mispronounces "Goethe."

Julia had good reason to partake in what scientists call the "men are pigs" bias. Women tend to approach social situations with an unconscious decision-making structure that assumes men are primarily interested in casual sex and nothing more. They're like overly sensitive smoke detectors, willing to be falsely alarmed because it's safer to err on the side of caution than to trust too willingly. Men, on the other hand, have the opposite error bias. They imagine there is sexual interest when none exists.

Julia went through cycles of hope and mistrust in just a few blinks of the eye. The tide of opinion, sadly, was running against Rob. Her inner smart-ass was going wild. But then, fortunately, he walked up and said hello.

The Meal

As destiny would have it, Rob and Julia were meant for each other. Despite what you've heard about opposites attracting, people usually fall in love with people like themselves. As Helen Fisher wrote in a chapter of *The New Psychology of Love*, "Most men and women fall in love with individuals of the same ethnic, social, religious, educational and economic background, those of similar physical attractiveness, a comparable intelligence, similar attitudes, expectations, values, interests, and those with similar social and communication skills." There's even some evidence that people tend to pick partners with noses of similar breadth to their own and eyes about the same distance apart.

One of the by-products of this pattern is that people tend to unwittingly pick partners who have lived near them for at least parts of their lives. A study in the 1950s found that 54 percent of the couples who applied for marriage licenses in Columbus, Ohio, lived within sixteen blocks of each other when they started going out, and 37 percent lived within five blocks of each other. In college, people are much more likely to go out with people who have dorm rooms on the same hallway or the same courtyard. Familiarity breeds trust.

Rob and Julia quickly discovered they had a lot in common. They had the same Edward Hopper poster on their walls. They had been at the same ski resort at the same time and had similar political views. They discovered they both loved *Roman Holiday*, had the same opinions about the characters in *The Breakfast Club*, and shared the same misimpression that it was a sign of sophistication to talk about how much you loved Eames chairs and the art of Mondrian.

Furthermore, they both affected discerning connoisseurship over extremely prosaic things such as hamburgers and iced tea. They both exaggerated their popularity while reminiscing about high school. They had hung out at the same bars and had seen the same rock bands on the same tours. It was like laying down a series of puzzle pieces that astoundingly matched. People generally overestimate how distinct their own lives are, so the commonalities seemed to them like a series of miracles. The coincidences gave their relationship an aura of destiny fulfilled.

Without realizing it, they were also measuring each other's intellectual compatibility. As Geoffrey Miller notes in *The Mating Mind*, people tend to choose spouses of similar intelligence, and the easiest way to measure someone else's intelligence is through their vocabulary. People with an 80 IQ will know words such as "fabric," "enormous," and "conceal" but not words such as "sentence," "consume," and "commerce." People with 90 IQs will know the latter three words, but probably not "designate," "ponder," or "reluctant." So people who are getting to know each other subconsciously measure to see if their vocabularies mesh, and they adapt to the other person's level.

The server stopped by their table, and they ordered drinks and then lunch. It is an elemental fact of life that we get to choose what we will order, but we do not get to choose what we like. Preferences are formed below the level of awareness, and it so happened that Rob loved cabernet but disliked merlot. Unfortunately, Julia ordered a glass of the former, so Rob had to select a glass of the latter, just to appear different. The food at their lunch was terrible, but the meal was wondrous. Rob had never actually been to this restaurant, but had selected it on the advice of their mutual friend, who was highly confident about his own judgments. It turned out to be one of those restaurants with ungraspable salads. Julia, anticipating this, had chosen an appetizer that could be easily forked and a main dish that didn't require cutlery expertise. But Rob had selected a salad, which sounded good on the menu, composed of splaying green tentacles that could not be shoved into his mouth without brushing salad dressing three inches on either side of his cheeks. In some retro-nostalgia for 1990s tall cuisine, his entrée was a three-story steak, potato, and onion concoction that looked like the Devils Tower from *Close Encounters of the Third Kind*. Getting a biteful was like chipping off a geological stratum from Mount Rushmore.

But none of it mattered, because Rob and Julia clicked. Over the main course, Julia described her personal history—her upbringing, her collegiate interests in communications, her work as a publicist and its frustrations, and her vision for the PR firm she would someday start, using viral marketing.

Julia leaned in toward Rob as she explained her mission in life. She took rapid-fire sips of water, chewing incredibly fast, like a chipmunk, so she could keep on talking. Her energy was infectious. "This could be huge!" she enthused. "This could change everything!"

Ninety percent of emotional communication is nonverbal. Gestures are an unconscious language that we use to express not only our feelings but to constitute them. By making a gesture, people help produce an internal state. Rob and Julia licked their lips, leaned forward in their chairs, glanced at each other out of the corners of their eyes, and performed all the other tricks of unconscious choreography that people do while flirting. Unawares, Julia did the head cant women do to signal arousal, a slight tilt of the head that exposed her neck. She'd be appalled if she could see her supposedly tough-as-nails self in the mirror at this moment, because there she was like any Marilyn Monroe wannabe—

doing the hair flip, raising her arms to adjust her hair, and heaving her chest up into view.

Julia hadn't yet realized how much she enjoyed talking to Rob. But the waitress noticed the feverish warmth on their faces, and was pleased, since men on a first date are the biggest tippers of all. Only days later did the importance of the meal sink in. Decades hence, Julia would remember the smallest detail of this lunch, and not only the fact that her husband-to-be ate all the bread in the breadbasket.

And through it all the conversation flowed.

Words are the fuel of courtship. Other species win their mates through a series of escalating dances, but humans use conversation. Geoffrey Miller notes that most adults have a vocabulary of about sixty thousand words. To build that vocabulary, children must learn ten to twenty words a day between the ages of eighteen months and eighteen years. And yet the most frequent one hundred words account for 60 percent of all conversations. The most common four thousand words account for 98 percent of conversations. Why do humans bother knowing those extra fifty-six thousand words?

Miller believes that humans learn the words so they can more effectively impress and sort out potential mates. He calculates that if a couple speaks for two hours a day, and utters on average three words a second, and has sex for three months before conceiving a child (which would have been the norm on the prehistoric savanna), then a couple will have exchanged about a million words before conceiving a child. That's a lot of words, and plenty of opportunities for people to offend, bore, or annoy each other. It's ample opportunity to fight, make up, explore, and reform. If a couple is still together after all that chatter, there's a decent chance they'll stay together long enough to raise a child.

Harold's parents were just in the first few thousand words of what, over the course of their lifetimes, would be millions and millions, and things were going fabulously. You'd think, if you listened to cultural stereotypes, that women are the more romantic of the sexes. In fact, there's plenty of evidence that men fall in love more quickly, and subscribe more to the conviction that true love lasts forever. So much of the conversation, for this first night and for several months thereafter, would be about getting Julia to let down her guard.

Rob would have been unrecognizable to his buddies if they could see him now. He was talking knowledgeably about his relationships. He seemed completely unaware of his own physical gifts, though he'd been known in other circumstances to stare admiringly at his own forearms for minutes at a time. All trace of cynicism was gone. Though men normally spend two-thirds of their conversational time talking about themselves, in this conversation he was actually talking about Julia's problems. David Buss's surveys suggest that kindness is the most important quality desired in a sexual partner by both men and women. Courtship largely consists of sympathy displays, in which partners try to prove to each other how compassionate they can be, as anybody who has seen dating couples around children and dogs can well attest.

Of course, there are other, less noble calculations going on as people choose their mates. Like veteran stock-market traders, people respond in predictable, if unconscious, ways to the valuations of the social marketplace. They instinctively seek the greatest possible return on their own market value.

The richer the man, the younger the woman he is likely to mate with. The more beautiful the woman, the richer the man. A woman's attractiveness is an outstanding predictor of her husband's annual income.

Men who are deficient in one status category can compensate if they are high in another. Several studies of online dating have shown that short men can be as successful in the dating market if they earn more than taller men. Guenter Hitsch, Ali Hortacsu, and Dan Ariely calculate that a man who is five foot six can do as well as a six-footer if he earns $175,000 a year more. An African American man can do as well with white women if he earns $154,000 more than a white man with similar attributes. (Women resist dating outside their ethnic group much more than men do.)

Along with everything else, Rob and Julia were doing these sorts of calculations unconsciously in their heads—weighing earnings-to-looks ratios, calculating social-capital balances. And every signal suggested they had found a match.

The Stroll

Human culture exists in large measure to restrain the natural desires of the species. The tension of courtship is produced by the need to slow down when the instincts want to rush right in. Both Rob and Julia were experiencing powerful impulsion at this point, and were terrified of saying something too vehement and forward. People who succeed in courtship are able to pick up the melody and rhythm of a relationship. Through a mutual process of reading each other and restraining themselves, their relationship will or will not establish its own synchronicity, and it is through this process that they will establish the implicit rules that will forever after govern how they behave toward each other.

"The greatest happiness love can offer is the first pressure of hands between you and your beloved," the French writer Stendhal once observed. Harold's parents were by this point engaging in the sort of verbal interplay that was less like conversation and more like grooming. When they got up from the table, Rob wanted to place his hand on the small of Julia's back to guide her to the door but was afraid she might be displeased by the implied intimacy. Julia silently regretted bringing her day bag, which was roughly the size of a minivan, and big enough to hold books, phones, pagers, and possibly a moped. She'd been afraid that morning that bringing a small bag would look too hopeful—too datelike—but here she was at one of the most important meals of her life, and she was misbagged!

Rob finally touched her arm as they walked out the door, and she looked up at him with that trusting smile. They walked down the sidewalk past the high-end stationery stores, unaware they were already doing the lovers' walk—bodies close to each other, beaming out at the space in front of them with a wide-open glee. Julia really felt comfortable with Rob. Throughout the meal he'd looked at her intently—not with that weird obsessive look Jimmy Stewart gave Kim Novak in *Vertigo*, but with an anchoring gaze that pulled her in.

For his part, Rob actually shivered as he escorted Julia back to her car. His heart was palpitating and his breathing was fast. He felt he'd been extraordinarily witty over lunch, encouraged by her flashing eyes. Vague sensations swept over him, which he didn't understand. Brazenly, he asked if he could see her tomorrow, and of course she said yes. He didn't want to just shake her hand, and a kiss was too forward. So he squeezed her arm and brushed his cheek against hers.

As Julia and Rob semi-embraced, they silently took in each other's pheromones. Their cortisol levels dropped. Smell is a surprisingly powerful sense in these situations. People who lose their sense of smell suffer greater emotional deterioration than people who lose their vision. That's because smell is a powerful way to read emotions. In one experiment conducted at the Monell Center, researchers asked men and women to tape gauze pads under their arms and then watch either a horror movie or a comedy. Research subjects, presumably well compensated, then sniffed the pads. They could somehow tell, at rates higher than chance, which pads had the smell of laughter and which pads had the smell of fear, and women were much better at this test than men.

Later in their relationship, Rob and Julia would taste each other's saliva and then collect genetic information. According to famous research by Claus Wedekind at the University of Lausanne, women are attracted to men whose human leukocyte antigen code of their DNA are most different from their own. Complementary HLA coding is thought to produce better immune systems in their offspring.

Aided by chemistry and carried along by feeling, Rob and Julia both sensed that this had been one of the most important interviews of their lives. In fact, it would turn out to be the most important two hours that each of them would ever spend, for there is no decision more important to lifelong happiness than the decision about whom to marry. Over the course of that early afternoon, they had begun to make a decision.

The meal had been delightful. But they had also just been through a rigorous intellectual exam that made the SAT seem like kindergarten. Each of them had spent the past 120 minutes performing delicate social tasks. They'd demonstrated wit, complaisance, empathy, tact, and timing. They'd obeyed a social script that applies to first dates in their culture. They had each made a thousand discriminating judgments. They had measured their emotional responses with discriminations so fine no gauge could quantify them. They had decoded silent gestures—a grin, a look, a shared joke, a pregnant pause. They had put each other through a series of screens and filters, constantly evaluating each other's performance and their own. Every few minutes they had admitted each other one step closer toward the intimacy of their hearts.

These mental tasks only seemed easy because the entire history of life on this earth had prepared them for this moment. Rob and Julia didn't need to take a course in making these sorts of social-bonding decisions the way they had taken a course in, say, algebra. The mental work was mostly done unconsciously. It seemed effortless. It just came naturally.

So far, they couldn't put their conclusions into words, because their sensations had not cohered into any conscious message. But the choice to fall in love would just sort of well up inside of them. It didn't feel like they had made a choice, but that a choice had made them. A desire for the other had formed. It would take each of them awhile to realize that a ferocious commitment to the other had already been made. The heart, Blaise Pascal observed, has reasons the head knows not of.

But this is how deciding works. This is how knowing what we want happens—not only when it comes to marriage but in many of the other important parts of life. Deciding whom to love is not a strange alien form of decision making, a romantic interlude in the midst of normal life. Instead, decisions about whom to love are more intense versions of the sorts of decisions we make throughout the course of life, from what food to order to what career to pursue. Decision making is an inherently emotional business.

Love's Role

Revolutions in our understanding of ourselves begin in the oddest ways. One of the breakthroughs that helped us understand the interplay between emotion and decision making began with a man named Elliot, whose story has become one of the most famous in the world of brain research. Elliot had suffered damage to the frontal lobes of his brain as the result of a tumor. Elliot was intelligent, well informed, and diplomatic. He possessed an attractively wry view of the world. But, after surgery, Elliot began to have trouble managing his day. Whenever he tried to accomplish something, he'd ignore the most important parts of the task and get sidetracked by trivial distractions. At work he'd set out to file some reports, but then would just sit down and start reading them. He'd spend an entire day trying to decide on a filing system. He'd spend hours deciding where to have lunch, and still couldn't settle on a place. He made foolish investments that cost him his life savings. He divorced his wife, married a woman his family disapproved of, and quickly divorced again. In short, he was incapable of making sensible choices.

Elliot went to see a scientist named Antonio Damasio, who evaluated him with a battery of tests. They showed that Elliot had a superior IQ. He had an excellent memory for numbers and geometric designs and was proficient at making estimates based upon incomplete information. But in the many hours of conversation Damasio had with Elliot, he noticed that the man never showed any emotion. He could recount the tragedy that had befallen his life without the slightest tinge of sadness.

Damasio showed Elliot gory and traumatic images from earthquakes, fires, accidents, and floods. Elliot understood how he was supposed to respond emotionally to these images. He just didn't actually feel anything. Damasio began to investigate whether Elliot's reduced emotions played a role in his decision-making failures.

A series of further tests showed that Elliot understood how to imagine different options when making a decision. He was able to understand conflicts between two moral imperatives. In short, he could prepare himself to make a choice between a complex range of possibilities.

What Elliot couldn't do was actually make the choice. He was incapable of assigning value to different options. As Damasio put it, "His decision-making landscape [was] hopelessly flat."

Another of Damasio's research subjects illustrated the same phenomenon in stark form. This middle-aged man, who had also lost his emotional functions through a brain injury, was finishing an interview session in Damasio's office, and Damasio suggested two alternative dates for their next meeting. The man pulled out his datebook and began listing the pros and cons of each option. For the better part of half an hour, he went on and on, listing possible conflicts, potential weather conditions on the two days in question, the proximity of other appointments. "It took enormous discipline to listen to all this without pounding the table and telling him to stop," Damasio wrote. But he and his fellow researchers just stood there watching. Finally Damasio interrupted the man's musings and just assigned him a date to return. Without a pause, the man said, "That's fine" and went away.

"This behavior is a good example of the limits of pure reason," Damasio writes in his book *Descartes' Error: Emotion, Reason, and the Human Brain*. It's an example of how lack of emotion leads to self-destructive and dangerous behavior. People who lack emotion don't lead well-planned logical lives in the manner of coolly rational Mr. Spocks. They lead foolish lives. In the extreme cases, they become sociopaths, untroubled by barbarism and unable to feel other people's pain.

Out of these and other experiences Damasio developed a theory, which he called the "somatic marker hypothesis," on the role of emotion in human cognition. Parts of the theory are disputed—scientists differ about how much the brain and the body interact—but his key point is that emotions measure the value of something, and help unconsciously guide us as we navigate through life—away from things that are likely to lead to pain and toward things that are likely to lead to fulfillment. "Somatic markers do not deliberate for us. They assist the deliberation by highlighting some options (either dangerous or favorable), and eliminating them rapidly from subsequent consideration. You may think of it as a system for automated qualification of prediction, which acts, whether you want it or not, to evaluate the extremely diverse scenarios of the anticipated future before you. Think of it as a biasing device."

As we go about our day, we are bombarded with millions of stimuli—a buzzing, blooming confusion of sounds, sights, smells, and motions. And yet amidst all this pyrotechnic chaos, different parts of the brain and body interact to form an Emotional Positioning System.

Like the Global Positioning System that might be in your car, the EPS senses your current situation and compares it to the vast body of data it has stored in its memory. It reaches certain judgments about whether the course you are on will produce good or bad outcomes, and then it coats each person, place, or circumstance with an emotion (fear or excitement, admiration or repugnance) and an implied reaction ("Smile" or "Don't smile"; "Approach" or "Get away") that helps us navigate our days.

Let's say someone touches your hand across a restaurant table. Instantly, the mind is searching the memory banks for similar events. Maybe there was a scene in *Casablanca* when Humphrey Bogart touched Ingrid Bergman's hand. Maybe there was a date in high school long ago. There was a distant memory of Mom, reaching across and holding hands with you during a childhood visit to McDonald's.

The mind is sorting and coding. The body is responding. The heart speeds. Adrenaline rises. A smile opens up. Signals are flowing from body and brain and back again in quick intricate loops. The brain is not separate from the body—that was Descartes' error. The physical and the mental are connected in complex networks of reaction and counter-reactions, and out of their feedback an emotional value emerges. Already the touch of the hand has been coated with meaning—something good, something delicious.

An instant later, a different set of loops open. This is the higher set of feedback routes between the evolutionarily older parts of the brain and the newer, more modern parts such as the prefrontal cortex. This set of information flow is slower, but more refined. It can take the reactions that have already been made by the first system and make finer distinctions among them. ("This hand reaching to touch me across the table is not quite like my mother's hand. It's more like the hand of other people I wanted to have sex with.") It can also flash warnings that lead to intelligent restraint. ("I'm so happy right now I want to pick up this hand and start kissing it, but I've got these other memories of freaking people out when I do things like that.")

Even through much of this stage there is still no conscious awareness, argues Joseph LeDoux, another prominent researcher in these vineyards. The touch of the hand has been felt and refelt, sorted and re-sorted. The body has reacted, plans have been hatched, reactions prepared, and all this complex activity has happened under the surface of awareness and in the blink of an eye. And this process happens not only on a date, with the touch of a hand. It happens at the supermarket when you scan an array of cereal boxes. It happens at the jobs fair when you look over different career options. The Emotional Positioning System is coating each possibility with emotional value.

Eventually, at the end of these complex feedbacks, a desire bursts into consciousness—a desire to choose that cereal or seek that job, or to squeeze the hand, to touch this person, to be with this person forever. The emotion emerges from the deep. It may not be a brilliant impulse; emotion sometimes leads us astray and sometimes leads us wisely. And it doesn't control. It can be overridden, but it propels and guides. As LeDoux writes, "The brain states and bodily responses are the fundamental facts of an emotion, and the conscious feelings are the frills that have added icing to the emotional cake."

Implications

This understanding of decision making leads to some essential truths. Reason and emotion are not separate and opposed. Reason is nestled upon emotion and dependent upon it. Emotion assigns value to things, and reason can only make choices on the basis of those valuations. The human mind can be pragmatic because deep down it is romantic.

Further, the mind or the self is no one thing. The mind is a blindingly complicated series of parallel processes. There is no captain sitting in a cockpit making decisions. There is no Cartesian theater—a spot where all the different processes and possibilities come together to get ranked and where actions get planned. Instead, as Nobel Laureate Gerald Edelman put it, the brain looks like an ecosystem, a fantastically complex associative network of firings, patterns, reactions, and sensations all communicating with and responding to different parts of the brain and all competing for a piece of control over the organism.

Finally, we are primarily wanderers, not decision makers. Over the past century, people have tended to conceive decision making as a point in time. You amass the facts and circumstances and evidence and then make a call. In fact, it is more accurate to say that we are pilgrims in a social landscape. We wander across an environment of people and possibilities. As we wander, the mind makes a near-infinite number of value judgments, which accumulate to form goals, ambitions, dreams, desires, and ways of doing things. The key to a well-lived life is to have trained the emotions to send the right signals and to be sensitive to their subtle calls.

Rob and Julia were not the best-educated people on earth, nor the most profound. But they knew how to love. As they sat at the restaurant, focusing more and more attention on each other, their emotions were sending a rapid stream of guidance signals and shaping whole series of small decisions, and thereby gradually reorienting their lives. "All information processing is emotional," notes Kenneth Dodge, "in that emotion is the energy that drives, organizes, amplifies and attenuates cognitive activity and in turn is the experience and expression of this activity."

Rob and Julia were assigning value to each other. They felt themselves swept along in some strong and delightful current that was carrying them toward someplace they deliriously wanted to go. This wasn't the sort of dissecting analysis Julia's inner smart-ass had used when she first glimpsed Rob. This was a powerful, holistic appraisal that followed an entirely different set of rules. Julia would fall in love and then invent reasons for her attraction later. That day she and Rob began wandering together down a path that would be the most rewarding of their lives.

CHAPTER 2

THE MAP MELD

ROB AND JULIA WERE WONDERFULLY HAPPY IN THE FIRST few months after their wedding, but they were also engaged, as newly-weds must be, in the map meld. Each of them had come into the marriage with a certain unconscious mental map of how day-to-day life worked. Now that their lives were permanently joined, they were discovering that their maps did not entirely cohere. It was not the big differences they noticed, but the little patterns of existence that they had never even thought of.

Julia assumed that dishes should be rinsed and put in the dishwasher as they are soiled. Rob assumed that dishes should be left in the sink for the day and then cleaned all at once in the evening. Julia assumed that toilet paper should roll clockwise so the loose sheets furl out the front. In Rob's house the toilet paper had always rolled counterclockwise so that the sheets furled out the back.

For Rob, reading the morning paper was a solitary activity done in silence by two people who happened to be sitting together. For Julia, the morning paper was a social activity and an occasion for conversation and observations about the state of the world. When Rob went to the grocery store, he bought distinct meal products—a package of tortellini, a frozen pizza, a quiche. When Julia went to the store she bought ingredients—eggs, sugar, flour—and Rob was amazed that she could spend $200 and when she came back there was still nothing for dinner.

These contrasts did not really bother them, for they were in that early stage of marriage when couples still have time to go running together and have sex afterward. In this mode, they slowly and sensitively negotiated the bargain of their new interdependence.

First came the novelty phase, when they were tickled by the interesting new habits each brought into the other's lives. For example, Rob was fascinated by Julia's ferocious attachment to sock wearing. Julia was game for any naked erotic activity he could fantasize about, so long as she was permitted to wear socks while performing it. She could work herself up into a sweaty, panting heat, but apparently blood flow didn't extend to her lower extremities, and if you really wanted to remove those white anklets, it would be like prying a rifle from the president of the NRA—you were going to have to rip them from her cold, dead toes.

Julia, meanwhile, had never seen anybody so much in the habit of buying toothpaste during every trip to the drugstore. Rob bought a tube a week, as if Martians were about to invade us for our Crest. She was also tickled by his pattern of attention. Rob was intensely interested in any event happening thousands of miles away, especially if it was covered by SportsCenter, but any event directly impinging upon his own emotions and inner state entered the zone of negative interest. He was incapable of focus.

Gradually they entered the second stage of map melding, the stage of precampaign planning. A house divided against itself cannot stand. Both Rob and Julia subliminally understood that the quirks that seemed so charming and lovable in the early stages of marriage—Julia's tendency to fire up the laptop in bed at six a.m., Rob's feigned Laddie Helpless in the face of any domestic chore—would cause the other to harbor homicidal urges once the first blush of matrimonial bliss expired.

And so they began to make little mental checklists of Things That Would Have to Change. But they were sensitive enough not to be Maoist about it. They had somehow absorbed the fact that cultural revolutions lead to angry backlashes or prolonged bursts of passive-aggressive withdrawal, and so reforming the other person's habits would have to be a gradual process.

Especially in the first few months, Julia watched Rob the way Jane Goodall watched chimpanzees, with rapt attention and with a sense of constant surprise about the behavior patterns he exhibited. The man had absolutely no interest in artisanal cheeses or any subtle flavors, yet get him within 150 yards of a Brookstone store in the mall, and suddenly he became rapt at the thought of indoor putting greens with automatic ball return. He considered himself a neat man, but neatness for him consisted of taking everything that had been cluttering the countertops and shoving them willy-nilly in the nearest available drawers. He never laid out the pieces he would need in preparation for some assembly project. His simply dove right into the project and spent hours in the middle of it trying to figure out where everything was. He was apparently smarter than every football coach he had ever watched, but lacked the foresight to see that leaving your shoes in the path that leads from the bed to the bathroom might create problems in the middle of the night.

Then there was the night of the movie ticket. One night, Rob was walking home from work and he walked past a theater that had seats available for a film he had wanted to see. He bought a ticket impromptu, as he had done many times during his bachelorhood, and called Julia to let her know that he'd texted some buddies to join him and that he'd be home late that night. He called in a happy, haphazard mood, and was utterly stunned when he sensed that the temperature on the other end of the call had dropped two hundred degrees. He could hear Julia doing the sort of breathing exercises one does when one is trying to restrain an impulse to put an ax in another person's head. It soon became clear that, in fact, he would not be going to the movies that night. It became clear that these sorts of spontaneous larks would no longer be a regular feature of his life and that marriage was not simply an extended phase of boyhood, but with serving dishes and regular sex.

Rob was made to understand, in phrases—interrupted by long glacial pauses—of the sort one uses when trying to explain something to a particularly stupid preschooler . . . that life from now on was going to involve a different level of commitment and joint planning and that a certain sort of carefree, what-do-I-want-for-myself-at-this-moment thinking would have to go.

Once this unconscious paradigm shift occurred in Rob's head, the relationship progressed relatively smoothly. Both issued their own domestic Monroe Doctrines, parts of their lives that they considered sacred, and where external meddling would be regarded as an act of war. Both were pleased by the loving acts of compromise each made on behalf of the other. Rob admired his own selfless nobility every time he remembered to put the toilet seat down. Julia silently compared herself to Mother Teresa every time she pretended to enjoy action movies.

And so commenced the division of marital labor. Both gravitated to areas of superior passion. For example, Rob somehow took control of all vacation planning, because he secretly considered himself the Robert E. Lee of the travel excursion, the brilliant tactician who could rise to any canceled flight, airport snafu, or hotel screwup. This meant Julia had to endure his Bataan Death March vacation schedule—six vineyards before lunch. But to her that was better than sitting down with a travel agent and going through hotel reservations. Julia, meanwhile, took over all aspects of the material surroundings. If Rob was unwilling to engage in discerning commentary during their trips to funky yet casual furniture stores, he could hardly expect to render the final judgments when the purchase decisions had to be made.

Marital satisfaction generally follows a U-shaped curve. Couples are deliriously happy during the first years of marriage. Their self-reported satisfaction declines and bottoms out when their children hit adolescence, then it climbs again as they enter retirement. Newly wed, Rob and Julia were indeed phenomenally happy and quite well suited for each other. And on most days they had sex.

Procreation

One day, about six months after their wedding, Julia and Rob woke up late and had brunch at a neighborhood place with country furniture and distressed wooden tables. Then they went shopping and grabbed sandwiches, which they ate on a bench in the park. They were alive to sensations of all sorts: the way the bread felt in their hands, the feel of stones they tossed into a pond. Julia absentmindedly watched Rob's hands as he used a little plastic knife to spread mustard across his sandwich. Her conscious thoughts were on the story she was telling him, but unconsciously she was becoming aroused. Rob was listening to her tale, but without even thinking about it, he was looking at a soft small crease in the skin of her neck.

In the back of his mind he was ready to have sex right then and there, if a conveniently sized bush could be found. People used to argue that men and women had the same desire for sex, but, on average, that's not true. Male desire is pretty steady and only dips in response to some invisible awareness of their partner's menstrual cycles. Studies in strip clubs have found that dancers' tips plunge 45 percent while they are menstruating, though the explanation for the drop is not clear.

That particular day in the park, Rob wanted Julia with all his body and all his soul. This wasn't merely a Darwinian reflex. Rob had all sorts of internal barriers that made it hard for him to express his emotions. His feelings were there, but they were hidden somewhere inside in a place where he couldn't easily grasp or understand them. Even in those moments when he did have a sense of what he was feeling, the words wouldn't come to help him express it. But during sex, his internal communication barriers dissolved. In the throes of passion, he went into a mental fog. He was no longer aware of his surroundings, or how he might be perceived. His emotions for Julia surfaced with their full force. He could feel his own emotions directly and express them unselfconsciously. The quickie acts of copulation that Julia sometimes granted him as a favor didn't really do this for him. But when they were both in the throes of passion together, Rob experienced the bliss of unencumbered communication that was the real object of his longing. There's something to the old joke that women need to feel loved in order to have sex and men need to have sex in order to feel loved.

Julia's desire was even more complicated. It was like a river with many tributaries. Like most women, Julia's interest in sex was influenced by how much testosterone her body produced at any given moment and by how she processed serotonin. It was influenced by the busyness of her day, her general mood, and the conversations she'd had with friends at lunch. It was influenced by images and sensations she wasn't even aware of—the sight of a piece of art, a melody, a field of flowers. Julia enjoyed looking at male bodies, female bodies, or anything in between. Like most women, she got lubricated even while looking at nature shows of animals copulating, even though consciously the thought of being aroused by animals was repellant.

Julia's sexual tastes were more influenced by culture than Rob's. Men want to do the same sexual acts regardless of education levels, but female sexual preferences differ by education, culture, and status level. Highly educated women are much more likely to perform oral sex, engage in same-sex activity, and experiment with a variety of other activities than less-educated women. Religious women are less adventurous than nonreligious women, though the desires of religious men are not much different than those of secular ones.

They say that foreplay for a woman is anything that happens twenty-four hours before intercourse. That evening, they watched a movie, had a drink, and before long they were playfully, then passionately, making love, heading toward the usual climax.

An orgasm is not a reflex. It's a perception, a mental event. It starts with a cascade of ever more intense physical and mental feedback loops. Touches and sensations release chemicals like dopamine and oxytocin, which in turn generate even more sensory input, culminating in a complex and explosive light show in the brain. Some women can achieve orgasms just by thinking the right thoughts. Some women with spinal cord injuries can achieve orgasm through the stimulation of their ears. Others can achieve orgasms through stimulation of the genitals that, because of a paralyzing accident, they are supposedly unable to feel. A woman in Taiwan could experience temporal-lobe seizures and shattering orgasms merely by brushing her teeth. A man studied by V. S. Ramachandran at UC San Diego felt orgasms in his phantom foot. His foot had been amputated, and the brain region corresponding to the foot had nothing to do. Since the brain is plastic and adaptive, sensations from the penis spread into the vacant real estate and the man felt his subsequent orgasms in a foot that didn't exist.

As they made love, Rob and Julia sent rhythmic vibrations through their minds and bodies. Julia had the mental traits that are associated with ease of orgasms—a willingness to surrender mental control, the ability to be hypnotized, the inability to control thoughts during sex—and she felt herself once again heading in the right direction. A few minutes later, their frontal cortexes partially shut down, while their senses of touch became ever more acute. They lost all remaining self-consciousness— any sense of time or where each other's bodies ended and theirs began. Sight became a series of abstract patches of color. The result was a pair of satisfying climaxes, and eventually, through the magic of the birds and the bees, a son.

CHAPTER 3

MINDSIGHT

I

T IS SAD TO REPORT THAT EVEN IN HER LATE TWENTIES, JULIA kept her Spring Break personality alive and on call. Responsible and ambitious by day, she would let her inner *Cosmo* girl out for a romp on Saturday nights. In these moods, she still thought it was cool to be sassy. She still thought it was a sign of social bravery to be a crude-talking, hard-partying, cotton candy lipstick–wearing, thong-snapping, balls-to-the-wall disciple in the church of Lady GaGa. She still thought she was taking control of her sexuality by showing cleavage. She thought the barbed wire tat around her thigh was a sign of body confidence. She was excellent entertainment at parties, always first in line for drinking games and bicurious female kissing. Ensconced in late-night throngs of group inebriation, she would walk perilously close to the line of skank-dom without ever quite going over.

Up until well into her pregnancy, it is fair to say that a truly maternal thought never crossed her mind. Harold, who was just forming in her womb at this point, was going to have to work if he was going to turn her into the sort of mother he deserved.

He began that work early and hard. As a fetus, Harold grew 250,000 brain cells every minute, and he had well over 20 billion of them by the time he was born. Soon his taste buds began to work, and he could tell when the amniotic fluid surrounding him turned sweet or garlicky, depending upon what his mother had for lunch. Fetuses swallow more of the fluid when sweetener is added. By seventeen weeks he was feeling his way around the womb. He began touching his umbilical cord and pressing his fingers together. By then he was also developing greater sensitivity to the world beyond. A fetus will withdraw from pain at five months. If somebody were to direct a bright flashlight directly at Julia's belly, Harold could sense the light and move away.

By the third trimester, Harold was dreaming, or at least making the same sorts of eye movements that adults make when they dream. It was at this point that the real work of Operation Motherhood could begin. Harold was still a fetus, with barely any of the features of what we would call consciousness, but already he was listening, and memorizing the tone of his mother's voice. After birth, babies will suck hard on a nipple in order to hear a recording of their mother's voice, and much less hard to hear a recording of another woman's voice.

He wasn't only listening to tones, but also to the rhythms and patterns he would need to understand and communicate. French babies cry differently than babies who have heard German in the womb because they've absorbed the French lilt of their mother's voices. Anthony J. DeCasper and others at the University of North Carolina at Greensboro had some mothers read *The Cat in the Hat* to their fetuses over a period of weeks. The fetuses remembered the tonal pattern of the story, and after they were born they'd suck more calmly and rhythmically on a pacifier than when they heard another story in a different meter.

Harold spent his nine months in the womb, growing and developing, and then one fine day, he was born. This wasn't a particularly important event as far as his cognitive development was concerned, though he had a much better view.

Now he could get to work on his mother in earnest, eliminating Julia, the party girl, and creating Supermom Julia. First, he would have to build a set of bonds between them that would supersede all others. A few minutes old, wrapped in a blanket and lying on his mother's chest, Harold was already a little bonding machine, and had a repertoire of skills to help him connect with those he loved.

In 1981 Andrew Meltzoff ushered in a new era of infant psychology when he stuck his tongue out at a forty-two-minute-old infant. The baby stuck her tongue out back at him. It was as if the baby, who had never seen a tongue in her life, intuited that the strange collection of shapes in front of her was a face, that the little thing in the middle of it was a tongue, that there was a creature behind the face, that the tongue was something other than herself, and that she herself had a corresponding little flap that she too could move around.

The experiment has been replicated with babies at different ages, and since then researchers have gone off in search of other infant abilities. They've found them. People once believed that babies were blank slates. But the more investigators look, the more impressed they have become with how much babies know at birth, and how much they learn in the first few months after.

The truth is, starting even before we are born, we inherit a great river of knowledge, a great flow of patterns coming from many ages and many sources. The information that comes from deep in the evolutionary past, we call genetics. The information revealed thousands of years ago, we call religion. The information passed along from hundreds of years ago, we call culture. The information passed along from decades ago, we call family, and the information offered years, months, days, or hours ago, we call education and advice.

But it is all information, and it all flows from the dead through us and to the unborn. The brain is adapted to the river of knowledge and its many currents and tributaries, and it exists as a creature of that river the way a trout exists in a stream. Our thoughts are profoundly molded by this long historic flow, and none of us exists, self-made, in isolation from it. So even a newborn possesses this rich legacy, and is built to absorb more, and to contribute back to this long current.

Though he still had no awareness of himself as a separate person, little Harold had a repertoire of skills to get Julia to fall in love with him. The first was his appearance. Harold had all the physical features that naturally attract a mother's love: big eyes, a large forehead, a small mouth and chin. These features arouse deep responses in all humans, whether they are on babies or Mickey Mouse or E.T.

He also had the ability to gaze. Harold would lie next to Julia and stare at her face. After a few months, he developed a seductive sense of timing—when to look to attract Julia's gaze, when to turn away, and then when to look back to attract her again. He would stare at her and she would gaze back. At an amazingly early age, he could pick out his mother's face from a gallery of faces (and stare at it longer). He could tell the difference between a happy face and sad face. He became extremely good at reading faces, at noting tiny differences in muscular movements around the eyes and mouth. For example, six-month-old babies can spot the different facial features of different monkeys, even though, to adults, they all look the same.

Then there was touch. Harold felt a primeval longing to touch his mother as much and as often as possible. As Harry Harlow's famous monkey experiments suggest, babies will forgo food in exchange for skin or even a towel that feels soft and nurturing. They'll do it because physical contact is just as important as nourishment for their neural growth and survival. This kind of contact was also a life-altering deliciousness for Julia. Human skin has two types of receptors. One type transmits information to the somatosensory cortex for the identification and manipulation of objects. But the other type activates the social parts of the brain. It's a form of body-to-body communication that sets off hormonal and chemical cascades, lowering blood pressure and delivering a sense of transcendent well-being. Harold would lie there on Julia's chest, suckling at her nipple, forging a set of intimate connections that stimulated the growing cells in his brain. Julia would find herself suffused with a deep sense of fulfillment that she had never imagined before. Once, she actually caught herself wondering, "What do I need sex for? This is so much more satisfying." This came from the woman who was voted "Most Likely to Appear in a *Girls Gone Wild* Video" while in college.

Then, and maybe most powerfully, there was smell. Harold just smelled wonderful. The subtle odor that arose from his hot little head penetrated deep into Julia's being, creating a sense of connection she had never imagined before.

Finally, there was rhythm. Harold began imitating Julia. Just a few months old, Harold would open his mouth when Julia opened hers. He'd move his head from side to side when she moved her head from side to side. Soon, he could copy hand gestures.

In looking into Julia's eyes, in touching her skin, in mimicking her gestures, Harold was starting a protoconversation, an unconscious volley of emotions, moods, and responses. Julia found herself playing along, staring into his eyes, getting him to open his mouth, getting him to shake his head.

Not long ago, a psychology class took advantage of the human capacity for this sort of protoconversation to play a trick on their professor. The class decided beforehand that they would look at him attentively when he lectured from the left side of the room but look away or appear distracted when he wandered over to the right side. As the class went on, the professor unconsciously stood more and more on the left side of the room. By the end, he was practically out the door. He had no idea what his students were doing, but he just felt better from that side of his room. His behavior was pulled by this invisible social gravity.

Of course Julia and Harold's protoconversation was much deeper. Harold kept up Operation Motherhood with steady and relentless persistence, week after week, month after month, breaking down her barriers, rewiring her personality, insinuating himself in her every thought and feeling, gradually transforming her very identity.

The Invasion

Julia's old personality battled back. You have to give her credit for that. She didn't just surrender to this new creature without a struggle.

For most of the first year, Julia would breast-feed Harold from a chair in the corner of his room. At her baby shower, her friends, very few of whom had babies themselves, gave her the sorts of things they considered essential for successful nurturing. She had the audio and video baby monitors, the air purifier, the Baby Einstein mobiles, the dehumidifier, the electronic photo displays, the visually stimulating floormat, the rattles for manual dexterity, and the aurally soothing ocean-currents noise machine. She would sit there amidst all the gizmos, breast-feeding him, looking like a milkmaid Captain Kirk in the chair of the starship *Enterprise*.

One night, about seven months into Harold's life, Julia was in the chair with Harold at her breast. The nightlight glowed softly and everything was quiet all around. It looked superficially like an idyllic maternal scene—a mother suckling her child, all filled with love and sweet affections. But if you could have read Julia's mind at that moment, here's what you would have found her saying: "Fuck! Fuck! Fuck! Help me! Help me! Will somebody please help me?"

At this moment—tired, oppressed, violated—she hated the little bastard. He'd entered her mind with tricks of sweet seduction, and once inside, he'd stomped over everything with the infant equivalent of jackboots.

He was half Cupid, half storm trooper. The greedy asshole wanted everything. Harold controlled the hours of her sleep, the span of her attention, the time she could shower, rest, or go to the bathroom. He controlled what she thought, how she looked, whether she cried. Julia was miserable and overwhelmed.

The average baby demands adult attention of one kind or another every twenty seconds. New mothers lose an average of seven hundred hours of sleep during that first year. Marital satisfaction plummets 70 percent, while the risk of maternal depression more than doubles. At the merest hint of discomfort Harold could let out a piercing scream that could leave Julia weeping in hysterics and Rob angry and miserable.

Exhausted, Julia would sit there in the chair, breast-feeding her little boy while thinking of the fat vessel she had become. Her thoughts raced through dark forests. She realized she would never again look as good in tight skirts. She'd never do anything on a whim. Instead, she'd get sucked into the vapid attitudes of the bourgeois mommy wars. She'd already come into contact with the pious breast-feeding crusaders (the über-boobers), the self-righteous playdate queens who would correct her parenting techniques (the sanctimommies), and the mopey martyr mommies who would bitch on endlessly about how rotten their lives were and how inconsiderate their husbands and parents had become.

She'd get involved in those numbingly dull playground conversations, and as Jill Lepore once noted, they'd be all the same. The mothers would all want forgiveness, and the fathers would all want applause.

She could say farewell to the partygoing life that gave her such pleasure. Instead, Julia saw a grim future spreading out before her—school lunches, recycling sermons, strep tests, ear infections, and hours and hours spent praying for nap time. To top it all off, women who give birth to boys have shorter life expectancies because the boys' testosterone can compromise their immune system.

Intertwined

Then, maybe a second after this anger and depression had flashed across her mind, Julia would lean back into the chair and hold Harold's head up to her nose. Then Harold would lie on her chest, grab her pinkie with his little hand, and start suckling again. Little tears of joy and gratitude would well up in her eyes.

Kenneth Kaye has suggested that human infants are the only mammalian infants who nurse in bursts, sucking for a few seconds then pausing while the nipple is still in the mouth, and then resuming for another round. This pause, Kaye theorizes, induces the mother to jiggle her baby. When the baby is two days old, mothers jiggle for about three seconds. When the baby is a few weeks old, the jiggle is down to two.

These movements sent Julia and Harold into a sort of ballet with its own rhythm. Harold paused, Julia jiggled; Harold paused, Julia jiggled. It was a conversation. As Harold aged, this rhythm would continue. He'd look at her, and she'd look at him. Their world was structured by dialogue.

It's almost musical the way the rhythm between mother and child evolves. Julia, no natural vocalist, found herself singing to him at the oddest moments—mostly, for some reason, songs from *West Side Story*. She read *The Wall Street Journal* to him in the morning and amused herself by reading every story that had to do with the Federal Reserve Board in motherese, the slow, exaggerated, singsong intonation that mothers in all cultures across the world use when speaking to their young.

Sometimes, as the months went by, she would begin impersonator training. She would mold her face into some expression and then get Harold to mimic until he looked like some celebrity. By scowling she could get him to look like Mussolini. By growling, Churchill. By opening her mouth and looking scared, Jerry Lewis. Sometimes when he smiled it was actually disconcerting. He gave a knowing, devious smile like some fraternity scuzzball who'd put a hidden camera in her shower.

Harold was so desperate to bond that, if the tempo of their conversation was interrupted, his whole world could fall to pieces. Scientists conduct a type of experiment they call "still-face" research. They ask a mother to interrupt her interactions with her child and adopt a blank, passive expression. Babies find this extremely disconcerting. They tense, cry, and fuss. Babies make a strenuous effort to regain their mother's attention, and if there is still no response they, too, become passive and withdrawn. That's because babies organize their internal states by seeing their own minds reflected back at them in the faces of others.

Except when Julia was completely exhausted, their conversations went on like a symphony. Harold's energy was regulated by her energy. His brain was built by her brain.

By the ninth month, Harold still had no sense of self-awareness. He was still limited in so many ways. But he had done what he needed to do to survive and flourish. He had intertwined his mind with the mind of another. Out of this relationship his own faculties would grow.

It's tempting to think that people grow like plants. You add nourishment to the seed, and an individual plant grows up. But that's not so. Mammal brains grow properly only when they are able to interpenetrate with another. Rat pups who are licked and groomed by their mothers have more synaptic connections than rat pups who aren't. Rats who are separated from their mothers for twenty-four hours lose twice as many brain cells in the cerebral and cerebellar cortices than rats who are not separated. Rats raised in interesting environments have 25 percent more synapses than those raised in ordinary cages. Though some mysterious emotional outpourings produce physical changes.

Back in the 1930s, H. M. Skeels studied mentally disabled orphans who were living in an institution but were subsequently adopted. After four years, their IQs diverged an amazing fifty points from those of the orphans who were not adopted. And the remarkable thing is that the kids who were adopted were not improved by tutoring and lecturing. The mothers who adopted them were also mentally disabled and living in a different institution. It was the mother's love and attention that produced the IQ spike.

By now, Harold's face lit up when Julia entered the room. This was good because Julia was coming apart at the seams. She hadn't slept well in months. She once considered herself relatively tidy, but now her house looked like a corner of Rome after a visit from the barbarian hordes. Franklin Roosevelt was able to launch the New Deal in the amount of time that had passed since her last witty observation. But in the mornings Harold let out a big smile and he got to live another day.

One morning, it dawned on Julia that she knew Harold better than any other person on earth. She knew the ways in which he needed her. She knew his difficulty in making transitions from one setting to another. She sensed, sadly, that he seemed to long for some sort of connection from her that she would never be able to offer.

Yet they had never actually exchanged a word of conversation. Harold didn't talk. They got to know each other largely through touch, tears, looks, smell, and laughter. Julia had always assumed that meanings and concepts came through language, but now she realized that it was possible to have a complex human relationship without words.

Mirror Neurons

Philosophers have long argued about the process people use to understand one another. Some believe that we are careful theorizers. We come up with hypotheses about how other people will behave, and then test those hypotheses against the evidence we observe minute by minute. In this theory, people come across as rational scientists, constantly weighing evidence and testing explanations. And there's clear evidence that this sort of hypothesis testing is part of how we understand one another. But these days most of the research points to the primacy of a rival hypothesis: that we automatically simulate others, and understand what others feel by feeling a version of what they are experiencing, in ourselves. In this view, people aren't cold theorizers who are making judgments about other creatures. They are unconscious Method actors who understand by sharing or at least simulating the responses they see in the people around them. We're able to function in a social world because we partially permeate each other's minds and understand—some people more, some people less. Human beings understand others in themselves, and they form themselves by reenacting the internal processes they pick up from others.

In 1992 researchers at the University of Parma in Italy were studying the brains of macaque monkeys, when they noticed a strange phenomenon. When a monkey saw a human researcher grab a peanut and bring it to his mouth, the monkey's brain would fire just as if the monkey were itself grabbing a peanut and bringing it to its own mouth, even though the monkey wasn't actually moving at all. The monkey was automatically simulating the mental processes it observed in another.

So was born the theory of mirror neurons, the idea that we have in our heads neurons that automatically re-create the mental patterns of those around us. Mirror neurons are not physically different from any other sort of neuron; it's the way the former are connected that seems to enable them to perform this remarkable task of deep imitation.

Over the last few years mirror neurons have become one of the most hyped and debated issues in all of neuroscience. Some scientists believe mirror neurons are akin to DNA, and will revolutionize our understanding of how people internally process outer experiences, how we learn from and communicate with others. Others think the whole idea is vastly overblown. They are quick to point out that the phrase "mirror neurons" is patently misleading because it suggests the mimicking skill is contained in the neurons, not in the networks in the brain. But there does seem to be a widely held view that monkey and human brains have an automatic ability to perform deep imitation, and in this way share mental processes across the invisible space between them. As Marco Iacoboni has observed, people are able to feel what others experience as if it were happening to them.

The monkeys in Parma not only mimicked the actions they observed, they seemed to unconsciously evaluate the intentions behind them. Their neurons fired intensely when a glass was picked up in a context that suggested drinking, but they did not fire the same way when an empty glass was picked up in a context that suggested cleaning up. The monkey's brains would not fire when scientists merely pantomimed picking up a raisin, but they did fire when the scientists picked up a real raisin. Their neurons fired in a certain characteristic pattern when they saw a scientist tearing a piece of paper, but they also fired in that same pattern when they merely heard a scientist tearing paper. In other words these weren't mere "monkey see, monkey do" imitations of physical actions. The way the brains reacted to an action was inextricably linked to the goal implied by the action. We sometimes assume that the mental process of perceiving an action is distinct from the mental process of evaluating an action. But in these examples, the processes of perception and evaluation are all intermingled. They share the same representational systems, the same network patterns in the brain.

Since those original experiments in Italy, many scientists, including Iacoboni, believe they have found mirror neurons in humans. Human mirror neurons help people interpret the intention of an action, although unlike monkey mirror neurons, they seem to be able to imitate an action even when no goal is detected. A woman's brain will respond with a certain pattern as she watches a person use two fingers to pick up a wineglass, but her brain will respond in a different way as she watches a person use two fingers and the same action to pick up a toothbrush. Her brain will respond one way when it watches another human in the act of speaking, but a different way when it watches a monkey in the act of chattering.

When people watch a chase scene in a movie, they respond as if they were actually being chased, except at lower intensity. When they look at pornography, their brains respond as if they were actually having sex, except at lower intensity. When Harold watched Julia look down lovingly at him, he presumably reenacted the activity in her brain, and learned how love feels and works from the inside.

Harold would grow up to be a promiscuous imitator, and this helped him in all sorts of ways. Carol Eckerman, a psychology professor at

Duke, has conducted research suggesting that the more a child plays imitation games, the more likely it is that the child will become an early fluent speaker. Tanya Chartrand and John Bargh found that the more two people imitate each other's movements, the more they like each other—and the more they like each other, the more they imitate. Many scientists believe that the ability to unconsciously share another's pain is a building block of empathy, and through that emotion, morality.

However the science on mirror neurons eventually shakes out, the theory gives us a vehicle to explain a phenomenon we see every day, and never as much as in the relationship between parents and child. Minds are intensely permeable. Loops exist between brains. The same thought and feeling can arise in different minds, with invisible networks filling the space between them.

Make 'Em Laugh

One day, months and months later, Julia, Rob, and Harold were sitting around the table at dinner when Rob, absentmindedly, dropped a tennis ball on the table. Harold exploded in peals of laughter. Rob dropped it again. Harold's mouth opened wide. His eyes crinkled. His body quaked. A little bump of tissue rose between his eyebrows, and the sound of rapturous laughter filled the room. Rob held the ball above the table, and they all sat there frozen in anticipation. Then he let it bounce a few times, and Harold exploded with glee, even louder than before. He sat there in his pajamas, his tiny hands oddly still, transported by laughter. Rob and Julia had tears coming out of their eyes, they were laughing so hard along with him. Rob kept doing it over and over. Harold would stare in anticipation of the ball being dropped and then let rip with squeals of delight when he saw it bounce, his head bobbing, his tongue trembling, his eyes moving delightedly from face to face. Rob and Julia matched him squeal for squeal, their voices blending and modulating with his.

These were the best moments of their days—the little games of peekaboo, the wrestling and tickling on the floor. Sometimes Julia would hold a little washcloth in her mouth over the changing table, and

Harold would grab it and hilariously try to cram it back in. It was the repetition of predictable surprise that sent Harold into ecstasy. The games gave him a sense of mastery—that he was beginning to understand the patterns of the world. They gave him that sensation—which is something like pure joy for babies—of feeling in perfect synchronicity with Mom and Dad.

Laughter exists for a reason, and it probably existed before humans developed language. Robert Provine of the University of Maryland has found that people are thirty times more likely to laugh when they are with other people than when they are alone. When people are in bonding situations, laughter flows. Surprisingly, people who are speaking are 46 percent more likely to laugh during conversation than people who are listening. And they're not exactly laughing at hilarious punch lines. Only 15 percent of the sentences that trigger laughter are funny in any discernable way. Instead, laughter seems to bubble up spontaneously amidst conversation when people feel themselves responding in parallel ways to the same emotionally positive circumstances.

Some jokes, like puns, are asocial and are often relished by those suffering from autism. But most jokes are intensely social and bubble up when people find a solution to some social incongruity. Laughter is a language that people use to bond, to cover over social awkwardness or to reinforce bonding that has already occurred. This can be good, as when a crowd laughs together, or bad, as when a crowd ridicules a victim, but laughter and solidarity go together. As Steven Johnson has written, "Laughing is not an instinctive physical response to humor, the way a flinch responds to pain or a shiver to cold. It's an instinctive form of social bonding that humor is crafted to exploit."

Night after night, Harold and his parents would try to fall into rhythm with one another. Sometimes they failed. Rob and Julia would be unable to get inside Harold's mind and figure out what he needed to soothe his agony. Sometimes they succeeded. And when they did, laughter was the reward.

If you had to step back and ask where Harold came from, you could give a biological answer, and explain conception and pregnancy and birth. But if you really wanted to explain where the essence of Harold—

or the essence of any person—came from, you would have to say that first there was a relationship between Harold and his parents. And that relationship had certain qualities. And then, as Harold matured and developed self-consciousness, those qualities became individualized, and came to exist in him even when he was apart from his parents. That is to say, people don't develop first and create relationships. People are born into relationships—with parents, with ancestors—and those relationships create people. Or, to put it a different way, a brain is something that is contained within a single skull. A mind only exists within a network. It is the result of the interaction between brains, and it is important not to confuse brains with minds.

As Samuel Taylor Coleridge once observed, "Ere yet a conscious self exists, the love begins; and the first love is love of another. The Babe acknowledges a self in the Mother's form years before it can recognize a self in its own."

Coleridge described how his own child, then three years old, awoke during the night and called out to his mother. "Touch me, only touch me with your finger," the young boy pleaded. The child's mother was astonished.

"Why?" she asked.

"I'm not here," the boy cried. "Touch me, Mother, so that I may be here."

CHAPTER 4

MAPMAKING

HAROLD HAD BEGUN HIS LIFE STARING AT MOM, BUT IT WASN'T long before the grubby world of materialism entered the picture. He didn't begin this phase longing for Porsches and Rolexes. At first, he was more of a stripes man—stripes and black-and-white checkered squares. After that he developed a thing for edges—edges of boxes, edges of shelves. He would stare at edges the way Charles Manson stared at cops.

Then, as the months went by, it was boxes, wheels, rattles, and sippy cups. He became a great leveler—consumed by the conviction that all matter should rest at its lowest possible altitude. Plates came off tables and onto the floor. Books came off shelves and onto the floor. Half-used boxes of spaghettini were liberated from their pantry prison and returned to their natural habitat across the kitchen floor.

The delightful thing about Harold at this stage was that he was both a psychology major and a physics major. His two main vocations were figuring out how to learn from his mother and figuring out how stuff falls. He'd look at her frequently to make sure she was protecting him, and then go off in search of stuff to topple. He possessed what Alison Gopnik, Andrew Meltzoff, and Patricia Kuhl call an "explanatory drive." Harold could sit for long stretches trying to fit different size boxes inside one another, and then when they were finally together, some primeval Sandy Koufax urge would come over him and they'd be flying down the stairs.

He was exploring and learning, but at this point in his life, Harold's thought processes were radically different from yours and mine. Young children don't seem to have a self-conscious inner observer. The executive-function areas in the front of the brain are slow to mature, so Harold did little controlled, self-directed thinking.

That meant he had no inner narrator that he thought of as himself. He couldn't consciously remember the past, or consciously connect his past actions to his present ones in one coherent timeline. He couldn't remember earlier thoughts or how he learned anything. Until he was eighteen months, he couldn't pass the mirror test. If you put a sticker on an adult chimpanzee's forehead or a dolphin's forehead, the animal understands that the sticker is on his own head. But Harold lacked that amount of self-awareness. To him the sticker was on the forehead of some creature in the mirror. He was very good at recognizing others, but he could not recognize himself.

Even up to age three, children don't seem to get the concept of self-consciously focused attention. They assume that the mind goes blank when there is no outside thing bidding for its attention. When you ask preschoolers if an adult they are watching is focusing her attention on part of a scene, they don't seem to understand what you are talking about. If you ask them if they can go long stretches of time without thinking at all, they say yes. As Alison Gopnik writes in *The Philosophical Baby*, "They don't understand that thoughts can simply follow the logic of your internal experience instead of being triggered from the outside."

Gopnik writes that adults have searchlight consciousness. We direct attention at specific locations. Harold, like all young children, had what Gopnik calls "lantern consciousness." It illuminated outward in all directions—a vivid panoramic awareness of everything. It was like being exuberantly lost in a 360-degree movie. A million things caught his attention in random bombardments. Here was an interesting shape! There was another! There was a light! There was a person!

Even that description understates the radical weirdness of Harold's consciousness at this point. The lantern metaphor suggests that Harold is illuminating and observing the world, and that the observer is somehow separate from what he sees. But Harold wasn't observing, he was immersing. He was vividly participating in whatever came across his mind.

The Task

At this point in his life, Harold had to learn the most the fastest. His job was to figure out what sort of environment he lived in and carve mental maps that would help him navigate it. Conscious, directed learning couldn't help him perform this task quickly, but unconscious immersion could.

Much of childhood—much of life—consists of integrating the chaotic billions of stimuli we encounter into sophisticated models, which are then used to anticipate, interpret, and navigate through life. As John Bowlby wrote, "Every situation we meet with in life is construed in terms of the representational models we have of the world about us and of ourselves. Information reaching us through our sense organs is selected and interpreted in terms of those models, its significance for us and for those we care for is evaluated in terms of them, and plans of action conceived and executed with those models in mind." Those internal maps determine how we see, what emotional value we assign to things, what we want, how we react, and how good we are at predicting what will come next.

Harold was in his most intense period of mapmaking. Elizabeth Spelke believes babies are born with a core knowledge of the world, which gives them a head start with this task. Infants know a rolling ball should keep rolling and that if it rolls behind something it should come out the other side. At six months, they can tell the difference between eight and sixteen dots on a page. They have a sense of mathematical proportion, though they obviously don't know how to count.

Before long, they are performing impressive acts of decoding. Meltzoff and Kuhl showed five-month-old babies silent videos of a face saying either "ahh" or "eee" and then played the babies audiotapes of each sound. The babies could correctly match the sound to the right face.

If you read an eight-month-old baby a phrase like "la ta ta" or "mi na na," within two minutes the baby will pick up the underlying rhyme scheme (ABB). Young children also use a phenomenally sophisticated statistical technique to understand language. When adults speak, all the sounds of the different words run together. But young children are able to discern that there is a high probability that the sound "pre" should go with the sound "ty" so "pretty" is one word. There is a high probability that "ba" will also go with "by" so "baby" is one word. Children can do these sorts of complex probability calculations even though their conscious capacities are barely online.

Only Connect

Harold's brain had over 100 billion cells, or neurons, in it. As Harold began making sense of the world, each of these neurons sent out branches to make connections with other neurons. The space where two branches for different neurons meet is called a synapse. Harold was making these connections at a furious pace. Some scientists calculate that humans create 1.8 million synapses per second from their second month in utero to their second birthday. The brain makes synapses to store information. Each thing we know is embodied in a network of neural connections.

By age two or three, each of Harold's neurons could have made an average of about 15,000 connections, though the unused ones will get pruned back. Harold could end up with something in the neighborhood of 100 trillion or 500 trillion or even 1,000 trillion synapses. If you want to get a sense of the number of potential connections between the cells in Harold's brain, contemplate this: A mere 60 neurons are capable of making 10^{81} possible connections with each other. (That's 1 with 81 zeroes after it.) The number of particles in the known universe is about one-tenth of this number. Jeff Hawkins suggests a different way to think about the brain. Imagine a football stadium filled with spaghetti. Now imagine it shrunk down to skull size and much more complicated.

In their book *The Scientist in the Crib*, Gopnik, Meltzoff, and Kuhl have a nice description of the process neurons use to connect with one another: "It's as if, when you used your cell phone to call your neighbor often enough, a cable spontaneously grew between your houses. At first, cells exuberantly attempt to connect to as many other cells as they can. Like phone solicitors, they call everyone, hoping someone will answer and say yes. When another cell does answer, and answers enough, a more permanent link gets laid down."

I want to pause here, because this process of synaptogenesis is part of the core of who Harold was. For millennia philosophers have sought a definition of the human self. What is it that makes a person ineffably herself, despite the changes that happen day by day and year by year? What is it that unifies all the different thoughts, actions, and emotions that pass through each of our lives? Where does the true self lie?

A piece of the answer lies in the pattern of synaptic connections. When we come across an apple, our sensory perceptions about that apple (its color, shape, texture, aroma, etc.) get translated into an integrated network of connected neurons that fire together. These firings, or electrochemical impulses, are not concentrated in one section of the brain. There is no apple section. The apple information is spread out in a vastly complicated network. In one experiment, a cat was taught to find food behind a door that was marked with a specific geometric shape. That one geometric form set off learning-related responses in over five million cells distributed throughout the cat's brain. In another experiment, the ability to distinguish the sound of "P" from the sound of "B" was represented in twenty-two sites scattered across the human brain.

When Harold saw a dog, a network of neurons fired. The more he saw a dog, the denser and more efficient the connections between the appropriate neurons grew. The more you see dogs, the faster and more complex your dog networks become, and the better you are at perceiving the general qualities of dogness and the differences between dogs. With effort, practice, and experience, you can improve the subtlety of your networks. Violinists have dense connections in the area of the brain related to their left hand, because they use it so much while playing their instrument.

You have a distinctive signature, a distinctive smile, and a distinctive way of drying yourself off after a shower because you perform these activities a lot and the corresponding networks of neurons are thus thickly connected in your brain. You can probably recite the alphabet from A to Z, because through repetition you have built that sequence of patterns in your head. You would probably have trouble reciting the alphabet from Z to A, because that sequence has not been reinforced by experience.

In this way, each of us has unique neural networks, which are formed, reinforced, and constantly updated by the eclectic circumstances of our lives. Once circuits are formed, that increases the chances the same circuits will fire in the future. The neural networks embody our experiences and in turn guide future action. They contain the unique way each of us carries himself in the world, the way we walk, talk, and react. They are the grooves down which our behavior flows. A brain is the record of a life. The networks of neural connections are the physical manifestation of your habits, personality, and predilections. You are the spiritual entity that emerges out of the material networks in your head.

Blending

As Harold went about his day, the sight of his mother's smile set off a certain pattern of synaptic firing, as did the sound of a scary truck. As he toddled around exploring his world, he built up his mind. One day when he was about five, he was running around the house and he did something amazing. He screamed, "I'm a tiger!" and he pounced playfully on Julia's lap.

This may seem like a simple thing, which all children do. After all, when we think of really difficult feats of thinking, we think about, say, calculating the square root of 5,041. (It's 71.) Saying "I'm a tiger" seems easy.

But that's an illusion. Any cheap calculator can calculate square roots. No simple machine is able to perform the imaginative construct involved in the sentence "I am a tiger." No simple machine can blend two complicated constructs such as "I," a little boy, and "a tiger," a fierce animal, into a single coherent entity. Yet the human brain is capable of performing this incredibly complicated task so easily, and so far below the level of awareness, we don't even appreciate how hard it is.

Harold could do this because of that ability to make generalizations, and because of his ability to make associations between generalizations—to overlay the gist of one thing with the gist of another. If you ask a sophisticated computer to find the door in a room, it has to calculate all the angles in the room, then look for certain shapes and ratios that correspond to the shapes and ratios of past doors that have been programmed into its memory banks. Because there are so many different kinds of doors, it has trouble figuring out what "door" means. But for Harold, or any human, this is a piece of cake. We store in our heads vague patterns of what rooms are like, and we know roughly where doors are in rooms, and finding them usually takes no conscious thought at all. We are smart because we are capable of fuzzy thinking.

We look at the variable patterns of the world and we form gists. Once we have created a gist, which is a pattern of firings, we can do a lot of things with it. We can take the gist of the dog, and then call up the gist of Winston Churchill we have stored in our head and we can imagine Winston Churchill's voice coming out of the dog's mouth. (It helps if the dog is a bulldog and there's already some overlap between the neural patterns so we can say, "This is sort of like that.")

This activity of blending neural patterns is called imagination. It seems easy but it is phenomenally complex. It consists of taking two or more things that do not exist together, blending them together in the mind, and then creating an emergent third thing that never existed at all. As Gilles Fauconnier and Mark Turner write in *The Way We Think*, "Building an integration network involves setting up mental spaces, matching across spaces, projecting selectively to a blend, locating shared structures, projecting backward to inputs, recruiting new structure to the inputs or the blend, and running various operations in the blend itself." And that is only the start of it. If you have a taste for incredibly intricate and sometimes impenetrable reasoning, read the work of scientists who are trying to piece together the exact sequence of events that go into imagination, or as they sometimes call it in that winsome way of theirs, double-scope integration.

In any case, Harold was a little demon at it. In the space of five minutes, he could be a tiger, a train, a car, his mom, a storm, a building, or an ant. For seven months when he was about four, he was persuaded that he was a sun creature born on the sun. His parents tried to get him to confess that he was actually an Earth creature born in a hospital, but he would grow quite grave and refuse to concede the point. Julia and Rob actually began to wonder if they'd given birth to some delusional psychotic.

In fact, he was just lost in his blends. When he got a little older, he created H-World, an entire universe established for the glorification of Harold (what researchers call a "paracosm"). In H-World, everybody was named Harold and all worshiped the king of H-World who was Harold himself. In H-World people ate certain foods—mostly marshmallows and M&Ms—and they had certain occupations—mostly of the professional-athlete variety. H-World even had its own history, events from fantasies gone by, which were recorded in the memory banks just like the history in the real world.

Throughout his life, Harold was really good at blending, generalizing, and storytelling. If you were to measure Harold's raw information-processing abilities, you would find that he was slightly above average, but nothing special. Yet he had an amazing ability to discern essences and play with neural patterns. That meant he was really good at creating models of reality, and models of possible alternate realities.

We sometimes think that imagination is cognitively easy because children can use it better than adults. In fact, imagination is arduous and practical. People who possess imaginative talents can say, "If I were you, I would do this. . . ." Or they can think, "I'm doing it this way now, but if I tried to do it that way, things might go faster." These double-scope and counterfactual abilities come in quite handy in real life.

Storytelling

Between the ages of four and ten, Harold would be sitting at the dinner table and he'd interject some snippet of TV dialogue or a commercial jingle, and it was always exactly appropriate to the conversation. He'd use difficult words appropriately, though if you asked him later what the word meant he couldn't consciously define it. He'd blurt out some ancient lyric from a Paul McCartney and Wings song, and it would be perfectly apt in that social situation. People would look at him in amazement and ask, "Is there a little old man in there?"

In reality, there was no hidden adult in Harold's brain. There was just a little pattern synthesizer. Rob and Julia organized his life. Day after day they had the same routines and the same expectations. These habits laid down certain fundamental structures in his mind. And out of this order, regularity, and discipline, Harold's mind went off on riotous adventures, in which he combined unlikely things in magical ways.

Rob and Julia would have been delighted with his imaginative abilities, but sometimes he seemed to have trouble with real life. They would see other kids peacefully holding on to the cart as they made their way up and down the aisles in the grocery store. Harold didn't do that. He was always pulling and struggling this way or that and had to be held or restrained. Other kids followed the teachers' instructions at his preschool, but Harold couldn't stay on task; he was always dashing off to do his own thing. Rob and Julia would get exhausted by his fits and tantrums, and tried to impose a little linearity into his life. He was a real problem on airplanes, and an embarrassment in restaurants. At parent-teacher conferences his teachers would remark that controlling Harold took up way too much of their time. He didn't seem to listen or follow instructions. Julia used to furtively look at the child-rearing guides in the bookstores, with the sinking sensation that she was raising a poster child for ADHD medications.

One evening, when Harold was in kindergarten, Rob passed by his room and Harold was splayed out across the floor, surrounded by little plastic figurines. There was a gathering of green army figurines off to his left, a mass of little Lego pirates flanking them, and a traffic jam of Hot Wheels cars challenging in from head on. Harold was in the middle scampering around, moving a Darth Vader figure behind enemy lines and crushing an unsuspecting G.I. Joe. A squad of army men confronted a gathering of Hot Wheels and fell back. Harold's voice rose and fell with the ebb and flow of battle. He kept up a steady play-by-play narrative, describing events as they unfolded and, occasionally, he'd rise to a sort of whispering "and the crowd goes wild" roar.

Rob stood in the doorway for about ten minutes and watched Harold go about his play. Harold glanced up, but then returned to the war. He gave a furious pep talk to one of his stuffed monkeys. He preached courage to a piece of plastic two inches tall. He soothed the hurt feelings of a car and scolded a stuffed turtle.

In his stories there were generals and privates, mommies and daddies, dentists and firemen. Very early in life, he seemed to have a very clear sense of what patterns of behavior these different social roles entailed. In one game, he'd play a warrior; in another, a doctor; in another, a chef—imagining how people in these roles think, enacting theories about other people's minds.

Many of Harold's stories were about his future life, and how he would win honor and fame. Rob, Julia, and their adult friends sometimes fantasized about money and comfort, but Harold and his playmates fantasized about glory.

One Saturday afternoon, Harold had a few buddies over to the house for a playdate. They were up in his room with his toys. Harold would announce they were firemen, and pretty soon they were busy imagining a fire in a house and gathering tools to fight it—a hose, a truck, a mass of axes. Each kid would assign himself a role in the master story. Rob snuck up there and stood in the doorway, watching. To his chagrin, Harold was a little Napoleon, telling his guests who got to drive the truck and who got to carry the hose. They would have elaborate negotiations over what was legitimate to do in the world of pretend, in the shared mental space they had constructed. Even in the free-form world of their imaginations, it was apparently still necessary to have rules, and they spent so much time talking about the rules, Rob got the impression that they were more important than the story itself.

Rob noticed that each boy tried to assert himself, and the games had a certain narrative arc, from calm to crisis to calm. First they played out a happy scene. Then something terrible would happen that would get them all worked up, and they would fight it together. Then, after victory, they would return to their earlier state of emotional tranquility.

Every story would end in triumph, a sort of "all better now" moment, with fame and glory for everyone involved.

After about twenty minutes playing Benjamin Spock and watching the kiddies, Rob got the urge to join in. He sat down with the boys, grabbed some figures, and joined Harold's team.

This was a big mistake. It was roughly the equivalent of a normal human being grabbing a basketball and inviting himself to play a pickup game with the Los Angeles Lakers.

Over the course of his adult life, Rob had trained his mind to excel at a certain sort of thinking. This is the kind that psychologist Jerome Bruner has called "paradigmatic thinking." This mode of thought is structured by logic and analysis. It's the language of a legal brief, a business memo, or an academic essay. It consists of stepping back from a situation to organize facts, to deduce general principles, and to ask questions.

But the game Harold and his buddies were playing relied on a different way of thinking, what Bruner calls the "narrative mode." Harold and his buddies had now become a team of farmers on a ranch. They just started doing things on it—riding, roping, building, and playing. As their stories grew and evolved, it became clear what made sense and what didn't make sense within the line of the story.

The cowboys began to work together and they began to squabble. Cows were lost. Fences were built. The cowboys formed teams when the tornados came through, and split apart when the danger passed.

And then the Invaders came. The narrative mode is a mythic mode. It contains another dimension, not usually contained in paradigmatic thinking—the dimension of good and evil, sacred and profane. The mythic mode helps people not only tell a story, but make sense of the emotions and moral sensations aroused by the story.

The boys reacted to the Invaders with alarm and dread. They scrambled about on the carpet, and lined up their plastic horses against the Invaders, but they screamed at one another, "There are too many of them!" All seemed lost. Then Harold produced a giant white horse, ten times larger than the other toys they were playing with. "Who's this?" he cried, and answered his own question: "It's the White Horse!" And he charged off into the Invaders. Two of the other boys switched teams and began hurling Invaders at the White Horse. An apocalyptic battle raged. The Horse crushed the Invaders. The Invaders bloodied the Horse. Before long the Invaders were dead, but the White Horse was dying, too. They put a cloth on his body and had a mournful funeral, and the Horse's soul went up to heaven.

Rob was like a warthog in a frolic of gazelles. Their imaginations danced while his plodded. They saw good and evil while he saw plastic and metal. After five minutes, their emotional intensity produced a dull ache in the back of his head. He was exhausted trying to keep up.

PRESUMABLY, ROB ONCE HAD the ability to perform these mental gymnastics. But then, he reflected, maturity set in. He could focus his attention better, but he could no longer put together odd juxtapositions the way he once had. His mind couldn't jump from association to association anymore. Later, when he told Julia he couldn't think in the random way Harold did, she simply replied, "Maybe he'll grow out of it."

Rob tried to agree. In the meantime, at least Harold's stories always ended happily. Dan P. McAdams argues that children develop a narrative tone, which influences their stories for the rest of their lives. Children gradually adopt an enduring assumption that everything will turn out well or badly (depending on their childhood). They lay down a foundation of stories in which goals are achieved, hurts healed, peace is restored, and the world is understood

After bedtime, Harold would be up in his room talking to his characters. His parents would be downstairs, exhausted and unable to hear exactly what he was saying. But they could hear the rise and fall of his voice as the stories danced in the air above him. They would hear him calmly explaining something. Reacting with alarm. Rallying his imaginary friends. He was in what Rob and Julia used to call his Rain Man mode, lost in his own spacey world. They'd wonder when exactly Harold would start joining the human race, if ever. But upstairs, while tutoring his monkeys, Harold drifted off to sleep.

CHAPTER 5

ATTACHMENT

ONE DAY, WHEN HAROLD WAS IN SECOND GRADE, JULIA CALLED him from the playroom to the kitchen table. She rallied her energy and told him it was time to do his homework. Harold ran through his normal gospel of homework avoidance. First, he told her he hadn't been assigned any homework. When that small fib cracked, he told her he'd already done it at school. This was followed by a series of ever less-plausible claims. He had done it on the bus. He had left the assignment at school. It was too hard, and the teacher had told the class they didn't have to do it. The homework was impossible because the teacher hadn't covered the material. It was not due for another week, and he would do it tomorrow, and so on and so on.

Having completed his nightly liturgy, he was asked to march to the front hall and retrieve his backpack. He did so with the energy of a convicted killer on his way to the execution chamber.

Harold's backpack was an encyclopedia of boyhood interests and suggested that Harold was well on his way to a promising career as a homeless person. Inside, if one dug down through the various geological layers, one could find old pretzels, juice boxes, toy cars, Pokemon cards, PSP games, stray drawings, old assignments, worksheets from earlier grades, apples, gravel, newspapers, scissors, and copper piping. The backpack weighed slightly less than a Volkswagen.

Julia pulled Harold's assignment folder from amid the wreckage. It is said that history moves in cycles, and this is true when it comes to the philosophy of homework-folder organization. In some ages, the three-ring binder is in vogue. In others, the double-sided cardboard folder prevails. The world's great educators debate the merits of each system, and their preferences seem to alternate according to some astrological cycle.

Julia found his assignment sheet, and realized with a sinking heart that the next sixty-five minutes would be spent completing the ten-minute assignment. The project's requirements were minimal—Harold would merely need a shoebox, six colored markers, construction paper, a three-foot display board, linseed oil, ebony, the toenail of a three-toed sloth, and some glitter glue.

Julia dimly suspected, and research by Harris Cooper of Duke University confirms, that there is only a tenuous correlation between how much homework elementary students do and how well they do on tests of the material or with other measures of achievement. She also suspected that this nightly homework ordeal served other purposes—to convince parents that their kids are getting a suitably rigorous education; to introduce the children to their future lives as spiritually crushed drones; or, more positively, to introduce children to the study habits they would need later in life.

In any case, Julia, trapped in the overpressured parenting life that everybody in her social class ridicules but few renounce, girded herself for the bribery and cajolery that would follow. She would, over the next few minutes, present Harold with an ever more elaborate series of incentives—gold stars, small pieces of candy, BMWs—all to induce him to do his homework. When these failed, as they inevitably would, she would wheel out the disincentives—threats to cut off TV privileges, to take away all computer games and videos, to write him out of her will, to imprison him in a cardboard box with nothing to eat but bread and water.

Harold would be able to resist all threats and incentives, either because he was not yet capable of calculating long-term pain versus temporary inconvenience, or because he knew his mother had no intention of ever cutting off the TV privileges, and thus putting herself in the position of having to entertain him all week.

In any case, Julia sat Harold down with his homework assignment at the kitchen table. She turned her back to get a glass of water, and 7.82 seconds later Harold handed her a sheet of paper claiming his homework was done. Julia looked down at the homework sheet, which looked like it contained three or four indecipherable markings that seemed to be in early Sanskrit.

This would mark the beginning of the nightly redo phase of the homework, when Julia would explain it was necessary to do his work slowly and carefully and in English if possible. Harold went through his normal protests, fell into another of his cycles of misery and internal chaos, and Julia knew that it would be another fifteen minutes of turmoil and disorder before he was in any mental shape to do the homework. It was as if she and Harold had to endure a phase of internal riot and protest before Harold would capitulate and be in a state capable of steady work.

One modern view of this situation is that Harold's freedom was being crushed by the absurd strictures of civilization. The innocence and creativity of childhood was being impinged and bound by the conformities of an overwrought society. Man is born free but is everywhere in chains.

But looking at her son, Julia didn't really get the sense that the unsupervised Harold, the non-homework Harold, the uncontrolled Harold was really free. This Harold, which some philosophers celebrate as the epitome of innocence and delight, was really a prisoner of his impulses. Freedom without structure is its own slavery.

Harold wanted to do his homework. He wanted to be a good student and please his teachers and his mother and father. But he was just unable. He somehow couldn't help that his backpack was a mess and his life was disorganized. Sitting at the table, he couldn't control his own attention. Something would happen by the sink and he'd check it out. Some stray thought would drive him toward the refrigerator, or to an envelope that happened to be lying near the coffee machine.

Far from being free, Harold was now a victim of the remnants of his own lantern consciousness, distracted by every stray prompt, unable to regulate his responses. He was smart enough to sense that he was spinning out of control. He could not reverse the turmoil welling up inside. So he would get frustrated and think he was bad.

Some evenings, to be honest, Julia made these moments worse by losing patience. At these tired, frustrated moments, she just told Harold to buckle down and get it over with. Why couldn't he complete these simple assignments, which he knew how to do, which should have been so easy for him?

That never worked.

But Julia had other resources. When Julia was young, her family moved around a lot. She switched schools and sometimes had trouble making new friends. At those times, she threw herself at her own mother, and relied on her company. They would take long walks together, and go out for tea together, and her mother, who was lonely, too, in the new neighborhood and had nobody she could talk to, would open up. She would tell young Julia about her nervousness in the new place, what she liked about it and what she didn't, what she missed and what she looked forward to. Julia felt privileged when her mother opened up in this manner. She was just a little girl at the time, but she had access to an adult viewpoint. She felt she was being admitted into a special realm.

Julia lived a very different life than the one her mother did. It was much easier in many respects. She spent an insane amount of time on superficialities—shopping for the right guest-room hand towels, following celebrity gossip. But she still had some of those internal working models in her head. Without thinking about it, without even realizing that she was replicating her mother's behavior, Julia sometimes would share her own special experiences with Harold. She wouldn't really think about it, but often when they were both on edge, when times were hard, she would just find herself talking about some adventure she'd had when she was young. She would give him privileged access into her life.

This particular evening, Julia saw Harold strangely alone, struggling with the stimuli and the random impulses within. She instinctively pulled him in, and brought him a bit inside her own life.

She told him a story. She told him, of all things, about a drive she had taken across the country with some friends after college. She described the rhythms of that drive, where they had stayed night after night, how the Appalachians had given way to the plains and then the Rockies. She described what it was like to wake up in the morning and see mountains in the distance and then drive for hours and still not reach them. She described the string of Cadillacs she had seen planted upright along the highway.

As she did this, his eyes were rapt upon her. She was treating him with respect and letting him into that most mysterious region—the hidden zone of his mother's life that had existed before his birth. His time horizon subtly widened. He got subtle intimations of his mother's girlhood, her maturity, his arrival, his growth, this moment now, and the adventures he would someday have.

And as Julia talked, she was tidying up. She was clearing space on the counters, removing the boxes and stray letters that had piled up during the day. Harold leaned in toward her, as if she were offering him water after a thirsty walk. Over the years, Harold had learned how to use her as a tool to organize himself, and during their little random conversation he started to do just that.

Julia looked over at Harold and noticed he had his pencil dangling from his mouth. He wasn't really chewing on it, just letting it hang softly between his teeth in the way he automatically did when he was thinking about something. He suddenly looked happier and more collected. With her story, Julia had triggered something—an implicit memory of what it was like to be calm and in control. She'd engaged him in the sort of extended conversation that he was still incapable of performing on his own. It was like a miracle, and Harold soon got his homework smoothly done.

But of course it wasn't a miracle. If there is one thing developmental psychologists have learned over the years, it is that parents don't have to be brilliant psychologists to succeed. They don't have to be supremely gifted teachers. Most of the stuff parents do with flashcards and special drills and tutorials to hone their kids into perfect achievement machines don't have any effect at all. Instead, parents just have to be good enough. They have to provide their kids with stable and predictable rhythms. They need to be able to fall in tune with their kids' needs, combining warmth and discipline. They need to establish the secure emotional bonds that kids can fall back upon in the face of stress. They need to be there to provide living examples of how to cope with the problems of the world so that their children can develop unconscious models in their heads.

Firmly Attached

Social scientists do their best to arrive at some limited understanding of human development. In 1944 the British psychologist John Bowlby did a study called *Forty-Four Juvenile Thieves* on a group of young delinquents. He noticed that a high percentage of the boys had been abandoned when they were young, and suffered from feelings of anger, humiliation, and worthlessness. "She left because I'm no good," they'd explain.

Bowlby noticed that the boys withheld affections and developed other strategies to cope with the sense of abandonment that plagued them. He theorized that what kids need most are safety and exploration. They need to feel loved by those who care for them, but they also need to go out into the world and to take care of themselves. Bowlby argued that these two needs, while sometimes in conflict, are also connected. The more secure a person feels at home, the more likely he or she is to venture out boldly to explore new things. Or as Bowlby himself put it, "All of us, from cradle to grave, are happiest when life is organized as a series of excursions, long or short, from the secure base provided by our attachment figures."

Bowlby's work helped shift thinking about childhood, and about human nature. Up until his day, psychologists tended to study individual behavior, not relationships. Bowlby's work emphasized that the relationship between a child and a mother or primary caregiver powerfully molds how that child will see herself and the world.

Before Bowlby's era, and even in the years beyond, many people focused on the conscious choices people made. The assumption was that people look at the world, which is simple, and then make decisions about it, which are complicated and hard. Bowlby focused on the unconscious models we carry around in our heads, which organize perception in the first place.

For example, a baby is born with a certain inborn trait, like irritability. But he is lucky enough to have a mother who can read his moods. She hugs him when he wants hugs and puts him down when he wants to be put down. She stimulates him when he wants stimulation and holds back when he needs tranquility. The baby learns that he is a creature who exists in dialogue with others. He comes to see the world as a collection of coherent dialogues. He also learns that if he sends signals, they will probably be received. He will learn to get help when he is in trouble. He will develop a whole series of suppositions about how the world works, and he'll rely on these suppositions as he ventures forth and meets other people (where these suppositions will either be validated or violated).

Children born into a web of attuned relationships know how to join in conversations with new people and read social signals. They see the world as a welcoming place. Children born into a web of threatening relationships can be fearful, withdrawn, or overaggressive. They often perceive threats, even when none exist. They may not be able to read signals or have a sense of themselves as someone worth listening to. This act of unconscious reality construction powerfully determines what we see and what we pay attention to. It powerfully shapes what we will end up doing.

There are many ways to define parental relationships, but Bowlby's protégé, Mary Ainsworth, figured that a crucial moment came when a child was separated from her attachment figure and compelled, even for a few minutes, to explore the world on her own. Ainsworth devised the Strange Situation Test to examine these transition moments between safety and exploration. In a typical permutation of the test, Ainsworth put a young child (usually between nine and eighteen months) and her mother in a room filled with toys that invite exploration. Then a stranger would enter the room. Then the mother would leave the baby with the stranger. Then the mother would return. Then the mother and the stranger would leave the baby alone. Then the stranger would return. Ainsworth and her colleagues closely observed the child at each of these transitions: How much did she protest when the mother left? How did she react when Mom returned? How did she react to the stranger?

Over the subsequent decades, the Strange Situation Test has been applied to thousands and thousands of children all around the world. About two-thirds of the children cry a bit when their mother leaves them in this test and then rush to her when she returns to the room. These children are said to be securely attached. About a fifth of the children don't make any outward display when their mother leaves, nor do they hurry over to her when she returns. These children are said to be avoidantly attached. The final group doesn't display coherent responses. They may rush back to Mom as she returns but also punch her in anger when she gets close. These children are said to have ambivalent or disorganized attachment styles.

These categories have the same flaws as all attempts to categorize human beings. Nonetheless, there is a mountain of research, known as attachment theory, which explores how different types of attachment are related to different parenting styles, and how strongly childhood attachments shape relationships and accomplishments over the course of a lifetime. It turns out that attachment, even at age one, correlates reasonably well with how people will do in school, how they will fare in life and how they will develop relationships later in life. The results of one test in infancy don't determine a life course. No one is locked into any destiny during childhood. But they give an insight into the internal working models that have been created by the relationship between parents and child, models that will then be used to navigate the world beyond.

Securely attached children have parents that are attuned to their desires and mirror their moods. Their mothers soothe them when they are alarmed and play happily with them when they are gleeful. These children do not have perfect parents or perfect relationships. Children are not fragile. Their parents can screw up, lose their tempers, and sometimes ignore their children's needs, and yet if the overall pattern of care is reliable, then their kids still feel secure in their presence. Another lesson is that there is no one right parenting style. Parents can deliver stern punishments, and as long as the child thinks the conversation is coherent and predictable, then the attachment will probably still be secure.

When parents do achieve this attunement with their kids, then a rush of oxytocin floods through their brains. Some scientists, with that special way of theirs, call oxytocin the "affiliative neuropeptide." It surges when people are enjoying close social bonds; when a mother is giving birth or suckling her child; after an orgasm, when two people in love gaze into each other's eyes; when friends or relatives hug. Oxytocin gives people a powerful feeling of contentment. In other words, oxytocin is nature's way of weaving people together.

Securely attached children tend to cope with stressful situations well. A study by Megan Gunnar of the University of Minnesota found that when you give a shot to a fifteen-month-old who is securely attached, he will cry at the pain, but the level of cortisol in his body will not rise. Insecurely attached children may cry just as loud, but they may not reach for their caregiver and their cortisol levels are more likely to shoot up, because they are accustomed to feeling more existential stress. Securely attached children tend to have more friends at school and at summer camp. In school, they know how to use teachers and other adults to succeed. They don't feel compelled to lean against and be near the teachers at all times. Neither do they hold themselves aloof from teachers. They come and go—establishing contact and breaking away. They also tend to be more truthful through life, feeling less of a need to lie to puff themselves up in other's eyes.

Avoidantly attached children tend to have parents who are emotionally withdrawn and psychologically unavailable. They don't communicate well with their children or establish emotional rapport. Sometimes they will say the right things, but their words are not accompanied by any physical gestures that communicate affection. In response, their children develop an internal working model in which they figure they have to take care of themselves. They learn not to rely on others and preemptively withdraw. In the Strange Situation Tests, they don't protest (at least on the outside) when their mothers leave the room, even though their heart rate goes up and internally they are all worked up. When left alone, they tend not to cry, but continue with their solitary play and exploration.

As they get older, these children seem, at first blush, astonishingly independent and mature. During the first weeks of school, their teachers rate them highly. But gradually it becomes clear that they are not developing close relationships with friends and adults. They suffer from higher levels of chronic anxiety and are unsure in social situations. In the book *The Development of the Person* by L. Alan Sroufe, Byron Egeland, Elizabeth A. Carlson and W. Andrew Collins, there is a description of an avoidantly attached child as he walks into a classroom: "He walked in a series of angles, like a sailboat tacking into the wind. By approximation, he eventually wound up near the teacher; then, turning his back toward her, he would wait for her to contact him."

Adults who are avoidantly attached tend not to remember much about their childhoods. They may describe their childhoods in generalities, but there was little that was emotionally powerful enough to lodge into recall. Often they have trouble developing intimate commitments. They may excel at logical discussion but react with deep unease when conversation turns to the emotions, or when asked to reveal themselves. They go through their days within a narrow emotional range, and are most at ease when alone. According to work done by Pascal Vrticka of the University of Geneva, adults who were avoidantly attached show less activation in the reward areas of the brain during social interaction. They are three times more likely to be solitary at age seventy.

Children with ambivalent or disorganized attachment patterns tend to have parents who are inconstant. They are there one minute, gone the next. They may be overly intrusive one hour, and then coldly aloof. The children have trouble developing consistent working models. They feel a simultaneous urge to run toward Mom and Dad and run away. When they are placed on the edge of a scary incline, even as early as twelve months, they don't look toward their mothers for help, the way secure babies do. They look away from their mothers.

Later in life, these children are more fearful than other children.

They are more likely to perceive threats, and to have trouble controlling their impulses. These kinds of stresses can have long-term influences. Girls who grow up in homes without a father tend to have their periods at earlier ages, even after controlling for other factors. They tend, in general, to be more promiscuous in adolescence. Children with disorganized attachment patterns tend to have higher rates of psychopathology at age seventeen. Children from disorganized homes have smaller, less densely connected brains because the traumatic shocks of their childhood have retarded synaptic development.

Again, all this is not to say that early attachment determines a life course. Adult outcomes do not rigidly follow attachment patterns. That's in part because some people seem to have tremendously resilient temperaments that allow them to overcome early disadvantages. (Even among people who are sexually abused as children, roughly a third show few serious aftereffects in adulthood.) And it's in part because life is complicated. A child with a poor attachment pattern with his mother might meet a mentor or an aunt who will teach him how to relate. Some children have the ability to "use" other people, to attract attachment figures even if their parents are not doing the job. But these early parental attachments do open up a pathway; they foster an unconscious working model of how the world works.

Many studies have traced how early attachment patterns influence people over the course of their lives. They've found, for example, that Germany has more avoidant babies than the United States, and Japan has more anxious ones. One of the most impressive studies is based in Minnesota and summarized in *The Development of the Person* by Sroufe, Egeland, Carlson and Collins.

Sroufe and his team have followed 180 children and their families for over three decades. They began testing about three months before the children were born (to evaluate the personalities of the parents), and they have observed, measured, and tested them in myriad ways since, in all aspects of their lives, and always with multiple rigorous independent observers.

The results of this study do not overturn common sense, but they do reinforce it in impressive ways. The first striking finding is most of the causal arrows flow from parent to child. It's obviously true that irritable or colicky children are harder to attach to and calm and sunny children are easier to attach to. Nonetheless, the key factor is parental sensitivity. Parents with communicative, interacting personalities tended to produce securely attached children. Parents with memories of good relationships with their own parents also tend to produce securely attached children. Sensitive parents can securely attach to difficult children and overcome genetic disadvantages.

Another striking finding is that people develop coherently. Children who were rated securely attached at one age, tended to get the same rating at another age, unless some horrible event intervened, like the death of a parent or abuse at home. "In general, our study strongly supported the predictive power of childhood experience," the authors write. Sensitive early care predicted competence at every subsequent age.

Third, attachment patterns correlated well with school performance. Some researchers think that, if they measure a kid's IQ, they can easily predict how well the kid will fare academically. The Sroufe study suggests that social and emotional factors are also incredibly powerful. Attachment-security and caregiver-sensitivity ratings were related to reading and math scores throughout the school years. Children with insecure or avoidant attachments were much more likely to develop behavior problems at school. Kids who had dominating, intrusive, and unpredictable caregivers at six months were much more likely to be inattentive and hyperactive by school age.

By observing quality of care measures at forty-two months, the Sroufe researchers could predict with 77 percent accuracy who would drop out of high school. Throwing in IQ and test-achievement data did not allow researchers to improve on that prediction's accuracy. The children who remained in school generally knew how to build relationships with their teachers and peers. At age nineteen, they reported having at least one "special" teacher who was "in their corner." Those who dropped out didn't know how to build relationships with adults. Most reported having no special teachers and "many of them looked at the interviewer as if an unfathomable question had been asked."

Attachment patterns in early childhood also helped predict the quality (though not the quantity) of other relationships later in life, especially romantic relationships. They strongly predict whether a child will go on to become a leader at school. They predict teenage self-confidence levels, social involvement, and social competence.

Children also tend to replicate their parent's behavior when they themselves have kids. Forty percent of the parents who had suffered from abuse while young went on to abuse their own children, while all but one of the mothers with a history of supportive care went on to provide adequate care for their own kids.

Sroufe and his team observed children with their parents as they played games and tried to solve certain puzzles. Then, twenty years later, they observed their subjects, now parents, play the same games with their own kids. Sometimes the results were eerily alike, as they describe in one case:

> When Ellis seeks help from his mother as he struggles with a problem, she rolls her eyes at the ceiling and laughs. When he finally manages to solve the problem, his mother says, "Now see how stubborn you were." Two decades later, as Ellis watches his son Carl struggle with the same problem, he leans away from the child, laughing and shaking his head. Later he taunts the child by pretending to raise the candy out of the box, then dropping it as the child rushes to try to get it. In the end he has to solve the problem for Carl and says, "You didn't do that, I did. You're not as smart as me."

The Complexity of Life

If you had asked Harold as an adult which sort of attachment style his parents had established, he would have told you he was securely attached. He remembered the happy holidays and the bonds with Mom and Dad. And it's true; most of the time his parents were attuned to his needs and Harold developed secure models. Harold grew into an open and trusting boy. Knowing that he'd been loved in the past, he assumed he'd be loved in the future. He had a tremendous hunger for social interaction. When things went wrong, when he fell into one of his self-hating moods, he didn't withdraw (much) or lash out (much). He threw himself at other people and expected that they would welcome him into their lives and help him solve his problems. He talked to others and asked for their help. He entered new environments, confident that he could make friends there.

But real life can never be completely reduced to a typology. Harold also suffered from certain terrors and felt certain needs that his parents could never comprehend. They simply had no experience with some of the things he was going through. It was as if he had a hidden spiritual layer that they lacked, terrors they could not understand, and aspirations they could not share.

When Harold was seven, he came to dread Saturdays. He would wake up in the morning, aware that his parents were going to go out that evening, as they almost always did. As the hours stretched by, he would tell himself that he must not cry when they left. He would pray to God during the afternoon, "Please, God, don't let me cry. Please don't let me cry."

He would be out in the backyard, looking at ants, or up in his room, playing with his toys, but thoughts of doom were never far away. He knew that parents were supposed to go out at night and boys were supposed to accept this bravely and without crying. But he knew this was a rule he could not follow, no matter how desperately he tried. Week after week, he dissolved into tears and scrambled toward them as they closed the door and left. For years, babysitters had clawed and wrestled and strained to hold him back.

His parents told him to be brave and to be a big boy. He knew and accepted the code he was supposed to follow, and he had a thorough knowledge of his own disgrace. The world was divided between boys who did not cry when their parents went out and him, alone—who could not do what he was supposed to do.

Rob and Julia tried various strategies to avoid these collapses. They reminded him that he went away to school every weekday without any fear or anxiety. But this didn't allay Harold's absolute certainty that he would cry and do wrong even though he desperately wanted to do right.

One afternoon, Rob caught Harold furtively sneaking around the house, turning on every light and closing every closet door. "Are you scared when we leave?" he asked. Of course Harold said no, meaning yes. Rob decided to take him on a little tour of the house to show him that there was nothing to be afraid of. They walked into every room, and Rob showed him how empty each was. Rob looked at the small empty rooms as incontrovertible proof that everything was safe. Harold looked into the vast empty chambers as incontrovertible proof that some formless evil was lurking there. "See? There's nothing to worry about," Rob said. Harold understood that this was the sort of thing adults said when they looked at something truly terrifying. He nodded glumly.

Julia sat him down for a conversation and she told him she wanted him to be brave. His Saturday-evening scenes were getting out of hand, she said. And this led to one of those comic misunderstandings that are woven into the fabric of childhood. Harold had never heard the expression "out of hand" before, and for some reason he imagined his punishment for crying would be that they would chop off his hands. He imagined some tall thin man in a long coat and long scraggly hair with stiltlike legs sweeping in with great scissors. A few weeks ago, he had decided—again, for confused reasons only a child can really follow—that he cried when his parents left because he ate his food too fast. And now he was going to lose his hands. He thought about blood spurting out from his wrists. He thought about trying to eat dinner with two stumps and whether he would still be able to eat too fast. All this was going through his head as Julia patiently talked to him, and he assured her he would not cry. Like a press secretary, there was an official position he knew he must repeat in public. Inside, he knew he would definitely cry.

Toward evening, he could hear his mother's hair dryer—a sign that the end was near. A solitary pot of water was boiling on the stove, for the macaroni and cheese he would eat alone. The babysitter arrived.

Rob and Julia put on their coats and headed for the door. Harold stood in the hall. The crying itself began as a series of slight tremors in his chest and stomach. Then he felt his torso heaving as he tried to hold it still. The pressure of tears welled up in his eyes, and he pretended they were not visible as he began to feel his nose tickle and his jaw tremble. Then his innards broke loose. He was convulsed by sobs, tears splashing down on the floor, making no attempt to hide them or wipe them away. This time he didn't move his feet or scramble to them. He just stood there alone in the hallway, with his parents at the door and the babysitter behind him, quaking in on himself.

"I'm bad. I'm bad," he thought. His shame welled up and swept over him. He was the boy who cries. And in the turmoil he got the causation wrong. It seemed that his parents were leaving because he was crying.

A few minutes after they left, Harold brought the blanket from his bed, surrounded himself with his stuffed-toy animals, and built a fort out of them. Children project souls into their favorite stuffed animals and commune with them in the way adults commune with religious icons. Years later he would remember a happy childhood, but it was interwoven with painful separations, confusions, misapprehensions, traumas, and mysteries. This is why all biographies are inadequate; they can never capture the inner currents. This is why self-knowledge is limited. Only a few remarkable people can sense the way early experience has built models in the brain. Later in life we build fictions and theories to paper over the mystery of what is happening deep inside, but in childhood, the inexplicableness of the world is still vivid and fresh, and sometimes hits with terrifying force.

CHAPTER 6

LEARNING

Popular, good-looking, and athletic children are the subjects of relentless abuse. While still young and impressionable, they are force-fed a diet of ugly duckling fables to which they cannot possibly relate. They are compelled to endure endless Disney movies that tell them that true beauty lies inside. In high school, the most interesting teachers favor the brainy students who are rendered ambitious by social resentments and who have time on Saturday nights to sit at home and develop adult-pleasing interests in Miles Davis or Lou Reed. After graduation the popular and good-looking have few role models save for local weathermen and game-show hosts, while the nerds can emulate any number of modern moguls, from Bill Gates to Sergey Brin. For as it is written, the last shall be first and the geek shall inherit the Earth.

And yet Harold, forever cheerful, carried the burden of his adolescent looks and popularity lightly. He'd had his growth spurt early, and had been a playground sports star through junior high. The other kids had caught up with him in size and surpassed him in ability, but he still played with a confidence that inspired deference and respect. Together, he and his thin-waisted, square-shouldered friends were notable for their ability to produce noise. Sound radiated out of their pores. They greeted one another explosively across the high-school hallways. If there was a water bottle at hand, they'd play an exuberant game of catch with it in the cafeteria, and everybody else had to flinch as the bottle went whizzing past. They swapped blowjob jokes with the pretty girls, which turned some male teachers into titillated spectators and reduced the sophomores into puddles of voyeuristic awe. They took delicious pride in the knowledge, never expressed but universally understood, that they were the kings of the school.

Harold's relationships with his friends involved maximum body contact and minimum eye contact. They were forever wrestling, shoving, and otherwise engaging in little prowess competitions. Sometimes it seemed entire friendships in that group were built around comic uses of the word "scrotum," and they were just as foul-mouthed with their female buddies. Harold went out with a string of cute girls—successively, as it turned out, from Egypt, Iran, Italy, and an old WASP family from England. Sometimes it seemed he was using Will and Ariel Durant's *Civilizations* series as a dating manual.

And yet he was well liked by adults. With his friends he was all "Yo! Douche bag!" but in parental and polite adult company he used a language and set of mannerisms based on the pretense that he'd never gone through puberty. Unlike many teenagers, he could be sensitive and polysyllabic, and at times he seemed sincerely moved by the global warming–awareness pep rallies that were so beloved by teachers and guidance counselors.

Harold's high school was structured like a brain. There was an executive function—in this case, the principal and the rest of the administrators—who operated under the illusion that they ran the school. But down below, amidst the lockers and in the hallways, the real work of the organism took place—the exchange of notes, saliva, crushes, rejections, friendships, feuds, and gossip. There were about 1,000 students and therefore roughly 500,000 relationships, the real substance of high-school life.

The people in the executive suites believed that the school existed to fulfill some socially productive process of information transmission—usually involving science projects on poster boards. But in reality, of course, high school is a machine for social sorting. The purpose of high school is to give young people a sense of where they fit into the social structure.

In 1954 Muzafer Sherif conducted a famous social-science experiment. He gathered a homogeneous group of twenty-two schoolboys from Oklahoma and took them to a campground in Robbers Cave State Park. He divided the eleven-year-old boys into two groups, who gave themselves the names the Rattlers and the Eagles. After a week of separation, the research team arranged for a series of competitive games between the two groups. Trouble started immediately. The Rattlers put their flag on the backstop of "their" baseball field. The Eagles tore it down and burned it.

After a tug-of-war match, the Rattlers raided the Eagles' cabins, trashed their property, and stole some clothing. The Eagles armed themselves with sticks and raided the Rattlers unit. When they returned, they prepared for the inevitable retaliation. They put stones in socks, so they could smash their enemies in the face.

The two groups developed opposite cultures. The Rattlers cursed, so the Eagles banned cursing. The Rattlers posed as toughs, so the Eagles organized prayer sessions. The experiment suggested what dozens of later experiments confirmed: People have a tendency to form groups, even on the basis of the most arbitrary characteristics imaginable, and when groups are adjacent, friction will arise.

In Harold's high school, nobody put rocks in socks. There, life was dominated by a universal struggle for admiration. The students divided into the inevitable cliques, and each clique had its own invisible pattern of behavior. Gossip was used to spread information on how each person in a clique was supposed to behave and to cast social opprobrium on those who violated the rules. Gossip is the way groups establish social norms. The person spreading the gossip gains status and power by demonstrating his superior knowledge of the norms. The person listening receives valuable information on how not to behave in the future.

At first, Harold's primary concern was being a good member of his clique. Social life absorbed his most intense energies. Fear of exclusion was his primary source of anxiety. Understanding the shifting rules of the clique was his most demanding cognitive challenge.

The students would burn out if forced to spend their entire day amidst the social intensity of the cafeteria and the hallway. Fortunately, the school authorities also schedule dormant periods, called classes, during which students can rest their minds and take a break from the pressures of social categorization. Students correctly understand, though adults appear not to, that socialization is the most intellectually demanding and morally important thing they will do in high school.

The Mayor

One day at lunchtime, Harold paused to look around the school cafeteria. High school would soon be over for him, and he wanted to absorb this scene. Around him he observed the primordial structures of high-school life. Individual students would come and go, but cafeteria geography was forever. From time immemorial, the school Royalty, the clique to which he now belonged, had sat at the table in the center of the room. The Honors kids sat by the window; the Drama Girls, by the door with the Pimpled Young Rockers hanging out hopefully nearby. The Faux Hippies tended to hang out by the trophy case; the Normals, along the tables by the bulletin boards, just to the right of a mix of fringier groups: the Hemp Brigades and the Pacific Thugs—the Asian-American kids who pretended not to do their homework.

Harold was Facebook friends with two or three people in each of these groups, for his gregariousness made him something of an ambassador from the nation of Jockdom to the rest of the school, and he spent large parts of his lunch period walking around the cafeteria exchanging greetings far and wide. As a freshman he'd hung out with whoever was proximate. Then sophomore and junior years he'd been tightly bound into his clique, but as a senior he'd found himself breaking out of it, both out of boredom with his same old friends and because he was growing secure enough in his identity to wander and enjoy people of all sorts.

You could practically see his posture change as he sauntered around the cafeteria, crossing from one cognitive neighborhood to another and falling into each clique's argot and social rituals. He took on the mood of rushed anxiety when he was with the Honors kids, who were extracurricular sluts and always had somewhere else they had to be. He put his arms around the waist of the leader of the black student group and made the sort of racially charged joke that make all the adults go tense but which the students don't seem to mind. The freshman jocks, who had to eat lunch on the floor near the lockers, were meek around him, and as a result he was gentle. The eyeliner girls, who cultivated a defensive wall of jaundiced disdain, actually looked cheerful for once.

"The real great man is the man who makes every man feel great," the British writer G. K. Chesterton wrote. Harold spread a little drop of good cheer wherever he landed. There'd be a group of adolescents sitting around in a circle, their heads bowed, as they silently texted each other notes across the table, and suddenly Harold would appear from above and they'd all look up beaming. "Howdy, Mayor!" one of them would jocularly shout out before Harold moved on, for he had developed a reputation for this sort of lunchroom canvassing.

The Social Sense

Harold had an ability to scan a room and automatically pick up a hundred small social dynamics. We all have a certain manner of scanning a sea of faces. For example, most people's gaze will linger on a redheaded person in any crowd because we're naturally drawn to the unusual. Most people will assume people with big eyes and puffy cheeks are weaker and more submissive than they are. (Perhaps in compensation, baby-faced soldiers in World War II and the Korean War were much more likely to win awards for valor than soldiers with more rugged features.)

Harold could intuit which groups permitted drug use and which groups didn't. He could tell which groups would tolerate country-music listening within its ranks and which groups would regard it as grounds for symbolic exclusion. He could tell, in each group, how many guys a girl could hook up with per year without being regarded as a skank. In some groups the number was three; in others, seven.

Most people automatically assume that the groups they don't belong to are more homogenous than groups they do belong to. Harold could see groups from the inside. When Harold would sit down with, say, the

Model UN kids, he could not only see himself with a bunch of brains, he could guess which one of them wanted to emigrate from the Geek quadrant and join the Honors/Athletes quadrant. He could sense who was the leader of any group, who was the jester, and who fulfilled the roles of peacemaker, daredevil, organizer, and self-effacing audience member.

He could pick out who had what role in any female troika. As the novelist Frank Portman has observed, the troika is the natural unit of high-school female friendship. Girl 1 is the hot one; Girl 2 is her side-kick; and Girl 3 is the less attractive one who is the object of the other two's loving condescension. For a time, Girls 1 and 2 will help Girl 3 with makeup and clothes and try to set her up with one of their boy-friends' less attractive friends. But eventually Girls 1 and 2 will let it be known how much hotter they are than Girl 3, and their ensuing bitter-ness toward her will become more and more obvious until they finally ostracize Girl 3 and replace her with a new Girl 3. The Girl 3s never quite have enough class-consciousness to collectivize and use their com-bined power to throw off the yoke of their oppression.

Harold had impressive social awareness. And yet as he sauntered down the hall and entered a classroom, a slight change came over him. Harold felt perfectly in control in the hallway. But somehow he couldn't achieve such mastery in class, with the reading material. His social ge-nius didn't seem to lead to academic genius. And in fact, the parts of the brain we use for social cognition are different than the parts we use for thinking about objects, abstractions, and other sorts of facts. People with Williams Syndrome have impressive social skills but are severely impaired when dealing with other tasks. Work by David Van Rooy sug-gests that no more than 5 percent of a person's emotional perceptive-ness can be explained by the sort of overall cognitive intelligence we track with an IQ score.

Sitting there in the classroom, waiting for the lecture to begin, Harold would lose the sense of command he possessed in the hallway. He looked over at the brains in the front of the room and decided he wasn't one of them. He could get B+'s and say productive things in the classroom discussions, but his was rarely the answer that made the teachers glow. Somewhere along the line, Harold had concluded that he could do decently well in school, but he was not intelligent, though if you had asked him what being intelligent means, he wouldn't have been able to give a precise answer.

Hot for Teacher

Harold settled into his seat in English class. Truth be told, Harold was sort of in love with his English teacher, which was embarrassing because she wasn't his type.

Ms. Taylor had resented the jocks back in her own high school. She'd been more of the sensitive artist in her teenage years. She'd formed her adult identity in accordance with Tom Wolfe's rule of the high-school opposite. This rule holds that in high school we all fall into social circles and become acutely aware of which personality types are our social allies and which are our social opposites. The adult personality—including political views—is forever defined in opposition to one's natural enemies in high school.

Ms. Taylor was thus forever destined to be in the camp of artistic sensitivity and opposed to the camp of athletic assertiveness. She was in the aloof-observer camp and opposed to the camp of the mindlessly energetic. She was in the camp of the more-emotional-than-thou rather than in the camp of the more-popular-than-thou. This meant she was always exquisitely attuned to her superior emotions, and it also meant, unfortunately, that if she wasn't having an engrossing emotional drama on any given day, she would try to make one up.

During young adulthood, she moved through her Alanis Morissette, Jewel, Sarah McLachlan phases. She marched and recycled and joined the boycotts of the virtuous. She could be counted upon to be moody at big events—proms, weddings, senior week at the beach—in a way that set her off from the carousing hordes of callow youth. She wrote embarrassingly sentimental notes in other people's yearbooks and impressively found her way to Hermann Hesse and Carlos Castaneda even though no one else her age had ever heard of them. She was something of a prodigy when it came to being overwrought.

But she grew up. She smoked in college, which gave her something dispassionate and cynical to do. She also had her years in Teach for America. During that time she saw what being really screwed up was all about, and it made her less enamored of her own crises.

When Harold met her, she was in her late twenties and teaching English. She listened to Feist, Yael Naïm, and the Arcade Fire. She read Dave Eggers and Jonathan Franzen. She was addicted to hand sanitizer and Diet Coke. She wore her hair too long and too natural, to show she wasn't on the job interview/law associate career track. She loved scarves and wrote letters longhand. She decorated her walls, even over her desk at home, with didactic maxims, most of them in the nature of Richard Livingstone's observation, "One is apt to think of moral failure as due to weakness of character: more often it is due to an inadequate ideal."

She could have grown into a normal person if she hadn't been subjected to the high-school English curriculum. It is one thing to have to read, over the course of a few years of one's life, *A Separate Peace, The Catcher in the Rye, Of Mice and Men, The Crucible, The Color Purple, The Scarlet Letter,* and *To Kill a Mockingbird.* It is another thing to have to teach these books, period after period, day after day, year after year. One cannot emerge unscathed.

They wheedled their way into her mind. And before long she became a matchmaker. She decided it was her role in life to look deep into her students' souls, diagnose their core longing, and then match that person with the piece of middlebrow literature that would uniquely change his life. She would stop her students in the hallway, and she would press a book into their hands, and with a trembling voice she would tell them, "You are not alone!"

It had never occurred to many of these kids that they were alone. But Ms. Taylor, perhaps overgeneralizing from her own life, assumed that behind every cheerleader, behind every band member, behind every merit scholar there was a life of quiet desperation.

And so she offered books as salvation. She saw books as a way to escape isolation and feel communion with Those Who Feel. "This book saved my life," she would tell her students, one by one, in hushed whispers after class. She would invite them into the church of those who are redeemed by high-school reading lists. She would remind them that when times are dark, when the suffering is unbearable, there is still Holden Caulfield to walk this path with you.

And then she would kvell. Her eyes would well up. Her heart would be touched. Sometimes just looking at her in this saccharine state was enough to give an average adult diabetes. But there was one other fact about Ms. Taylor that was undeniable. She was a great teacher. Her emotional neediness was all directed to the task of reaching teenagers, and in that business subtlety and reticence have no place. All of the sentimental qualities that made her hard to take in adult company made her a superstar at school.

Her Method

Ms. Taylor was one of those teachers who understand that schools are structured on a false view of human beings. They are structured on the presupposition that students are empty crates to be filled with information.

She couldn't forget the fact that other people are weirder and more complex than we can ever know. She taught adolescents, so the brains of her students were going through a period of tumult that is almost like a second infancy. With the onset of puberty, humans enter a period of ruthless synaptic pruning. As a result of this tumult, teenagers' mental capacities don't improve in a straight line. In some studies, fourteen-years-olds are less adept at recognizing other people's emotions than nine-year-olds. It takes a few more years of growth and stability before they finally catch up with their former selves.

Then of course there are the hormone hurricanes. The pituitary glands in her female students are suddenly churning to life. Just as in early childhood, estrogen is flooding their brains. That deluge produces a sudden leap in both critical thinking skills and emotional sensitivity. Some teens are suddenly sensitive to light and dark. Their moods and perceptions change minute to minute, depending on hormonal surges.

In the first two weeks of a teenage girl's menstrual cycle, for example, surging estrogen levels seem to make the brain hyper and alert. Then in the final weeks a wave of progesterone sedates brain activity. You can tell a teenage girl that her jeans are cut too low, Louann Brizendine writes, and one day she'll ignore you. "But catch her on the wrong day of her cycle and what she hears is that you're calling her a slut, or telling her she's too fat to wear those jeans. Even if you didn't say or intend this, it's how her brain interprets your comment."

As a result of hormonal surges, boys and girls begin to react differently to stress. Girls react more to relationship stress, and boys, with ten times more testosterone pumping around in their bodies, react to assaults on their status. Both have a tendency to freak out at the oddest moments. At other times, they can be astonishingly awkward. Ms. Taylor wondered why her students were generally incapable of smiling naturally in front of a camera. Plagued by self-consciousness, they put on these uncomfortable half-smiles that made them look like they're going to the bathroom.

Her general presumption was that while she's trying to teach English, every single boy in her class is secretly thinking about masturbation. Every single girl in her class is secretly feeling lonely and cut off.

Ms. Taylor would look out over a sea of faces in her classes. She'd have to remind herself that those placid and bored expressions are deceiving. There's mayhem within. When she puts a piece of information in front of a student, that kid's brain doesn't just absorb it in some easily understandable fashion. As John Medina writes, the process is more "like a blender left running with the lid off. The information is literally sliced into discrete pieces as it enters the brain and splattered all over the insides of our mind." "Don't exaggerate the orderliness of their thoughts," she'd tell herself. The best she could hope to do was to merge old patterns already there with new patterns from what she was trying to teach. As a young teacher, she ran across a book called *Fish Is Fish*. It's about a fish who becomes friends with a frog. The fish asks the frog to describe the creatures that exist on land. The frog complies, but the fish can't really grasp what he's saying. For people, the fish imagines fish who walk on their tailfins. For birds, the fish imagines fish with wings. Cows are fish that have udders. Ms. Taylor's students were like that. They had models, imposed by their experience, which caused them to create their own constructions of everything she said.

Don't think the methods teenagers use to think today are the same methods they will use tomorrow. Some researchers used to believe that people had different learning styles—that some people are right brain and some are left brain; some are auditory and some are visual learners. There's almost no credible evidence to support this view. Instead, we all flip back and forth between different methods, depending on context.

Of course, Ms. Taylor wanted to impart knowledge, the sort of stuff that shows up on tests. But within weeks, students forget 90 percent of the knowledge they learn in class anyway. The only point of being a teacher is to do more than impart facts; it's to shape the way students perceive the world, to help a student absorb the rules of a discipline. The teachers who do that get remembered.

She didn't so much teach them as apprentice them. Much unconscious learning is done through imitation. She exhibited a way of thinking through a problem and then hoped her students participated along with her.

She forced them to make mistakes. The pain of getting things wrong and the effort required to overcome error creates an emotional experience that helps burn things into the mind.

She tried to get students to interrogate their own unconscious opinions. Making up your mind, she believed, is not like building a wall. It's more a process of discovering the idea that already exists unconsciously. She wanted kids to try on different intellectual costumes to see what fit.

She also forced them to work. For all her sentimentality, she did not believe in the notion that students should just follow their natural curiosity. She gave them homework assignments they did not want to do. She gave them frequent tests, intuitively sensing that the act of retrieving knowledge for a test strengthens the relevant networks in the brain. She pushed. She was willing to be hated.

Ms. Taylor's goal was to turn her students into autodidacts. She hoped to give her students a taste of the emotional and sensual pleasure discovery brings—the jolt of pleasure you get when you work hard, suffer a bit, and then something clicks. She hoped her students would become addicted to this process. They would become, thanks to her, self-teachers for the rest of their days. That was the grandiosity with which Ms. Taylor conceived of her craft.

The Hunt

Harold found Ms. Taylor absurd for the first few weeks and then unforgettable forever after. The most important moment of their relationship came one afternoon as Harold was moving from gym class to lunch. Ms. Taylor had been lurking in the hallway, camouflaged in her earth tones against the lockers. She spotted her prey approaching at normal speed. For a few seconds, she stalked him with a professional calm and patience, and then during a second when the hallway crowds parted and Harold was vulnerable and alone, she pounced. She pressed a slim volume into Harold's hand. "This will lift you to greatness!" she emoted. And in a second she was gone. Harold looked down. It was a used copy of a book called *The Greek Way* by a woman named Edith Hamilton.

Harold would remember that moment forever. Later, Harold would learn that *The Greek Way* has a tainted reputation among classicists, but in high school, it introduced him to a new world. It was a world alien yet familiar. In classical Greece, Harold found a world of combat, competition, teams, and glory. Unlike in his own world, he found a world in which courage was among the highest virtues, in which a warrior's anger could propel history, in which people seemed to live in bold colors. There was little in Harold's milieu that helped him come into his own masculinity, but classical Greece provided him a language and set of rules.

Edith Hamilton's book also introduced him to a sensation that he had not experienced before, of being connected to something ancient and profound. Hamilton quoted a passage from Aeschylus: "God, whose law it is that he who learns must suffer. And even in our sleep pain that cannot forget, falls drop by drop upon the heart, and in our own despite, against our will, comes wisdom to us by the awful grace of

God." Harold did not fully understand that passage, but he sensed that somehow it carried an impressive weight.

He followed Hamilton's book with others, reading on his own, in search of that sensation of connecting with something mystical across the ages. He had always studied and paid attention in the manner of a professional student, in order to get into the sort of college he would be proud to mention at parties. But he began to read about Greece in a different way, with a romantic yearning to discover something true and important. He read this material out of a sense of need. He went on to read popular histories. He saw movies about ancient Greek life (most of them bad), such as *300* and *Troy*. In a high-school fashion, he dipped into Homer, Sophocles, and Herodotus.

Ms. Taylor watched all this with exuberant attention, and one day they met during a free period to chart a plan of study.

It started, of course, under bare fluorescent lights, in a normal classroom, while she and Harold sat at desks slightly too small for their own legs. Harold had decided, or been cajoled, into doing his senior honors paper on some as yet undetermined aspect of ancient Greek life, and Ms. Taylor was going to be his faculty advisor. So Harold sat there listening to her as she went on excitedly about the project ahead. Her enthusiasm was contagious. It was fun to talk with her one-on-one. Studies of language acquisition have found that the quickest learning comes from face-to-face tutoring. The slowest learning comes from video- or audiotapes. Plus, there was something alluring about having a smart, attractive older woman talking about a mystery of intense interest to him.

Ms. Taylor's theory about Harold was that he was a popular, athletic high-school boy who also showed flashes of idealism. She'd noticed it in their classroom discussions—a desire for loftiness, a desire to be part of something higher than normal life. Ms. Taylor had originally given Harold that Hamilton book because the ancient Greeks offer boys a vision of greatness that seemed to inspire them. When they met, she suggested that Harold write his senior paper linking classical Greek life to some aspect of high-school life. Ms. Taylor was a big believer in the idea that creativity comes when two disparate fields crash in one mind, like two galaxies merging in space. She was a big believer in the notion that everybody should have two careers, two perspectives for looking at the world, each of which provided insights into the other. In her case, she was a teacher by day and, less successfully but not less important, a singer-songwriter by night.

Step One

The first stage of Harold's project would be knowledge acquisition. Ms. Taylor told him to keep reading books about Greek life and bring her back a list of five he had read. She didn't give him an organized curriculum; she wanted him to find these books the way adults find books when they get interested in a subject, by browsing Amazon or the bookstore— by word of mouth and by chance. She wanted him to get information from different kinds of books and different kinds of authors so that his unconscious would actively work to weave it all together.

In the first stage, it didn't matter if Harold's research was a little dilettantish. Benjamin Bloom has found that teaching doesn't have to be brilliant right away: "The effect of this first phase of learning seemed to be to get the learner involved, captivated, hooked, and to get the learner to need and want more information and expertise." So long as Harold was curious and enjoying his quest, he'd be developing a feel for Greek life, a certain base level of knowledge about how the Athenians and the Spartans lived, fought, and thought. This concrete knowledge would serve as the hook upon which all subsequent teaching would be hung.

Human knowledge is not like data stored in a computer's memory banks. A computer doesn't get better at remembering things as its database becomes more crowded. Human knowledge, on the other hand, is hungry and alive. People with knowledge about a topic become faster and better at acquiring more knowledge and remembering what they learn.

In one experiment, third graders and college students were asked to memorize a list of cartoon characters. The third graders had much better recall, because they were more familiar with the subject matter. In another experiment, a group of eight- to twelve-year-olds who had been classified as slow learners and a group of adults with normal intelligence were each asked to recall a list of pop stars. Again, the younger, "slow learners" did much better. Their core knowledge improved performance.

Ms. Taylor was helping Harold lay down some core knowledge. Harold read about the Greeks whenever he had the chance. At home. On the bus. After dinner. This made a difference. Many people believe you should set aside a specific place to do your reading, but a large body of research shows that people retain information better when they alternate from setting to setting. The different backgrounds stimulate the mind and create denser memory webs.

After a few weeks, he came back with five books he had read—popular histories of the battles of Marathon and Thermopylae, a biography of Pericles, a modern translation of the *Odyssey*, and a book comparing Athens to Sparta. These books, willy-nilly, filled in his picture of the life, values, and the world of ancient Greece.

Step Two

In their second session, Ms. Taylor praised Harold for his hard work. Researcher Carol Dweck has found that when you praise a student for working hard, it reinforces his identity as an industrious soul. A student in this frame of mind is willing to take on challenging tasks, and to view mistakes as part of the working process. When you praise a student for being smart, on the other hand, it conveys the impression that achievement is an inborn trait. Students in that frame of mind want to continue to appear smart. They're less likely to try challenging things because they don't want to make mistakes and appear stupid.

Then Ms. Taylor told Harold to go back and look over everything he had read so far, starting with the Edith Hamilton book that had been his first entry into Greek life. Ms. Taylor wanted Harold to automatize his knowledge. The human brain is built to take conscious knowledge and turn it into unconscious knowledge. The first time you drive a car, you have to think about every move. But after a few months or years, driving is done almost automatically. Learning consists of taking things that are strange and unnatural, such as reading and algebra, and absorbing them so steadily that they become automatic. That frees up the conscious mind to work on new things. Alfred North Whitehead saw this learning process as a principle of progress: "Civilization advances by extending the number of operations which we can perform without thinking about them."

Automaticity is achieved through repetition. Harold's first journey through his Greek books may have introduced him to his subject, but on his second, third, and fourth journeys, he would begin to entrench it deep down. Ms. Taylor had told her students a hundred times that it is far better to go over material for a little bit, repetitively, on five consecutive nights than it is to cram in one long session the night before an exam. (No matter how often she repeated this point, this was one lesson her students never seemed to automatize.)

Ms. Taylor wanted Harold to slip back into the best learning rhythm. A child in a playroom instinctively understands how to explore. She starts with Mom, and then ventures forth in search of new toys. She returns to Mom for security and then repeats her ventures forth. Then it's back to Mom and out again to explore.

The same principle applies to learning in high school and beyond. It is a process of what Richard Ogle, the author of *Smart World*, calls reach and reciprocity. Start with the core knowledge in a field, then venture out and learn something new. Then come back and reintegrate the new morsel with what you already know. Then venture out again. Then return. Back and forth. Again and again. As Ogle argues, too much reciprocity and you wind up in an insular rut. Too much reach and your efforts are scattershot and fruitless. Ms. Taylor wanted to slip Harold into this rhythm of expansion and integration.

Harold groaned when she told him to read everything again. He thought he'd be bored out of his mind, going back and reading the same books he'd already finished. He was stunned to find that the second time through they were different books. He noticed entirely different points and arguments. Sentences he had highlighted seemed utterly pointless now, whereas sentences he had earlier ignored seemed crucial. The marginalia he had written to himself now seemed embarrassingly simpleminded. Either he or the books had changed.

What had happened, of course, is that as he had done more reading; he had unconsciously reorganized the information in his brain. Thanks to a series of internal connections, new aspects of the subject seemed important and old aspects, which had once seemed fascinating, now seemed mundane. He had begun to inhabit the knowledge differently and see it in a new way. He had begun to develop expertise.

Harold was not a real expert in ancient Greek history, of course, or ready for his exams at Oxford. But he had crossed the white-belt threshold of expertise. He had come to see that learning is not entirely linear. There are certain breakthrough moments when you begin to think of and see the field differently.

The easiest way to understand this is to examine the expertise that chess grandmasters possess. In one exercise, a series of highly skilled players and a series of nonplayers were shown a series of chessboards for about five to ten seconds each. On each board twenty to twenty-five pieces were arrayed, as if in an actual game. The participants were later asked to remember the positions on the board. The grandmasters could remember every piece on every board. The average players could remember about four or five pieces per board.

It is not that the chess grandmasters were simply a lot smarter than the others. IQ is, surprisingly, not a great predictor of performance in chess. Nor is it true that the grandmasters possess incredible memories. When the same exercise was repeated, but the pieces were arrayed randomly, in a way that did not relate to any game situation, the grandmasters had no better recall than anyone else.

No, the real reason the grandmasters could remember the game boards so well is that after so many years of study, they saw the boards in a different way. When average players saw the boards, they saw a group of individual pieces. When the masters saw the boards, they saw formations. Instead of seeing a bunch of letters on a page, they saw words, paragraphs, and stories. A story is easier to remember than a bunch of individual letters. Expertise is about forming internal connections so that little pieces of information turn into bigger networked chunks of information. Learning is not merely about accumulating facts. It is internalizing the relationships between pieces of information.

Every field has its own structure, its own schema of big ideas, organizing principles, and recurring patterns—in short, its own paradigm. The expert has absorbed this structure and has a tacit knowledge of how to operate within it. Economists think like economists. Lawyers think like lawyers. At first, the expert decided to enter a field of study, but soon the field entered her. The skull line, the supposed barrier between her and the object of her analysis, had broken down.

The result is that the expert doesn't think more about a subject, she thinks less. She doesn't have to compute the effects of a range of possibilities. Because she has domain expertise, she anticipates how things will fit together.

Step Three

Ms. Taylor's third step was to help bring Harold's tacit knowledge of Greek life to the surface. After the weeks of reading, and then more weeks of rereading, she asked him to keep a journal. In it he would describe both his thoughts about Greek life and his own time in high school. She told him to let his mind go free, to let his thoughts bubble up from his unconscious, and to not worry for the time being about what he was writing or how good it might be.

Her basic rule was that a student should be 75 percent finished with a paper before he sits down to write it. Before composition starts, there should be a long period of gestation, as he looks at the material in different ways and in different moods. He should give his mind time to connect things in different ways. He should think about other things and allow insights to pop into his head. The brain doesn't really need much conscious pushing to do this. It is such an anticipation machine, it is always and automatically trying to build patterns out of data. A telephone transmits only 10 percent of the tones in a voice, and yet from that, any child can easily build a representation of the person on the other end of the line. This is what the brain does easily and well.

Ms. Taylor wanted Harold to write a journal because she wanted Harold to retrieve the knowledge that was buried inside in as frictionless a way as possible. She wanted him to go off on a reverie, and convert the intuitions he had developed into language. She was a firm believer in Jonah Lehrer's dictum "You know more than you know." She wanted to give him an exercise that would allow him to wander around the problem in a way that might seem haphazard and wasteful, because the mind is often most productive when it is the most carefree.

Harold would save that journal for the rest of his life, though he was always tempted to burn it because he didn't want his descendents to see his overwrought adolescent musings. At first he would just write a word in the center of a page and then scribble the ideas or thoughts that popped into his head in a cluster around it, and sometimes a peripheral thought would become the center of its own cluster.

He wrote a lot about the passions of Greek heroes. He compared the anger of Achilles to his own anger at various situations, and in his telling he came off as the slightly more heroic character of the two. He wrote a lot about courage, and copied down a passage Edith Hamilton wrote about Aeschylus: "Life for him was an adventure, perilous indeed, but men are not made for safe havens."

He wrote about pride, copying Aeschylus's own passage, "All arrogance will reap a harvest rich in tears. God calls men to a heavy reckoning for overweening pride." He tended to be the hero of his own stories, feeling more and seeing better than his classmates. But at his best, the Greek passages did lift him up and give him a sense of profound connection to an age long past and men and women long dead. "I make honorable things pleasant to children," one Spartan teacher boasted, and this contact with excellence inspired Harold. He experienced a feeling of historical ecstasy late one night reading and writing a journal entry about Pericles' funeral oration. He began to share the Greek sense of the dignity and significance of life. He also began, especially in his later journal passages, to make judgments and connections. He wrote one passage about the difference between the warlike Achilles and the subtle Odysseus. He began to notice the ways in which he was different from the Greeks. There were troubling passages where they

seemed to lack all sympathy. They were great in expressing the competitive virtues—like seeking glory—but they were not so great when it
came to the compassionate virtues—like extending a sympathetic hand
to those suffering or in need. They seemed to lack an awareness of
grace, of God's love even for those who didn't deserve it.

After a few weeks, Ms. Taylor asked to see Harold's journal. He was
reluctant to share it, because so many personal thoughts had found their
way in there. With a male teacher he never would have allowed himself
that vulnerability. But he trusted her, and one weekend he let her take it
home.

She was struck by its nearly schizophrenic quality. Sometimes
Harold wrote in a portentous Gibbonesque voice. Sometimes he wrote
like a child. Sometimes he was cynical, sometimes literary, and sometimes scientific. "The mind wheels," Robert Ornstein has written. "It
wheels from condition to condition, from emergency to quiescence,
from happiness to concern. As it wheels among different states, it se-
lects the various components of the mind which operate in that state."

There didn't seem to be one Harold represented in this journal, but
dozens of them and Ms. Taylor wasn't sure which one she would find as
she turned each page. Ed school had not prepared her for the multiplic-
ity inside the mind of even a single student. "How do you teach a classroom of Sybils," Ms. Taylor wondered, "who are breaking apart and
re-forming moment by moment in front of you?" Still, she was thrilled.
This happened only once every few years—to have a student seize on
her suggestion and leap so far ahead.

Step Four

After a few weeks, Ms. Taylor decided Harold was ready to move on to
the fourth and final stage of the exercise. The best learners take time to
encode information before they begin work on their papers. And
Harold had now spent months encoding and re-encoding information.
It was time to make an argument and bring it all to a point.

Harold had drawn a picture called "Pericles at the Prom" in one of
his journal entries. It showed a guy in a toga in the middle of kids in

tuxes and gowns. Ms. Taylor suggested that he use that as his paper title. She noticed that in his journal Harold seemed to alternate between passages on his Greek studies and passages on his high-school life. But creativity consists of blending two discordant knowledge networks. She wanted him to integrate his thoughts on Greece with his thoughts about himself.

Harold sat at home, with his books and journal pages spread out on the floor and bed before him. How to turn all of this into one twelve-page paper? He read, with some embarrassment, some of his old journal entries. He dipped into some of his books. Nothing was coming together. He texted his friends. He played a few games of solitaire. He went on Facebook. He dipped back into some of the old books. He kept interrupting himself and starting over. A person who is interrupted while performing a task takes 50 percent more time to complete it and makes 50 percent more errors. The brain doesn't multitask well. It needs to get into a coherent flow, with one network of firings leading coherently to the next.

The problem was that Harold was not mastering his data. It was mastering him. He was hopping from one fact to another, but had found no overall scheme with which to organize them. In a small way he was temporarily like Solomon Shereshevskii, the Russian journalist born in 1886, who could remember everything. In one experiment, researchers showed Shereshevskii a complex formula of thirty letters and numbers on a piece of paper. Then they put the paper in a box and sealed it for fifteen years. When they took the paper out, Shereshevskii could remember it exactly.

Shereshevskii could remember, but he couldn't distill. He lived in a random blizzard of facts, but could not organize them into repeating patterns. Eventually he couldn't even make sense of metaphors, similes, poems, or even complex sentences.

In small form, Harold was in the middle of that kind of impasse. He had a certain paradigm he used when thinking about high school. He had another paradigm he used when thinking about the Greeks. But they weren't meshing together. He had no core argument for his paper. Being a normal seventeen-year-old kid, he quit for the night.

The next night, he turned off his phone and closed the web browser. He resolved to focus his attention, exile himself from the normal data smog of cyber-connected life, and get something done.

Instead of starting with his own writing, he went back and read Pericles' funeral oration from *The Peloponnesian War*. The virtue of reading classic authors is that they are more likely to set your mind racing, and of all the things Harold had read, that speech fired his imagination most. In one passage, for example, Pericles celebrated Athenian culture: "We cultivate refinement without extravagance and knowledge without effeminacy; wealth we employ more for use than for show, and place the real disgrace of poverty not in owning to the fact but in declining to struggle against it."

Harold was moved and uplifted. It wasn't even so much the substance but the lofty cadences and the heroic tone. The spirit of the speech entered his mind and his mood changed. He began to think about heroism, about men and women achieving immortal glory through valor, dedicating their lives to the service of their nation. Pericles celebrated excellence and offered models for imitation.

Harold began to think about the different kinds of Greek heroes he had read about: Achilles, the furious man of war; Odysseus the clever leader who seeks to return to his wife and family; Leonidas, who surrendered his life at Thermopylae; Themistocles, who saved his country through deceit and manipulation; Socrates, who gave his life for truth, and Pericles, the gentleman and statesman.

Over the next few hours, Harold thought about these different flavors of greatness. He intuited that somewhere the key to his paper lay in comparing their styles, or in finding some common thread. Somehow his unconscious mind was telling him that he was on the right track. He had that feeling you get when an answer is on the tip of your tongue.

For the first time since he'd begun the writing stage, his attention was truly focused on the task at hand. He looked at his books and journal entries again for examples of different types of heroism. He was possessed by what Steven Johnson calls a "slow hunch." He had a vague, hard-to-explain sense that he was heading in the right direction, but it would take many delays and much circling around until a solution popped into his head.

We are always besieged by different pieces of information bidding for attention. But in his aroused state, Harold shut out everything that didn't have to do with Greek ideas of heroism. Music that might have annoyed him suddenly was rendered mute. Sounds and colors disappeared. Scientists call this the "preparatory phase." When the brain is devoting serious attention to one thing, then other areas, like the visual cortex or the sensory regions, go dark.

Over the next hour or two, Harold pushed himself. He searched for a way to write a paper on heroism, both in Greek and contemporary life. His focus had narrowed but he still did not have an argument. So he went over his books and journal entries yet again to see if some point or argument leaped out at him.

It was hard and frustrating work, like pushing on a series of doors and waiting for one to break open. And yet none of the patterns that popped into Harold's head bound his thoughts. He started writing notes to himself. He'd come up with an idea and then see a stray piece of paper and realized that he'd come up with the same idea a few hours ago and had already forgotten about it. To make up for the limitations of his short-term memory, he began arranging his notes and journal entries into piles on the floor. He hoped that this process of shuffling his notes would somehow bring some coherence. He put notes on courage in one pile and notes on wisdom into another, but over time the piles began to seem arbitrary. He was loosening his imagination. Sometimes an answer seemed to hang just a few millimeters out of reach. He would follow a hunch, a subtle signal from the mental regions beneath consciousness. But he still had no overall concept. Harold had reach but no reciprocity. He was tired and at an impasse.

Once again, he called it a day and went to bed. It turned out to be the smartest thing he could possibly do. There's a controversy among scientists about what sleep accomplishes, but many researchers believe that during sleep the brain consolidates memories, organizes the things that have been learned that day, and reinforces the changes in the brain that have been ushered in by the previous day's activity. The German scientist Jan Born gave a group of people a series of math problems and asked them to discover the rule necessary to solve them. The people who slept for eight hours between work sessions were twice as likely to solve the problems as those who worked straight through. Research by Robert Stickgold and others suggests that sleep improves memory by at least 15 percent.

Harold lay in bed after his night's sleep, watching the sunlight shimmer off the treetops outside his window. His mind wandered, thinking about his day, his paper, his friends, and a random series of other things. In these sorts of early-morning states, people's right-brain hemispheres are unusually active. That means his mind wandered over remote domains, not tightly focused on one thing. His mental state was loose and casual. Then something happened.

If scientists had his brain wired up at this moment, they would have noticed a jump in the alpha waves emanating from the right hemisphere. Joy Bhattacharya of the University of London has found that these waves jump about eight seconds before a person has the insight necessary to solve a puzzle. A second before an insight, according to Mark Jung-Beeman and John Kounios, the area that processes visual information goes dark, shutting out distraction. Three hundred milliseconds before insight there is a spike of gamma rhythm, the highest frequency produced by the brain. There is a burst of activity in the right temporal lobe, just above the right ear. This is an area, Jung-Beeman and Kounios argue, that draws together pieces of information from wildly different areas of the brain.

Harold experienced a blast of insight, his "Eureka!" moment. Something big had just burst forth from inside him. His eyes went wide. He felt an intense and instantaneous burst of ecstasy. Yes, that's it! His mind had leaped across some uncharted void and integrated his thinking in a new way. He knew in an instant that he had solved his problem, that he had a theme for his paper, before he could even really say what the solution was. Patterns that had not fit together suddenly felt as if they did. It was a sensation more than a thought, a feeling of almost religious contact. As Robert Burton wrote in his book *On Being Certain*, "Feelings of *knowing*, *correctness*, *conviction* and *certainty* aren't deliberate conclusions and conscious choices. They are mental sensations that *happen* to us."

His core insight involved motivation. Why did Achilles risk his life? Why did the men at Thermopylae lay down theirs? What did Pericles seek for himself and for Athens? What does Harold seek for himself at school? Why does he want his team to win state championships?

The answer to all these questions is a Greek word he had come across in his reading: *thumos*. All his life Harold had been surrounded by people with a set of socially approved motivations: to make money, to get good grades, to get into a good college. But none of these really explained why Harold did what he did, or why the Greek heroes did what they did.

The ancient Greeks had a different motivational structure. *Thumos* was the desire for recognition, the desire to have people recognize your existence, not only now but for all time. *Thumos* included the desire for eternal fame—to attract admiration and to be worthy of admiration in a way that was deeper than mere celebrity. Harold's culture didn't really have a word for that desire, but this Greek word helped explain Harold to himself.

All his life, he had been playing games in his imagination. He had imagined himself as a boy winning the World Series, throwing the perfect pass, saving his favorite teachers from mortal peril. And in each fantasy, his triumph had been deliriously witnessed by family, friends, and the world around him. This fantasizing, in its childish way, was the product of *thumos*, the desire for recognition and union, which underlay the other drives for money and success.

The thymotic world was a more heroic world than the bourgeois, careerist one Harold saw all around him. In the modern world in which he lived, the common assumption is that all human beings are attached at the earliest and lowest level. All human beings are descended from common ancestors and share certain primitive traits. But the Greeks tended to assume the opposite, that human beings were united at the highest level: There are certain ideal essences, and the closer one is to taking possession of the eternal excellence, the closer one is to this common humanity. *Thumos* is the drive to rise up to those heights. It is the dream of the perfect success, when all that is best within oneself blends with all that is eternal in the universe in perfect synchronicity.

Harold's insight consisted of taking the vocabulary of Greek motivation—*thumos, arete,* eros—and applying it to his life. Harold was really combining two idea spaces, making the Greek world more comprehensible to him and his own world more heroic.

He began furiously writing notes to himself for his paper, describing how the thymotic drive, this drive for recognition, explained all sorts of high-school behavior. He made connections he had never made before and mixed together old information in new ways. At times he felt as though the paper was writing itself. The words just poured out of him unbidden. When he was deeply in the rush of it, he almost felt like he didn't exist. Only the task existed, and it was happening to him, not because of him.

Editing and polishing the paper was still not easy, but it came. Ms. Taylor was delighted by the product. It was a little overheated in places, and parts were painfully earnest. But Harold's rapture came across in every paragraph. The process of writing this paper had taught him how to think. His insight gave him a new way to understand himself and his world.

Greek Gifts

Ms. Taylor had guided Harold through a method that had him surfing in and out of his unconscious, getting the conscious and unconscious processes to work together—first mastering core knowledge, then letting that knowledge marinate playfully in his mind, then willfully trying to impose order on it, then allowing the mind to consolidate and merge the data, then returning and returning until some magical insight popped into his consciousness, and then riding that insight to a finished product. The process was not easy, but each ounce of effort and each moment of frustration and struggle pushed the internal construction project another little step. By the end, he was seeing the world around him in a new way. There was, as the mathematician Henri Poincaré observed, "an unsuspected kinship . . . between facts, long known, but wrongly believed to be strangers to one another." Harold no longer had to work to apply qualities like *thumos* to the world around him; they simply became the automatic categories of his mind, the way he perceived new situations.

When he was in kindergarten and first grade, Harold struggled to learn to read, but then it came naturally to him. Suddenly reading wasn't about piecing together words; he could concentrate on the meanings. As a senior in high school, he had similarly internalized some Greek thought, and now he could automatically apply it to his life moment by moment.

He would go off to college and he would sit in classes as required, but he understood those classes would be only the first stage of his learning. He would have to spend nights writing random thoughts in his journal. He would organize his thoughts on the floor. He would have to stew and struggle and then maybe a few times in his life, while taking a shower or walking to the grocery store, some insight would come to him and make all the difference. This would be his method for escaping passive institutional learning. This would be the way he would build for himself a mind that is not stuck in an inherited rut, but which jumps from vantage point to vantage point, applying different patterns to new situations to see what works and what doesn't, what will go together and what will not, what is likely to emerge from the confusion of reality and what is not likely to emerge. This would be his path to wisdom and success.

CHAPTER 7

NORMS

E RICA, WHO WOULD SPEND SO MUCH OF HER LIFE INTER-
twined with Harold, started out in a very different place than he. At age
ten, she almost got arrested.

She and her mom had moved into a friend's apartment in a public-
housing project. Their new neighborhood had a charter school called
the New Hope School, which was in a new building, with new basketball hoops with nets, and with new art studios. The students wore elegant maroon and gray uniforms. Erica was desperate to go there.

Her mother took her down to the social welfare agency, and waited
in a hallway for over an hour. When they finally got in, the caseworker
told them that Erica couldn't even qualify for the lottery to go there because she didn't have legal residence in the neighborhood.

The social workers spent their days besieged by impossible requests. To make their lives manageable, they developed a brusque and
peremptory way of talking. They kept their eyes focused down at their
papers, and sped through the supplicants who came streaming through
the doors. They spoke in municipal-government jargon that nobody
else could understand and challenge. Their first instinct was always to
say no.

The moms had no confidence in settings like that—in an office with
people in business dress. Half the time, they couldn't understand what
the caseworker was saying and were afraid of revealing how little they

knew about the rules. They put on a mask of apathy and sullenness to disguise their nervousness. Most of the time, they just accepted whatever judgment the caseworker rendered and went home. They'd make up some story to explain their humiliation for their friends later on.

Erica's mom was following the pattern. They'd moved into this neighborhood three months before, but the truth is they had no legal status there. It was a friend's apartment, and Erica's mom didn't want to raise a fuss about the school and risk getting evicted from her home. When the caseworker kept repeating that she had "no authorization" to be in the school district, Erica's mom stood up and got ready to leave.

Erica refused to budge. She could already imagine the way her mom would be on the bus ride home—cursing the caseworker, spewing out all the anger she should have let loose right here in the office. Plus, the caseworker was a bitch—chewing gum, looking down on them. She'd barely looked up from her papers to make even a show of eye contact. She hadn't even tried to smile.

Erica gripped the chair as her mom stood and headed toward the exit. "I wanna go to New Hope," she said stubbornly.

"You have no legal residence in the district," the caseworker repeated. "You have no authorization."

"I wanna go to New Hope." Erica had no argument, no logic, just some furious sense that her mother shouldn't take this shit lying down. Her mother, now alarmed, pleaded with her to get up and leave. Erica wouldn't go. She gripped the chair harder. Her mom tugged. Erica wouldn't release. Her mom hissed at her in quiet fury, desperate not to make a scene. Erica wouldn't budge. Her mom yanked her, and the chair fell over with Erica still in it.

"You want me to call the cops?" the caseworker hissed. "You want to go across the street?" The juvenile-detention center was across the street.

Erica held on and soon three or four people were tugging at her at once, including some sort of security guard. "I wanna go to New Hope!" She was crying now, her face a mask of tears and anger. Eventually they got her loose. The rent-a-cop screamed at her. Her mom took the furious little girl back home.

Her mom didn't scold her or even say a word. They rode home silently. That night her mom washed Erica's hair in the sink, and they talked sweetly about other things.

ERICA'S MOTHER, AMY, was the most downwardly mobile member of her family. Her parents had emigrated from China, and all her other relatives were doing well. But Amy suffered with recurrent long bouts of mania and depression. When her spirits were up, she had phenomenal energy and she'd be off doing the model-minority thing. In her early twenties she spent months each at several different colleges, training academies, and learning centers. She trained as a medical technician. She learned computer software in the hopes of becoming an IT professional. She would work two jobs and just plug away with a doggedness she said she'd inherited from her ancient Chinese peasant stock.

During these prosperous months, she'd take Erica out to the all-you-could-eat buffet at Golden Corral and buy her new clothing and shoes. She'd also try to run her life. She'd tell Erica what to wear and which of her friends she wasn't permitted to see (most of them—they carried germs). She assigned Erica extra reading so she'd "run ahead" of the other children. Amy even taught her Chinese calligraphy, with brushes she'd kept packed away in the closet. There was a lightness and rhythm to her brushstrokes that Erica hadn't known her mother possessed. "When you do calligraphy, you must think in a different way," her mom would tell her. For a couple of years, Erica even took skating lessons.

But then there were the down times. Amy would go from slave driver to nullity in a matter of days, leaving Erica to play the role of mother. It was normal to find bottles of Bacardi and Manischewitz Cream and weed and mirrors with cocaine dust around the apartment. Amy wouldn't shower or wear deodorant. Nothing at home would get done. When Erica was a baby, and depression struck, her mom would put Pepsi in her baby bottle just to get her to shut up. Later, she would feed her Cheerios for dinner. They'd go for days on a diet of bologna from the corner bodega. When she was nine, Erica learned how to call a cab so she could take her mother to the emergency room for what she told everybody were heart palpitations. She learned to live in the dark, because her mom would tape shut the curtains.

During these times, her dad didn't come around. Her dad was Mexican American. (The genetic combination accounted for her striking looks.) Erica's dad was a mixed bag—charming and bright but not exactly Mr. Reliable. On the negative side, he seemed incapable of holding reality in his mind. If he was driving drunk and hit a fire hydrant, he would invent a lavish tale to explain that his car had been rammed by a runaway bus. He would give strangers invented versions of his life story. He would tell lies so glaring, even young Erica could see through them.

Furthermore, he talked constantly about his self-respect. His self-respect prevented him from taking any job that involved serving others. His self-respect caused him to flee whenever Amy got domineering. He'd disappear for weeks and months and then show up with Pampers, even when Erica was five or six. He came and went and yet complained that Amy and Erica were sucking away all his money.

On the other hand, Erica didn't hate him, the way some of her friends hated their dads who came and went. When he was around, he was funny and compassionate. He remained close to his own parents, brothers, and cousins and often included Erica in large family get-togethers. He'd bring Erica and her various stepsiblings around to picnics and parties. He was very proud of her then, and told everybody how smart she was. He never went to jail and he never abused her, but somehow he could never stay on task. He had momentary enthusiasms but nothing ever amounted to anything.

Both of Erica's parents were desperately in love with her. In the early days, they wanted to marry and build a traditional home. According to a Fragile Families study, 90 percent of couples who are living together when their child is born plan on getting married someday. But, as is typical, Erica's parents never performed the deed. According to the Fragile Families research, only 15 percent of those unmarried couples who planned on being married actually did so by the time of their child's first birthday.

There were many reasons they never actually got hitched. They faced very little social pressure to actually do it. They didn't entirely trust each other. They never could afford the glorious wedding of their dreams. They were afraid of divorce and the pain that would spread all around. Most important, the cultural transmission belt had snapped. For at least a few decades in American life, it was simply assumed that couples with children would get married—that this was part of entering adulthood. But somehow those life scripts no longer got passed along, at least in certain subcultures, so a decision that had once been automatic and canalized in the brain now required conscious intention. Marriage was no longer the default option. It took specific initiative. For Erica's parents, it never quite happened.

What was Erica's socioeconomic status? It depended on the month. There were times, when her mom was productive and her dad was around, when she lived a middle-class life. But in other years they slipped back toward poverty and into a different cultural milieu. These downward slides sent them hurtling back into disorganized neighborhoods. One month they'd be living in a neighborhood with intact families and low crime. But then they couldn't make the rent, and they'd have to scramble to find a place in a different neighborhood, with empty lots, high crime, and a varied array of living arrangements from apartment to apartment.

Erica would remember those scenes all her life—the small plastic bags to carry stuff away, saying good-bye to the comforts of the middle class, getting crammed into the spare room of some relative or friend, and then the dreary first visit to the decrepit empty apartment in some half-abandoned neighborhood, which would be their new temporary home.

There were fewer jobs in these new neighborhoods. There was less money. There were fewer men, because so many were in prison. There was more crime. But it wasn't just the material things that were different. Modes of thought and habits of behavior were different, too.

The people in the poorer neighborhoods wanted the same things as everybody else wanted—stable marriages, good jobs, orderly habits. But they lived within a cycle of material and psychological stress. Lack of money changed culture, and self-destructive culture led to lack of money. The mental and material feedback loops led to distinct psychological states. Some people in these neighborhoods had lower aspirations or no aspirations at all. Some had lost faith in their ability to control their own destinies. Some made inexplicable decisions that they knew would have terrible long-term consequences, but they made them anyway.

Many people in these neighborhoods were exhausted all the time from work and stress. Many lacked self-confidence even while making a great show of pretending they had plenty of it. Many lived on edge, coping with one crisis after another. There were more horrible stories. A girl Erica knew stabbed and killed a classmate in a moment of passion, effectively ruining her life at fifteen. Erica decided that in these neighborhoods you could never show weakness. You could never back down or compromise. You could never take shit from anybody.

To cope with the disorder, the moms set up sharing networks, and would help one another out with child care, food, and anything else. They looked after one another within the networks, but they were alienated from almost everything beyond—the government, the world of middle-class jobs. They radiated distrust—most of it earned. They assumed everyone was out to get them: Every shopkeeper would shortchange them; every social worker would take something away.

In short, each cognitive neighborhood had a different set of rules of conduct, a different set of unconscious norms about how one should walk, say hello, view strangers, and view the future. Erica handled the moves between these two different cultures with surprising ease, at least on the surface. It was like jumping from one country to another. In the country of the middle class, men and women lived in relatively stable arrangements, but in poverty country they did not. In middle class country, children were raised to go to college. In poverty country they were not.

Annette Lareau, of the University of Pennsylvania, is the leading scholar of the different cultural norms that prevail at different levels of American society. She and her research assistants have spent over two decades sitting on living-room floors and riding around in the backseats of cars, observing how families work. Lareau has found that educated-class families and lower-class families do not have parenting styles that are on different ends of the same continuum. Instead, they have completely different theories and models about how to raise their kids.

Educated-class kids like Harold are raised in an atmosphere of what Lareau calls "concerted cultivation." This involves enrolling the kids in large numbers of adult-supervised activities and driving them from place to place. Parents are deeply involved in all aspects of their children's lives. They make concerted efforts to provide a constant stream of learning experiences.

The pace is exhausting. Fights about homework are normal. But the children raised in this way know how to navigate the world of organized institutions. They know how to talk casually with adults, how to perform before large audiences, how to look people in the eye and make a good impression. They sometimes even know how to connect actions to consequences.

When Lareau showed lower-class parents the schedule one of her educated-class families stuck to, the lower-class parents were horrified by the pace and the stress. They figured the educated-class kids must be incredibly sad. Lower-class child-rearing, Lareau found, is different. In these homes, there tends to be a much starker boundary between the adult world and the children's world. Parents tend to think that the cares of adulthood will come soon enough and that children should be left alone to organize their own playtime. When a girl Lareau was watching asked her mother to help her build a dollhouse out of boxes, the mother said no, "casually and without guilt"—because playtime was deemed inconsequential, a child's sphere and not an adult's.

Lareau found that lower-class children seemed more relaxed and vibrant. They had more contact with their extended families. Because their parents couldn't drive them from one activity to another, their leisure time was less organized. They could run outside and play with whatever group of kids they found hanging around the neighborhood. They were more likely to play with kids of all ages. They were less likely to complain about being bored. They even asked their mom's permission before getting food out of the refrigerator. "Whining, which was pervasive in middle-class homes, was rare in working-class and poor ones," Lareau wrote.

Harold's childhood fit into the first of Lareau's categories. Erica's childhood was so chaotic she sort of bounced between styles—sometimes her mother doted on her; sometimes she had no mother, only a patient she had to care for and nurse back from the edge.

The lower-class mode has many virtues, but it does not prepare children as well for the modern economy. In the first place, it does not cultivate advanced verbal abilities. Language, as Alva Noë has written, "is a shared cultural practice that can only be learned by a person who is one among many in a special kind of cultural ecosystem." Erica's home, like the homes of most working-class kids, was simply quieter. "The amount of talking in these homes varies," Lareau wrote, "but overall, it is considerably less than in middle-class homes."

Harold's parents kept up a constant patter when he was around. In Erica's home, the TV was more likely to be on all the time. Erica's mom was simply too exhausted to spend much energy on childlike conversation. Scientists have done elaborate calculations to measure the difference in word flows between middle-class and lower-class households. A classic study by Betty Hart and Todd Risley of the University of Kansas found that by the time they are four, children raised in poor families have heard 32 million fewer words than children raised in professional families. On an hourly basis, professional children heard about 487 "utterances." Children growing up in welfare homes heard about 178.

And it wasn't just the quantity; it was the emotional tone. Harold was bathed in approval. Every miniscule accomplishment was greeted with a rapturous paean to his magnificent abilities. Erica heard nearly as many discouraging statements as encouraging ones. Harold's parents quizzed him constantly. They played trivia games and engaged in elaborate duels with mock insults. They were constantly explaining to him why they had made certain decisions and imposed certain restrictions, and Harold felt free to argue with them and offer reasons why they were wrong. Harold's parents also corrected his grammar, so that by the time it came to taking standardized tests, he didn't actually have to learn the rules of the language. He just went with whatever answer sounded best. These differences in verbal environment have been linked in study after study to differences in IQ scores and academic achievement.

In short, Harold's parents didn't just give him money. They passed down habits, knowledge, and cognitive traits. Harold was part of a hereditary meritocratic class that reinforces itself through genes and strenuous cultivation generation after generation.

Erica didn't have most of these invisible advantages. She lived in a much more disrupted world. According to Martha Farah of the University of Pennsylvania, stress-hormone levels are higher in poor children than in middle-class children. This affects a variety of cognitive systems, including memory, pattern awareness, cognitive control (the ability to resist obvious but wrong answers), and verbal facility. Poor children are also much less likely to live with two biological parents in the home. Research with small mammals has found that animals raised without a father present were slower to develop neural connections than those raised with a father present, and as a result have less impulse control. It is not only a shortage of money and opportunity. Poverty and family disruption can alter the unconscious—the way people perceive and understand the future and their world.

The cumulative effects of these differences are there for all to see. Students from the poorest quarter of the population have an 8.6 percent chance of getting a college degree. Students in the top quarter have a 75 percent chance of earning a college degree. As Nobel Prize–winning economist James J. Heckman had found, 50 percent of lifetime-earnings inequality is determined by factors present in the life of a person by age eighteen. Most of these differences have to do with unconscious skills— that is, attitudes, perceptions, and norms. The gaps in them open up fast.

Emergence

When Erica was in eighth grade—not in the New Hope School, but in an old-fashioned public school—two young Teach for America alumni started a new charter high school nearby, called simply the Academy. It was meant to pick up the kids who graduated from New Hope, and it had a similar ethos—with uniforms, discipline, and special programs.

The founders had started out with a theory about poverty: They didn't know what caused it. They figured it arose from some mixture of the loss of manufacturing jobs, racial discrimination, globalization, cultural transmission, bad luck, bad government policies, and a thousand other factors. But they did have a few useful observations. They didn't think anybody else knew what caused poverty either. They believed that it was futile to try to find one lever to lift kids out of poverty, because there was no one cause for it. They believed if you wanted to tackle the intergenerational cycle of poverty, you had to do everything at once.

When they first conceived of the Academy, they worked up a presentation for donors, which they later discarded because almost none of the donors understood it. But the premise behind the presentation was still dear to their hearts. The premise was that poverty is an emergent system.

Through most of human history, people have tried to understand their world through reductive reasoning. That is to say, they have been inclined to take things apart to see how they work. As Albert-László Barabási wrote in his influential book *Linked*, "Reductionism was the driving force behind much of the twentieth century's scientific research. To comprehend nature, it tells us, we must decipher its components. The assumption is that once we understand the parts, it will be easy to grasp the whole. Divide and conquer; the devil is in the details. Therefore, for decades we have been forced to see the world through its constituents. We have been trained to study atoms and superstrings to understand the universe; molecules to comprehend life; individual genes to understand complex behavior; prophets to see the origins of fads and religions." This way of thinking induces people to think they can understand a problem by dissecting it into its various parts. They can understand a person's personality if they just tease out and investigate his genetic or environmental traits. This deductive mode is the specialty of conscious cognition—the sort of cognition that is linear and logical.

The problem with this approach is that it has trouble explaining dynamic complexity, the essential feature of a human being, a culture, or a society. So recently there has been a greater appreciation for the structure of emergent systems. Emergent systems exist when different elements come together and produce something that is greater than the sum of their parts. Or, to put it differently, the pieces of a system interact, and out of their interaction something entirely new emerges. For example, benign things like air and water come together and sometimes, through a certain pattern of interaction, a hurricane emerges. Sounds and syllables come together and produce a story that has an emotional power that is irreducible to its constituent parts.

Emergent systems don't rely upon a central controller. Instead, once a pattern of interaction is established, it has a downward influence on the behavior of the components.

For example, let's say an ant in a colony stumbles upon a new food source. No dictator ant has to tell the colony to reorganize itself to harvest that source. Instead, one ant, in the course of his normal foraging, stumbles upon the food. Then a neighboring ant will notice that ant's change in direction, and then a neighbor of that ant will notice the change, and pretty soon, as Steven Johnson puts it, "Local information can lead to global wisdom." The entire colony will have a pheromone superhighway to harvest the new food source. A change has been quickly communicated through the system, and the whole colony mind has restructured itself to take advantage of this new circumstance. There has been no conscious decision to make the change. But a new set of arrangements has emerged, and once the custom has been set, future ants will automatically conform.

Emergent systems are really good at passing down customs across hundreds or thousands of generations. As Deborah Gordon of Stanford discovered, if you put ants in a large plastic tray, they will build a colony. They will also build a cemetery for dead ants, and the cemetery will be as far as possible from the colony. They will also build a garbage dump, which will be as far as possible from both the colony and the cemetery. No individual ant worked out the geometry. In fact, each individual ant may be blind to the entire structure. Instead individual ants followed local cues. Other ants adjusted to the cues of a few ants, and pretty soon the whole colony had established a precedent of behavior. Once this precedent has been established, thousands of generations can be born and the wisdom will endure. Once established, the precedents exert their own downward force.

There are emergent systems all around. The brain is an emergent system. An individual neuron in the brain does not contain an idea, say, of an apple. But out of the pattern of firing of millions of neurons, the idea of an apple emerges. Genetic transmission is an emergent system. Out of the complex interaction of many different genes and many different environments, certain traits such as aggressiveness might emerge.

A marriage is an emergent system. Francine Klagsbrun has observed that when a couple comes in for marriage therapy, there are three patients in the room—the husband, the wife, and the marriage itself. The marriage is the living history of all the things that have happened between husband and wife. Once the precedents are set, and have permeated both brains, the marriage itself begins to shape their individual behavior. Though it exists in the space between them, it has an influence all its own.

Cultures are emergent systems. There is no one person who embodies the traits of American or French or Chinese culture. There is no dictator determining the patterns of behavior that make up the culture. But out of the actions and relationships of millions of individuals, certain regularities do emerge. Once those habits arise, then future individuals adopt them unconsciously.

Poverty, the two Academy founders believed, is an emergent system, too. The people who live in deep poverty are enmeshed in complex ecosystems no one can fully see and understand.

In 2003 Eric Turkheimer of the University of Virginia published a study that showed that growing up in poverty can lead to a lower IQ. Journalists naturally asked him: What can be done to boost IQ development in poor children? "The honest answer to the question is that I don't think there *is* anything in particular about the environment that is responsible for the effects of poverty," he wrote later. "I don't think there is any single thing in an impoverished environment that is responsible for the deleterious effects of poverty."

Turkheimer had spent years trying to find which parts of growing up with a poor background produced the most negative results. He could easily show the total results of poverty, but when he tried to measure the impact of specific variables, he found there was nothing there. He conducted a meta-analysis of forty-three studies that scrutinized which specific elements of a child's background most powerfully shaped cognitive deficiencies. The studies failed to demonstrate the power of any specific variable, even though the total effect of all the variables put together was very clear.

That doesn't mean you do nothing to alleviate the effects of poverty. It means you don't try to break down those effects into constituent parts. It's the total emergent system that has its effects. As Turkheimer notes, "No complex behaviors in free-ranging humans are caused by a linear and additive set of causes. Any important outcome, like adolescent delinquent behavior, has a myriad of interrelated causes, and each of these causes has a myriad of potential effects, inducing a squared-myriad of environmental complexity even before one gets to the certainty that the environmental effects co-determine each other, or that the package interacts with the just-as-myriad effects of genes."

For scientists, this circumstance leads to what Turkheimer calls the "Gloomy Prospect." There is no way to pin down and clarify the causes of human behavior or trace the sources of this or that behavior. It is possible to show how emergent conditions, like poverty or single parenthood, can roughly affect big groups. It is of course possible to show correlations between one thing and another, and those correlations are valuable. But, it is hard or impossible to show how A causes B. Causation is obscured in the darkness of the Gloomy Prospect.

For the founders of the Academy, the lesson was: Fixate on whole cultures, not specific pieces of poverty. No specific intervention is going to turn around the life of a child or an adult in any consistent way. But if you can surround a person with a new culture, a different web of relationships, then they will absorb new habits of thought and behaviors in ways you will never be able to measure or understand. And if you do surround that person with a new, enriching culture, then you had better keep surrounding them with it because if they slip back into a different culture, then most of the gains will fade away.

The founders figured they would start not just a school but a counterculture. Their school would be an immersive environment that would give lower-class kids access to an achievement ethos. It couldn't be totally hostile to the culture in which they lived, or else they would just reject it. But it would insist on the sort of norms, habits, and messages that had allowed the founders, sons of doctors and lawyers, to go to college. Their school would bluntly acknowledge that we live in an unequal and polarized society. It would declare forthrightly that poor kids need different sorts of institutional support than middle-class kids.

Their school would be "parent neutral," which was a polite way of saying they would blot out the culture the poor kids' parents were unconsciously handing down. The sociologist James Coleman had once found that parents and community have a greater effect on achievement than school. The founders of the Academy decided that their school would not just be a bunch of classrooms where math and English were taught. It would also be a neighborhood and a family. The school the pair envisioned would train the kids to see childhood as a ladder to college, a ladder out.

The difficult thing about emergence is that it is very hard in emergent systems to find the "root cause" of any problem. The positive side is that if you have negative cascades producing bad outcomes, it is also possible to have positive cascades producing good ones. Once you have a positive set of cultural cues, you can get a happy avalanche as productive influences feed on and reinforce one another.

There was no way Erica was going to not be in this school. By the time she was in eighth grade, Erica had grown taller and prettier but no less stubborn. Some deep dissatisfaction had crept into her blood. She screamed at her mother and loved her fiercely, a tangle too complex for anybody to understand. On the streets with her peers, she argued, overreacted, and sometimes fought. At school she was both an excellent student and a problem. Somehow it had gotten into her head that life is a battle, and she lived on a warlike footing, antagonizing people for no good reason.

She was sometimes a bitch to people who were trying to help her. She knew she was being a bitch, and she knew it was wrong, but she didn't stop. When she looked in the mirror, her motto was "I am strong." She persuaded herself she hated her school, which she didn't. She persuaded herself she hated her neighborhood, which she sort of did. Here was her true genius. She somehow understood she couldn't change herself on her own. She couldn't remain in her current environment and just turn her prospects around by force of individual willpower. She would always be subject to the same emotional cues. They would overpower conscious intention.

But she could make one decision—to change her environment. And if she could change her environment, she would be subject to a whole different set of cues and unconscious cultural influences. It's easier to change your environment than to change your insides. Change your environment and then let the new cues do the work.

She spent the first part of eighth grade learning about the Academy, talking to students, asking her mother, and quizzing her teachers. One day in February, she heard that the board of the school had arrived for a meeting, and she decided in her own junior-warrior manner that she'd demand that they let her in.

She snuck into the school when a group of kids came out the back door for gym class, and she made her way to the conference room. She knocked, and entered the room. There was a group of tables pushed toward the middle of the room, with about twenty-five adults sitting around the outside of them. The two Academy founders were sitting in the middle on the far side of the tables.

"I would like to come to your school," she said loud enough for the whole room to hear.

"How did you get in here?" somebody at the table barked.

"May I please come to your school next year?"

One of the founders smiled. "You see, we have a lottery system. If you enter your name, there is a drawing in April—"

"I would like to come to your school," Erica interrupted, launching into the speech she had rehearsed in her head for months. "I tried to get into New Hope when I was ten, and they wouldn't let me. I went down to the agency and I told the lady, but she wouldn't let me. It took them three cops to get me out of there, but I'm thirteen now, and I've worked hard. I get good grades. I know appropriate behavior. I feel I deserve to go to your school. You can ask anyone. I have references." She held out a piece of binder paper with her teachers' names on it.

"What's your name?" the founder asked.

"Erica."

"You see, we have rules about this. Many people would like to come to the Academy, so we decided the fairest thing to do is to have a lottery each spring."

"That's just a way of saying no."

"You'll have as fair a chance as anyone."

"That's just a way of saying no. I need to go to the Academy. I need to go to college."

Erica had nothing more to say. She just stood there silently. She decided it would take some more cops to take her away.

Sitting across from the founders was a great fat man. He was a hedge-fund manager who had made billions of dollars and largely funded the school. He was brilliant, but had the social graces of a gnat. He took a pen from his pocket and wrote something on a piece of paper. He looked at Erica one more time, folded the paper, and slid it across the table to the founders. They opened it up and read the note. It said, "Rig the fucking lottery."

The founders were silent for a moment and looked at each other. Finally, one of them looked up and said in a low voice. "What did you say your name was?"

"Erica."

"Listen, Erica, at the Academy we have rules. We have one set of rules for everybody. Those rules we follow to the letter. We demand discipline. Total discipline. So I'm only going to say this to you once. If you ever tell anybody about bursting in here and talking to us like that, I will personally kick you out of our school. Are we clear about that?"

"Yes, sir."

"Then write your name and address on a piece of paper. Put it on the table, and I will see you in September."

The fat man heaved himself up out of his chair and handed Erica his pen and a little pad. She had never seen a pen like that, except on TV. She wrote out her name and address and her Social Security number, just to make sure, and she left.

When she was gone the members of the board just looked at one another. Then after a few seconds, everybody was sure she was out of earshot. The hedge-fund guy broke out into a grin. The room erupted in a wave of joyful laughter.

CHAPTER 8

SELF-CONTROL

THE ACADEMY CERTAINLY WAS A SHOCK FOR ERICA. IN THE FIRST place, it went on forever. School at the Academy lasted from eight in the morning until five in the evening. Erica also had to go on Saturday and for several weeks over the summer. Students who were performing below grade level spent twice as much time in school as other American students, and even students performing at grade level spent 50 percent more time there. Second, the school provided everything. There were the usual English and math classes—actually she took two separate English classes every day. But there was also a health clinic, psychological counseling, full meal services, and evening activities.

But the biggest shock was the emphasis on behavior. The Academy started from the ground up. It taught its students to look at someone who was talking to them, how to sit up in class, how to nod to signal agreement, how to shake hands and say hello on first meeting. Erica and her classmates spent the entire first session of her music class learning how to file into the room and take their seats. During the first weeks of school, they were taught how to walk down the hall, how to carry their books, how to say, "Excuse me," if they bumped into one another. The teachers told them that, if they did the small stuff right, the big stuff would be much easier to master later on. Middle-class kids may have learned these lessons automatically, but many of the kids at the Academy had to be taught.

Another big shock was the chanting. Every school day began with what they called "school-wide circle time." Every student gathered in the gym and they performed raps and chants together. They had a Respect Chant. They had a Knowledge-Is-Power call-and-response. They had a College Chant, in which they screamed out the names of prominent universities and vowed to make it to one of them. At the end of each rally, a gym teacher asked them the Questions: Why are you here? To get an education! How do you get it? Hard work! What do you do? Work hard! What do you use? Self-discipline! Where are you going? College! Why? To be master of my own destiny! How are you going to get there? Earn it! What is earned? Everything is earned!

Each class had its own graduation date. But the year was not the year they would graduate from the Academy. It was the year they would graduate from college four years later. Each classroom had an identity, but it was not Room 215 or Room 111. It was the name of the college the teacher who taught in it had attended: Michigan, Claremont, Indiana, or Wellesley. College was the Promised Land. College was the elevated circle these students would someday join.

In class, Erica learned about things she had never even heard about—life in Thailand and ancient Babylon. She was tested and assessed every six weeks, and the tests were used to mark her progress. If she surpassed expectations, she earned Scholar Dollars, with which she could buy privileges like free time and field trips. Her favorite class was orchestra, where she was taught to read music and started to play the Brandenburg Concerto. She made the honor roll her second term, which meant she could wear a blue shirt to school, instead of the white ones that were the standard uniform. Putting on that shirt for the first time, at an assembly in front of the whole school, was the single proudest event of her life up until that moment.

After school, she played tennis. Erica had never played an organized sport before. She had never so much as picked up a racket. But a few years earlier, two African American tennis stars had come to the school and donated money to build four tennis courts out back. A coach came in every day to teach the game. Erica decided she wanted to be on the team.

Erica became a much more serious student at the Academy, but there was something ferocious about the way she took up tennis. She became obsessed by it. She spent hours every afternoon pounding a ball against the wall. She put tennis posters on the walls of her room at home. She learned the geography of the world by learning about where tennis stars were born and where the tournaments were held. During freshman and sophomore years, in particular, she organized her life around the little yellow ball.

Tennis was serving some larger cosmic purpose in her mind. Walter Lippmann once wrote that "above all the other necessities of human nature, above the satisfaction of any other need, above hunger, love, pleasure, fame—even life itself—what a man most needs is the conviction that he is contained within the discipline of an ordered existence." For a few years tennis organized Erica's identity.

Erica was strong and fast, and though she never admitted it to anyone, she became convinced, even for just these two years, that tennis could be her path to fortune and fame. She saw herself at Wimbledon. She saw herself at the French Open. She saw herself back at the school telling future students how it had all begun.

Her e-mail address was tennisgirl1. Her online passwords had to do with tennis. The doodles on her notebooks were about tennis. Day after day, she picked up tips from the coach, read the online tennis sites, and watched tennis on TV. And day after day, her tennis improved. But there was an anger in her game that scared everyone around her. She was a determined and somewhat serious person in most of the realms of her life, but not an angry one. On the court, she was driven by impatience for everyone and everything. She never talked on the court or bantered with her partners. When she was winning, people relaxed around her, but when she was losing, they kept out of her way. If she had a bad practice session on the court, it ruined the rest of her day, and she went home foul and cranky.

At first the coach called her Little Mac, since her attitude was like John McEnroe's, but one day it got scary. It was the spring of her sophomore year, and her team was playing at an upper-middle-class school in the suburbs. By this point, Erica was the second-ranked girl on the team, playing a singles match late in the afternoon. Her coach watched her first service game from behind the fence and had a sinking sensation right away. Her first serve went long. Her second serve hit the bottom of the net. By the time she was down three games to zero, her form was in disarray. On volleys, her shoulder was flying open. On serves, her arm was dipping down, and she was practically serving sidearm, blasting the ball anywhere but into the other court.

Her coach told her to count to ten, relax, and regain her composure, but she looked at him like a feral animal, her brows furrowed with rage and frustration. Soon she was standing flatfooted awaiting the serve, paying more attention to her own frustration than to the ball. Her returns hit the net, went long or wide, and after each one she'd bark, "Fuck!" to herself.

The coach started peppering her with advice. Keep your shoulder in. Move your feet. Work on your toss. Rush the net. But she was stuck in some spiral of disorganization. She hit the ball as hard as possible, and each error seemed to vindicate some tide of self-hatred rising inside. For reasons that would never be clear, she began sabotaging her own game, hitting volleys deep into the fence behind the court, not even trying to return serves she could have made a try at. She stomped off the court during side changes and threw her racket on the ground beneath her chair. After one bad volley, she wheeled and threw her racket against the fence. Her coach lit into her: "Erica! Grow up or get out!"

Erica hit the next serve for an ace and glared at him. Her next serve was in, but was called out. "Are you fucking crazy?" Erica screamed. All games stopped. Erica slammed her racket to the ground. "Are you fucking crazy?" She stormed the net and looked like she was going to throttle anybody who got in her way. Her opponent, the line judge, her teammates—everybody physically recoiled. She was overflowing with steam and fury.

She knew at that very moment she was doing wrong, but it felt so good. She wanted to punch someone and see a face explode in a flash of blood. She felt some surge of power and domination as she looked at the people drawing back nervously around her. She was looking for somebody to humiliate.

For several long seconds, nobody approached. Eventually, she stormed off the court and sat in her chair, looking down. She blamed everybody but herself. The assholes of the world, the ball, the racket, her opponent. Finally, her coach came over, as furious as she was. He grabbed her arm and barked, "You're outta here. Let's go."

She yanked it away. "Don't you fucking touch me!" But she got up and started walking toward the bus, three strides ahead of him. She slammed her fist against the metal side of the bus as she stepped on, and stomped on down the aisle. She threw her gear against the wall, and herself onto the back bench. She sat there for an hour and a half, while the rest of the matches finished, and then stewed silently as they all rode back to school.

THERE WAS NO REACHING her that afternoon. She had no remorse. No fear of getting into trouble at the Academy or at home. She was stubborn, unyielding, and harsh when anybody tried to talk with her.

By the time the team got back to school, everybody was talking about how Erica had gone crazy on the court. The next day they stopped the school, which is what the administrators did when something terrible had happened. Classes were cancelled, and every student and teacher gathered for an hour in the gym for an assembly on sportsmanship. They never mentioned Erica's name, but everybody knew she had caused it. Teachers and administrators pulled her aside that day— some harsh, some soft—but none of what they said registered.

Temperament

By the next evening, though, the whole episode was beginning to look different. Erica cried into her pillow. She felt a wave of humiliation and shame.

By this age, her mother, Amy, was no match for Erica. Her personality wasn't as strong. But she knew what it was like to behave in ways that were inexplicable to yourself. She wondered if she'd simply passed these genes on to her daughter, and all Erica's fine qualities were about to be overshadowed by the dark ones inherited from dear old Mom.

She also wondered if these were just the storms of Erica's adolescence, or whether this would be her life now and forever. All human beings have inherited from the distant past an automatic ability to respond to surprises and stress, the so-called fight-or-flight response. Some people, even from the earliest age, seem to flee from stress and pain. Some, like Erica, fight.

Some newborns startle more easily than others. Their heart rate shoots up more than others when confronted with strange situations, and their blood pressure rises. Their bodies react more vividly. In 1979 psychologist Jerome Kagan and his colleagues presented five hundred infants with a series of unfamiliar stimuli. About 20 percent of the babies cried vigorously and were labeled "high reactive." Another 40 percent showed little response and were labeled "low reactive." The rest were in between.

A decade or so later, Kagan ran the same children through a battery of experiences that were designed to induce performance anxiety. About a fifth of those who had been labeled "high reactive" still responded sharply to stress. A third of the "low reactives" still maintained their sense of calm. Most of the kids had matured and were now in the middle range. Very few of the kids had jumped from the high reactive to low reactive or vice versa.

In other words, kids are born with a certain temperament. That temperament is not a track that will guide them through life. It is, as E. O. Wilson has argued, a leash. Erica, like all kids, was born with a certain disposition, whether to be high strung or preternaturally calm, whether to be naturally sunny or naturally morose. Her disposition would evolve over the course of her life, depending on how experience wired her brain, but the range of this evolution would have limits. She might grow from high strung to moderately tempered, but her personality would probably not flip from one extreme to another. And once that basic home state was established, her moods would oscillate around that mean. She might win the lottery and be delighted for a few weeks, but after a time she would return to that home state and her life would be no happier than if she'd never won it. On the other hand, she might lose a husband or a friend, but she would, after some period of grief and agony, return to that home state.

Amy was worried. Erica had some dangerous fire inside. Even early on, it was clear that Erica's moods oscillated more wildly than most. She seemed to startle intensely when something unexpected happened (people who startle easily experience more anxiety and dread through life). Some researchers distinguish between dandelion children and orchid children. Dandelion kids are more even-tempered and hardier. They'll do pretty well wherever you put them. Orchid children are more variable. They can bloom spectacularly in the right setting or wither pitifully in the wrong one. Erica was an orchid, perched dangerously between success and catastrophe.

As Amy sat there, wondering blankly about Erica's future, she was experiencing that pervasive depth of worry that the parents of adolescents all know. She herself had been one of those kids who became overly defensive at the first sign of perceived frustration, who misinterpret normal situations as menacing ones, who perceive anger when it isn't there, feel slights that aren't intended, who are victim to an imagined inner world, which is more dangerous than the outer world they actually inhabit.

People who live with that sort of chronic stress suffer cell loss in their hippocampus, and with it loss of memory, especially the memory of good things that have happened to them. Their immune systems weaken. They have fewer minerals in their bones. They accumulate body fat more easily, especially around the middle. They live with long-term debilitating deficits. A study of engineers who worked up to ninety hours a week for six months on an extremely stressful project had higher levels of cortisol and epinephrine, two chemicals associated with stress, for up to eighteen months later, even though all of them had taken four- to five-week vacations after the project was over. The effects of stress can be long lasting and corrosive.

That night, a full thirty hours after the tennis meltdown, Amy still wasn't sure how much she could ease her daughter's stress and shame.

So she just sat there with her hand on Erica's back, and rather pitifully helped her cope. After about fifteen minutes, they were both a little restless, and they got up and started making dinner. Erica made a salad. Amy got the pasta out from the pantry. She and Erica were doing something together. They were doing something that calmed their minds and restored their equilibrium. Somehow, Erica was seeing the world calmly again. At one point while she was slicing tomatoes, Erica looked up and asked her, "Why am I a person I can't control?"

This was actually quite an important question. Research by Angela Duckworth and Martin Seligman found that self-control is twice as important as IQ in predicting high-school performance, school attendance, and final grades. Other researchers disagree that self-control trumps IQ, but there is no question self-control is one of the essential ingredients of a fulfilling life.

"It feels like it wasn't even me," Erica told her mother during one of their conversations about the event. "It was like it was some strange angry person who had hijacked my body. I don't understand where this person came from or what she was thinking. I'm afraid she's going to come back again and do something terrible."

The Famous Marshmallow

Around 1970 Walter Mischel, then at Stanford and now at Columbia, launched one of the most famous and delightful experiments in modern psychology. He sat a series of four-year-olds in a room and put a marshmallow on the table. He told them they could eat the marshmallow right away, but that he was going to go away and if they waited until he returned he would give them two marshmallows. In the videos of the experiment you can see Mischel leave the room, and then the children squirming, kicking, hiding their eyes, and banging their heads on the table, trying not to eat the marshmallow on the table in front of them. One day, Mischel used an Oreo instead of a marshmallow. A kid picked up the cookie, slyly ate the creamy filling and carefully put it back in its place. (That kid is probably now a U.S. senator.)

But the significant thing is this: the kids who could wait several minutes subsequently did much better in school and had fewer behavioral problems than the kids who could wait only a few minutes. They had better social skills in middle school. The kids who could wait a full fifteen minutes had, thirteen years later, SAT scores that were 210 points higher than the kids who could wait only thirty seconds. (The marshmallow test turned out to be a better predictor of SAT scores than the IQ tests given to four-year-olds.) Twenty years later, they had much higher college-completion rates, and thirty years later, they had much higher incomes. The kids who could not wait at all had much higher incarceration rates. They were much more likely to suffer from drug- and alcohol-addiction problems.

The test presented kids with a conflict between short-term impulse and long-term reward. The marshmallow test measured whether kids had learned strategies to control their impulses. The ones who learned to do that did well in school and life. Those that hadn't found school endlessly frustrating.

The kids who possessed these impulse-control abilities had usually grown up in organized homes. In their upbringing, actions had led to predictable consequences. They possessed a certain level of self-confidence, the assumption that they could succeed at what they set out to do. Kids who could not resist the marshmallows often came from disorganized homes. They were less likely to see the link between actions and consequences and less likely to have learned strategies to help them master immediate temptations.

But the crucial finding concerned the nature of the strategies that worked. The kids who did poorly directed their attention right at the marshmallow. They thought if they looked right at it they could somehow master their temptation to eat it. The ones who could wait distracted themselves from the marshmallow. They pretended it wasn't real, it wasn't there, or it wasn't really a marshmallow. They had techniques to adjust their attention.

In later experiments, Mischel told the children to put a mental frame around the marshmallow—to imagine that what they were seeing was a picture of a marshmallow. These children could wait on average three times longer than the children who did not imagine a picture.

Children who were told to imagine the marshmallow was a fluffy cloud could also wait much longer. By using their imagination, they encoded their perceptions of the marshmallow differently. They distanced themselves from it and triggered different, less-impulsive models in their heads. The children who could control their impulses triggered cool ways of perceiving the marshmallow. The children who could not triggered hot ways: they could see it only as the delicious temptation it really was. Once those in the latter group engaged these hot networks in their brain, it was all over. There was no way they were not going to pop the marshmallow into their mouths.

The implication of the marshmallow experiment is that self-control is not really about iron willpower mastering the hidden passions. The conscious mind simply lacks the strength and awareness to directly control unconscious processes. Instead, it's about triggering. At any moment there are many different operations running or capable of running at an unconscious level. People with self-control and self-discipline develop habits and strategies that trigger the unconscious processes that enable them to perceive the world in productive and far-seeing ways.

Character Reconsidered

Human decision making has three basic steps. First, we perceive a situation. Second, we use the power of reason to calculate whether taking this or that action is in our long-term interest. Third, we use the power of will to execute our decision. Over the centuries, different theories of character have emerged, and along with them, different ways of instilling character in the young. In the nineteenth century, most character-building models focused on Step 3 of the decision-making process—willpower. Victorian moralists had an almost hydraulic conception of proper behavior. The passions are a wild torrent and upstanding people use the iron force of will to dam it, repress it, and control it.

In the twentieth century, most character-building models focused on Step 2 of the decision-making process—the use of reason to calculate interests. Twentieth-century moralists emphasized consciousness-raising techniques to remind people of the long-term risks of bad behavior. They reminded people that unsafe sex leads to disease, unwanted pregnancy, and other bad outcomes. Smoking can lead to cancer. Adultery destroys families and lying destroys trust. The assumption was that, once you reminded people of the foolishness of their behavior, they would be motivated to stop.

Both reason and will are obviously important in making moral decisions and exercising self-control. But neither of these character models has proven very effective. You can tell people not to eat the French fry. You can give them pamphlets about the risks of obesity. You can deliver sermons urging them to exercise self-control and not eat the fry. And in their nonhungry state, most people will vow not to eat it. But when their hungry self rises, their well-intentioned self fades, and they eat the French fry. Most diets fail because the conscious forces of reason and will are simply not powerful enough to consistently subdue unconscious urges.

And if that is true of eating a fry, it is also true of more consequential things. Preachers issue jeremiads against the evils of adultery, but this seems to have no effect on the number of people in the flock who commit the act—or on the number of preachers themselves who do it. Thousands of books have been written about the sin of greed, but every few years greed runs self-destructively rampant. There is near-universal agreement that spending on material things doesn't produce joy and fulfillment, and yet millions of people run up huge credit-card debt. Everyone knows killing is wrong, and yet genocide happens. Terrorists convince themselves it is righteous to murder the innocent.

For decades people have tried to give drug users information about the dangers of addiction; teenagers, information on the risks involved in unprotected sex; students, about the negative consequences of dropping out of school. And yet the research is clear: Information programs alone are not very effective in changing behavior. For example, a 2001 survey of over three hundred sex-education programs found that, in general, these programs had no effect on sexual behavior or contraceptive use.

Classroom teaching or seminar–consciousness raising has little direct effect on unconscious impulses. Sermons don't help either.

The evidence suggests reason and will are like muscles, and not particularly powerful muscles. In some cases and in the right circumstances, they can resist temptation and control the impulses. But in many cases they are simply too weak to impose self-discipline by themselves. In many cases self-delusion takes control.

The nineteenth- and twentieth-century character-building models were limited because they shared one assumption: that Step 1 in the decision-making process—the act of perception—is a relatively simple matter of taking in a scene. The real action involved the calculation about what to do and the willpower necessary to actually do it.

But, as should be clear by now, that's wrong. The first step is actually the most important one. Perceiving isn't just a transparent way of taking in. It is a thinking and skillful process. Seeing and evaluating are not two separate processes, they are linked and basically simultaneous. The research of the past thirty years suggests that some people have taught themselves to perceive more skillfully than others. The person with good character has taught herself, or been taught by those around her, to see situations in the right way. When she sees something in the right way, she's rigged the game. She's triggered a whole network of unconscious judgments and responses in her mind, biasing her to act in a certain manner. Once the game has been rigged, then reason and will have a much easier time. They will be up to the task of guiding proper behavior.

For example, some students walk into a classroom with no innate respect for whatever teacher they may find there. When they get angry or frustrated, they'll curse at the teacher, ignore him, humiliate him, or even punch or throw a chair at him. Other students, on the other hand, do walk into the room with an innate respect for the teacher. They know, without thinking about it, that they are supposed to defer to him—that there are certain ways you act in front of a teacher and certain ways you don't. They may get angry or annoyed, but they will express those feelings out of class. It would never occur to them to scream, curse, or throw a chair at a teacher. If someone were to do it in their presence, they'd gasp with shock and horror.

Where did that innate respect come from? How did it come to be that the mere act of seeing the teacher triggered certain parameters in their minds? The answers are lost in Gloomy Prospect. The answers are lost in the midnight river of the unconscious. But somehow, over the course of their lives, they have had certain experiences. Maybe they came to respect the authority of their parents and now extend that mental frame to authority figures in general. Maybe they have absorbed certain stories in which they observed people treating teachers in a certain way. Maybe they have absorbed certain small habits and norms about classroom behavior that put a leash on the sort of behavior they consider unacceptable there. Out of these myriad influences, a certain pattern of perception has emerged, a certain way of seeing. Having learned to see a teacher in a certain way, they would never even consider punching one in the face, except in the realm of faraway fantasy, which they know they will never enact.

Similarly, upright people learn to see other people's property in a way that reduces the temptation to steal. They learn to see a gun in a way that reduces their temptation to misuse it. They learn to see young girls in a way that reduces the temptation to abuse them. They learn to see the truth in a way that reduces the temptation to lie.

This learning-to-see model emphasizes that it is not one crucial moment that shapes a character. Character emerges gradually out of the mysterious interplay of a million little good influences. This model emphasizes the power of community to shape character. It's very hard to build self-control alone (and if you're in a community of obese people, it's very hard to stay thin alone). It also emphasizes the power of small and repetitive action to rewire the fundamental mechanisms of the brain. Small habits and proper etiquette reinforce certain positive ways of seeing the world. Good behavior strengthens certain networks. Aristotle was right when he observed, "We acquire virtues by first having put them into action." The folks at Alcoholics Anonymous put the sentiment more practically, with their slogan "Fake it until you make it."

Timothy Wilson of the University of Virginia puts it more scientifically: "One of the most enduring lessons of social psychology is that behavior change often precedes changes in attitude and feelings."

Rematch

People looked at Erica strangely in the days and weeks after the explosion. Erica looked at herself strangely. But months passed. Life at the Academy meant following a thousand small rules. Don't start eating until everybody at the cafeteria table is seated. Always put your paper napkin on your lap first. Always stand up when a teacher enters the room. Never chew gum when you are in uniform, even if you're just walking home. It's not how Academy students conduct themselves.

These thousand little rules became second nature to Erica, as to almost all the students. She found her diction changing, especially when she addressed strangers. She found her posture evolving, so that she adopted an almost military bearing.

These little routines were almost always about self-discipline in one way or another. They were about delaying gratification or exercising some small act of self-control. She didn't really think about them this way. The rules were just the normal structure of life for a student such as herself. But they had a pervasive effect on how she lived at school, eventually at home, and even on the tennis court.

By junior year, Erica wasn't quite so obsessed with tennis, but she had developed a way of mentally preparing for each match. She was using what you might call the Doctrine of Indirect Self-Control. She was manipulating small things in order to trigger the right responses about the big things.

She'd sit on the bench before a match and play in her head the voices of airplane pilots she had heard, mostly in the movies. They always had such a deliberately calm manner as they came over the intercom. It put her in the right frame of mind. Then she would go through certain tricks and habits, match after match: Always lay your water bottles in the same spot near the net. Always put your racket cover under your chair with the same side facing up. Always wear the same mismatched sweatbands on your wrist. Always step over the lines on the way onto the court. Always draw a line with the right sneaker at the spot from which you will do your serving. Always think about serving five aces in a row. If you don't actually feel you're going to serve aces, just pretend. If your body impersonates an attitude long enough, then the mind begins to adopt it.

Once on the court, Erica had strict rules for herself. There were two locales in her universe: on the court and off the court. Off the court is for thinking about the past and future; on the court is for thinking about the present. When Erica was about to serve, she thought about three things: spin, location, and velocity. If she found herself thinking about something else, she would step back, bounce the ball a few times, and then resume.

Erica would not allow herself to have a conception of her opponent. She would not allow herself to think about line calls. Her performance would be judged by how the ball left her racquet, and nothing else was within her control. Her own personality was not at the center. Her talent wasn't at the center. Her ego and self-worth were not at the center. The task was at the center.

By putting the task at the center, Erica could quiet the conscious self. She could direct her attention away from her own qualities—her expectations, her nerve, her reputation—and she could lose herself in the game. She could prevent herself from thinking too much, which is death to peak performance. She could merge with the patterns of the craft. She could fall back on the many hours of practice when she had done the same thing over and over and laid down certain models in her mind. And when she did this, her self-control was just outstanding, and nothing could ruffle her.

When playing a game like tennis or baseball or soccer, athletes' brains are engaged in complicated cycles of perception, reperception, and correction. Research by Claudio Del Percio of Sapienza University in Rome has found that, while engaging in difficult tasks, star athletes' brains are actually quieter than nonathletes' brains. They have prepared their minds to perform these sorts of tasks so it takes much less mental labor to excel. They also see what is happening much more clearly. Salvatore Aglioti, also of Sapienza, assembled a group of basketball and nonbasketball players to watch movies of free throws. The movies stopped just after the ball was released from the hand, and the athletes had to guess if the ball went in the basket. The basketball players were much better at this. They did it by activating the parts of their brains that control hand and muscle motion. They reenacted the free throw and felt it as if they themselves were performing the task. In short, expert players experience sports differently than nonexperts.

Ninety-five percent of the time Erica's regimen worked. She worried less her junior year, and she played better. There were occasions, though, when her composure slipped. She felt the demon of her anger slipping the chain and about to go off on a romp.

She had a ritual for this, too. She would think about her anger and she would say to herself, "That is not who I am. That is an experience that is happening within me." She imagined a grassy field. On one side was the angry dog of her anger. But on the other was the tennis player who had won her last five matches. She would imagine herself wandering away from the dog and over to the tennis player.

She was trying to establish the right distance between herself and the world. She was practicing the form of self-monitoring that Daniel J. Siegel calls "mindsight." She was reminding herself that she had a say in triggering which inner self would dominate her behavior. All she had to do was focus her attention on one internal character rather than another. This wasn't easy. Sometimes the act of focusing attention required an immense display of mental force. But it was doable. William James was among the first to understand the stakes involved in these sorts of decisions: "[T]he whole drama of voluntary life hinges on the amount of attention, slightly more or slightly less, which rival motor ideas might receive. . . . Effort of attention is thus the essential phenomenon of the will." Those who have habits and strategies to control their attention can control their lives.

As Erica aged, she got better at shifting attention from one impulse to another, and triggering different models in her head. The orchid seemed more likely to bloom.

Inspiration

After a few years in the Academy, she was different. The downside was that she was now somewhat estranged from her old neighborhood friends and even from her parents. They thought she'd entered a cult. The good news was that she had discovered how to work.

One day, a middle-aged Hispanic woman visited the Academy. This woman had started a restaurant company and now owned a chain of restaurants spread around the country. She was thin, well dressed in a conservative business suit, and extremely calm. Erica was transfixed. She could imagine a path between the current life she was leading now, and the sort of elevated life the woman was leading. After all, that woman had traveled that path.

Erica was suddenly consumed by a burning desire to be a business leader. In a short time, she went from a normal hardworking Academy student to a member of the club of the extremely ambitious. She bought an organizer book and portioned her day into color-coded blocs. She gradually changed her wardrobe. Her clothing was so prim, precise, and neat, she began to look like a ghetto Doris Day. She somehow got hold of a used desk set, and divided her assignments into an inbox and an outbox. It was as though her entire being had been suddenly occupied by the ethos of Switzerland. She was meticulous, disciplined, and ready to rise. Something had lit the furnace of the little engine of ambition, which from this day forth would know no rest.

CHAPTER 9

CULTURE

RESEARCHERS HAVE SPENT MANY YEARS EXPLORING THE jungles of the human mind in search of the source of ambition. They've found some traits that highly driven people tend to share, and Erica had many of them.

Ultra-driven people are often plagued by a deep sense of existential danger. Historians have long noticed that an astonishing percentage of the greatest writers, musicians, artists, and leaders had a parent die or abandon them while they were between the ages of nine and fifteen: The list includes Washington, Jefferson, Hamilton, Lincoln, Hitler, Gandhi, and Stalin, just to name a few. Erica hadn't lost a parent. But her mother disappeared psychologically from time to time, and her father did physically. Like so many other ambitious people, she was haunted by the knowledge that life is precarious. Unless she scrambled to secure some spot in the world, everything could be destroyed by a sudden blow.

Highly ambitious people often have met someone like themselves who achieved great success. It could be a person from their town, from their ethnic background, or with some other connection, who showed the way and fired their sense of possibility.

It's amazing how little it takes to spark the imitation instinct. A few years ago, two researchers, Geoff Cohen and Greg Walton, gave Yale students a short biography of a man named Nathan Jackson, who had become a successful mathematician. But they altered one key detail in some of the biographies. In half the cases, the researchers made sure Jackson's birthday matched that of the student who was reading the bio. Then Cohen and Walton gave all the students some math problems to solve. The students who had read the essays with the matching birthdays worked on the problems 65 percent longer than the students without the matching birthdays. These students felt a sudden sense of kinship with Jackson, and were motivated to imitate his success.

Highly ambitious people often possess some early talent that gave them some sense of distinction. It didn't have to be a huge talent. Maybe they were among the better speakers in their fifth-grade class. Maybe they were among the best mathematicians in their small town. But it was enough so that the achievement became a kernel of their identity.

Ambitious people often have a vision of an elevated circle they might join. There's a common prejudice that ambitious people are driven to surpass their fellows, to be better than everybody else. In fact, most ambitious people are driven to achieve membership in some exclusive group or club.

Erica had met the Hispanic restaurant owner at the Academy, and that encounter opened up a conviction that anything was possible for her. She would go to the newsstand and buy copies of *Fast Company*, *Wired*, and *Bloomberg Businessweek*. She imagined herself working at a small new company, part of a band of brothers working together for a common cause. She'd clip ads from other magazines showing people at parties in Manhattan, or gathering at a home in Santa Monica or Saint-Tropez. She'd tape them to the walls around her room. They became the shimmering subjects of her longing, the places she would someday belong.

Erica's teachers praised her for being a hard worker, for being efficient and meticulous. She began to think of herself as a person who could get things done.

In 1997 Gary McPherson studied 157 randomly selected children as they picked out and learned a musical instrument. Some went on to become fine musicians and some faltered. McPherson searched for the traits that separated those who progressed from those who did not. IQ was not a good predictor. Neither were aural sensitivity, math skills, income, or a sense of rhythm. The best single predictor was a question McPherson had asked the students before they had even selected their instruments: How long do you think you will play? The students who planned to play for a short time did not become very proficient. The children who planned to play for a few years had modest success. But there were some children who said, in effect: "I want to be a musician. I'm going to play my whole life." Those children soared. The sense of identity that children brought to the first lesson was the spark that would set off all the improvement that would subsequently happen. It was a vision of their future self.

Work

Some people live in romantic ages. They tend to believe that genius is the product of a divine spark. They believe that there have been, throughout the ages, certain paragons of greatness—Dante, Mozart, Einstein—whose talents far exceeded normal comprehension, who had an otherworldly access to transcendent truth, and who are best approached with reverential awe.

We, of course, live in a scientific age. Vast amounts of research have now been conducted on early achievement, and collected in volumes like the *Cambridge Handbook of Expertise and Expert Performance*. The prevailing view is that geniuses are largely built, not born. In the flinty and overly prosaic view that is now dominant, even Mozart's early abilities were not the product of some supernatural gift. His early compositions were not acts of genius, researchers argue. Mozart was a very good musician at an early age, but he would not stand out among today's top child performers.

What Mozart had, it's maintained, was the same thing many extraordinarily precocious performers have—a lot of innate ability, the ability to focus for long periods of time, and an adult intent on improving one's skills. Mozart played a lot of piano at a very young age, so he got his ten thousand hours of practice in early, and then he built from there.

The latest research suggests a prosaic, democratic, even puritanical view of how fantastic success is achieved. The key factor separating geniuses from the merely accomplished is not a divine spark. Instead, what really matters is the ability to get better and better gradually over time. As K. Anders Ericsson of Florida State University has demonstrated, it's deliberate practice. Top performers spend more hours (many more hours) rigorously honing their craft. As Ericsson has noted, top performers devote five times more hours to become great than the average performers devote to become competent.

John Hayes of Carnegie Mellon studied five hundred masterworks of classical music. Only three of them were published within the first ten years of the composer's career. For all the rest, it took a decade of solid, steady work before they could create something magnificent. The same general rule applies to Einstein, Picasso, T. S. Eliot, Freud, and Martha Graham.

It's not just the hours, it's the kind of work done in those hours. Mediocre performers practice in the most pleasant way possible. Great achievers practice in the most deliberate and self-critical way. Often they break their craft down to its smallest constituent parts, and then they work on one tiny piece of the activity over and over again. At the Meadowmount music camp, students spend three hours covering one page of music. They play the music five times more slowly than normal. If somebody nearby can hear the music and recognize the tune, they are not playing slowly enough. At the Spartak Tennis Club, students have rallies without a ball. They simply work on pieces of their technique.

Benjamin Franklin taught himself to write in the following manner: He would read an essay in *The Spectator,* the best-written magazine of his day. He would write notes on each sentence of the essay on a separate piece of paper. Then he would scramble the notes and return to them after a few weeks. Then he would try to organize the notes in the proper order and use them to recreate the original essay. This is how he taught himself structure. When he discovered that his vocabulary lagged behind the original *Spectator* authors, he switched to another technique. He would translate each essay, sentence by sentence, into poetry. Then a few weeks later he would try to reconvert the poetry back into prose.

As Daniel Coyle notes in his book *The Talent Code*, "Every skill is a form of memory." It takes hard work and struggle to lay down those internal structures. In this way, brain research reinforces the old-fashioned work ethic.

Execution

Schoolwork structured Erica's life during her high-school years. It was the activation of some inner nature. She didn't have one great teacher who changed her life. Instead, the Academy's atmosphere subtly inculcated certain habits of order, discipline, and regularity. Erica loved organizing her assignment book. She loved making checklists and checking off each task as she finished it. If, by high-school graduation, you had asked her to list one outstanding trait she possessed, she would have said, "I am an organized person." She had a desperate need to get things right. In this way, she was drawn to the world of business. Successful people tend to find those milieus where the gifts they possess are most highly valued.

We can all point to charismatic business leaders who lead like heroes on horseback. But most business leaders are not of that sort. Most are the sort of calm, disciplined, determined leaders Erica wanted to be.

In 2009 Steven Kaplan, Mark Klebanov, and Morten Sorenson completed a study called "Which CEO Characteristics and Abilities Matter?" They relied on detailed personality assessments of 316 CEOs and measured their companies' performances. There is no one personality style that leads to corporate or any other kind of success. But they found that the traits that correlated most powerfully with success were attention to detail, persistence, efficiency, analytical thoroughness, and the ability to work long hours. That is to say, the ability to organize and execute.

These results are consistent with a lot of work that's been done over the past few decades. In 2001 Jim Collins published a best-selling study called *Good to Great*. He found that many of the best CEOs were not flamboyant visionaries. They were humble, self-effacing, diligent, and resolute souls who found one thing they were really good at and did it over and over again. They did not spend a lot of time on internal motivational campaigns. They demanded discipline and efficiency.

That same year Murray Barrick, Michael Mount, and Timothy Judge surveyed a century's worth of research into business leadership. They, too, found that extroversion, agreeableness, and openness to new experience did not correlate well with CEO success. Instead, what mattered was emotional stability and conscientiousness—being dependable, making plans, and following through.

These sorts of dogged but diffident traits do not correlate well with education levels. CEOs with law or MBA degrees do not perform better than CEOs with college degrees. These traits do not correlate with salary or compensation packages. Nor do they correlate with fame and recognition. On the contrary, a study by Ulrike Malmendier and Geoffrey Tate found that CEOs get less effective as they become more famous and receive more awards.

Erica didn't dream of becoming flashy and glamorous. She hungered for control. She prized persistence, order, attention to detail.

Family and Tribe

But there are many minds wheeling about in the unconscious. During her senior year, Erica found herself unexpectedly sucked back into a maelstrom. She found the primeval callings of home, family, and tribe reaching out and claiming her in ways she never anticipated.

The complications started when she applied for early decision to the University of Denver and was accepted. Her SATs weren't quite good enough to earn her admission, but her background helped.

When the acceptance letter from Denver arrived, Erica was thrilled, but she was thrilled in a different way than somebody in Harold's social class would have been. Erica's attitude was that she came from a neighborhood where the tough survive and the weak are eaten. For her, Denver admission wasn't a merit badge in honor of her wonderful self. It wasn't a prestigious window sticker her mom could stick on the car. It was the next front in the battle of life.

She brought the acceptance letter separately to her mother and to her father. That's when all hell broke loose. You have to remember that Erica had a split background, half Mexican and half Chinese. She had two extended families, and she spent time with each of them.

In some ways, both families were the same. People on both sides were ferociously loyal to their kin. When people around the world are asked whether they agree with the statement "Regardless of the qualities and faults of one's parents, one must always love and respect them," 95 percent of Asians and 95 percent of Hispanics say they agree, compared to, say, only 31 percent of Dutch respondents and 36 percent of Danes.

Both of Erica's extended families would go out for large and long picnics in the parks on Sunday afternoons, and while the food was different, the atmosphere was similar. The grandparents sat in the same sorts of blue folding chairs in the shade. The kids formed little packs.

But there were differences. It was hard to put those differences into words. Every time she tried to explain the contrasts between her Mexican and Chinese relatives, she ended up lapsing into stale ethnic clichés. Her father's extended family inhabited a world of Univision, soccer, merengue, rice and beans, pig's feet, and El Dieciséis de Septiembre. Her mother's family inhabited a world of woks, ancestor stories, shopkeeper's hours, calligraphy, and ancient sayings.

But the important differences were as pervasive as they were elusive. There were different kinds of messes in the kitchens, different smells that greeted you at the front door. The families told different kinds of jokes about their own kind. Erica's Mexican relatives joked about how late they were to everything. Her Chinese relatives joked about which uncouth cousin spit on the floor.

Erica had a different personality depending on what home she visited. With her father's Mexican relatives, she stood closer to people. She was louder. Her arms hung more loosely around her body. With her mother's relatives, she was more deferential, but when it came time to reach across for a serving platter at the dinner table, she was more aggressive. She was a picky eater with her Mexican relatives but ate the grossest things imaginable with her Chinese ones. In the different contexts she had different ages. With her father's family, she acted like a fully sexualized woman. With her mother's family she still acted like a girl. Years hence, after she had finished her education and made her way in the world, she would come back and visit these relatives, and she would immediately slip back into her old girlhood personas. "A man has as many social selves as there are individuals who recognize him and carry an image of him in their mind," William James once wrote.

The Denver admissions letter created problems at both sets of homes. Everybody in Erica's families was, on one level, thrilled that she had gotten into such a fine school. But their pride was a possessive pride, and beneath their happiness, there were layers of suspicion, fear, and resentment that took a long time to unpack.

The Academy had already opened up rifts between her and her relatives. The school had imparted certain unconscious messages. You are your own project, and your goal in life is to fulfill your own capacities. You are responsible for yourself. Success is an individual achievement. The members of her extended families did not necessarily share these presuppositions.

Her Mexican relatives were wary of the changes that had already come over her personality. Like most Mexican Americans, Erica's relatives were assimilating into mainstream American life. By the time they have lived in the United States for thirty years, 68 percent of Latinos own their own home. By the third generation, 60 percent of Mexican American immigrants speak only English in the home. But Erica's Latino relatives had little experience with the world of elite higher education. They suspected, probably correctly, that if Erica went off to Denver, she would never really be one of them again.

They had a sense of cultural boundaries. Within their own world, they had their heritage and culture, which was deep, enriching, and profound. Outside the boundaries, they felt, there was no heritage. The culture was thin and spiritually inert. Why would anybody want to live on that sparse ground?

Erica's Chinese relatives also feared she was about to drift away into some loose amoral world. They wanted her to succeed, but through the family, near the family, and among the family.

They began pressuring her to go to college closer to home, to schools that were less prestigious than Denver. Erica tried to explain the difference. She tried to explain how useful it was to go to a competitive school. They didn't seem to get it. They didn't seem to understand the thrill she felt at the prospect of moving away and striking out on her own. Erica began to realize that though she looked like them and loved them, she perceived the topography of reality in slightly different ways.

Scholars like Shinobu Kitayama of Kyoto University, Hazel Markus of Stanford, and Richard Nisbett of the University of Michigan have spent years studying the different ways Asians and Westerners think and perceive. The core lesson of Nisbett's work is contained in a famous experiment in which he showed pictures of a fish tank to Americans and Japanese, and asked them to describe what they saw. In case after case, the Americans described the biggest and most prominent fish in the tank. The Japanese made 60 percent more references to the context and background elements of the scene, like the water, rocks, bubbles, and plants in the tank.

Nisbett's conclusion is that, on the whole, Westerners tend to focus narrowly on individuals taking actions, while Asians are more likely to focus on contexts and relationships. His argument is that since at least the time of classical Greece, Western thought has emphasized individual action, permanent character traits, formal logic, and clearly delineated categories. For an even longer period, Asian thought has emphasized context, relationships, harmony, paradox, interdependence, and radiating influences. "Thus, to the Asian," Nisbett writes, "the world is a complex place, composed of continuous substances, understandable in terms of the whole rather than in terms of the parts, and subject more to collective than personal control."

This is a wide generalization obviously, but Nisbett and many other researchers have fleshed it out with compelling experimental results and observations. English-speaking parents emphasize nouns and categories when talking with their children. Korean parents emphasize verbs and relationships. Asked to describe video clips of a complex airport scene, Japanese students pick out many more background details than American students.

When shown a picture of a chicken, a cow, and some grass and asked to categorize the objects, American students generally lump the chicken and the cow because they are both animals. Chinese students are more likely to lump the cow and the grass because cows eat grass, and so have a relationship with it. When asked to describe their day, American six-year-olds make three times more references to themselves than Chinese six-year-olds.

The experiments in this line of research are diverse. When presented with a dialogue of a mother and daughter arguing, American subjects were likely to pick a side, either the mother or daughter, and describe who was right. Chinese subjects were more likely to see merit in both positions. When asked about themselves, Americans tend to exaggerate ways in which they are different and better than the crowd, while Asians exaggerate the traits they have in common and the ways they are interdependent. When asked to choose between three computers—one of which had more memory, one of which had a faster processor, and one of which was in the middle on both—American consumers tend to decide which trait they value most and then choose the computer with the highest performance on that trait. Chinese consumers tend to choose the middle computer, which has a mid-ranking on both traits.

Nisbett has found that Chinese and Americans use different scanning patterns to see the world. When looking at something like the *Mona Lisa*, Americans tend to spend more time looking at her face. The Chinese eyes perform more saccades, jerky eye movements, between the focal object and the background objects. This gives them a more holistic sense of the scene. On the other hand, separate research has found that East Asians have a tougher time distinguishing fearful from surprised expressions and disgusted from angry expressions, because East Asians spent less time focused on the expressions around the mouth.

Erica's Mexican and Chinese relatives couldn't have told you how culture influenced them, beyond the vague stereotypes, but they did have a sense that people in their group possessed a distinct way of thinking, that their way of thinking embodies certain values and leads to certain accomplishments. It's spiritual death to leave that behind.

Authenticity

Relatives from both sides urged Erica to stay close to home. Any kid in Harold's social class would have shrugged off these pleas. Of course, he would go off to college. To people in Harold's circle, personal growth mattered most. But for members of Erica's cultures, family mattered most. Erica found that she was attached to these people in a way that preceded individual choice. Their preconceptions were implanted in her brain, too.

Then there were her childhood friends. Many of her oldest friends had rejected the values of the Academy. She'd gone down one cultural path, and they'd gone down another—toward gangsta rap, tats, and bling. They had decided—consciously or not—to preserve their integrity as outsiders. Instead of selling out to the mainstream culture, they lived in opposition to it. These kids—white, black, brown, and yellow—divided their world into white culture, which was boring, repressive, and dweeby, and black rapper culture, which was glamorous, sexy, dangerous, and cool. Their sense of integrity was more important to them than future income (or else they just didn't want to apply themselves and were rationalizing). In any case, they went down a spiral of countercultural opposition. The way they dressed, the way they walked, the way they sat, the way they acted around adults—all these things made them admired among their peers but precluded high-school success. As a matter of self-respect, they were rude to any adult who might help them. They told Erica she was a fool to go off to that country club, where everybody would look down on her. They told her she'd come back to the hood in her pink preppie sweaters and her khaki shorts. They wanted to be rich, but hated the rich at the same time. She knew they were half teasing, but she was more than half upset.

In the weeks around graduation, Erica thought about her life. She could barely remember the hours she had spent studying. Her most vivid memories involved hanging out on the street and on the playground—fooling around with her friends, going out on her first dates, getting drunk behind the warehouses, playing Double Dutch while high at the Boys & Girls Club. She had spent so many hours trying to get away from this place, but she loved it nonetheless, more fiercely because it was so ugly.

The summer after high-school graduation should have been a time of ease and celebration, but Erica would forever after remember it as the Summer of "Authenticity." Her friends called her "Poindexter" or just "Denver"—as in "Hey, here comes Denver! Isn't she late for her foursome?"

So of course she smoked more weed that summer than ever before. Of course she hooked up with more guys. Of course she listened to more Lil Wayne and more Mexican music and did everything to rebut the neighborhood impression that she'd been whitewashed. Things became bad at home with her mother. She'd be out until 3 a.m., sleeping over unannounced at other people's homes, and showing up at noon the next day. Her mother didn't know if she even had the right to control her anymore. The girl was eighteen. But she worried more than ever. Her dreams for her daughter were suddenly in peril. Something terrible could happen—a shooting, a drug arrest. It was as though the culture of the street had reached out from beyond the grave and was pulling her daughter back in.

One Sunday afternoon, Erica came home and found her mother dressed, angry, and standing by the door. Erica had promised to be home early so they could go to a family picnic together, but Erica had forgotten. She got angry when her mother reminded her of it all, and grumpily stormed off to her room to get dressed. "Too busy for me!" her mother screamed. "Not too busy for the gangbangers!" Erica wondered where her mom got that word.

There were about twenty aunts, uncles, cousins, and grandparents at the picnic. They were delighted to see Erica and her mom. Hugs all around. One man handed her a beer, which had never happened before. The picnic was fun. The loud ones talked and talked. Stories were told. As usual, Erica's mom sort of faded into the background. She was the disappointment in the family, and so she was relegated to a silent corner of family life. But she seemed to be following along and soaking up the company.

Around about hour three, the older folks were sitting around some tables while the kids were still running around. Some of the uncles and aunts began talking about Denver. They told her about the other kids her age who were going to local colleges. They told her about the Chinese way, the family businesses, the loans that went out from relative to relative. They told her about their own accomplishments and their own lives and as the minutes passed, they ratcheted up the pressure. Don't go to Denver. Stay here. The future is bright here. They weren't even subtle. They harangued and pushed. "It's time to come back to your people," an uncle said. Erica looked at her empty plate. Your family— they can get under your skin in a way no one else can. Tears began to well up in her eyes.

Then a quiet voice could be heard from the other end of the table. "Leave her alone." It was her mother. The picnic table went silent. What followed wasn't even a speech. Her mother was so nervous and yet so furious, she just issued a series of disjointed statements. "She's worked so hard. . . . It's her dream. . . . She has earned the right to go. . . . You don't see her in her room night after night. You don't see how much she has overcome, what has happened at home." Finally she just looked around at her relatives. "I've never wanted anything so much in all my life, for her to go to that place and do this thing."

The little speech didn't stop all discussion. The uncles still thought she was wrong, and they still harangued. But the balance of forces had shifted in Erica's head. Her mom had stood up for her in front of the family. Erica's sense of conviction came back to her, and once she had dug into a position, there was no moving her.

The Club

Leaving was still not easy. Leaving your childhood home is never easy. In 1959, when the writer Eva Hoffman was thirteen, her family emigrated from Poland to Canada. Poland lingered forever after in the recesses of her mind. "The country of my childhood lives within me with a primacy that is a form of love," she wrote years later. "It has fed me language, perceptions, sounds, the human kind. It has given me colors and the furrows of reality, my first loves. The absoluteness of those loves can never be recaptured. No geometry of the landscape, no haze in the air, will live in us as intensely as the landscapes that we saw as the first, and to which we gave ourselves wholly, without reservation."

But Erica did go, and in early September, she found herself in a dorm in Denver.

Elite universities are great inequality machines. They are nominally open to all applicants regardless of income. They have lavish financial-aid packages for those who cannot afford to pay. But the reality is that the competition weeds out most of those who are not from the upper middle class. To fulfill the admissions requirements, it really helps to have been raised in the atmosphere of concerted cultivation. It helps to have had all the family reading time, the tutors, the coaches, and the extracurricular supervision.

Denver gave Erica a chance to be around affluent people and to see how they behaved with one another. She learned how they socialized, how they greeted each other, how they slept with each other, what a guy in that culture said when he wanted to get into your pants, and what a girl in that culture said to keep him out. Denver was like a cultural-exchange program. She didn't know the phrase when she got there, but at Denver Erica acquired what the great sociologist Pierre Bourdieu called "cultural capital"—the tastes, opinions, cultural references, and conversational styles that will enable you to rise in polite society.

Actually, it wasn't the students' wealth that shocked Erica and shook her confidence. She found she could easily look down on the guy who wrecked his BMW one day and had his family drop off a Jaguar the next. It was the knowledge. She'd worked hard at the Academy to prepare herself for Denver. But some of these kids had been preparing their whole lives. They'd been to where the Battle of Agincourt had taken place. They'd been to China and spent a summer in high school teaching kids in Haiti. They knew who Lauren Bacall was, and where F. Scott Fitzgerald went to school. They seemed to get every reference the professors threw out. A professor would make some reference to

Mort Sahl or Tom Lehrer, and they'd all chuckle knowingly. They knew how to structure papers in ways that she had never been taught. She took a look at those kids and thought about her friends back in the neighborhood who were still working at the mall or hanging out on the street. Her friends back home weren't just four years behind these Denver kids. They were forever behind.

Erica took econ, poli-sci, and accounting classes. She hung around the business school and sat in when visiting lecturers stopped by. She was very hardheaded and practical. But something bothered her about these classes. In many of them, Erica was taught by economists and political scientists who assumed that human beings are pretty much the same. You put some incentives in front of them, no matter what their cultural differences, and they will respond in predictable, law-governed, and rational ways.

This assumption makes social science a science. If behavior is not governed by immutable laws and regularities, then quantitative models become impossible. The discipline loses its predictive value. It's all just fuzzy, context-driven subjectivity.

And yet Erica grew up among many people who did not respond in predictable ways to incentives. Many of her friends had dropped out of high school when all the incentives pointed the other way. Many of them made decisions that were simply inexplicable, or they had not made decisions at all because they were in the grip of addictions, mental illnesses, or other impulsions. Furthermore, cultural differences simply played too large a role in her life. What really mattered, it seemed to her, was self-interpretation. The way people defined themselves had a huge impact on how they behaved and responded to situations. None of this seemed to have any role in the courses she was taking.

So Erica was drawn, despite her well-laid plans, in a different academic direction. She didn't abandon all the pre-MBA-type courses. But she supplemented them. She found herself drawn, of all places, to anthropology. She wanted to study cultures—how they differed and how they clashed.

It was, at first blush, a wildly impractical subject for an aspiring mogul to study. But Erica, being Erica, quickly turned it into a strategic

business plan. Her whole life had been about clashing cultures—
Mexican/Chinese, middle class/lower class, the ghetto/the Academy,
the street/the university. She already understood what it was like to
merge different cultures. In a globalizing world this knowledge would
probably come in handy. At college she would learn how some companies created successful corporate cultures and how some failed at this
task. She would learn about how global corporations handled cultural
diversity. In a business world filled with engineers and finance people,
she would know culture. This would be her unique selling proposition.
There would always be a market for skills like that. After all, how many
female Chinese-Chicana workaholics from the ghetto does anybody
know?

The Extended Mind

Millions of years ago, animals roamed the earth. As Michael Tomasello
has argued, smarter animals such as apes are actually pretty good at
coming up with innovative solutions to common problems. What they
are not good at is passing down their discoveries to future generations.
Nonhuman animals don't seem to have the impulse to teach. You can
teach a chimpanzee sign language, but the chimp won't teach sign language to his fellows or to his children so that they might talk to one another.

Humans are different. Humans begin life far behind other animals.
Humans have a diffuse set of genetic instructions, so when they are
born, and for years afterward, they can't survive on their own. As the
great anthropologist Clifford Geertz put it, man is an "unfinished animal. What sets him off most graphically from nonmen," Geertz continued, "is less his sheer ability to learn (great as that is) than how much
and what particular sorts of things he *has* to learn before he is able to
function at all."

Humans succeed because they have the ability to develop advanced
cultures. Culture is a collection of habits, practices, beliefs, arguments,
and tensions that regulates and guides human life. Culture transmits

certain practical solutions to everyday problems—how to avoid poison-ous plants, how to form successful family structures. Culture also, as Roger Scruton has observed, educates the emotions. It consists of nar-ratives, holidays, symbols, and works of art that contain implicit and often unnoticed messages about how to feel, how to respond, how to di-vine meaning.

An individual human mind couldn't handle the vast variety of fleet-ing stimuli that are thrust before it. We can function in the world only because we are embedded in the scaffold of culture. We absorb ethnic cultures, institutional cultures, regional cultures, which do most of our thinking for us.

The human race is not impressive because towering geniuses pro-duce individual masterpieces. The human race is impressive because groups of people create mental scaffolds that guide future thought. No individual could build a modern airplane, but modern companies con-tain the institutional knowledge that allows groups to design and build them.

"We build 'designer environments' in which human reason is able to far outstrip the computational ambit of the unaugmented biological brain," the philosopher Andy Clark writes. Unlike other animals, he continues, humans have the ability to dissipate reasoning—to build so-cial arrangements that contain the bodies of knowledge.

Human brains, Clark believes, "are not so different from the frag-mented, special-purpose, action-oriented organs of other animals and autonomous robots. But we excel in one crucial respect: We are masters at structuring our physical and social worlds so as to press complex co-herent behaviors from these unruly resources. We use intelligence to structure our environment so that we can succeed with less intelligence. Our brains make the world smart so that we can be dumb in peace! Or, to look at it another way, it is the human brain plus these chunks of ex-ternal scaffolding that finally constitutes the smart, rational inference engine we call mind. Looked at that way, we are smart after all—but our boundaries extend further out into the world than we might have ini-tially supposed."

Cultures That Work

Erica took courses in sociology, psychology, history, literature, marketing, and behavioral economics—anything she thought might help her understand the shared scaffolding of the human mind.

All cultures share certain commonalities, stored in our genetic inheritance. Anthropologists tell us that all cultures distinguish colors. When they do, all cultures begin with words for white and black. If the culture adds a word for a third color, it is always red. All humans, for example, register the same basic facial expressions for fear, disgust, happiness, contempt, anger, sadness, pride, and shame. Children born without sight display emotion on their faces the same way as children born with sight. All humans divide time into past, present, and future. Almost all fear, at least at first, spiders and snakes, creatures that threatened their Stone Age ancestors. All human societies produce art. They all disapprove, at least in theory, of rape and murder. They all dream of harmony and worship God.

In his book *Human Universals*, Donald E. Brown lists traits that people in all places share. The list goes on and on. All children fear strangers and prefer sugar solutions to plain water from birth. All humans enjoy stories, myths, and proverbs. In all societies men engage in more group violence and travel farther from home than women. In all societies, husbands are on average older than their wives. People everywhere rank one another according to prestige. People everywhere divide the world between those inside their group and those outside their group. These tendencies are all stored deep below awareness.

But nobody lives in a universal thing called culture. They live only in specific cultures, each of which differ from one another. Plays written and produced in Germany are three times as likely to have tragic or unhappy endings than plays written and produced in the United States. Half of all people in India and Pakistan say they would marry without love, but only 2 percent of people in Japan would do so. Nearly a quarter of Americans say they are often afraid of saying the wrong things in social situations, whereas 65 percent of all Japanese say they are often afraid. In their book *Drunken Comportment*, Craig MacAndrew and Robert B. Edgerton found that in some cultures drunken men get into fights, but in some cultures they almost never do. In some cultures drunken men grow more amorous, but in some cultures they do not.

Researchers from the University of Florida observed couples having coffee in different cities around the world. In London, couples rarely touch each other. In Paris, 110 touches were observed per coffee. In San Juan, Puerto Rico, it was 180.

As Nicholas A. Christakis and James H. Fowler report in their book *Connected*, 10 percent of working-age Americans report suffering back pain, but 45 percent of the people in Denmark do, as do 62 percent of the people in Germany. Some Asian cultures have very low back-pain rates, but many people there do suffer from *koro*, a condition in which men become afflicted by the feeling that their penises are retracting into their bodies. The treatment involves asking a trusted family member to hold the penis twenty-four hours a day until the anxiety goes away.

If you bump into a man on the street in the American North, the testosterone level in his bloodstream will not rise appreciably. But if you bump into a man on the street in the American South, where a culture of honor is more prevalent, there will probably be a sharp spike in cortisol and testosterone production. Cities in the South are twice as likely to have words like "gun" in their names (Gun Point, Florida), whereas cities in the North are more than twice as likely to have words like "joy" in their names.

A cultural construct like language can change the way people see the world. Guugu Yimithirr, an aboriginal tongue in Australia, is one of the world's geographical languages. People don't say, "Raise your right hand" or "Step backward." They say, "Raise your north hand" or "Step east." People who speak geographical languages have amazing orientation senses. They always know which way is north, even in caves. A speaker of the language Tzeltal from Mexico was blindfolded and spun around twenty times. He still had no trouble pointing, north, south, east, and west.

In this way, culture imprints some patterns in our brains and dissolves others. Because Erica grew up in the United States, she had a distinct sense of when something was tacky, even though she couldn't have easily defined what made it so. Her head was filled with what Douglas Hofstadter calls "comfortable but quite impossible to define abstract patterns," which were implanted by culture and organized her thinking into concepts such as: sleazeballs, fair play, dreams, wackiness, crackpots, sour grapes, goals, and you and I.

Erica learned that a culture is not a recipe book that creates uniformity. Each culture has its own internal debates and tensions. Alasdair MacIntyre points out that each vital culture contains a continuity of conflict, which allows divergent behavior. Furthermore, in the age of globalization, cultures are not converging. They seem to be growing farther apart.

She also learned that not all cultures are equal. She knew she wasn't supposed to think this. She had been at Denver long enough to know that she was supposed to think all cultures were wonderful and they were all wonderful in their own unique way. But she wasn't some rich kid from a suburban high school. She couldn't afford that kind of bullshit. She needed to know what led to success and what led to failure. She looked at the world and at history, looking for clues and useful lessons she could use.

She came across a Stanford professor named Thomas Sowell, who wrote a series of books called *Race and Culture*, *Migrations and Cultures*, and *Conquests and Cultures* that told her some of the things she needed to know. Erica knew she was supposed to disapprove of Sowell. All her teachers did. But his descriptions jibed with the world she saw around her every day. "Cultures do not exist as simply static 'differences,' to be celebrated," Sowell wrote. They "compete with one another as better and worse ways of getting things done—better and worse, not from the standpoint of some observer, but from the standpoint of the peoples themselves, as they cope and aspire amid the gritty realities of life."

Erica had noticed that some groups seemed to outcompete their neighbors and peers. Haitians and Dominicans share an island, but the Dominicans have a GDP per capita that is nearly four times higher than that of their neighbors. They have life expectancies that are eighteen years longer and literacy rates 33 percentage points higher. Jews and Italians both lived on the Lower East Side of Manhattan during the first half of the twentieth century, but the Jews rose out much more quickly.

She noticed that some groups made themselves winners wherever they settled. The Lebanese and the Gujarati Indians became successful merchants in different societies with different conditions all around the world. In Ceylon in 1969, the Tamil minority provided 40 percent of all university students in the sciences, including 48 percent of all engineering students and 49 percent of all medical students. In Argentina, 46 percent of the businessmen in *Who's Who* were foreign born. In Chile, three-quarters of the heads of large industrial enterprises were immigrants or the children of immigrants.

In American schools, Chinese American kids raced ahead. By the time they enter kindergarten, Chinese Americans are four months ahead of Latino children in letter recognition and other pre-reading skills. They take more demanding high-school courses than the average American student. They do much more homework each night. They are more likely to be punished at home if they earn a grade lower than an A−. Roughly 54 percent of Asian Americans between the ages of twenty-five and twenty-nine have graduated from college, compared to 34 percent of native-born white Americans.

These cultural differences can produce stunning inequalities. Asian Americans have a life expectancy of eighty-seven years compared with seventy-nine years for whites and seventy-three years for African Americans. In Michigan, a state with a struggling economy, the Asian American life expectancy is ninety, while for the average white person it's seventy-nine and for the average African American it's seventy-three. Income and education levels are also much higher. The average Asian American in New Jersey lives an amazing twenty-six years longer and is eleven times more likely to have a graduate degree than the average American Indian in South Dakota.

Erica also noticed that some cultures are more corrupt than others. In their study, "Cultures of Corruption," Raymond Fisman and Edward

Miguel took advantage of a natural experiment. Until 2002 diplomats in New York City could avoid parking fines. Fisman and Miguel analyzed the data from 1,700 consular personnel and their families to see who took advantage of their immunity and who didn't. They found that diplomats from countries that rank high on the Transparency International corruption index piled up huge numbers of unpaid tickets, whereas diplomats from countries that ranked low on the index barely got any at all. Between 1997 and 2002, diplomats from Kuwait picked up 246 parking violations per diplomat. Diplomats from Egypt, Chad, Nigeria, Sudan, Mozambique, Pakistan, Ethiopia, and Syria also had incredible numbers of violations. Meanwhile diplomats from Sweden, Denmark, Japan, Israel, Norway, and Canada had no violations at all. Even thousands of miles away from home, diplomats still carried their domestic cultural norms inside their heads. The results were not influenced by salary, age, or any other of the measured controls.

Erica noticed, in sum, that certain cultures are better adapted for modern development than others. In one class she was assigned a book called *The Central Liberal Truth* by Lawrence E. Harrison. People in what he calls progress-prone cultures assume that they can shape their own destiny. People in progress-resistant cultures are more fatalistic. People in progress-prone cultures assume that wealth is the product of human creativity and is expandable. People in progress-resistant cultures have a zero-sum assumption that what exists will always be.

People in progress-prone cultures live to work, he argues. People in progress-resistant cultures work to live. People in progress-prone cultures share other values. They are more competitive; they are more optimistic; they value tidiness and punctuality; they place incredible emphasis on education; they do not see their family as a fortress in a hostile world, they see it as a gateway to the wider society; they internalize guilt and hold themselves responsible for what happens; they do not externalize guilt and blame others.

Erica became convinced that this cultural substructure shaped decisions and behavior more than most economists or most business leaders realized. This was where the action was.

Memo to Herself

Late in her college career, Erica opened up her laptop and wrote a memo to herself. She tried to write some lessons or rules that would help encapsulate what she'd learned by studying cultural differences. The first maxim she wrote to herself was "Think in Networks."

Society isn't defined by classes, as the Marxists believe. It's not defined by racial identity. And it's not a collection of rugged individualists, as some economic and social libertarians believe. Instead, Erica concluded, society is a layering of networks.

When she was bored, she would actually sit down and draw up network charts for herself and her friends. Sometimes she'd put a friend's name in the middle of a piece of paper and then draw lines to all the major attachments in that person's life, and then she'd draw lines showing how strongly those hubs were attached to one another. If she'd gone out with friends the night before, she might draw a chart showing how all the people in the group were socially attached.

Erica felt sure she'd understand people better if she saw them linked and in context. She wanted to train herself to think of people as embedded creatures, whose decisions emerge from a specific mental environment.

"Be the Glue," Erica wrote next. She would look at her charts of the networks and she would ask herself, "What do those lines connecting people consist of?" In a few special cases, it's love. But in most workplaces, and most social groups, the bonds are not that passionate. Most relationships are bound by trust.

Trust is habitual reciprocity that becomes coated by emotion. It grows when two people begin volleys of communication and cooperation and slowly learn they can rely upon each other. Soon members of a trusting relationship become willing to not only cooperate with each other but sacrifice for each other.

Trust reduces friction and lowers transaction costs. People in companies filled with trust move flexibly and cohesively. People who live in trusting cultures form more community organizations. People in more trusting cultures have wider stock market–participation rates. People in trusting cultures find it easier to organize and operate large corporations. Trust creates wealth.

Erica noticed that there are different levels and types of trust in different communities, different schools, different dorms, and different universities. In his classic study *The Moral Basis of a Backward Society*, Edward Banfield noticed that peasants in southern Italy shared a great deal of trust with members of their own family, but were very suspicious of people outside their kinship boundaries. This made it hard for them to form community groups or to build companies that were bigger than the family unit. Germany and Japan have high levels of social trust, enabling them to build tightly knit industrial firms. The United States is a collective society that thinks it is an individualistic one. If you ask Americans to describe their values, they will give you the most individualistic answers of any nation on the planet. Yet if you actually watch how Americans behave, you see they trust one another instinctively and form groups with alacrity.

Erica decided she would never work in a place where people didn't trust one another. Once she got a job, she would be the glue. She would be the one organizing outings, making connections, building trust. She would carry information from person to person. She would connect one worker to another. If everybody around her drew a network chart of their life, she'd be on every one.

The final maxim Erica wrote to herself that day was, "Be an Idea-Space Integrator." Erica noticed that the greatest artists often combined what Richard Ogle in his book *Smart World* calls two mental spaces. Picasso inherited the traditions of Western art, but he also responded to the masks of African art. The merging of these two idea spaces created *Les Demoiselles d'Avignon* and Picasso's fantastic burst of creativity.

Erica resolved that she would always try to stand at the junction between two mental spaces. In organizations, she would try to stand at the junction of two departments, or fill in the gaps between departments. Ronald Burt of the University of Chicago has a concept he calls structural holes. In any society there are clumps of people doing certain tasks. But between those clumps there are holes, places in between where there are no people and there is no structure. These are the places where the flow of ideas stops, the gaps separating one part of a company from another. Erica would occupy space in those holes. She would span the distance from one group of people to another—reach out to discordant clumps and bring their ideas together. In a world of discordant networks and cultures, she would find her destiny and her role.

CHAPTER 10

INTELLIGENCE

ERICA DIDN'T HAVE TO FIND HER WAY IN BUSINESS. BUSIness found her. Recruiters had been chasing her since her junior year in college all the way through business school, and she fended them off like an heiress in a Victorian novel, carefully guarding herself for the right suitor.

She flirted with finance, got serious for a time with a tech company, but eventually decided to start her career with one of the elite consulting firms. The firm gave her a choice. She could join one of what they called the "functional-capability groups" or one of the "clientele–industry sector" groups. This was no choice at all because she didn't really know what either did.

She chose an FCG, because somehow it sounded cooler, and wound up working for a man named Harrison. Three days a week, Harrison would gather his team for a meeting about the research projects they were working on. The meetings weren't held around a table with a speakerphone in the middle like an altar, the way normal meetings were. Harrison, with his own quirky ideas, had hired some interior designer to build a different conversation space. Instead, his team sat on low padded chairs in a vast open area that looked like a big living room.

The arrangement was supposed to be flexible and allow small groups to huddle, but instead it allowed large groups of men to be mutually avoidant. They'd come in at ten a.m. and plop their coffees and papers on the floor, sink down into their chairs, and subtly adjust them so they were slightly askew. The chairs would be in a rough circle, but each became slightly misaligned so that one guy would be looking at the window, another guy would be looking at a piece of corporate art on the wall, and a third would be facing the door. The members of the team could go an entire hour without ever making eye contact, even as they were talking together happily and productively.

Harrison was about thirty-five, pale, large but nonathletic, and utterly brilliant. "What's your favorite power law?" he asked Erica during one of her first meetings with the unit. Erica didn't really know what one was.

"It's a polynomial with scale invariance. Like Zipf's law." Zipf's law, Erica was told later, states that the most common word in any language will appear exactly twice as frequently as the next common word, and so on down to the least common. The largest city in any large nation will be twice as populous as the next largest city, and so on down the line.

"Or Kleiber's law!" Another worker chimed in. Kleiber's law states that there is a constant relationship between mass and metabolism in any animal. Small animals have faster metabolisms and big animals have slower ones, and you can plot the ratio of mass to metabolism of all animals on a straight line, from the smallest bacteria to the largest hippopotami.

The whole room was suddenly aflame with power laws. Everybody but her had their favorites. Erica felt astoundingly slow-witted next to these guys, but happy she'd get to work with them.

Every day's meeting was another intellectual-fireworks display. They'd plop down into their chairs—lower and lower as their meeting progressed until they were practically horizontal with their bellies sticking up and their wing tips crossed in front of them—and about once a meeting there'd be some brilliant outburst. One day they spent an hour arguing over whether "jazz" was the best of all possible words to select when you are playing Hangman.

"Suppose Shakespeare plays had titles like Robert Ludlum thrillers?" one of the crew wondered one day.

"The Rialto Sanction," somebody suggested immediately.

"The Elsinore Vacillation," another chirped, for *Hamlet*.

"The Dunsinane Reforestation," cried another, for *Macbeth*.

These guys had been marked out as geniuses before they could walk. It seemed as though they'd all been whizzes at College Bowl or debate. Harrison once mentioned that he'd dropped out of med school because it was too easy. If somebody mentioned that somebody in another company was smart, he'd ask, "But is he smart like us?" Erica played a little betting game with herself. She allowed herself to eat one M&M for every second that passed between the time Harrison mentioned the name of somebody and the time he noted whether or not they went to Harvard, Yale, or MIT.

Then there were the silences. If they weren't having fierce debates about methodologies and data sets, the whole group was perfectly content to sit in silence—for seconds and minutes at a time. For urban-ethnic Erica, this was torture. She'd sit upright in her own chair, staring at her feet, repeating a mantra silently to herself, "I will not break this silence. I will not break this silence. I will not break this silence."

Erica would wonder how these geniuses could sit mutely this way. Maybe it was just that they were mostly men and the few other women in her group had over the years learned to adapt to the male culture. Erica had, of course, grown up with the popular notion that men are less communicative and empathetic than women. And there is plenty of scientific evidence to support that. Male babies make less eye contact with their mothers than female babies, and the higher the testosterone level in the womb during the first trimester of pregnancy, the lower the eye-contact level will be. Simon Baron-Cohen of Cambridge surveyed the research literature on male communication and feelings and concluded that men are more curious about systems and less curious about emotions. They are, on average, more drawn to rules-based analyses of how inanimate objects fit together. Women are, on average, better empathizers. They do better in experiments in which they are given partial clues and have to guess a person's emotional state. They are generally better at verbal memory and verbal fluency. They don't necessarily talk more than men, but they seem to take turns more while talking, and they are more likely to talk about others while men are much more likely to talk about themselves. Women are much more likely to seek somebody else's help when they're in a stressful situation.

But Erica had been around groups of guys before, and it was not always like this. This culture was peculiar, and it was shaped from the top down. Harrison had turned social awkwardness into a form of power. The more cryptic he became, the more everyone had to attend to him.

He ate the same lunch every day: cream-cheese-and-olive sandwiches. As a boy he'd developed a formula to help him predict the winners of dog races, and now his business was to look out for hidden patterns. "Did you read the footnotes in the company report?" he asked Erica mysteriously, after the group had acquired a new client. "They're about to experience a crossover moment." She pored over the footnotes and still had no clue what he was talking about.

He studied charts for hour upon hour—stock prices, annual cocoa-production levels, weather patterns, and cotton output.

He could be deeply impressive. Clients respected him even if they didn't love him. CEOs were humble in his presence. Everybody believed that Harrison could look at a page of numbers and tell them if they'd be bankrupt or booming five years out. Harrison shared this reverential attitude toward his own intelligence. He was certain about many things—everything, actually—but he was most certain about two propositions: He was really smart, and most people in the world were not.

For a few years, Erica enjoyed working with this man, even with all the weirdness attached. She liked watching him talk about modern philosophy. He was avid about bridge. He loved any intellectual game with a fixed set of rules. Sometimes she helped him apply his insights, which were always dazzlingly complex, into the language of everyday reality. But gradually she began to notice something. The department wasn't doing very well. The reports were brilliant but the business sucked. New clients would come, but they would rarely last. People would use their services for specific projects, but they never brought the team on board as trusted advisors.

It took Erica a surprisingly long time to come to this realization, but once she did, she looked at her group with a different and more critical

eye. The meetings went on forever, she realized, but there was little actual debate. Instead everybody would bring little bits of information
that confirmed theories Harrison had concocted years before. Erica felt
as though she were watching courtiers bring candies to the king and
then watching him savor them in everybody's presence.

Harrison's favorite locution was "That's all you need to know!" He'd
make some sharp, pithy observation about a complex situation, and
then he'd bark it out: "That's all you need to know!" It occurred to
Erica that sometimes it wasn't all you needed to know, but the conversation was effectively over.

Then there was the Model. Many years before, Harrison had had a
big success restructuring a consumer bank. He was a legend in the
banking community. Now every time a bank came to him he tried to
implant that model. He tried in big banks and little banks, urban banks
and rural banks. When he tried to implant that model in different nations, Erica tried to wheel out her cultural expertise. One meeting she
tried to explain the *Varieties of Capitalism* approach pioneered by Peter
Hall and David Soskice. Different national cultures, she said, have different motivational systems, different relationships to authority and to
capitalism. Germany, for example, has tight interlocking institutions
like work councils. It also has labor markets that make it hard to hire
and fire people. These arrangements mean that Germany excels at in-
cremental innovation—the sort of steady improvements that are common in metallurgy and manufacturing. The United States, on the other
hand, has looser economic networks. It is relatively easy to hire and fire
and start new businesses. The United States thus excels at radical innovation, at the sort of rapid paradigm shifts prevalent in software and
technology.

Harrison dismissed her with a wave of the hand. Different countries
excelled at different things because of different government regulations. Change the regulations and you change the cultures. Erica tried
to argue that regulations emerge from cultures, which are deeper and
longer lasting. Harrison had turned away. Erica was a valuable employee, but she was not smart enough to bother arguing with.

Harrison didn't just treat her this way. He treated clients this way, too. He ignored arguments that didn't fit his mental framework. He had his group prepare long presentations in which they presumed to lecture people about the industries they'd spent their whole lives mastering. They made presentations deliberately opaque as a way of demonstrating their own expertise. They didn't understand that different companies have different risk tolerances. They didn't understand that a particular CFO might be in a power struggle with a particular CEO and they should be careful not to make the latter's life more difficult. There was no piece of office politics so obvious that they couldn't be oblivious to it, no attempt at empathic accuracy they could not fail. For Erica, no day was complete unless Harrison and his team had committed some incredible faux pas. She spent the final five months of her tenure at the firm going home each day with one question on her mind: How could people who are so smart be so fucking stupid?

Beyond IQ

This turns out to be a revealing question. Harrison had built an entire lifestyle and career around reverence for IQ. He generally hired people on the basis of intelligence; socialized with people on the basis of intelligence. He impressed clients by telling them he'd unleash a team of Ivy Leaguers on their problems.

And to some extent Harrison's faith in intelligence was justified. Researchers have studied IQ pretty extensively over the decades and know a lot about it. The IQ scores a person gets in childhood are reasonably predictive of the scores he or she gets as an adult. People who are good at one kind of intellectual skill tend to be good at many others. People who are really good at verbal analogies tend to also be good at solving math problems and reading comprehension, though they may be less good at some other mental skills, such as memory recognition.

The ability to do well on these sorts of tests is significantly influenced by heredity. The single strongest predictor of a person's IQ is the IQ of his or her mother. People with high IQs do better in school and in school-like settings. As Dean Hamer and Peter Copeland note, "In study after study, IQ is the single best predictor of school performance."

If you want to lead a business, it probably helps to have an IQ over 100. If you want to go into nuclear physics, it probably helps to have an IQ over 120.

But there are a couple of problems with Harrison's emphasis on IQ. In the first place, it is surprisingly malleable. Environmental factors can play a huge role in shaping IQ. A study of black children in Prince Edward County, Virginia, found that they lost an average of six IQ points for every missed year of school. Parental attention also seems to matter. Firstborns tend to have higher IQs than secondborns, who tend to have higher IQs than thirdborns. This effect disappears, however, when there is more than a three-year gap between children. The theory is that mothers talk to their firstborns more and use more complicated sentences. They have to divide their attention when they have young children born closely together.

The broadest evidence of IQ malleability is the Flynn Effect. Between 1947 and 2002, IQ levels across the developed world rose steadily by about three percentage points per decade. This was found across many countries, across many age groups, and in many different settings, and it's stark evidence of an environmental component to IQ.

Interestingly, scores did not rise across all sections of the IQ test. People in 2000 were no better at the vocabulary and reading-comprehension portions of the test than people in 1950. But they were much better at the sections designed to measure abstract reasoning. "Today's children," James R. Flynn writes, "are far better at solving problems on the spot without a previously learned method for doing so."

Flynn's explanation is that different eras call forth different skills. The nineteenth-century society rewarded and required more concrete-thinking skills. Contemporary society rewards and requires more abstract-thinking skills. People who have a genetic capacity to reason abstractly use those skills more and more, and hence get better and better at them. Their inherited skills are multiplied by their social experiences, and the result is much, much higher IQ scores.

However, once you get beyond the school environment, it's not a very reliable predictor of performance. Controlling for other factors, people with high IQs do not have better relationships and better marriages. They are not better at raising their children. In a chapter of *Handbook of Intelligence*, Richard K. Wagner of Florida State University surveys the research on IQ and job performance and concludes, "IQ predicts only about 4 percent of variance in job performance." In another chapter of the handbook, John D. Mayer, Peter Salovey, and David Caruso conclude that at best IQ contributes about 20 percent to life success. There is great uncertainty about these sorts of numbers. As Richard Nisbett puts it, "What nature hath joined together, multiple regression cannot put asunder." But the general idea is that once you get past some pretty obvious correlations (smart people make better mathematicians), there is a very loose relationship between IQ and life outcomes.

One famous longitudinal study known as the Terman study followed a group of extremely high-IQ students (they all scored 135 or above). The researchers expected these brilliant young people to go on to have illustrious careers. They did fine, becoming lawyers and corporate executives, for the most part. But there were no superstar achievers in the group, no Pulitzer Prize winners or MacArthur Award winners. In a follow-up study by Melita Oden in 1968, the people in the group who seemed to be doing best had only slightly higher IQs. What they had was superior work ethics. They were the ones who had shown more ambition as children.

Once a person crosses the IQ threshold of 120, there is little relationship between more intelligence and better performance. A person with a 150 IQ is in theory much smarter than a person with a 120 IQ, but those additional 30 points produce little measurable benefit when it comes to lifetime success. As Malcolm Gladwell demonstrated in *Outliers*, the Americans who won Nobel Prizes in Chemistry and Medicine did not mostly go to Harvard and MIT, the schools at the tippy-top of the cognitive ladder. It was simply enough that they went to good schools—Rollins College, Washington State, Grinnell. If you are smart enough to get into a good school, you're smart enough to excel—even in academic spheres like chemistry and medical research. It's not important that you are in the top 0.5 percent. A study of 7,403 Americans who participated in the National Longitudinal Survey of Youth, conducted by Jay Zagorsky of Ohio State, found no correlation between accumulating large wealth and high IQ.

Harrison's mistake was to equate IQ with mental ability. The reality is that intelligence is a piece of mental ability, but it is not the most important piece. People who score well on IQ tests are good at logical, linear, and computational tasks. But to excel in the real world, intelligence has to be nestled in certain character traits and dispositions. To draw a parallel, a soldier may be phenomenally strong. If you gave him a test involving push-ups and pull-ups, he would do very well. But unless he possesses courage, discipline, technique, imagination, and sensitivity, he probably won't survive amidst the chaos of the battlefield. In the same way, a thinker may be very smart but unless she possesses moral virtues such as honesty, rigor, and fair-mindedness, she probably won't succeed in real life.

In his book *What Intelligence Tests Miss*, Keith E. Stanovich lists some of the mental dispositions that contribute to real world performance: "The tendency to collect information before making up one's mind, the tendency to seek various points of view before coming to a conclusion, the disposition to think extensively about a problem before responding, the tendency to calibrate the degree of strength of one's opinions to the degree of evidence available, the tendency to think about future consequences before taking action, the tendency to explicitly weight pluses and minuses of a situation before making a decision, and the tendency to seek nuance and avoid absolutism."

In other words, there is a big difference between mental force and mental character. Mental character is akin to moral character. It is forged by experience and effort, carved into the hinterland of the mind.

Clocks and Clouds

The science writer Jonah Lehrer sometimes reminds his readers of Karl Popper's distinctions between clocks and clouds. Clocks are neat, orderly systems that can be defined and evaluated using reductive methodologies. You can take apart a clock, measure the pieces, and see how they fit together. Clouds are irregular, dynamic, and idiosyncratic.

It's hard to study a cloud because they change from second to second. They can best be described through narrative, not numbers.

As Lehrer has noted, one of the great temptations of modern research is that it tries to pretend that every phenomenon is a clock, which can be evaluated using mechanical tools and regular techniques. This is surely true of the study of intelligence. Researchers have spent a great deal of time studying IQ, which is relatively stable and quantifiable, and relatively little time studying mental character, which is cloud-like.

Raw intelligence is useful for helping you solve well-defined problems. Mental character helps you figure out what kind of problem you have in front of you and what sort of rules you should use to address it. As Stanovich notes, if you give people the rules they need to follow in order to solve a thinking problem, then people with higher IQs do better than people with low IQs. But if you don't give them the rules, people with high IQs do no better, because coming up with the rules to solve a problem and honestly evaluating one's performance afterward are mental activities barely related to IQ.

Mental force and mental character are only lightly correlated. As Stanovich puts it, "Many different studies involving thousands of subjects have indicated that measures of intelligence display only moderate to weak correlations (usually less than .30) with some thinking dispositions (for example, actively open-minded thinking, need for cognition) and near zero correlation with others (such as conscientiousness, curiosity, diligence.)"

Many investors, for example, are quite intelligent, but behave self-destructively because of their excessive faith in their intelligence. Between 1998 and 2001 the Firsthand Technology Value mutual fund produced an annualized total return of 16 percent. The average individual investor in this fund, however, lost 31.6 percent of his or her money over this time. Why? Because the geniuses thought they could get in and out of the market at the right moments. They missed the important up days and caught the devastating down ones. These people, who are quite smart, performed worse than if they had been stolid and stupid.

Other people score well on IQ tests but can't hold down a job. James

J. Heckman of the University of Chicago and others compared the workplace performance of high-school graduates with those who dropped out of high school but took the GED exams. The GED recipients are as smart as high-school grads who do not go on to college, but they earn less than these high-school grads. In fact, they have lower hourly wages than do high-school dropouts, because they possess fewer of the so-called noncognitive traits like motivation and self-discipline. GED recipients are much more likely to switch jobs. Their labor-force participation rates are lower than that of high-school grads.

At the very top of intellectual accomplishment, intelligence is nearly useless in separating outstanding geniuses from everybody else. The greatest thinkers seem to possess mental abilities that go beyond rational thinking narrowly defined. Their abilities are fluid and thoroughly cloudlike. Albert Einstein, for example, would seem to be an exemplar of scientific or mathematical intelligence. But he addressed problems by playing with imaginative, visual, and physical sensations. "The words of the language, as they are written or spoken, do not seem to play any role in my mechanism of thought," he told Jacques Hadamard. Instead, he said that his intuitions proceed through "certain signs and more or less clear images" that he could manipulate and combine. "The above mentioned elements are, in my case, of visual and some of muscular type," Einstein observed.

"I can only think in pictures," the physicist and chemist Peter Debye declared. "It's all visual." He said that when working on a problem he saw fuzzy images, which he tried to progressively clarify in his mind and then eventually, after the problem was largely solved, he would clarify the pictures in the form of mathematics. Others proceed acoustically, rehearsing certain sounds associated with certain ideas. Others do so emotionally: "You had to use your feelings," Debye explained, "What does the carbon atom *want* to do?"

Wisdom doesn't consist of knowing specific facts or possessing knowledge of a field. It consists of knowing how to treat knowledge: being confident but not too confident; adventurous but grounded. It is a willingness to confront counterevidence and to have a feel for the vast spaces beyond what's known. Harrison did not rate highly on any of these character traits.

Time to Go

Erica was in an office filled with people with impressive brains who nonetheless couldn't find their way out of a paper bag. As the months went by, she became more and more impatient with their shortcomings, and more dumbfounded by their ability to miss opportunities and repeat their mistakes. Here, as so often in her new life, Erica felt like a semi-outsider. Maybe it was because her upbringing was so different, or her skin color was different, or for some other reason, but she seemed more aware of the irrational, darker, and passionate side of life. One day, when she was at her most exasperated, she half-jokingly decided that she had been put on this earth to fulfill a Mission from God: to save the white man from himself.

Because the Almighty is a testing God, he had sent down upon this earth upper–middle class suburban kids who went to white-bread high schools, polo-shirt colleges, and light beer–sipping business schools and then were spit out into the world of bottled-water corporate America and who never got closer to reality than occasional forays into turnpike rest stops. Their worldviews rested upon an assumption of pristine equilibrium. As long as everybody was civil and genial, the way they were, then their way of thinking made sense. As long as everything was neat and orderly, they could retreat and live inside the formulas they'd learned in school.

But, much of the time, because the world is not neat and gentle, they were the babes of the universe. They fell for Bernie Madoff schemes, subprime mortgages, and derivatives they didn't understand. They were suckers for every moronic management fad, every bubble mania. They wandered about in the mist, blown about by deeper forces they could not understand.

Fortunately, God, in his infinite and redeeming mercy, had also sent down a tight-abbed, small-boned Chinese-Chicana woman to rescue the innocents. This hard-assed, chip-on-her-shoulder, hyper-organized human Filofax would liberate the overprotected masses from the six-delta PowerPoint bullet points and introduce them to the underworld of reality. God had raised his servant in chaos and squalor so that she might be armed with enough knowledge, drive and vinegar in her bloodstream to jostle the White Man from the comfort of his categories and help him see hidden forces that actually drive the mind. God had armed Erica with the strength and the bad attitude she would need so she would take up the yellowish-brown woman's burden and pave the way for the salvation of the Earth.

As the months went by, she grew increasingly bored, and frustrated by the groupthink. She took long walks at night, fantasizing about what she would do if she ran her own department or her own firm, and as she strode she would furiously type her ideas into the memo section of her iPhone. During these walks she felt almost euphoric, like she was destined to do some great thing. She realized that her imagination had raced beyond her current job. She was restless. There was no going back.

Erica began to think about creating her own consulting firm. She decided to coolly weigh the pros and cons of such a venture, but with her emotions racing ahead, she rigged the exercise from the start. She exaggerated the pros, minimized the cons, and vastly overestimated how easy it would be.

Erica told Harrison she was leaving. She set up the world corporate headquarters of her new firm on her dining-room table, and she worked with a sort of mania that was a wonder to behold. She called every old mentor, client, and contact. She barely slept. She was flooded with ideas about things she could do with the firm. She would sit down and remind herself that she needed to find one narrow niche, but she couldn't help herself—the flood of scattershot ideas just kept coming. She felt liberated not having to follow the guardrails of some other person's thinking. She was going to create a consulting firm that would be unlike any other. It would be humanist in the deepest sense. It would treat people not as data points, but as the fully formed idiosyncratic creatures they are. She was utterly convinced she would succeed.

CHAPTER II

CHOICE ARCHITECTURE

SOMETIME BACK IN THE PHARAOHS' DAY, A SHOPKEEPER DIScovered he could manipulate the unconscious thoughts of his customers simply by manipulating the environment in his store. Merchandisers have been following his lead ever since. For example, shoppers in grocery stores usually confront the fruit-and-vegetable section first. Grocers know that shoppers who buy the healthy stuff first will feel so uplifted they will buy more junk food later in their trip.

Grocers know that the smell of baked goods stimulates shopping, so many bake their own bread from frozen dough on the premises each morning and then pump the bread smell into the store throughout the day. They also know that music sells goods. Researchers in Britain found that when French music was pumped into a store, sales of French wines skyrocketed. When German music was played, German wine sales grew.

At the shopping mall, low-volume stores are generally near the exits. People haven't yet made the transition from the outside world to the inner shopping world so they barely notice those first few establishments. In department stores, the women's shoe section is generally next to the women's cosmetics section (while the clerk is going back to find the right size shoe, bored customers are likely to wander over and find some makeup they might want to try later).

Consumers frequently believe products placed on the right side of a display are of higher quality than those on the left. Timothy Wilson and

Richard Nisbett put four identical pairs of panty hose on a table and asked consumers to rate them. The farther to the right a pair was on the table, the higher the rating the women gave it. The rightward-most pair was rated highest by 40 percent of the customers, the next one by 31 percent, the next by 17 percent, and the leftward-most by 12 percent. All of the customers but one (a psychology student) denied that location made any difference in their selection, and none noticed that the products were exactly the same.

At restaurants, people eat more depending on how many people they are dining with. People eating alone eat least. People eating with one other person eat 35 percent more than they do at home. People dining in a party of four eat 75 percent more, and people dining with seven or more eat 96 percent more.

Marketing people also realize that people have two sets of tastes, one for stuff they want to use now and one for stuff they want to use later. For example, when researchers asked customers what movies they would like to rent to watch later, they generally pick art films such as *The Piano*. When they are asked what movie they want to watch tonight, they pick blockbusters such as *Avatar*.

Even people shopping for major purchases often don't know what they want. Realtors have a phrase, "Buyers lie," because the house many people describe at the beginning of their search is nothing like the one they actually prefer and buy. Builders know that many home decisions are made in the first seconds upon walking in the door. A California builder, Capital Pacific Homes, structured its high-end spec houses so that upon entering the customer would see the Pacific Ocean through the windows on the main floor, and then the pool through an open stairway leading to the lower level. The instant view of water on both levels helped sell these $10 million homes. Later cogitation was much less important.

The Struggle

Erica loved these kinds of hidden patterns. (Like most people, she thought they applied to others but of course not to herself.) She figured she could build her consulting business by gathering data about these unconscious behavioral patterns, especially the ones tied to cultural differences, and then she could sell the information back to companies.

She began collecting information on African American shoppers, Hispanic shoppers, coastal and heartland shoppers. She was especially intrigued by the difference between upscale and downscale shoppers. For all of human history the rich had worked fewer hours than the poor, but over the past generation that trend had been inverted. Attitudes about leisure had become inverted, too. While lower–middle class shoppers wanted video games and movies for the weekends, so they could relax, the rich wanted books and exercise regimens, so they could improve.

Erica developed a collection of analyses about these consumer trends and was ready to pitch her material to potential clients. From the first, building this business was harder than she anticipated. She wrote to companies she thought she could help, called executives she'd met, hounded their assistants. Very few got back to her. During her first few months on her own, Erica's personality changed. Until now, she had had the usual array of human needs: food, water, sleep, affection, relaxation, and so on. Now she had only one need: clients. Every thought, every dinner conversation, and every chance meeting was evaluated on that basis. She was anxious about being productive each day, but the more anxious she was, the less productive she became. In addition, she fell into an anxiety spiral. She would concentrate on getting enough sleep each night, but the more she concentrated on sleep, the less she could actually get. She worked doggedly to absorb new information, but the more frantically she strived to absorb new knowledge, the less she actually remembered.

Erica had always been an owl. Most people are alert in the morning. About 10 percent are at their most alert around noon. But about 20 percent of the adult population is most alert after six p.m., the owls. But during this period of her life, Erica's evening alertness turned into all-night insomnia. Time changed shape. It had once flowed at a peaceful, steady pace. Now it was a furious current roaring by. When she pulled into a gas station, she silently calculated how many e-mails she could send on her BlackBerry while her tank was filling up. During every pause before an elevator she brought her phone out of her pocket and was texting. She ate at her desk so that she could e-mail while she chewed. Television and movies dropped out of her life. Her neck began to hurt and her back was sore. In the morning she'd stare at furious scribbles she had written to herself the night before, completely unable to decipher them.

She did things she never thought she would do—cold-calling potential clients and then silently swallowing their dismissive disdain. She'd started this business with dreams of success, but once it was under way she was primarily motivated by fear of failure. It was the thought of the looks she would get from friends and colleagues if her business failed that drove her onward. It was the prospect of having to tell her mother that she'd gone bankrupt.

She'd been a driven person since the Academy, but now she became a detail fanatic. She presented potential clients with little binders of her ideas and proposals. If a page was out of line, if one of the plastic spiral things was bent, she went to Code Red. The rest of the world might be lackadaisical, but not she.

And Erica believed in her product. She believed there were hidden currents of knowledge and, if she could only get her clients to see them, she would change the world. She would give people deeper ways to perceive reality, new powers to serve and succeed. But there were a few roadblocks in her way. When she talked about culture, her potential clients had no idea what she meant. They knew vaguely that culture was important. They used the phrase "corporate culture" with reverence. But still the concept had no concreteness to them. They had been trained to master spreadsheets and numbers. They couldn't quite bring themselves to take sociological or anthropological categories seriously. To them it was like molding air.

Furthermore, when Erica spoke about different ethnic cultures they broke out in hives. It was one thing for a Chinese-Latina woman to talk about shopping preferences of blacks and whites, urban Jews and rural Protestants. But the mostly white executives had been trained by a generation of consciousness-raising to never, never, never talk in these terms. Never make a generalization about a group of people, never make observations about a minority group, and for God's sake, never make any comments of this sort in public! That was career suicide. They could laugh when Chris Rock made ethnic jokes. They could listen as Erica noted cultural differences. But they themselves could never, ever go there without facing racism charges, discrimination suits, and boycotts. When Erica asked them to think in ethnic and cultural terms, they had the sudden urge to flee the room in terror.

Erica also had the misfortune to launch her company at the high-water mark of the neuromappers. These were glamorous neurologists who went from business conference to business conference with multicolor fMRI brain scans, promising to unlock the secret synaptic formula to selling toilet paper or energy bars.

The typical neuromapper was a six-foot, shaved-head, cool academic who traipsed into marketing conventions in a leather jacket, jeans, and boots, carrying a motorcycle helmet as though he'd just come in from a neuroscientists' revival of *Grease*. He'd be followed around by a camera crew for Finnish television, making a documentary of his life and ideas, and he'd whisper his faux intimacies to his clients while covering the lavalier microphone that was forever clipped to his T-shirt.

His PowerPoint presentation would be polished like fine chrome. He'd start with a series of optical illusions, like the one about the two tabletops that seem totally different but which are exactly the same size and shape, or the picture of the old lady that suddenly flips in the mind's eye and becomes a beautiful woman in a hat. By the time he was done with the optical illusions the businesspeople were practically wetting their pants in wonder. This was even cooler than the free key chains and tote bags they'd gotten in the vendor area outside.

Then he'd flip on the fMRI scans and start talking about the left- and right-brain differences and his theories of reptilian-brain impulses. Somewhere deep inside this spiel there was some serious science, but it was submerged under layers of pizzazz. The brain scans were awesome. He'd explain that from the top down the brain looks like a rounder version of Ohio. Then he'd get excited as the scans would roll by. Look, a sip of Pepsi makes the front of the brain—around Cleveland, Akron, and Canton—light up. Look! A Frito Lay chip makes the area around Mansfield light up, with a little activity also in Columbus! Look what happens when you give people an image of FedEx. Dayton turns orange! Toledo is red!

A breakfast cereal really should be exciting the medial frontal cortex, he'd declare. Commercials with LeBron James should set the ventral premotor cortex on fire! You want to lodge your brand, he tells everyone, in the ventral striatum! You've got to get the client emotionally involved!

This was science with sex appeal! This was not Erica's vague talk about culture. This was colors on a screen produced by multimillion-dollar machinery that you can see and measure. The neuromappers had their exclusive NeuroFocus Insight System or their NeuroFramework Product Strategy services. They could pinpoint the pure brain essences that would unlock the selling code! Well, of course the executives loved it. Of course every time Erica went in to pitch her services she hit a wall of apathy. Her potential clients wanted somebody who could paint their dorsolateral prefrontal activation bright green! Erica was out of phase with the marketing fads.

One day Erica was pitching her expertise to the CEO of an auto-parts company. He interrupted her after about ten minutes. "You know, I respect you. We're the same," he said, "but you are boring me. I just don't relate to what you are offering."

Erica couldn't think of any rejoinder.

"Why don't you try a different approach? Instead of telling me what you're offering, why don't you ask me what I want?" Erica wondered if he was putting the moves on her. But he continued. "Ask me what makes me unhappy. Ask me what keeps me up at night. Ask me what part of my job I wish somebody would take care of for me. It's not about you. It's about me."

Erica realized this was no pickup line. It was a life lesson. She didn't make a sale to that guy. She left his office confused, her mind jumbled. But the meeting did change everything. From now on her approach was "I'll do whatever you need." She would find a way to use her tools to solve whatever problem the clients threw at her. She would come at them and she would say, "What do you want me to do? How can I serve?"

Erica took herself out for a walk one day and thought this thing through. She was failing to sell cultural segmentation. She didn't want to join the ranks of the neuromappers because she noticed that the advice they derived from their science was actually quite banal. What could she possibly offer?

It never occurred to her to quit. As Angela Duckworth of the University of Pennsylvania has argued, people who succeed tend to find one goal in the distant future and then chase it through thick and thin. People who flit from one interest to another are much, much less likely to excel at any of them. School asks students to be good at a range of subjects, but life asks people to find one passion that they will follow forever.

Behavioral Economics

Erica figured she needed to find some field of expertise she could bring to her client's problems. She needed some body of knowledge that related to her interest in culture and deep decision making, but which also was palatable in the marketplace. She had to find a language to describe consumer psychology that businesspeople could understand— something familiar and scientific. And that's how she came upon behavioral economics.

Over the previous decade a group of economists had worked to apply the insights of the cognitive revolution to their own field. Their chief argument, which appealed to Erica a great deal, was that classical economics got human nature partially or largely wrong. The human being imagined by classical economics is smooth, brilliant, calm, and perpetually unastonished by events. He surveys the world with a series of uncannily accurate models in his head, anticipating what will come next. His memory is incredible; he is capable of holding a myriad of decision-making options in his mind, and of weighing the trade-offs involved in each one. He knows exactly what he wants and never flip-flops between two contradictory desires. He seeks to maximize his utility (whatever that is). His relationships are all contingent, contractual, and ephemeral. If one relationship is not helping him maximize his utility, then he trades up to another. He has perfect self-control and can restrain impulses that may prevent him from competing. He doesn't get caught up in emotional contagions or groupthink, but makes his own decisions on the basis of incentives.

Classical economists readily concede that this sort of person doesn't actually exist. But they argue that this caricature is close enough to reality to allow them to build models that accurately predict real human behavior. Moreover, the caricature allows them to build rigorous mathematical models, which are the measures of true genius in the economics profession. It allows them to turn economics from a soft squishy muddleheaded field like psychology into a hard, rigorous, and tough-minded field like physics. It allows them to formulate laws that govern the study of behavior, and wield the mighty powers of numbers. As M. Mitchell Waldrop put it, "Theoretical economists use their mathematical prowess the way great stags of the forest use their antlers: to do battle with one another and to establish dominance. A stag who doesn't use his antlers is nothing."

Behavioral economists argue that the caricature is not accurate enough to produce reliable predictions about real events. Two psychologists, Daniel Kahneman and Amos Tversky, were the pioneers. Then their insights were picked up by economists proper: including Richard Thaler, Sendhil Mullainathan, Robert Schiller, George Akerlof, and Colin Camerer. These scholars investigate cognition that happens below the level of awareness. Rationality is bounded by emotion. People have a great deal of trouble exercising self-control. They perceive the world in biased ways. They are profoundly influenced by context. They are prone to groupthink. Most of all, people discount the future; we allow present satisfaction to blot out future prosperity.

As Dan Ariely writes in his book *Predictably Irrational*, "If I were to distill one main lesson from the research described in this book, it is that we are pawns in a game whose forces we largely fail to comprehend. We usually think of ourselves as sitting in the driver's seat, with ultimate control over the decisions we make and the direction our life takes; but, alas, this perception has more to do with our desires—with how we want to view ourselves—than with reality."

Behavioral economists argue that stray intuitions, such as a sense of fairness, have powerful economic effects. Pay scales are not only set by what the market will bear. People demand salaries that seem fair, and managers have to take these moral intuitions into account when setting pay scales.

Behavioral economists look for the ways real human beings depart from the rational ideal. There is peer pressure, overconfidence, laziness, and self-delusion. People sometimes take out extended warranties when they buy appliances even though these warranties almost never justify the cost. Health officials in New York thought that if they posted calorie information near the menu boards at fast-food restaurants, people might eat more healthily. In fact, diners actually ordered slightly more calories than before the law went into effect.

Classical economists often believe that economies as a whole tend toward equilibrium, but behavioral economists are more likely to analyze the way shifts in the animal spirits—in confidence, trust, fear, and greed—can lead to bubbles, crashes, and global crises. If the fathers of classical economics knew what we know now about the inner workings of the human mind, some behavioral economists argue, there is no way they would have structured the field as it is.

Behavioral economics came much closer to explaining the reality Erica saw around her every day. She also recognized immediately that this field offered her a way to describe the mind's hidden processes in a language that would be familiar to MBA grads in corporations across America.

Deep in her heart, Erica did not think the way the behavioral economists did. She saw cultures first. She saw society as an organic creature—a complex growth of living relationships. The behavioral economists may be behavioral, but they were still economists. That is to say, the behavioral economists acknowledged complexities and errors that the classical economists ignored, but they still argued that human errors were predictable, systemic, and expressible in mathematical for-

mulas. Erica suspected they were trimming their sails. If they acknowledged that behavior was not law-governed—if it was too unpredictable
to be captured in mathematics and models—then they would no longer
be economists. They wouldn't get published in economic journals or
get to go to economic conferences. They'd have to move their offices
over to the psychology departments, a big step down in the academic
pecking order.

Nonetheless, just as the behavioral economists had an incentive to
pretend that what they were doing was still rigorous, tough-minded science, so did Erica. Her clients respected science. They, too, had been
trained to think of society as a mechanism. If she had to adopt some of
their mind-set in order to get them to listen to her, so be it.

Erica decided she would build her consulting business not on cultural segmentation, which the market wasn't ready for, but on behavioral economics, which was hot and in demand.

Heuristics

Erica read the major behavioral economists. Behind every choice, they
said, there is a choice architecture, an unconscious set of structures that
helps frame the decision. This choice architecture often comes in the
forms of heuristics. The mind stores certain "if . . . then . . ." rules of
thumb, which get activated by context and can be trotted out and applied in appropriate or near-appropriate circumstances.

First, for example, there is priming. One perception cues a string of
downstream thoughts that alters subsequent behavior. If you ask test
subjects to read a series of words that vaguely relate to being elderly
("bingo," "Florida," "ancient"), when they leave the room they will
walk more slowly than when they came in. If you give them a group of
words that relate to aggressiveness ("rude," "annoying," "intrude"),
they will be quicker to interrupt somebody in conversation after the experiment is supposedly over.

If you tell somebody stories about high achievement just before they
perform some test or exercise, they will perform better than if you had
not told them those stories. If you merely use the words "succeed,"

"master" and "achieve" in a sentence, they will do better. If you describe what it is like to be a college professor, they will do better on knowledge tests. On the other hand, if you play into negative stereotypes, they will do worse. If you remind African American students that they are African Americans just before they take a test, their scores will be much lower than if you had not reminded them. In one case, Asian American women were reminded of their ethnicity before a math test. They did better. Then they were reminded they were women. They did worse.

Priming can work in all sorts of ways. In one experiment, some students in a group were asked to write down the first three digits of their phone number and then all were asked to guess the year of Genghis Khan's death. The students who wrote down the digits were more likely to guess he lived in the first millennium, with a three-digit death year.

Another heuristic involves anchoring. No piece of information is processed in isolation. Mental patterns are contagious, and everything is judged in comparison to something else. A $30 bottle of wine may seem expensive when surrounded by $9 bottles of wine, but it seems cheap when surrounded by $149 bottles of wine (which is why wine stores stock those superexpensive wines that almost nobody actually buys). The manager of a Brunswick pool-table store tried an experiment. One week he showed customers to his lowest priced pool table first, at $329, and then worked his way up. The ones who bought any table that week spent on average $550. The next week he showed customers to the $3,000 table first and worked his way down. That week, the average sale topped $1,000.

Then there is framing. Every decision gets framed within a certain linguistic context. If a surgeon tells his patients that a procedure may have a 15 percent failure rate, they are likely to decide against it. If he tells them the procedure has an 85 percent success rate, they tend to opt for it. If a customer at a grocery store sees some cans of his favorite soup on a shelf, he is likely to put one or two in the cart. If there is a sign that says "Limit: twelve per customer," he is likely to put four or five in the cart. Dan Ariely asked students to write down the last two digits of their Social Security number and then bid on a bottle of wine and other products. Students with high Social Security numbers (between 80 and

99) bid, on average, $56 for a cordless keyboard. Students with lower numbers (1–20) bid $16 on average. The high-digit students bid 216 to 346 percent higher than the low-digit students because they were using their own numbers for a frame.

Then there are expectations. The mind makes models of what it thinks will happen, which colors its perceptions of what is actually happening. If you give people a hand cream and tell them it will reduce pain, you are building a set of expectations. People really feel their pain diminish, even if the cream is just hand lotion. People who are given a prescription pain reliever they are told costs $2.50 a pill experience much more pain relief than those given what they are told is a 10-cent pill (even though all the pills are placebos). As Jonah Lehrer writes, "Their predictions became self-fulfilling prophecies."

Then there is inertia. The mind is a cognitive miser. It doesn't like to expend mental energy. As a result people have a bias toward maintaining the status quo. TIAA-CREF offers college professors a range of asset-allocation options for their retirement accounts. According to one study, most of the participants in those plans make zero allocation changes during their entire professional careers. They just stick with whatever was the first option when they signed up.

Then there is arousal. People think differently depending on their state of mind. A bank in South Africa worked with Harvard economist Sendhil Mullainathan to conduct an experiment to see what sort of loan-solicitation letters worked best. They sent out different letters with different photographs on them, and they sent out different letters offering different loan rates. They found that the letter with photographs of a smiling woman did particularly well among men. The picture of the smiling woman increased demand for loans among men as much as lowering the interest rate by five percentage points.

Dan Ariely asked men a set of questions both when they were in an aroused state (Saran wrap–covered laptops, masturbation, you don't want to know) and a nonaroused state. In the nonaroused state, 53 percent of the men said they could enjoy sex with someone they hated. In the aroused state, 77 percent said they could. In the nonaroused state, 23 percent said they could imagine having sex with a twelve-year-old

CHOICE ARCHITECTURE   *183*

girl. In the aroused state, 46 percent said they could imagine it. In the nonaroused state, 20 percent said they would try to have sex with their date after she said no. In the aroused state, 45 percent said they would keep trying.

Finally, there is loss aversion. Losing money brings more pain than winning money brings pleasure. Daniel Kahneman and Amos Tversky asked people if they would accept certain bets. They found that people needed the chance of winning $40 if they were going to undergo a bet that might cost them $20. Because of loss aversion investors are quicker to sell stocks that have made them money than they are to sell stocks that have been declining. They're making self-destructive decisions because they don't want to admit their losses.

Rebirth

Gradually Erica acquired a new vocabulary to define unconscious biases. But the work behavioral economists do on campus doesn't automatically translate into the sort of work a consultant does in a boardroom. Erica needed to find a way to translate the research into usable advice.

For a few weeks, as her savings dwindled, Erica wrote memos to herself on how this could be done. When she had finished she looked them over and came to a profound realization. This was not the sort of thing she was good at. She was going to need to hire someone who could really play with ideas, who could take academic findings and find ways to apply them in the real world.

She asked around. She asked friends in the consulting world. She sent mass e-mails. She posted a little note on Facebook. Finally, through a friend of a friend, she heard about a young man who was good with ideas, who was available and who she could probably afford. The man's name, of course, was Harold.

CHAPTER 12

FREEDOM AND COMMITMENT

OR THE FIRST EIGHTEEN YEARS OF HIS LIFE, HAROLD HAD engaged in a sort of highly structured striving. During childhood, he had been extravagantly supervised, coached, and mentored. His missions had been clearly marked: get good grades, make the starting team, make adults happy.

Ms. Taylor had introduced a new wrinkle into his life—a love of big ideas. Harold discovered he loved world historical theories, the grander the better. Sometimes he would get so swept up in ideas, you had to chase him around with a butterfly net.

In college, Harold made another discovery. He could be interesting. In college, there were two different status economies. There was the daytime economy, when students interacted with adults and were at their resume-padding, mentor-pleasing best. Harold didn't really stand out in this world, where he was surrounded by students whose conversation consisted mostly of how much work they had to do.

But then there was the nighttime economy, an all-student mosh pit of sarcasm and semen-related gross-out humor. In this economy, worldly accomplishments were irrelevant, and the social rewards went to those with the wittiest sensibilities.

Harold and his friends were sensibility gymnasts. They could pull off hilarious routines of irony, camp, ridicule, and self-referential, postmodern pseudo-mockery. Nothing they said was ever meant literally, and the trick to entering their social set consisted in knowing exactly how many layers of irony surrounded each conversational display.

He and his friends knew what the cruelest and funniest YouTube videos were before anyone else. They debated Coen brothers movies and the cultural significance of the *American Pie* series. They were briefly enthralled by the open-source software movement as a new mode of social organization. They wondered what is the optimal level of fame—Brad Pitt or Sebastian Junger? They favored the kind of music that is more fun to talk about than to listen to—intellectual neo-House music and self-consciously retro electro-funk. They cultivated the sort of weird obsessions that can come only through months of nonschoolwork-related Internet surfing. They shared an interest in the radical Dutch traffic engineer Hans Monderman.

In other generations, the campus avant-garde debated Pauline Kael and the meaning of Ingmar Bergman films, but Harold and his friends assumed that technology would produce bigger social changes than art or cultural products. They moved first from iPod to iPhone to iPad, and if Steve Jobs had come out with an iWife they would have been married on launch day. They were not only early adopters; they were early discarders, ditching each fad just as it hit the mainstream. They had finished their titanium-necklace phases by eighth grade, and by college they were sick of whimsical furniture. They scoffed at kids who had gumball machines in their rooms, though Harold found it witty when a friend used an airplane-service cart as an at-home liquor cabinet.

Harold was pretty good at these sensibility contests, but overall he was overshadowed by his roommate. In the initial housing application, he'd asked to be paired with a student who had low grades but high SAT scores. When he walked into his dorm room for the first time, there was Mark, dripping in sweat and wearing one of those sleeveless undershirts like Marlon Brando wore in *A Streetcar Named Desire*.

Mark was from L.A. He was about six two with hard, muscled shoulders and a dark handsome face. He wore a scruffy three-day growth of beard on his face, and his hair was perpetually shaggy, like one of those sensitive stud novelists at the Iowa Writers' Workshop. He'd already put a sliding board in the room, for impromptu late-night exercise, and had brought his own bed frame to college—believing that bachelors should always invest in a good bed frame.

Mark was willing to risk humiliation in order to have fun and organized his life as a series of picaresque adventures, designed to produce adrenaline bursts. For example, during his freshman year, he decided, on a lark, to enter the Golden Gloves boxing tournament, billing himself the Kosher Killer. He decided he wouldn't train for his bouts, just blog about boxing. He was escorted by a posse of ring girls dressed as morticians, carrying a coffin as he walked in for the fight. He was knocked out by a real boxer in eighty-nine seconds, but not before his story was covered by every TV news show in the city.

One month, Mark tried to get on *American Idol*. The next, he took up kitesurfing and ended up hanging out with the owner of an NBA basketball team. He had four thousand Facebook friends and on nights out Mark would spend half the night texting, juggling different social and hook-up options. He lived in what he called "Intense World," a constant search for adrenaline and fond memories.

Harold was never quite sure how seriously to take his roommate. Mark would leave little sarcastic Post-it notes around the room—"Go Ahead! Be a Manwhore!"—designed for his own amusement. He made lists of everything: women he'd slept with, women he'd seen naked, people who'd hit him, people who would do community service even if they didn't have to. One day Harold picked up an issue of *Men's Health*, which Mark had left around the apartment, and he found some seemingly earnest marginalia next to an article on exfoliation: "So True! . . . Exactly!"

Once a leader, Harold was now a follower. Mark was Gatsby and Harold, who had once been so assertive, was Nick Carraway, the narrator. He spent the stray hours of his youth marveling at Mark's manic energy and trailing along to share in the fun.

The writer Andrea Donderi argues that the world is divided between Askers and Guessers. Askers feel no shame when making requests and are willing to be told no without being hurt. They'll invite themselves over as a guest for a week. They'll ask for money, to borrow the car, a boat, or a girlfriend. They have no compunction about asking and do not take offense when they are refused.

Guessers hate asking for favors and feel guilty when saying no to other people's requests. In Guess culture, Donderi writes, you avoid putting a request into words unless you're sure the answer will be yes. In Guess culture you never say no to someone else directly. You make excuses. Every request, made or received, is fraught with emotional and social peril.

Mark lived in Ask culture, and Harold lived in Guess culture. This occasionally caused problems between them. Sometimes Harold even thought of buying some self-help books—an entire genre designed to teach Guessers how to be Askers. But it never actually came to that. Besides, to a nineteen-year-old kid, Mark was irresistible. He was always happy, always moving, and always fun. He was like the poster boy of youthful vitality. After graduating from college he set off on a grand world tour, blithely unconcerned with how he would organize the rest of his life. He had assumed since early adolescence that he was destined to be the Omnivore Guardian of Taste. He would take charge of some field—movies, TV, music, design, fashion, or something else, and impose his delightful sensibility on a grateful world.

"Hey, High Thinking!" He called out one day just before graduation. High Thinking was his nickname for Harold. "Do you want to share an apartment while I travel the globe?" So Harold spent the next few years sharing an apartment with a man who wasn't there. Mark's bedroom would sit idle for months, and then occasionally he would breeze into town, bringing a wake of European heiresses and adventure stories.

Harold went on to earn a degree in global economics and foreign relations. He also figured out how to ace job interviews. Instead of being polite, deferential, and demure at these interviews, he was his late-night irreverent self. The bored interviewers inevitably loved it, or at least those at any place he actually wanted to work did.

After college he went through a pseudo–Peace Corps phase of do-good think tankery. He worked at the Social Change Initiative, the

Foundation for Global Awareness, and Common Concerns before serving as a senior fellow at Share, a clean-water distribution NGO founded by an aging rock star. Tiring of private-jet philanthropy, he then went through his editorial-associate phase. He applied for jobs at *The Public Interest, The National Interest, The American Interest, The American Prospect, Foreign Policy and Foreign Affairs,* and *National Affairs.* While working as an associate editor, he edited essays advocating the full range of oxymoronic grand strategies: practical idealism, moral realism, cooperative unilateralism, focused multilateralism, unipolar defensive hegemony, and so on and so on. These essays were commissioned by executive editors who had been driven insane by attending too many Davos conferences.

The jobs sounded exciting on the outside, but they often involved doing a lot of unnecessary research. Harold had spent the years before college graduation in upper-level seminars discussing Tolstoy, Dostoyevsky, and the problem of evil. He spent the years after graduation operating a Canon copying machine.

It became obvious to him, as he stood there trying not to be hypnotized by the cruising green light of the machine, that he had become information-age Canon fodder. The organizations and journals he worked for were run by paunchy middle-aged adults who had job security and a place in society. People in his cohort, on the other hand, were transient young things who seemed to be there mostly to provide fact-checking and sexual tension.

His parents were growing increasingly anxious, because their son, a few years out of college now, seemed adrift. Harold's own mental state was more complicated. On the one hand, he didn't feel any particular pressure to settle into a groove and become an adult yet. None of his friends were doing it. They were living in an even more slapdash manner than he was—spending their twenties doing a little teaching, a little temping, a little bartending. They seemed to move from city to city with amazing promiscuity. Cities have become the career dressing rooms for young adults. They have become the place where people go in their twenties to try on different identities. Then, once they know who they are, they leave. Thirty-eight percent of young Americans say they would like to live in Los Angeles, but only 8 percent of older Americans would. Harold's friends would show up in San Francisco one year and then Washington, D.C., the next. Everything changed except their e-mail addresses.

On the other hand, Harold desperately wanted to know what he was supposed to do with his life. He dreamed of finding some calling that would end all uncertainty and would give his life meaning. He longed for some theme that would connect one event in his life to another and replace the jarring sensation he had that each of his moments was unconnected to what came before and after. He dreamed that someday some all-knowing mentor would sit him down and not only tell him how to live but why he was here. But his Moses never came. Of course he could never come, because you can only discover your vocation by doing it, and seeing if it feels right. There's no substitute for the process of trying on different lives, and waiting to find one that fits.

In the meantime, Harold found himself evolving in ways he didn't particularly like. He had developed a personality based on sensibility snobbery. He hadn't accomplished much of anything yet, but at least he could feel good about his superior sensibility. He watched those comedy shows that exploit young people's status anxiety by ridiculing famous people who are professionally accomplished but personally inferior.

At the same time, he could be a shameless suck-up. He found himself dashing across cocktail receptions to make a nice impression before a superior. He discovered that the higher people rise in the world, the larger the dose of daily flattery they need in order to maintain their psychic equilibrium. He became very good at delivering it.

Harold also discovered that it's socially acceptable to flatter your bosses by day so long as you are blasphemously derisive about them while drinking with your buddies at night. He marveled at the college losers who'd spent the four years at school in friendless isolation watching sitcoms, and who were now promising young producers and Hollywood's flavors of the month. The adult world seemed mysterious and perverse.

The Odyssey Years

Harold was part of a generation that inaugurated a new life phase, the odyssey years. There used to be four life phases—childhood, adolescence, adulthood, and old age. Now there are at least six—childhood, adolescence, odyssey, adulthood, active retirement, and old age. Odyssey is the decade of wandering that occurs between adolescence and adulthood.

Adulthood can be defined by four accomplishments: moving away from home, getting married, starting a family, and becoming financially independent. In 1960, 70 percent of American thirty-year olds had accomplished these things. By 2000, fewer than 40 percent had done the same. In Western Europe, which has been leading this trend, the numbers are even lower.

The existence of this new stage can be seen in a range of numbers, which have been gathered by scholars such as Jeffrey Jensen Arnett in his book *Emerging Adulthood*, Robert Wuthnow in his book *After the Baby Boomers*, Joseph and Claudia Allen in their book *Escaping Endless Adolescence*, and by William Galston of the Brookings Institution.

People around the world are shacking up more and postponing marriage. In the early 1970s, 28 percent of Americans had lived with a partner before marriage. By the 1990s, 65 percent of Americans had. Between 1980 and 2000 the median age of first marriage had increased by between five and six years in France, Germany, the Netherlands, and the United Kingdom, an astonishing shift in lifestyles in such a short time. In 1970 a fifth of Americans at age twenty-five had never been married. By 2005, 60 percent had never been married.

As Wuthnow demonstrates, people around the developed world are spending more years in school and taking more time to finish their education. The average college graduate in 2000 took 20 percent longer to earn a degree than the average student in 1970.

The changes have been caused by several interrelated phenomena. People are living longer, and so have more time to settle on a life course. The economy has become more complicated, with a broader array of career possibilities, so it takes awhile for people to find the right one. Society has become more segmented, so it takes longer for people to find the right psychological niche. Women are better educated than before and more likely to be working full-time. In 1970 only 26 percent of women were working out of the home fifty weeks a year in the United States. By 2000, 45 percent were. Many of these women want to, or feel compelled to, postpone marriage and family until they are professionally established.

Finally, young people are ambivalent about adulthood. As Arnett argues, they want the security and stability adulthood brings, but they don't want to settle into a daily grind. They don't want to limit their spontaneity or put limits on their dreams.

These changes had profound effects on the way Harold and his cohort imagined their life courses. For example, earlier generations assumed that a young person should get married and then together as a couple go out and get established in the world. But people in Harold's social class generally took a different view. First you got established. Then when you were secure and could afford a wedding, you got married.

Harold and his friends were not rebels. By and large, they still wanted a stable marriage, two kids, a house in the suburbs, and a secure income. People in the current generation are more likely than those of previous generations to say that parents should sacrifice their own happiness for the sake of their children. But the former had been raised amid peace and (for the most part) prosperity, so they had an amazing confidence in their ability to realize their dreams. Around 96 percent of eighteen- to twenty-nine-year-old Americans agree with the statement "I am certain that someday I will get to where I want to be in life." They were very, even insanely, impressed with their own specialness. In 1950 a personality test asked teenagers if they considered themselves an important person. Twelve percent said yes. By the late 1980s, 80 percent said yes.

Despite his assumption that everything would turn out well in the end, Harold found himself living in an under-institutionalized world. Because the Odyssey stage of life was so new, groups and customs had

not yet arisen to give it structure. He didn't belong to any religious con-
gregation (young people today are much less likely to attend church
than young people were in the 1970s). He didn't have any clear ethnic
identity. His view of the world wasn't shaped by any local newspaper or
single opinion leader (he surfed the Web). His worldview wasn't
molded by any world historical event such as the Depression or World
War II. He wasn't even bound down by acute financial pressures. Between the ages of eighteen and thirty-four, the average American receives $38,000 in subsidies from Mom and Dad, and Harold, too, relied
on some help to pay the rent.

He lived in a social landscape with astonishingly few guardrails.
Some days he felt as though he was waiting for a set of opinions, habits,
and goals to harden in his mind. The social critic Michael Barone argues that the United States produces moderately impressive twenty-
year-olds but very impressive thirty-year-olds. He says that the hard
pressures and choices that hit people during their wide-open, unsupervised twenties forge a new and much better kind of person.

Harold wasn't sure about that, since he seemed to spend a disturbing amount of time on a friend's ragged couch playing Call of Duty:
Black Ops. But at least he did have moments of intense pleasure, and he
did have a great group of friends.

The Group

In the years between living with his parents and living with his wife,
Harold lived with the Group. The Group was a gang of friends who
lived in the same limbo state as he. They were between twenty-two and
thirty. The core had attended college together, but they'd accumulated
a gang of selected friends along the way, so now there were roughly
twenty people hanging about in their circle.

Most of them had dinner together once a week at a local diner, including Mark when he was around. They formed a softball team and
some of them played volleyball together, too. They had orphan dinners
on Thanksgiving and Christmas for Group members who couldn't
make it home to be with their folks. They lent each other money, drove

each other to the airport, helped each other load U-Hauls and generally provided all the services that people from an extended family might provide for one another in a more traditional society.

Harold was sure that his group was filled with the most talented proto-geniuses that had ever been assembled. One of them was a singer-songwriter, another was doing her medical residency, a third did art and graphic design. Even the ones who had boring jobs had interesting sidelights—hot-air ballooning, extreme sports, or great potential as a future contestant on *Jeopardy!*. There was an unofficial ban against Groupcest, dating within the group. But an exception was made if the couple involved got really serious about each other.

The Group conversations were the most exhilarating part of Harold's life at this time. They spent hours talking at cafés, bars, and parties—repeating dialogue from *30 Rock* episodes, complaining about bosses, coaching each other for job interviews, and debating serious issues such as whether or not people over forty should still be allowed to wear sneakers in public when not working out. They had uproarious nostalgic conversations about who had puked on whom in college. They sent each other philosograms—little pseudo-profound texts such as "Don't you think my narcissism is my most interesting feature?" They handed out Whuffies, a reputational currency from a Cory Doctorow novel, that were awarded to people who did things that made them no money but which were creative or just nice. They spent a lot of their time discussing core questions such as which of them was smart enough or ruthless enough to make it in the real world.

Researchers have done a lot of work over the past few years analyzing social networks. It turns out almost everything is contagious. If your friends are obese, you are more likely to be obese. If your friends are happy, you're more likely to be happy. If your friends smoke, you smoke. If they feel lonely, you feel lonely. In fact, Nicholas Christakis and James H. Fowler have found that a person's friends have more influence on whether he or she will be obese than a person's spouse.

But to be honest, Harold loved spending time with the Group because he didn't have to worry if it served any utility or not. Being part of the Group was an end in itself. More time with his friends meant more of a feeling of being alive, and there was no higher purpose involved. They'd get together for hours on end in great swirling bouts of talk. Very frequently they'd dance. Most societies have some form of ritualized group dancing. Modern American society has done away with a lot of that (except for square dancing and a few other specialties). Now most dancing is done by couples, as a preparation for sex. But when the Group got together they would all dance. They'd gather at a bar or an apartment, and they would form this big mob of dancers—a cloud of people with no set pairings or formations. They'd each move about the mob, engaging one or another, man or woman, and then they'd move on to another part of the shape-shifting cloud. The dancing wasn't about anything. It wasn't about wooing. It wasn't about seduction. It was just the physical exuberance of being together.

Fate

And then one day, or really over the course of forty-eight hours, fate intervened. Harold was out with Mark and some Group friends at a sports bar, watching the World Cup. The match was coming to its climax, with a few minutes to go, when Mark elbowed him on the shoulder with a thought that had just popped into his head: "Hey, do you want to move to L.A. and become a TV producer with me?"

Harold looked at him for a second and then back at the game. "Have you really thought this through?"

"I don't need to. It's my Destiny. It's what I was meant to do." The match went back and forth. Everybody in the bar was screaming, and Mark sketched out the life they would lead. Produce a few trashy shows at first—maybe infomercials and cop shows. Then take a few years off with their money and have fun. Then do something more legit. Then buy some houses in various parts of the world and have more fun. Then do big dramas on HBO and change the world. The great thing, as Mark described it, is that you'd make boatloads of money, have total freedom, and never be tied down to one thing or one project or one idea. It was perfect liberty.

The funny thing is, Harold had no doubt that Mark would achieve everything he set out to do. He had what Harold had once called "Universally Synchronous Superficiality." That is to say, Mark was exactly as shallow as the market would bear. He was never tempted to be too complicated or too experimental. What he liked, the world liked. What he hated, the world hated—or at least that portion of the world who lived and died for early-evening TV and Saturday night at the movies.

Still, Harold resisted. "That's no way to live," he replied. And so began the debate, the debate they had been heading toward since that day years earlier when Harold had first walked in on Mark in the dorm room. It was the debate between freedom and commitment, about whether life is happier footloose or firmly rooted.

Mark made his case, then Harold made his, and neither made any points that would strike you as particularly original. Mark painted a picture of endlessly exciting diversions—traveling the world and trying new things. He contrasted it with the world of middle-aged drudgery, going to work at the same job and home to the same wife, drinking yourself to sleep to cover up your life of quiet desperation.

Harold took the other side. He painted a picture of loving relationships and stable bonds—old friends over for dinner, watching the kids grow up, making a difference in a town and community. He contrasted that to a life of shallow fripperies—zipless sex, vacuous possessions, showy luxuries, and a sad and lonely old age.

This is an old debate—the debate between *On the Road* and *It's a Wonderful Life*. To the extent that social science can solve debates like this, the data is on Harold's side.

In recent years, researchers have spent a lot of time investigating what makes people happy. They do it mostly by asking people if they are happy and then correlating their answers with other features of their lives. The method seems flimsy, but it produces surprisingly stable and reliable results.

The first thing they have found is that the relationship between money and happiness is complex. Richer countries tend to be happier countries, and richer people tend to be happier than poorer people, but the relationship is not that strong; it depends on how you define happiness, and it is the subject of fierce debate among the experts. As Carol

Graham writes in her book *Happiness Around the World*, Nigerians rate themselves just as happy as the Japanese, even though Japan's GDP per capita is almost twenty-five times higher than theirs. The percentage of Bangladeshis who report themselves satisfied with their lives is twice as high as the percentage of Russians. Living standards in the United States have risen dramatically over the past fifty years. But this has produced no measurable uptick in happiness. On the other hand, the United States has become a much more unequal society. This inequality doesn't seem to have reduced national happiness either, even among the poor.

Winning the lottery produces a short-term jolt of happiness, but the long-term effects are invisible. The happiness gain you get from moving from poor to middle class is greater than the gain you get moving from middle to upper class; the happiness curve flattens out. People aren't happiest during the middle-aged years, when they are winning the most promotions. They are happiest in their twenties and their sixties, when their careers are just starting or winding down. People who place tremendous emphasis on material well-being tend to be less happy than people who don't.

The next clear finding from research is that people are pretty bad at judging what will make them happy. People vastly overvalue work, money, and real estate. They vastly undervalue intimate bonds and the importance of arduous challenges. The average Americans say that if they could make only $90,000 more a year, they could "fulfill all their dreams." But the evidence suggests they are wrong.

If the relationship between money and happiness is complicated, the relationship between social bonds and happiness is not. The deeper the relationships a person has, the happier he or she will be. People in long-term marriages are much happier than people who aren't. According to one study, being married produces the same psychic gain as earning $100,000 a year. According to another, joining a group that meets even just once a month produces the same happiness gain as doubling your income.

People who have one recurrent sexual partner in a year are happier than people who have multiple partners in a year. People who have more friends have lower stress levels and longer lives. Extroverts are happier than introverts. According to research by Daniel Kahneman, Alan B. Krueger, David Schkade, and others, the daily activities most associated with happiness are all social—having sex, socializing after work, and having dinner with friends—while the daily activity most injurious to happiness—commuting—tends to be solitary. The professions that correlate most closely with happiness are also social (being a corporate manager, a hairdresser, or a health- or care provider), while the professions most injurious to happiness are either perversely social (being a prostitute) or less social (being a machinery operator).

As Roy Baumeister summarizes the evidence, "Whether someone has a network of good relationships or is alone in the world is a much stronger predictor of happiness than any other objective predictor."

In what became their lifelong How-to-Live debate, Mark cited movies and rock songs that celebrated freedom and the open road. Harold said all those movies and lyrics were just marketing strategies for adolescents. Adults should want two things, he said, and these were the two things he wanted from his own life: First, he wanted to have a successful marriage. If you have a successful marriage, it doesn't matter how many professional setbacks you endure, you will be reasonably happy. If you have an unsuccessful marriage, it doesn't matter how many career triumphs you record, you will remain significantly unfulfilled.

Then, Harold continued, he wanted to find some activity, either a job or a hobby, which would absorb all his abilities. He imagined himself working really hard at something, suffering setbacks and frustrations, and then seeing that sweat and toil lead to success and recognition.

He knew that his two goals were in conflict. Marriage might drain time away from his vocation, and his vocation might steal time he could be spending with his friends. He had no idea how he'd navigate those problems. But these were the things he wanted, and neither of them were compatible with the sort of peripatetic, freewheeling life Mark was interested in. Harold had grown up in a culture that, for forty years, had celebrated expressive individualism, self-fulfillment, and personal liberation. But he sensed that what he needed was more community, connection, and interpenetration. He couldn't bring out his best self alone. He could only do it in conjunction with other people.

Erica

Life is filled with strange correspondences. You spend months looking for a good job and then two land at your feet in a day. You spend years looking for a soul mate and then find yourself drawn to two people simultaneously. The day after Harold had his debate with Mark, and effectively closed off one life course for himself, he found himself with another offer. A different life course opened before him.

It came in the form of an e-mail. There was a lunch invitation. It was from a woman named Erica, a friend of a friend. She said she was looking for someone who would help her build her business, and she'd heard that he might be just the person to do that. He checked her out on Facebook and saw a small-boned, attractive Latina-Asian woman. Harold didn't know about working with her. But he wouldn't mind getting to know her. Harold wrote Erica back and said he'd be delighted to meet for lunch. He pretended to be interested in the job, but all sorts of romantic fantasies were already burbling in his mind.

CHAPTER 13

LIMERENCE

AROLD AND ERICA HAD THEIR FIRST MEETING AT A STAR-bucks, where she had arranged a job interview. She made sure to get there first, so she could assume the role of host. He arrived in a suit, but carrying a backpack, which displeased her. She had a coffee waiting for him on the table, and he sat down and introduced himself. He seemed lively and pleasant, though his manners were a tad casual for her taste.

"Let's do our small talk after," Erica said after about a minute, cutting him off. "I want to tell you who I am and what I'm looking for." She briskly ran down a history of her life and a description of the consulting firm she had started. She was completely honest about the difficulties she had experienced so far. "I want someone who can dive into behavioral economics and similar research and find a unique selling proposition—a set of tools we will possess that will help us meet client needs." She spoke rapidly because, though she would never admit it to herself, she was uncomfortable and a little nervous.

Harold was practically a professional interviewee. He'd been through dozens and by now had his disarming shtick down cold. He didn't get to use it this time. Instead he stiffened in response to her clipped, efficient tone. He liked her, though. He was entranced by her background and her tough, driven demeanor. He especially liked the fact that she didn't ask what he hoped to be doing in ten years, or any of those other bullshit questions.

Her queries were precise and practical. Did he know who Daniel Kahneman was? (No.) What sort of research projects had he conducted in the past? (He exaggerated his responsibilities, but not too much.) Had he done fact-checking? (Yes.) It was only at the end that she got to some unusual questions. She asked him to describe the culture at his college. What was the difference between working at a policy magazine and a for-profit business?

The interview took only twenty-five minutes. She hired him. He asked for $55,000 a year and she told him the job would pay $60,000, with raises as business picked up.

She had no office, so they met about three times a week in her kitchen, and then he'd go work at home. She kept her kitchen spare, to give it some semblance of a professional atmosphere, and always kept the door to the bedroom closed. There were no magnets on the refrigerator door. There were no pictures of friends or family that Harold could see. On the other hand, he was impressed by her cutlery and flatware. Harold was still using the utensils he had acquired in college—the drying rack for the dishes, the same six pots and pans, a bottle opener he'd gotten free from a beer distributor. Erica, who was basically his age, had an adult's kitchen.

There were parts of the business he did not see. She never let him meet potential clients. He didn't know how much work went into getting a meeting. She'd drop him an e-mail with the name of a possible client, the nature of the problem they were hoping to solve, and a list of the things they would have to do to win the account. Harold would dive into his research, sleeping during the day, working at night, and then he'd arrange to come by her place to present what he had found. She would greet him kindly but firmly, with Chinese tea and sliced carrots.

Business began to pick up. There was a brisk rhythm of proposals and research projects. One company wanted to find ways to break down the wall between its engineers and marketing people. Another wanted to find ways to market banking to young people. Erica would give Harold instructions about what she wanted and tips about where to find the information, and he felt comfortable with her and really enjoyed the work. If there was a period when their relationship blossomed, it was during editing.

Erica would secure a client, then do a series of meetings with them. She'd send Harold off on a research project. He'd write a bunch of memos, and then she'd use them to draft a report that would go to the client. About two-thirds of Harold's work was doing the research and writing the memos, but a good third was going over her drafts and helping her improve them.

The first time they sat down together Erica almost cried with gratitude. Harold had the ability to read something and really see what the person was trying to get at. When he gave his reactions to her drafts, Erica had this overwhelming sense of being fully listened to and deeply understood. Harold could take a stray wisp of an idea, and get enthralled by it. He'd gush over parts of her draft, making her feel like an absolute star. He'd underline some sections three times and look at her in absolute wonder for having produced them. Then, he'd look at the bad parts as gold mines that just hadn't come in yet. Erica had a tendency to pile up vague, high-minded sentences as a way to cover up a concept that was still fuzzy in her mind. Harold would clear them away, and chop off sections that simply didn't work. Then he'd fill in the holes. He developed an ability to write in her voice and to think in her style, and he made her sound smarter than she really was. He was a tremendous editor. He derived pleasure from sublimating his own ego and writing in another's name.

After six months, they spoke in their own code, with just a few letters indicating what still had to be done. She loosened up in her notes back, telling a few jokes. "I just couldn't get this to work," she wrote once, which for her was a major show of vulnerability. If he found some new fact, he'd call her up, flushed with enthusiasm. Sometimes they'd go out for chicken wings and edit the reports together. Once, when she was out of town with a client he ended an e-mail note with "I miss you." She BlackBerried back, "I miss you, too."

She had no conscious interest in finding a man then, and Harold was nothing like the sort of man she hoped someday to get involved with. He wasn't as tough as she was. He wasn't destined for corporate greatness. He was the sort of guy she could eat alive. But over the months, she found she had real affection for him. He was a genuinely good person. From the bottom of his soul, he wanted her to succeed.

One afternoon, after a hard stretch of work, Harold suggested they go biking. Erica hadn't ridden a bike in years and didn't own one. Harold said they could borrow his roommate's. They drove to his apartment, where Erica had never been, met his strapping and overly charming roommate, whom Erica had never seen, and then went out for a ride. Erica wore her workout gear and Harold had on just regular shorts, a T-shirt, and was kind enough to let Erica use the less dorky of the two bike helmets. They rode for about ten miles, and of course Erica had to accelerate past him up the hills, just to show she could. They got to a steep hill overlooking the water, and Erica began to break away once again, laughing as she outdistanced him. About thirty yards farther on, Harold blew by her. He didn't just pass her. He blasted by her like she was going backward. He had a huge smile on his face, and he was barely breathing. She had no idea he had that power in him.

Harold stopped at the top of the hill and watched her huff up. He still had the huge grin on his face, and she was laughing between her gasps, when their eyes met as she pulled up alongside him. Erica looked into Harold's eyes more deeply than she ever had, and saw through them into some of the things he liked and cherished: his flag-football games, his backpack filled with Great Books, his excitement for her and for their projects together.

They stood astride their bikes on the top of the hill, looking out at the view of the water, and Erica slipped her hand into Harold's. Harold was surprised at how rough and hard her palm felt to the touch, and how lovely.

Status Sonar

A few weeks later, Harold sat alone in his apartment, feeling that his life was going tremendously well. All human beings go through life with a fully operational status sonar. We send out continual waves of status

measurements and receive a stream of positive or negative feedback signals that cumulatively define our place in society. Harold looked around
at his loft. PING. A plus signal came back. He loved its open space and
high ceilings. Harold contemplated his abs. PING. A negative signal
came back. He really should go to the gym more. Harold looked at his
face in the mirror. PING. A neutral signal came back. No sculpted
cheekbones, but it could be worse.

All day long the status sonar hums along—a stream of pluses, minuses, and neutrals building in the mind, producing either happiness,
anxiety, or doubt. The status sonar isn't even a conscious process most
of the time; it is just the hedonic tone of existence. Much of life, Mark
had told Harold, consists of trying to maximize the number of pluses in
the stream and minimize the number of minuses. Much of life is a series
of adjustments to plus up the flow.

The problem is, nobody's status sonar is accurate. Some people are
status exaggerators. They wildly inflate their spot in the pecking order.
They are sixes but they think they are eights and when they ask out
women who are nines they are flummoxed when they get rejected.
Other people are status minimizers. These people will never apply for
jobs for which they are amply qualified because they assume they'll be
crushed by the competition.

The most successful people are mildly delusional status inflators.
They maximize their pluses, thus producing self-confidence, and decide
their minuses are not really that important anyway, thus eliminating
paralyzing self-doubt.

After millennia of male domination, men are big status inflators. A
global survey by Adrian Furnham of University College, London,
found that men everywhere overestimate their own intelligence. Another study revealed that 95 percent of American men believe they are
in the top 50 percent when it comes to social skills. Women are more
likely to be status deflaters. Women underestimate their IQ scores by
an average of about five points.

Harold's sonar sensor was like a finely crafted Swiss watch. It was
balanced, sensitive, and appropriately forgiving. Like most happy peo-

ple, Harold judged himself by his intentions, his friends by their deeds, and his rivals by their mistakes. The PINGs continued. The pluses flowed.

And when Harold imagined himself with Erica, well, it was like a surging torrent of pluses. Stendhal observed that each person's first great love is fueled by ambition. Harold wasn't merely excited by Erica as a person. He was excited by the whole aura of the hard-charging rags-to-riches girl. He was excited at the thought of the places they would go together. He imagined them together, trading delightful mock insults at dinner parties, like Beatrice and Benedick in *Much Ado about Nothing*.

But there was also something deeper going on. All his life, Harold had lived at a certain level, but now he had discovered deeper compulsions. Coming to this realization was like living in a house all your life and suddenly falling through a trapdoor to find there had been a level underground all along, and then to find another level beneath that, and another level and another. As Matthew Arnold put it:

> Below the surface-stream, shallow and light,
> Of what we say we feel—below the stream,
> As Light, of what we think we feel—there flows
> With noiseless current strong, obscure and deep,
> The central stream of what we feel indeed.

Harold couldn't go five minutes without thinking about Erica. If he was walking down the street alone, he thought he saw her face in the crowd every few blocks. He rarely ate, and neglected his friends. Harold's whole mood was elevated. Things that used to bore him he now found delightful. People who used to annoy him now seemed warm and friendly. When martins mate, they flutter frantically from branch to branch in a state of hypercharged delirium. Harold now had the energy to stay up all night, to work without breaks.

His mind raced back to certain precious episodes since she had first slipped her hand into his—eating a Chinese dinner in her apartment, their first lovemaking. When he was out running, he would concoct elaborate fantasies in which he heroically saved her from harm (something about the act of running, and the primal chemicals it released in his brain, brought out these Walter Mitty imaginings).

Then, at another moment he might be swept up in fear of losing her. There's a nineteenth-century poem by a Kwakiutl Indian that captures the crush of Harold's sweet and searing sensations: "Fires run through my body—/the pain of loving you./Pain runs through my body with the fires of my love for you./Sickness wanders my body with my love for you./ . . . /Pain like a boil about to burst with my love for you./I remember what you said to me./I am thinking of your love for me./I am torn by your love for me."

According to studies by Faby Gagné and John Lydon, 95 percent of those in love believe that their current partner is above average in looks, intelligence, warmth, and sense of humor (while they describe their former lovers as closed-minded, emotionally unstable, and generally unpleasant). Harold was no different. He practiced a most delicious form of self-deception and saw Erica as perfect in every way.

Harold was experiencing what Stendhal called "crystalization." In his essay, "Love," Stendhal described a salt mine near Salzburg, where workers would throw leafless branches into one of the abandoned parts of the mine. Then, when they would retrieve the branches two or three months later, they would find them covered with shimmering, diamondlike crystals, beautiful beyond all reckoning. "What I have called crystalization," Stendhal wrote, "is a mental process which draws from everything that happens new proofs of the perfection of the loved one."

This is what the unconscious scouts do: They coat people, places, and objects with emotional significance. They coat the objects of our love with shimmering and irresistible light. They induced Harold to love Erica even more. It meant he had no interest in other women. It meant he had no dreams but her.

Motivation

If you had asked Harold how Erica made him feel, he would have told you he felt as if some superior force from outside had taken over his life.

He could now understand why the pagans had conceived of love as a god. It really did feel as if some supernatural entity had entered his mind, reorganized everything, and lifted him to some higher realm.

And the odd thing is if you had looked inside Harold's brain while he was in this enchanted state, you would not have found some separate and magical part aflame. Helen Fisher's research into the brain activity of people who are deeply and madly in love reveals that it's some of the prosaic, furnacelike parts of the brain that are actually most active at moments of intense romantic feeling—parts like the caudate nucleus and the ventral tegmental area (VTA). The caudate nucleus, for example, helps us perform extremely mundane tasks. It preserves muscle memory, so we remember how to type or ride a bike. It integrates huge amounts of information, including childhood memories.

But the caudate nucleus and the VTA are also parts of something else, the reward system of the mind. They produce powerful chemicals like dopamine, which can lead to focused attention, exploratory longings, and strong, frantic desire. Norepinephrine, a chemical derived from dopamine, can stimulate feelings of exhilaration, energy, sleeplessness, and loss of appetite. Phenylethylamine is a natural amphetamine that produces feelings of sexual excitement and emotional uplift.

As Fisher wrote in her book *Why We Love*, "The caudate helps us detect and perceive a reward, discriminate between rewards, *prefer* a particular reward, anticipate a reward, and expect a reward. It produces motivation to acquire a reward and plans specific movements to obtain a reward. The caudate is also associated with the acts of paying attention and learning."

In other words, love isn't separate from everyday life. It is a member of a larger family of desires. Arthur Aron of Stony Brook University argues that on an fMRI machine, the brain of a person experiencing the first burst of love looks, in some ways, like the brain of a person in the midst of a cocaine rush. Neuroscientist Jaak Panksepp argues that the experience of opiate addiction mimics the pleasure lovers feel being around each other. In each case, people are gripped by a desire that takes over their lives. Inhibitions fall. The object of desire becomes the object of an obsession.

Aron argues that love is not an emotion like happiness or sadness. Love is a motivational state, which leads to various emotions ranging from euphoria to misery. A person in love has the keenest possible ambition to achieve a goal. A person in love is in a state of need.

Harold had not been notably ambitious so far, but now he was in the grip of some deep and monumental force. In *The Symposium*, Plato treats love as the attempt to reunite two halves of a single being. And indeed, Harold's love made him feel incomplete. Even when they fought, it was better to be with Erica in misery than to be without her in happiness. Even if he did nothing else, he had to erase the boundaries between them and meld their souls together.

The Urge to Merge

Wolfram Schultz is a neuroscientist at Cambridge University who did research on monkeys in hopes of understanding Parkinson's disease. He would squirt apple juice in their mouths and observe a little surge in the dopamine neurons in their brains. After a few squirts, he noticed that the dopamine neurons began to fire just before the juice arrived. He set up an experiment in which he sounded a tone and then delivered the juice. After just a few rounds, the monkeys figured out that the tone preceded the juice. Their neurons begin to fire at the sound of the tone, not with the delivery of the juice. Schultz and his colleagues were baffled. Why didn't these neurons simply respond to the actual reward, the juice?

A crucial answer came from Read Montague, Peter Dayan, and Terrence Sejnowski. The mental system is geared more toward predicting rewards than in the rewards themselves. The mind creates predictive models all day long—for example, that tone will lead to this juice. When one of the models accurately anticipates reality, then the mind experiences a little surge of reward, or at least a reassuring feeling of tranquility. When the model contradicts reality, then there's tension and concern.

The main business of the brain is modeling, Montague argues. We are continually constructing little anticipatory patterns in our brain to help us predict the future: If I put my hand here, then this will happen. If I smile, then she'll smile. If our model meshes with what actually happens, we experience a little drip of sweet affirmation. If it doesn't, then there's a problem, and the brain has to learn what the glitch is and adjust the model.

This function is one of the fundamental structures of desire. As we go through our days, the mind generates anticipatory patterns, based on the working models stored inside it. Often there's tension between the inner models and the outer world. So we try to come up with concepts that will help us understand the world, or changes in behavior that will help us live in harmony with it. When we grasp some situation, or master some task, there's a surge of pleasure. It's not living in perpetual harmony that produces the surge. If that were so, we'd be happy living on the beach all our lives. It's the moment when some tension is erased. So a happy life has its recurring set of rhythms: difficulty to harmony, difficulty to harmony. And it is all propelled by the desire for limerence, the desire for the moment when the inner and outer patterns mesh.

This yearning for harmony, or limerence, can manifest itself in small mundane ways. People experience a small spark of pleasure when they solve a crossword puzzle or when they sit down and find a perfectly set table that meets their standard of "just so."

The desire for limerence can also manifest itself in odd ways. People are instinctively drawn to the familiar. For example, Brett Pelham of the State University of New York at Buffalo has shown that people named Dennis and Denise are disproportionately likely to become dentists. People named Lawrence and Laurie are disproportionately likely to become lawyers. People named Louis are disproportionately likely to move to Saint Louis, and people named George disproportionately move to Georgia. These are some of the most important choices in people's lives, and they are influenced, if only a bit, by the sound of the name they happen to be given at birth and the attraction to the familiar.

The desire for limerence drives us to seek perfection in our crafts. Sometimes, when we are absorbed in some task, the skull barrier begins to disappear. An expert rider feels at one with the rhythms of the horse she is riding. A carpenter merges with the tool in his hands. A mathematician loses herself in the problem she is solving. In these sublime moments, internal and external patterns are meshing and flow is achieved.

The desire for limerence propels us intellectually. We all like to be told how right we are (some radio and cable-TV pundits make millions reinforcing their audience's inner models). We all feel a surge of pleasure when some clarifying theory clicks into place. We all like to feel in harmony with our surroundings. As Bruce Wexler argues in *Brain and Culture*, we spend much of the first halves of our lives trying to build internal models that fit the world and much of the last halves trying to adjust the world so it fits the inner models. Much late-night barroom conversation involves someone trying to get other people to see the world as we do. Nations don't clash only over land, wealth, and interests; they fight to compel others to see the world as they do. One of the reasons the Israeli-Palestinian conflict has been so stubbornly unresolved is that each side wants the other to accept its historical narrative.

Most people are deeply moved when they return to their childhood home, to the place where their mental models were first forged. When we return to the town where we grew up, it is the details that matter most—the way the drugstore is in the same place as it was when we were young, the same fence around the park, the angle of the sun in the winter, the crosswalk we used to traverse. We don't love these things for their merits, because the crosswalk is the best of all possible crosswalks. The mind coats home with a special layer of affection because these are the patterns we know. "The child will love a crusty old gardener who has hardly ever taken any notice of it and shrink from the visitor who is making every attempt to win its regard," C. S. Lewis once observed. "But it must be an *old* gardener, one who has 'always' been there—the short but seemingly immemorial 'always' of childhood."

The desire for limerence is at its most profound during those transcendent moments when people feel themselves fused with nature and with God, when the soul lifts up and a feeling of oneness with the universe pervades their being.

Most important, people seek limerence with one another. Within two weeks of being born, babies will cry if they hear another baby in distress, but not if they hear a recording of their own crying. In 1945 the Austrian physician René Spitz investigated an American orphanage. The orphanage itself was meticulously clean. There was a nurse for every eight babies. The babies were well fed, but they were left alone all day, in theory to reduce their exposure to germs. Sheets were hung between the cribs for the same reason. Despite all the sanitary precautions, 37 percent of the babies in the orphanage died before reaching age two. They were missing one essential thing they needed to live—empathetic contact.

People gravitate toward people like themselves. When we meet new people, we instantly start matching our behavior to theirs. It took Muhammad Ali, who was just about as quick as anybody ever, 190 milliseconds to detect an opening in his opponent's defenses and begin throwing a punch into it. It takes the average college student 21 milliseconds to begin synchronizing her movement unconsciously with her friends.

Friends who are locked in conversation begin to replicate each other's breathing patterns. People who are told to observe a conversation begin to mimic the physiology of the people having the conversation, and the more closely they mimic the body language, the more perceptive they are about the relationship they are observing. At the deeper level of pheromones, women who are living together often share the same menstrual cycles.

As the neuroscientist Marco Iacoboni notes, "Vicarious" is not a strong enough word to describe the effect of these mental processes. When we sense another's joy, we begin to share that person's laughter as if it were our own. When we see agony, even up on a movie screen, that agony is reflected in our brains, in paler form, as if it were our own.

"When your friend has become an old friend, all those things about him which had originally nothing to do with the friendship become familiar and dear with familiarity," C. S. Lewis writes. A friend's love, Lewis continues, "free from all duties but those which love has freely assumed, almost wholly free from jealousy, and free without qualification from the need to be needed, is eminently spiritual. It is the sort of love one can imagine between angels."

Once people feel themselves within a group, there is a strong intuitional pressure to conform to its norms. Solomon Asch conducted a famous experiment in which he showed people three different lines of obviously different length. Then he surrounded the test subjects with a group of people (secretly working for Asch) who insisted that the lines were the same length. Faced with this group pressure, 70 percent of the research subjects conformed at least once, reporting that the lines were the same length. Only 20 percent refused to conform to this obvious falsehood.

Bliss

We don't teach this ability in school—to harmonize patterns, to seek limerence, to make friends. But the happy life is defined by these sorts of connections, and the unhappy life is defined by a lack of them.

Emile Durkheim demonstrated that people with few social connections are much more likely to commit suicide. In *Love and Survival*, Dean Ornish surveyed research on longevity and concluded that solitary people are three to five times more likely to die prematurely than socially engaged people.

Achieving limerence, on the other hand, can produce an overwhelming feeling of elevation. When the historian William McNeill was in the U.S. Army in 1941, he was taught, in boot camp, how to march. Soon, this act of marching with his fellows began to alter his own consciousness:

> Words are inadequate to describe the emotion aroused by the prolonged movement in unison that drilling involved. A sense of pervasive well-being is what I recall; a strange sense of personal enlargement; a sort of swelling out, becoming bigger than life, thanks to participation in collective ritual.

Millions of soldiers have risked and surrendered their lives in war because of the primordial connection they felt toward their fellows. Families are often held together through thick and thin by that feeling.

Social life is held together by the lower-level version of that feeling we call trust. And for most of us, the strongest longing for limerence takes the form of that intense desire we have to meld with the special other—love.

This drive, this longing for harmony, is a never-ending process—model, adjust, model, adjust—guiding us onward.

Eros Reconsidered

Today, when we hear the word "eros," we think of something quite distinct and compartmentalized—sex. Erotica is separated in the bookstore from the other books. But this is the narrow, chopped-up meaning of eros that we have inherited from a sex-centered culture. In the Greek understanding, eros is not just the desire for orgasm, sex, or even genetic transmission. The Greeks saw eros as a generalized longing for union with the beautiful and the excellent.

People driven by lust want to have orgasms with each other. But people driven by eros want to have a much broader fusion. They want to share the same emotions, visit the same places, savor the same pleasures, and replicate the same patterns in each other's minds. As Allan Bloom wrote in *Love & Friendship*, "Animals have sex and human beings have eros, and no accurate science is possible without making this distinction."

People sometimes say neuroscience is destroying the soul and the spirit. It reduces everything to neurons, synapses, and biochemical reactions. But in fact neuroscience gives us a glimpse of eros in action. It helps us see the dance of the patterns between friends and lovers.

Harold and Erica were never more alive than in the first weeks of their love for each other. One afternoon they were sitting on the couch at Harold's place, watching an old movie. "I know you," Erica said after a lull, apropos of nothing, peering into Harold's eyes. Then a few minutes later she fell asleep on Harold's chest. Harold went on watching the movie and shifted her head a bit so he could be comfortable. She made a soft nuzzling sound.

Then Harold brushed his hand over her hair and face. Her breathing quickened and slowed with the pace of his touch, but still her eyes were closed and she didn't stir. Harold had never noticed how deeply she could sleep. He lost all interest in the movie and just watched her there.

He picked up her arm and put it around his neck. She made a sweet puckering gesture with her lips, but remained asleep. Then he put her arm back down on her side. She nestled back into his chest. After that he just watched her doze, measuring the rise and fall of her chest, a feeling of tender protectiveness sweeping over him. "Remember this moment," he thought.

Not that everything was perfect. Each found that they still had deep unconscious inhibitions that blocked the union they sought most. There were still frictions and conflicts.

The longing for limerence doesn't automatically produce perfect romances or easy global harmony. We spend large parts of our lives trying to get others to accept our patterns—and trying to resist this sort of mental hegemony from others. On a broader scale, people don't just connect; they compete to connect. We compete against one another to win the prestige and respect and attention that will help us bond with one another. We seek to surpass one another in earning one another's approval. That's the logic of our complicated game.

But especially during those first eighteen months, Harold and Erica experienced a sort of worldly magic. They worked together. They ate together. They slept together and fit together in nearly every respect. They tasted the synchronicity that is the essence of all great professions of love: "Love you? I *am* you." "We are one, / One flesh; to lose thee were to lose myself."

CHAPTER 14

THE GRAND NARRATIVE

As Erica's career grew brighter, her house got darker. She and Harold had started their consulting firm when they were both twenty-eight. For the next few years everything went great. They racked up clients. They hired new people—eighteen in all. They bought new phones and nice printers. Their time was consumed by consulting projects—during the day, at night, and on weekends. Occasionally they would carve out time for vacations, for friends and even dinner dates alone. But there was never time for chores around the house they bought. Everything began to fray at the edges. If a lightbulb burned out, it would stay in the socket for months while Erica and Harold learned to navigate their way in the dark. The cable went out in their downstairs TV, but neither had time to call the cable company and take care of it. Windows cracked. Gutters filled with leaves. Stains lodged in carpets. They adapted to each peripheral dysfunction, content to trade professional achievement for domestic decay.

After about four years, though, the company began to fall apart. A recession hit. Physically, nothing changed. The buildings and the people were all there. But the psychology was different. One moment everyone talked heroically about embracing risk, the next they were terrified. Consulting contracts, which had seemed essential for long-term growth, were now perceived as useless luxuries. Companies slashed them back.

Dozens of friends disappeared from Erica's life. These were clients she'd played tennis with, gone on trips with, invited into her home. They worked at companies she advised, and the bonds of trust and camaraderie between them were real.

But when the contracts were cut, the relationships dissolved. Erica noticed her witty sarcastic e-mails no longer generated responses. Calls went unreturned. It wasn't that people stopped liking her. They just didn't want to hurt her. They were cutting off her contract, and they didn't want to cause her pain by telling her, so they just withdrew. Erica began to recognize the dishonesty of niceness. The desire to not cause pain was just an unwillingness to have an unpleasant conversation. It was cowardice, not consideration.

The office grew quiet. It was hard in turn for Erica's staff to see her helpless in this way. She couldn't show fear, but they all felt it within her. "Nothing is over until it's over," she would tell them, calm and focused. But the money was not coming in. The banks were unhappy. Lines of credit dried up. She was paying employees off her credit card, and begging new clients for work.

Finally, the biggest contract disappeared. She called the CEO asking for a renewal. It was hard to hear her vulnerable like that, her life's work resting on one call. And the CEO lied to her nicely like the others had. It was just a blip in the relationship, he said. They'd be back in a year or so, blah, blah, blah. She couldn't tell him that, without his contract, her company wouldn't last a week. It was the death sentence, and yet as she hung up the phone she found she wasn't shaking. She wasn't hyperventilating. "So this is what it feels like to fail," she thought. The emotional impact came only an hour or so later. She retreated to the ladies' room, heaving with sobs. She wanted to go home and crawl into bed.

At the end of the week, she gathered her staff. They sat around the conference room, trading gallows humor. Erica looked across at them, the individuals who would soon be unemployed. There was Tom, who carried a laptop at all times and typed every significant thing he heard into a file. There was Bing, who was so mentally hyperactive she could only get through half a sentence before she started on the next one. There was Elsie, who had no confidence in herself; Alison, who platonically shared a bed with her roommate to save money; and Emilio, who kept antacid pills in a row atop his computer. People were stranger than you could imagine.

In moments of crisis she became eerily calm. She announced that she had no choice but to close the firm. Gone. Belly-up. She told them the national economy had gone wrong and it was nobody's fault, but then she spoke too long and her mind naturally started rehearsing things she might have done differently. There was something inside her that had trouble with the concept of "nobody's fault." It wanted to assign some concrete blame, justified or not. Then she started giving the old entrepreneur's mantra that there is no such thing as failure. Failure is just a step in the process of learning. Nobody was comforted.

For a few weeks after that, there was still stuff to do. Sell the office supplies. Write letters. But then there was nothing. Erica was shocked at how disorienting this was. All her life she had worked. Suddenly she lived in a pathless universe.

She had thought she might actually like a little tranquility. But it was terrible. "There is no craving or demand of the human mind more constant and insatiable than that for exercise and employment," the Scottish philosopher David Hume wrote, "and this desire seems the foundation of most of our passions and pursuits."

Her thoughts began to disintegrate. After a few weeks, she had trouble organizing an argument or composing a memo. She was exhausted all the time, though she never actually did anything. She longed for some difficulty to overcome.

Eventually, she began to scaffold her days. She had long been a member of a gym, but barely went as she struggled to save her firm. Now she worked out feverishly. She dressed each morning and went to Starbucks, where she sat with her briefcase, phone, and laptop. Going out among the employed was tough—like being a sick person in the land of the healthy, an internal exile. She watched the great mass of coffee sippers trudging thoughtlessly back to their offices. They had obligations; she didn't. She rotated between different Starbucks so it wouldn't be so obvious she had no place else to go.

In an essay for *The Atlantic*, Don Peck summarized the research findings on the psychological costs of unemployment. People who suffer long-term bouts of unemployment are much more likely to suffer depression, even years later. For the rest of their lives, they cling more tightly to jobs, and become more risk averse. They are much more likely to become alcoholics and beat their spouses. Their physical health deteriorates. People who lose jobs at thirty have life spans a year and a half shorter than people who never lost a job. Long-term unemployment, some researchers have found, is the psychic equivalent to the death of a spouse.

Erica's relationship with Harold suffered. Growing up as he had, Harold assumed that your worth depends on who you are. Erica assumed that your worth depends on what you do. Harold always had these random interests he was happy to throw himself into. He spent the first few weeks reading. Erica needed the upward climb, the mission. Harold was willing to take any job that seemed interesting, and before long he got a job as a program officer for a historical society. Erica needed a job that would set her once again on the path to dominance. She'd sit in Starbucks, calling her old contacts, looking for an opening at the vice-president level or above. The calls were almost never returned, and soon her expectations slipped. She began thinking about entrepreneurial opportunities. She could open a smoothie franchise, a Mongolian grill, a nanny agency, a spicy-pickle supplier. She could start a company of pet butlers. These were not exactly the career paths she had ever considered before.

After a few months, a friend told her that Intercom, the cable company, was looking for somebody to help with strategic planning. She had always hated that company. The service was awful, the repairmen were ill-trained, the customer support was slow, the CEO was famously narcissistic. Of course none of that mattered now. She applied.

The interviewer kept her waiting and then greeted her with a condescending amiability. "We have the smartest people on earth working here," he told her. "It's a pleasure coming to work each day. It's like *The Best and the Brightest*."

Erica wondered if this guy had missed the Vietnam parts of that book.

Of course he started talking about himself. "I owe it to myself to live up to the highest standards. I owe it to myself to provide legendary excellence." This phrase was apparently a buzzword that had been circling around in the company propaganda. As the session went on, he turned into a little jargon machine. "At the end of the day, we try not to boil the ocean but just look for the best win-wins," he told her. Apparently people at this company were always drilling down and disintermediating the dialogue. They were driving maximum functionality, with end-to-end mission-critical competence to incent high-level blue-ocean change.

Erica sat there with a smile pasted on her face. She appeared eager and supplicating. She debased herself. When he asked her what she wanted to do at the company, she slipped into the argot and threw it all back at him. She would save self-loathing for after she got the job.

He said he would call in a week, but it took two. She had her phone on vibrate the whole time, and every little tingle, real or imagined, sent her grabbing for the thing. The call finally came. Follow-up interviews were arranged and after another month or so she was an employee once again. She had a nice office. She began going to meetings and found herself surrounded by the lords of self-esteem.

Overconfidence

The human mind is an overconfidence machine. The conscious level gives itself credit for things it really didn't do and confabulates tales to create the illusion it controls things it really doesn't determine. Ninety percent of drivers believe they are above average behind the wheel. Ninety-four percent of college professors think they are above-average teachers. Ninety percent of entrepreneurs think that their new business will be a success. Ninety-eight percent of students who take the SAT say they have average or above-average leadership skills.

College students vastly overestimate their chances of getting a high-paying job, traveling abroad, and staying married when they reach adulthood. When shopping for clothes, middle-aged people generally choose clothes that are too tight on the grounds that they're about to lose a few pounds, even though the vast majority of people in their age bracket get wider year by year. Golfers on the PGA tour estimate that 70 percent of their six-foot putts drop in the hole, when in reality 54 percent of the putts from that distance actually make it in.

This overconfidence comes in many varieties. People overestimate their ability to control their unconscious tendencies. They buy health-club memberships but then are unable to work up the willpower to go. People overestimate how well they understand themselves. Half of all students at Penn State said they would make a stink if somebody made a sexist comment in their presence. When researchers arranged for it to actually happen, only 16 percent actually said anything.

People overestimate what they know. Paul J. H. Schoemaker and J. Edward Russo gave executives questionnaires to measure how much they knew about their industries. Managers in the advertising industry gave answers that they were 90 percent confident were correct. In fact, their answers were wrong 61 percent of the time. People in the computer industry gave answers they thought had a 95 percent chance of being right; in fact, 80 percent of them were wrong. Russo and Schoemaker gave their tests to more than two thousand people and 99 percent overestimated their success.

People not only overestimate what they know, they overestimate what they can know. Certain spheres of life, like the stock market, are too complex and too random to be able to predict near-term events with any certainty. This seems to have no effect on actual behavior, as the entire stock-picking industry demonstrates. Brad Barber and Terrance Odean analyzed over sixty-six thousand trades from discount broker accounts. The traders who were the most confident did the most trades and underperformed the overall market.

People get intoxicated by their own good luck. Andrew Lo of MIT has demonstrated that when stock traders experience a series of good days, the dopamine released into their brains creates a surge of overconfidence. They believe they've achieved this good fortune themselves; they have figured out the market. They become blind to downside risk.

People overestimate their ability to understand why they are making certain decisions. They make up stories to explain their own actions, even when they have no clue about what is happening inside. After they've made a decision, they lie to themselves about why they made the decision and about whether it was the right one in the circumstances. Daniel Gilbert of Harvard argues that we have a psychological immune system that exaggerates information that confirms our good qualities and ignores information that casts doubt upon them. In one study, people who were told they had just performed poorly on an IQ test spent a lot more time reading newspaper articles on the shortcomings of IQ tests. People who had been given a glowing report from a supervisor developed an increased interest in reading reports about how smart and sagacious that supervisor was.

And the telling thing is that self-confidence has very little to do with actual competence. A great body of research finds that incompetent people exaggerate their own abilities more grossly than their better-performing peers. One study found that those who scored in the bottom quartile on tests of logic, grammar, and humor were especially likely to overestimate their abilities. Many people are not only incompetent, they are in denial about how incompetent they are.

So it is fair to say that human beings are generally overconfident. But Erica's colleagues at Intercom not only rode the steed of arrogance, they took it out for a parade. The CEO, Blythe Taggert, never met an organization he didn't want to transform. When he came to the company he declared war on entrenched bureaucracy and "old thinking." The result was that his revolutionary fervor sometimes turned into a contempt for experienced managers and time-tested practices. He issued middle-of-the-night memos, often composed off the top of his head, which caused chaos in department after department. He was guided by aphorisms and rules that sounded good in speeches but often had nothing to do with real-life situations. He'd impatiently sit through presentations that had taken weeks to prepare, then he'd absentmindedly observe, "These ideas don't really bite me in the ass," and he'd stroll out while his acolytes laughed.

He was so eager to be seen as a heroic innovator, he led the company through a series of acquisitions into markets and niches nobody really understood. The company became too big to manage, and in his quest

for the latest and most cutting-edge techniques, he tolerated accounting practices and organizational charts that were too complex to
fathom.

He spoke first at every meeting. He had such definite views that few
were willing to challenge or question him after he was done. The senior
management team, meanwhile, encouraged this diversification into new
sectors. The theory seemed to be that by spreading into many markets
with many products it would be possible to diversify risks. The reality
was that the more sectors they entered, the less they knew about any
one of them. This strategy empowered executives who did deals and
marginalized executives who had spent their lives in a specific market
and had concrete knowledge of how it worked.

The company spent more time managing its structure than improving its products. Hoping to find a single measure that could be used to
compare results across a wide variety of product lines, managers devised
pseudo-objective success criteria. These success metrics had only tan-
gential relationships to long-term growth. Managers spent more time
trying to figure out how they could game the metrics than in actually
producing sustainable results.

The finance and accounting departments, with the CEO's approval,
became enamored of arcane risk-management devices that seemed brilliant to the very few who claimed to understand them, but which mud-
died risk analysis in real life. Erica noticed that nobody colored in the
future in the PowerPoint charts. At every other company, past data was
shown on a white background and future projections were distinguished with a yellow background or a dotted line. These folks, the
team of assholes, were so confident of their predictive abilities they
didn't bother. They were embedded in a macho culture in which admit-
ting they didn't know something was not an option.

The odd thing was that as the company got more diverse the executives became more conformist. There were people in many different
sectors in offices spread throughout the world. You'd think this config-
uration would yield a range of viewpoints and expectations that would
balance each other out. But time and time again, instant communications and instant judgments based on those communications created a

herd mentality and an astonishing culture of intellectual homogeneity. Time and time again, people made the same one-way bets at the same time. Maybe this is what happens when a whole company (or a whole global economy) lives off its BlackBerries and makes decisions at the speed of electrons.

While all this was happening, the chairman and the CEO were making ever more lavish claims about the company's success. During the conference calls, the sales meetings, and the self-congratulatory corporate retreats, there would be one grandiose boast after another—that this was the greatest corporation in America, that this was the most innovative company in the world.

The most frustrating thing of all was that, in meeting after meeting, Erica had nothing to add. It's not that she didn't see huge problems in the company. There were big hairy monsters everywhere you looked. It's just that the mode of analysis was a closed language. Erica had her own way of looking at things and her own vocabulary, which emphasized culture, social life, and psychology. All of her new colleagues had a different way of seeing, based on amassing huge piles of data and then devising formulas and building systems. The two modes seemed non-overlapping.

Maybe it was in B-School, maybe it was somewhere else, but the team of assholes had been trained in certain methodologies. They had been trained to turn management into a science. They didn't really grow up steeped in the features of a specific product. They were trained to study organizations. Some did Dynamic Systems Theory, some did Six Sigma Analysis, or the Taguchi Method or Su-Field Analysis (structural-substance field analysis). There was TRIZ, a Russian-made model-based technology for producing creativity. There was Business Process Reengineering. Erica looked this one up on Wikipedia. According to one of the management books quoted on the site, BPR "escalates the efforts of JIT [Just In Time] and TQM [Total Quality Management] to make process orientation a strategic tool and a core competence of the organization. BPR concentrates on core business processes, and uses specific techniques within the JIT and TQM 'toolboxes' as enablers, while broadening the process vision."

Erica read sentences like that, or heard them at meetings, and she just had no clue how they applied to the problems at hand. The sounds just sort of bounced off her brain. The people who uttered them seemed to value precision and clarity. They sought to be scientific. But the jargon just seemed to float in the air.

The Rationalist Version

Of course these management whizzes did not come into being by accident. John Maynard Keynes famously wrote that "practical men, who believe themselves to be quite exempt from any intellectual influences, are usually the slaves of some defunct economist." The people Erica now worked with were the slaves of a long philosophic tradition. This tradition, rationalism, tells the story of human history as the story of the progress of the logical, conscious mind. It sees human history as a contest between reason, the highest human faculty, and passion and instinct, our animal natures. In the upbeat version of this story, reason gradually triumphs over emotion. Science gradually replaces myth. Logic wins out over passion.

This historical narrative usually begins in ancient Greece. Plato believed the soul was divided into three parts: reason, spirit, and appetite. Reason seeks truth and wants the best for the whole person. Spirit seeks recognition and glory. Appetite seeks base pleasures. For Plato, reason is like a charioteer who must master his two wild and ill-matched horses. "If the better elements of the mind which lead to order and philosophy prevail," Plato wrote, "then we can lead a life here in happiness and harmony, masters of ourselves."

In classical Greece and Rome, according to this narrative, the party of reason made great strides. But after the fall of Rome, the passions reasserted themselves. Europe fell into the Dark Ages. Education suffered, science lay dormant, superstition flourished. Things began to pick up again during the Renaissance with the developments in science and accounting. Then, during the seventeenth century, scientists and technologists created new forms of machinery and new ways to think about society. Great investigators began to dissect and understand their world. The metaphor, "the world is a machine," began to replace the metaphor, "the world is a living organism." Society was often seen as a clock with millions of moving pieces, and God was the Divine Clockmaker, the author of an exquisitely rational universe.

Great figures like Francis Bacon and René Descartes helped create a different way of thinking—the scientific method. Descartes aimed to begin human understanding anew. He would start from scratch and work logically and consciously through every proposition to see, step by step, what was true and certain. He would rebuild human understanding on a logical foundation. In this scientific age, the mind could not, Bacon urged, be "left to take its own course, but guided at every step." What was needed was a "sure plan" and a new reliable methodology.

In this new mode of thought, the philosopher and scientist must begin by purging his mind of prejudice, habit, and prior belief. He must establish a cool, dispassionate distance from the subject of his inquiry. Problems must be broken down into their discrete parts. He must proceed consciously and methodically, beginning with the simplest element of the problem and then proceeding step by step toward the complex. He must develop a scientific language that will avoid the vagueness and confusion of ordinary language. The aim of the whole method is to arrive at certain lawlike generalizations about human behavior—to arrive at certainty and truth.

The scientific method brought rigor to where there had once been guesswork and intuition. In the realm of physics, chemistry, biology, and the other natural sciences, the results were awesome to behold.

Inevitably, rationalist techniques were applied to the science of organizing society, so that progress in the social realm could be as impressive as progress in the scientific one. The philosophies of the French Enlightenment compiled a great encyclopedia, trying to organize all human knowledge in one reference book. As Dumarsais declared in the encyclopedia, "Reason is to the philosopher what grace is to the Christian. Grace moves the Christian to act, reason moves the philosopher."

As the centuries passed, social scientists tried to create a science of human nature. They worked to create models that would enable them to predict and mold human activity. Political scientists, international-relations professors, and others developed complex models. Management consultants conducted experiments to better understand the science of corporate leadership. Politics became organized around abstract ideologies, grand systems that connect everything into one logically consistent set of beliefs.

This rationalist mode of thought is omnipresent and seems natural and inevitable. The rationalist tradition proved seductive. It promised certainty, to relieve people of the anxiety caused by fuzziness and doubt. People's perceptions about human nature seem to be influenced by the dominant technology of their time. In the mechanical and then the industrial age, it was easy to see people as mechanisms and the science of human understanding as something akin to engineering or physics.

Rationalism gained enormous prestige during the nineteenth and twentieth centuries. But it does contain certain limitations and biases. This mode of thought is reductionist; it breaks problems into discrete parts and is blind to emergent systems. This mode, as Guy Claxton observes in his book *The Wayward Mind*, values explanation over observation. More time is spent solving the problem than taking in the scene. It is purposeful rather than playful. It values the sort of knowledge that can be put into words and numbers over the sort of knowledge that cannot. It seeks rules and principles that can be applied across contexts, and undervalues the importance of specific contexts.

Moreover, the rationalist method was founded upon a series of assumptions. It assumes that social scientists can look at society objectively from the outside, purged of passions and unconscious biases.

It assumes that reasoning can be fully or at least mostly under conscious control.

It assumes that reason is more powerful than and separable from emotion and appetite.

It assumes that perception is a clear lens, giving the viewer a straightforward and reliable view of the world.

It assumes that human action conforms to laws that are akin to the laws of physics, if we can only understand what they are. A company, a society, a nation, a universe—these are all great machines, operated through immutable patterns of cause and effect. Natural sciences are the model that the behavioral sciences should replicate.

Eventually, rationalism produced its own form of extremism. The scientific revolution led to scientism. Irving Kristol defined scientism as the "elephantiasis of reason." Scientism is taking the principles of rational inquiry, stretching them without limit, and excluding any factor that doesn't fit the formulas.

Over the past centuries, many great errors and disasters have flowed from the excessive faith in pure reason. At the end of the eighteenth century, revolutionaries in France brutalized the society in the name of beginning the world anew on rational grounds. Social Darwinists imagined they had discovered the immutable laws of human evolution, which could be used to ensure the survival of the fittest. Corporate leaders under the influence of Frederick Taylor tried to turn factory workers into hyper-efficient cogs. In the twentieth century, communists tried to socially reengineer whole nations, attempting to create, for example, a New Soviet Man. In the West, Le Corbusier and a generation of urban planners sought to turn cities into rational machines—factories for traffic—by clearing away existing neighborhoods and replacing them with multilane highways and symmetrical housing projects cut off from the older city. Technocrats from affluent nations tried to plant large-scale development schemes across the developing world without much concern for the local context. Financial analysts at the big banks and the central banks thought they had mastered economic cycles and created a "Great Moderation."

In short, the rationalism method has yielded many great discoveries, but when it is used to explain or organize the human world, it does have one core limitation. It highly values conscious cognition—what you might call Level 2 cognition—which it can see, quantify, formalize, and understand. But it is blind to the influence of unconscious—what you might call Level 1 cognition—which is cloudlike, nonlinear, hard to see, and impossible to formalize. Rationalists have a tendency to lop off or diminish all information that is not calculable according to their methodologies.

Lionel Trilling diagnosed the problem in *The Liberal Imagination* when he noted that so long as politics or commerce "moves toward organization, it tends to select the emotions and qualities that are most susceptible to organization. As it carries out its active and positive ends it unconsciously limits its view of the world to what it can deal with, and unconsciously tends to develop theories and principles, particularly in relation to the nature of the human mind, that justify its limitation." As a result, "it drifts toward a denial of the emotions and the imagination. And in the very interest of affirming its confidence in the power of the mind, it inclines to constrict and make mechanical its conception of the mind."

Rationalism looks at the conscious mind, and assumes that that is all there is. It cannot acknowledge the importance of unconscious processes, because once it dips its foot in that dark and bottomless current, all hope of regularity and predictability is gone. Rationalists gain prestige and authority because they have supposedly mastered the science of human behavior. Once the science goes, all their prestige goes with it.

This scientism has expressed itself most powerfully, over the last fifty years, in the field of economics. Economics did not start out as a purely rationalist enterprise. Adam Smith believed that human beings are driven by moral sentiments and their desire to seek and be worthy of the admiration of others. Thorstein Veblen, Joseph Schumpeter, and Friedrich Hayek expressed themselves through words not formulas. They stressed that economic activity was conducted amidst pervasive uncertainty. Actions are guided by imagination as well as reason. People can experience discontinuous paradigm shifts, suddenly seeing the same situation in radically different ways. John Maynard Keynes argued that economics is a moral science and reality could not be captured in universal laws calculable by mathematics. Economics, he wrote, "deals with introspection and with values... it deals with motives, expectations, psychological uncertainties. One had to be constantly on guard against treating the material as constant and homogenous."

But over the course of the twentieth century, the rationalist spirit came to dominate economics. Physicists and other hard scientists were achieving great things, and social scientists sought to match their rigor and prestige. The influential economist Irving Fisher wrote his doctoral dissertation under the supervision of a physicist, and later helped build a machine with levers and pumps to illustrate how an economy works. Paul Samuelson applied the mathematical principles of thermodynamics to economics. On the finance side, Emanuel Derman was a physicist who became a financier and played a central role in developing the models for derivatives.

While valuable tools for understanding economic behavior, mathematical models were also like lenses that filtered out certain aspects of human nature. They depended on the notion that people are basically regular and predictable. They assume, as George A. Akerlof and Robert Shiller have written, "that variations in individual feelings, impressions and passions do not matter in the aggregate and that economic events are driven by inscrutable technical factors or erratic government action."

Within a very short time economists were emphasizing monetary motivations to the exclusion of others. Homo Economicus was separated from Homo Sociologus, Homo Psychologicus, Homo Ethicus, and Homo Romanticus. You ended up with a stick figure view of human nature.

The Disaster

Taggert and his team didn't study intellectual history. Rationalism was just around them in the air they breathed, shaping their assumptions and methods in ways they did not appreciate. The rationalist mentality was in the economics courses they took in college, the strategy courses they took in business school, and the management books they read every day. It was the mentality that narrowed useful information down to the sort of thing that could be captured on PowerPoint slides.

As the recession deepened and lingered, Erica watched them make a series of disastrous moves that threatened to destroy the company. Forced to cut costs, they first cut every single practice that might have fostered personal bonds. For example, they took the company phone number off the Web site so it was nearly impossible for a customer with a problem to call and talk to a human being. They eliminated all the company gatherings that used to build camaraderie. They cut office space. Some people who had worked for decades to get a real office now found themselves in ego-destroying cubicles. The floor plan had looked so efficient when the management team had presented it.

Jim Collins argues that institutional decline is like a staged disease. Companies can look fine on the outside but already be sick within, and once they get sick, there is a certain progression they follow on the way to their doom. If that's true, then the cable company went through all of the phases all at once.

At first, the Intercom executives were thrilled by the economic slow-down. "In China, the word for 'crisis' also means 'opportunity'!" they would tell one another. They saw sliding revenues as a call to enact all their experiments. The launched off on a hyperactive process of reorganization and restructuring. They relieved division heads, and put in new people. They put out a new long-term strategy called Leapfrog Growth. They were going to grow the company at all costs, pour money into sectors that promised 10 percent growth, and get rid of divisions that were just crawling along. "We no longer have the luxury of doing what we've always done," Taggert would bark out at meetings. "We have to rip up the playbook. Think anew."

Soon, there were even more acquisitions. Taggert, bored with running a cable company, bought a television network. Now he could hang around with the stars. He could go to dinner parties and talk about the prime-time lineup. He didn't bother to think about whether a company providing a technical service could really mesh with a company providing artistic product.

There were other acquisitions—a biotech firm, an online appliance store. Erica watched her colleagues as they got swept up in the seduction of doing the deal. After each one, a triumphant memo would go around the executive suits. This deal allows us to "double our reach . . . transform our company. . . . In a single move we revolutionize the landscape. . . . This is an absolute gamechanger. . . . We now have a blockbuster product that will herald a new era. . . . Today we witness a new dawn and a new beginning." Each deal was supposed to be the silver bullet that pulled the company out of its slide, but weeks and months later, the slide was still there, only with more debt.

As everything new was being polished, everything old was being squeezed. Old suppliers were squeezed, contractors were cut back, old employees were told to do more with less. A lifeboat mentality began to pervade the company—month by month, the weak were thrown overboard, and the survivors gripped the gunnels more tightly. Morale suffered. Customer engagement plunged. When bad news came in, there was a search for those responsible, but somehow responsibility could never be assigned. Each decision had been made by a layering of committees. When everyone was responsible, no one was.

Erica watched the debacle with grim disgust. She had withstood the death of her own company, which was more or less unavoidable. Now she was going to be part of one of the worst management fiascos in the history of capitalism. Who was going to hire her after that?

Month after month, the numbers got worse and worse. One day she was at a meeting when a new set of revenue numbers were announced. "You must have that wrong," one of Taggert's butt boys responded. Erica heard a spontaneous groan from the back of the room. No one else seemed to notice, but when propriety allowed, Erica swiveled her head over to see who had made the noise. It was a jowly older guy, with white hair, wearing a white short-sleeve shirt, and a red and blue rep tie. She'd seen this guy at many of the bigger meetings, but she had never heard him say anything. She stared at him. He had his eyes down, staring at his meaty hands. Then he looked up and their eyes locked. He smirked, and she turned away.

After the meeting she followed him down the hallway, and eventually pulled up alongside him. "What did you think?" she ventured. He just looked at her suspiciously.

"Pathetic," she finally whispered.

"Fucking pathetic. Unbelievably fucking pathetic," he replied.

And so Project Valkyrie was born.

The guy's name was Raymond. He'd worked for the company for thirty-two years. They couldn't get rid of him because no one else knew the technology, but they put him in a job far away from decision making where he ended up cleaning up other people's messes. Through him, Erica learned there were others in the company just as disgusted as she was—a lot of them, actually. They set up a dissident underground. They had a samizdat network on their private e-mail accounts. At first they just bitched and moaned, and then they planned. Erica persuaded them this action was a matter of survival. If the company went down, they'd all be destroyed. If the company went down, then an institution they had spent their lives building would be gone. Surely they weren't going to just sit there and await their fates. Surely something could be done.

CHAPTER 15

MÉTIS

ERICA SPENT HER DAYS BEING APPALLED BY TAGGERT AND his minions. At night, sometimes late at night, she'd come home and vent to Harold. Harold couldn't really help her with concrete business advice. He'd drifted away from the corporate world over the years. But he did try to give her some help on how to think about her problems.

Harold was now deeply ensconced at the Historical Society. He'd begun writing catalogue copy for the exhibitions, but he'd been promoted and now was a curator and helped organize exhibitions. The Historical Society was a sleepy old institution, started in the nineteenth century, with countless artifacts in its storerooms. Harold would spend spare hours down in the basement, poking through old boxes and files. Sometimes he'd go into the vault, where the Society's most precious treasures were stored.

Foremost among these was a dress an actress had worn at Ford's Theatre the day Lincoln was shot. Just after the assassination, she had rushed up to the presidential box and had nestled Lincoln's head in her lap as people tried to treat his wound. The dress had a loud floral print, and Lincoln's bloodstains splattered all over it.

One day, early in his tenure, Harold had gone down to the basement alone, put on white gloves, and slowly pulled the dress from its box. He laid it gently across his lap. It is hard to describe the feelings of reverence that swept through him at that moment. The historian Johan

Huizinga came closest: "A feeling of immediate contact with the past is a sensation as deep as the purest enjoyment of art; it is an almost ecstatic sensation of no longer being myself, of overflowing into the world around me, of touching the essence of things, of through history experiencing the truth."

When he was lost in his artifacts, Harold felt he had reached through time and entered another age. The longer he worked at the Society, the more he immersed himself in the past. He'd organize an exhibition on a certain period—the Victorian age, the American Revolution, or some time long before—and he'd go on eBay and purchase little prints, newspapers and knickknacks from the period. He'd hold them in his hands and imagine the hands that had held them. He'd stare at them through a magnifying glass and try to cross the centuries.

Going into his office was like going into a lost age. Save for his laptop and his books, there was nothing at all made in Harold's lifetime— the furniture, the pens, the prints, the busts, and the carpets. Harold wouldn't have wanted to actually live in an age of warriors or an age of aristocrats, but he was stirred by old ideals—classical Greek honor, Medieval chivalry, the Victorian code of the gentleman.

After one exhibit, a publisher noticed Harold's catalogue copy and asked him to write a book about Samuel F. B. Morse. After that, Harold churned out mid-list history books and biographies at the rate of about one every two years. He never became a David McCullough. For some reason he never took on the really big figures—Napoleon, Lincoln, Washington, Franklin Roosevelt. But he focused on admirable, accomplished men and women, and in a quieter way gave his readers models of how to live.

At the time Erica was struggling with Taggert, Harold was working on a book about the British Enlightenment. He was doing a group portrait of David Hume, Adam Smith, Edmund Burke, and some of the thinkers, politicians, economists, and conversationalists who had dominated eighteenth-century British thought. One evening he told Erica about the difference between the French and British Enlightenments, because he thought it might be useful to her at work.

The French Enlightenment was led by thinkers like Descartes,

Rousseau, Voltaire, and Condorcet. These were philosophers who confronted a world of superstition and feudalism and sought to expose it to the clarifying light of reason. Inspired by the scientific revolution, they had great faith in the power of individual reason to detect error and logically arrive at universal truth. Taggert and his team were the dumbeddown children of the French Enlightenment.

But, Harold told her, there was a different Enlightenment going on at roughly the same time. Leaders of the British Enlightenment acknowledged the importance of reason. They were not irrationalists. But they believed that individual reason is limited and of secondary importance. "Reason is and ought only to be the slave of the passions, and can never pretend to any other office than to serve and obey them," David Hume wrote. "We are generally men of untaught feelings," Edmund Burke asserted. "We are afraid to put men to live and trade each on his own private stock of reason, because we suspect that this stock in each man is small."

Whereas the leaders of the French Enlightenment spoke the language of logic, science, and universal rules, the leaders of the British Enlightenment emphasized the power of the sentiments and the affections. In effect, members of the British Enlightenment based their view of human nature on the idea that behavior is largely shaped by the unconscious, Level 1 cognition. Early in his career, Edmund Burke wrote a book on aesthetics called *A Philosophical Inquiry into Our Ideas of the Sublime and Beautiful.* He had noticed that there is a great deal of commonality in what people find beautiful. Human beings are not blank slates to be filled in by education. They are born and raised with certain preferences, affections, and aversions. The "senses and imagination captivate the soul before understanding is ready either to join with them or to oppose them," he wrote.

Whereas the members of the French Enlightenment imagined a state of nature in which autonomous individuals formed social contracts for their mutual benefit, members of the British Enlightenment stressed that people are born with a social sense, which plays out beneath the level of awareness. People are born with a sense of "fellow feeling," a natural sympathy for other people's pain and pleasure. They are guided by a desire to be admired and to be worthy of admiration. Morality, these writers argued, flows from these semiconscious sentiments, not from logical deductions derived from abstract laws.

Whereas the children of the French Enlightenment tended to see society and its institutions as machines, to be taken apart and reengineered, children of the British Enlightenment tended to see them as organisms, infinitely complex networks of living relationships. In their view, it's often a mistake to dissect a problem into discrete parts because the truth is found in the nature of the connections between the things you are studying. Context is crucial. Abstract universals are to be distrusted. Historical precedents are more useful guides than universal principles.

The members of the British Enlightenment made a distinction between change and reform. Change is an engineering process that replaces the fundamental nature of an institution. Reform is a medicinal process that preserves the essence while repairing wounds and reviving the essence. Harold tried to explain how the methods of the British Enlightenment might help Erica understand Taggert's failings and think about alternative ways of proceeding.

The Next Question

And in truth, this debate between pure reason on one side and intuition and affection on the other is one of the oldest. Intellectual history has oscillated between rationalist and romantic periods, or as Alfred North Whitehead put it, between eras that are simpleminded and those that are muddleheaded. During simpleminded periods, rationalist thinkers reduced human behavior to austere mathematical models. During muddleheaded eras, intuitive leaders and artists guide the way. Sometimes imagination grows too luxuriant. Sometimes reason grows too austere.

The cognitive revolution of the past thirty years has provided a new burst of insight into these old questions. The new findings strongly indicate that the British Enlightenment view of human nature is more accurate than the French Enlightenment view. Thinkers from the French Enlightenment imagined that we are Rational Animals, distinguished from other animals by our power of logic. Marxists and others in the nineteenth and twentieth centuries imagined that we are Material Animals, shaped by the physical conditions of our lives. But the thinkers from the British Enlightenment were right to depict us as Social Animals.

But this raises new questions: Level 1 processes are important, but exactly how smart are they? How much should we trust them?

These were not issues in the old days when the passions and sentiments were thought to be brutish, unruly, and primitive—Dr. Jekyll's Mr. Hyde. But now we know they are more subtle and sophisticated than that. What we don't have is a consensus description of our unconscious strengths and weaknesses.

Some researchers argue that whatever its merits, the unconscious is still best seen as a primitive beast or an immature child. In their book *Nudge*, Richard Thaler and Cass Sunstein, then of the University of Chicago, say that the conscious Level 2 is like Mr. Spock—mature, reflective, and far-seeing. Unconscious Level 1, they say, is like Homer Simpson—an impulsive, immature goofball. When the alarm clock rings at five a.m., the mature Spock knows that it's in his best interest to get out of bed, but Homer just wants to throw the thing across the room.

And there's some truth to that goofball view of Level 1. The unconscious is subjective. It treats information like a fluid, not a solid. When information gets stored in the brain, it doesn't just get filed away. It seems to get moved about. The recall process of a seventy-year-old activates different and more scattered parts of the brain than the recall process of a twenty-six-year-old. Memory doesn't actually retrieve information. It reweaves it. Things that happen later can transform your memory of something that happened before. For these and many other reasons, your unconscious data-retrieval system is notoriously unreliable.

One day after the space shuttle *Challenger* exploded, Ulric Neisser asked a class of 106 students to write down exactly where they were when they heard the news. Two and a half years later, he asked them the same question. In that second interview, 25 percent of the students gave completely different accounts of where they were. Half had significant errors in their answers and less than 10 percent remembered with any real accuracy. Results such as these are part of the reason people make mistakes on the witness stand when they are asked months later to recall a crime. Between 1989 and 2007, 201 prisoners in the United States were exonerated on the basis of DNA evidence. Seventy-seven percent of those prisoners had been convicted on the basis of mistaken eyewitness accounts.

The unconscious is also extremely sensitive to context—current feelings influence all sorts of mental activities. Research by Taylor Schmitz of the University of Toronto suggests that when people are in a good mood, they have better peripheral vision. In another experiment a group of doctors was given a small bag of candy and another group was given nothing. Then they were all asked to look at a patient's history and make a diagnosis. The doctors who got the candy were quicker to detect the liver problem than those who didn't.

Happiness researchers go around asking people if their lives are happy. They've noticed that when they ask on sunny days, people are more likely to say their entire lives are happy, whereas if they ask on rainy days the wet weather changes their entire global perspective on the state of their existence. (Though if people are told to consciously reflect on the day's weather, the effect goes away.)

In one ingenious experiment researchers asked young men to walk across a rickety bridge in British Columbia. Then, while their hearts were still thumping from the frightening bridge, a young woman approached them to fill out a questionnaire. She gave them her phone number, under the pretext of doing further research. Sixty-five percent of the men from the bridge called her later and asked for a date. Only 30 percent of the men she approached while they were sitting on a bench called later. The bridge guys were so energized by the rickety bridge, they attributed their excitement to the woman who met them on the other side.

Then there is the problem of immediate rewards. The unconscious is impulsive. It wants to have good feelings now. After all, Level 1 evolved to protect us from immediate pain, the kind that might result from being jumped by a lion.

As a result, we may be aware of our long-term desire to lose weight, but we want the donut now. We may know the virtues of objective perspective, but we still love hearing a commentator affirm a position we already share. Fans at a baseball game become utterly convinced that their own player beat the tag at home plate, while the fans of the other team select their perceptions differently and arrive at the pleasing conclusion that he was out. "We hear and apprehend only what we already half know," Henry David Thoreau observed.

Then there is the problem of stereotypes. The unconscious mind finds patterns. It even finds them where none exist and makes all sorts of vague generalizations. For example most people believe shooters in a basketball game go through hot and cold streaks. They detect the pattern. But a mountain of research has found no evidence of hot and cold streakiness in the NBA. A shooter who has made two consecutive shots is as likely to miss his third attempt as his career shooting percentage would predict.

People are also quick to form stereotypes about one another. Research subjects were asked to guess the weight of a certain man. When they were told he was a truck driver, they guessed more. When told he was a dancer, they guessed less. Most people, no matter how well intentioned, no matter what their race, harbor unconscious racial prejudices. As part of Project Implicit, psychologists at the University of Virginia, the University of Washington, and Harvard have administered hundreds of thousands of tests in which they flash white or black faces and ask test takers to make implicit associations. This project's work indicated that 90 percent of the people showed unconscious bias. The prejudices against the elderly in similar studies were even more profound.

Finally, the unconscious mind is really bad at math. For example, consider this problem: Let's say you spent $1.10 on a pen and pad of paper. If you spent a dollar more for the pad than the pen, how much did the pen cost? Level 1 wants to tell you that the pen cost 10 cents, because in its dumb, blockheaded way, it wants to break the money into the $1 part and the 10-cent part, even though the real answer is that you spent 5 cents for the pen.

Because of this tendency, people are bad at calculating risks. Level 1 develops an inordinate fear of rare but spectacular threats, but ignores threats that are around every day. People fear planes, even though everybody knows car travel is more dangerous. They fear chain saws, even though nearly ten times more people are injured each year on playground equipment.

Overall, the unconscious mind has some serious shortcomings when it comes to making good decisions. So there is a reason Taggert and his deference committee went to college and B-School, a reason why they mastered methodical ways of analyzing data. But there is another side to this coin. There are things Level 1 sees that Level 2 just doesn't. There are reasons to think that the unconscious mind is quite smart indeed.

The Hidden Oracle

In the first place, conscious processes are nestled upon the unconscious ones. It is nonsensical to talk about rational thought without unconscious thought because Level 2 receives its input and its goals and its directional signals from Level 1. The two systems have to intertwine if a person is going to thrive. Furthermore, the unconscious is just more powerful than the conscious mind. Level 1 has vast, implicit memory systems it can draw upon, whereas Level 2 relies heavily upon the working memory system, the bits of information that are consciously in mind at any given moment. The unconscious consists of many different modules, each with its own function, whereas the conscious mind is just one module. Level 1 has much higher processing capacity. Measured at its highest potential, the conscious mind still has a processing capacity 200,000 times weaker than the unconscious.

Moreover, many of Level 1's defects are the flip side of its virtues. The unconscious is very sensitive to context. Well, sometimes it's really important to be sensitive to context. The unconscious treats information like a fluid, not a solid. Well, sometimes situations are ambiguous and it is useful to be flexible. The unconscious is quick to make generalizations and to project stereotypes. Well, daily life would be impossible if you didn't rely on generalizations and stereotypes. The unconscious can be fuzzy. Well, most of life is conducted amidst uncertainty, and it's useful to have mental processes that can handle uncertainty.

If you want to get a sense of the difficult tasks the unconscious performs day to day, start with some of the most basic. The unconscious monitors where your body parts are at any moment through a sixth sense called proprioception. The physician Jonathan Cole documented the case of Ian Waterman, who suffered nerve damage and lost parts of this unconscious sense. Through a process of painstaking work over many years, Waterman was able to use conscious thinking to monitor his body. He laboriously taught himself to walk again, to get dressed, and even to drive a car. The problem came when he was standing in the kitchen one night and there was a power outage. He could not see where his limbs were and hence could not control them. He collapsed to the floor into a tangle of body parts.

This unconscious ability to converse with the sensations of the body is not trivial. The body delivers messages that are an integral part of thinking, in all sorts of strange ways. If you read people an argument while you ask them to move their arms in a "pushing away" direction, they will be more hostile to the argument than if you read it to them while they are making a "pulling in" movement. A brain could not work if it was just sitting in a jar somewhere, cut off from motor functions.

The unconscious is also capable of performing incredibly complex tasks without any conscious assistance. It takes conscious attention to learn to drive, but once the task is mastered, the knowledge gets sent down to the unconscious, and it becomes possible to drive for miles and miles while listening to the radio and talking to a passenger and sipping coffee without consciously attending to the road. Without even thinking about it, most people treat strangers courteously, avoid needless confrontations, and feel pained by injustice.

The unconscious is responsible for peak performance. When a beginner learns a task, there is a vast sprawl of brain activity. When an expert does it unconsciously, there is just a little pulse. The expert is performing better by thinking less. When she's at the top of her game, the automatic centers of her brain are controlling her movements. The sportscasters would say she's "unconscious." If she were to think more about how to swing her golf club or sing her aria, she would do worse. She would, as Jonah Lehrer observes, be "choking on thought."

Then there is perception. As it absorbs data the unconscious simultaneously interprets, organizes, and creates a preliminary understanding. It puts every discrete piece of information in context. Blindsight is one of the most dramatic illustrations of unconscious perceptions. People who have suffered damage to the visual areas of the brain, usually as the result of strokes, cannot consciously see. But Beatrice de Gelder of Tilburg University asked a man with this damage to walk down a cluttered hallway. He deftly zigzagged down the hall, navigating around the obstacles to get to the other end. When scientists flash cards with shapes on them to other sufferers of this "blindness," they guess the shapes on the card with impressive accuracy. The unconscious proceeds when conscious sight is gone.

These perceptual skills can be astonishingly subtle. Many chicken farms employ professional chicken sexers. They look at newly hatched chicks and tell whether the chicks are male or female even though, to the untrained eye, the chicks all look the same. Experienced sexers can look at eight hundred to one thousand chicks an hour and determine their gender with 99 percent accuracy. How do they figure it out? They couldn't tell you. There is just something different about the males and females, and they know it when they see it.

In a test that has been conducted by many researchers, subjects are told to follow an X as it jumps from one quadrant of a computer screen to another. The movement of the X is governed by a complex formula in which the location of the next X appearance is governed by the previous sequence of appearances. Nonetheless, subjects can guess where the X will appear at a rate better than that of chance, and their guesses improve the longer they play the game. When researchers change the formula in the middle, the subject's performance deteriorates, though they have no idea why.

Studies of American soldiers in Iraq and Afghanistan, meanwhile, suggest that some soldiers are much better than others at scanning a scene and detecting tiny clues—an out-of-place rock, an odd-looking pile of garbage—where there might be a roadside bomb in the area. Sgt. First Class Edward Tierney does not understand how he knew that a certain car contained a bomb and decided to take the evasive action that saved his life. "My body suddenly got cooler; you know, that danger feeling," he told Benedict Carey of *The New York Times.*

In a landmark study, Antonio and Hanna Damasio and their colleagues asked their subjects to play a card game. They were given $2,000 and told to choose cards from four decks. If they picked good cards, they would win money. If they picked bad cards, they would lose. The decks were stacked. Two of the decks had slightly disproportionate numbers of very good cards and the other decks had disproportionate numbers of bad ones. By the fiftieth turn, many of the subjects declared that they "liked" certain decks better than others, though they could not tell you why. As soon as their tenth turn, some started sweating slightly as they reached for the risky deck.

The unconscious mind's next great achievement is the ability to construct implicit beliefs. The Swiss doctor Édouard Claparède conducted a small experiment with one of his patients, who suffered from amnesia. He had to introduce himself each time he came to see her. But during one visit he concealed a pin in his hand. When they shook hands, the pin pricked her hand. The next time he came to see her, she still did not recognize him. He had to introduce himself all over again. She was happy to "meet" him but when he held out his hand for their traditional handshake, she refused to shake it. Unconsciously she had learned to associate his hand with pain.

This sort of implicit learning pervades every aspect of life. For example, there is no computer powerful enough to catch a fly ball. It would have to calculate too many trajectories to get the glove to hit the exact spot where the ball would land. But even a ten-year-old eventually learns the implicit rule that enables you to catch a ball. If a fly ball is hit to you, you look at the ball at a certain angle. You run toward where the ball is hit while keeping the angle of your gaze constant. If the angle drops, then speed up. If the angle rises, slow down. That one implicit rule will guide you to where the ball will land.

This ability to accumulate implicit heuristics applies to things even more important than baseball. The unconscious seems to encode information in two ways. There is what scientists call "verbatim encoding," which seeks to encode exactly what happened during a certain event. There is also fuzzy-trace theory, which posits that the unconscious also tries to derive a gist, an imprecise rendering of an event that can be pulled out and applied the next time some vaguely similar event happens. If every time you went to a funeral you remembered the exact details of your behavior at all past funerals, you would get bogged down in useless details. But if you remember the gist of how to behave at a funeral—what to wear, how to walk, what tone of voice to adopt—then you will have a general idea of the socially acceptable form of behavior.

Implicit beliefs and stereotypes organize your world, and are absolutely essential to performing the normal activities of life. They tell you what sort of behavior you are likely to find when you attend a party, what sorts of people you are likely to see if you go to a *Star Trek* convention or a Bible study group or a rock concert. The unconscious understands the world by building generalizations.

By using these flexible tools, the unconscious is quite good at solving complex problems. The general rule is that conscious processes are better at solving problems with a few variables or choices, but unconscious processes are better at solving problems with many possibilities and variables. Conscious processes are better at solving problems when the factors are concretely defined. Unconscious processes are better when everything is ambiguous.

In one experiment Ap Dijksterhuis and Loran F. Nordgren of the University of Amsterdam and colleagues gave a group of subjects a complex string of forty-eight pieces of information about four different apartments. One of the apartments was made more convenient and attractive than the others (it was described in positive ways, while the others were described in mixed or negative ways). Then the subjects were split into three groups. One group was asked to choose the best apartment immediately. Another group was given a few minutes to think about it. A third group was told they would make a choice in a few minutes, but was then distracted during that entire period with another unrelated task.

Fifty-nine percent of the people in the distracted group chose the favored apartment, compared to 47 percent of those in the conscious
thinkers group and 36 percent of those in the one for immediate
choosers. While they were distracted, their Level 1 processes had been
churning away. Because they had relied upon Level 1 with its superior
processing capacity, they had made a holistic choice, factoring in the
full array of variables. The conscious thinkers tended to pick out just a
few characteristics, and couldn't process the whole. The immediate
choosers did worst, illustrating the important point that unconscious
thinking is not the same as snap-judgment thinking. Level 1 does better
when it has time to think, just as Level 2 does.

Timothy Wilson did an experiment, later replicated by Dijksterhuis,
in which he gave students a choice of five different art posters, and then
later surveyed to see if they still liked their choice. People who were
told to consciously scrutinize their choices were least happy with their
posters weeks later. People who looked at the poster briefly and then
chose later were happiest. Dijksterhuis and his colleagues then replicated the results in the real world with a study set in IKEA. Furniture
selection is one of the most cognitively demanding choices any consumer makes. The people who had made their IKEA selections after
less conscious scrutiny were happier than those who made their purchase after a lot of scrutiny. At a nearby store called De Bijenkorf, where
the products on sale tend to be simpler, people who relied on conscious
scrutiny were happier.

The unconscious is a natural explorer. Whereas conscious thought
tends to march step by step and converge on a few core facts or principles, unconscious thought tends to spread out through a process of associations, venturing into what Dijksterhuis calls the "dark and dusty
nooks and crannies of the mind." Level 1 therefore produces more creative links and unlikely parallels. Unconscious thought can take in many
more factors. It naturally weighs the importance of various factors as
they come into view. It restlessly scurries about—many parallel
processes at a time—as the conscious mind is busy with other things,
trying to match new situations with old models or trying to rearrange
the pieces of a problem until they create a harmonious whole. It chases

vibes and metaphors in search of connections, patterns, and similarities. It uses the whole panoply of psychological tools—emotions as well as physical sensations.

We tend to think of Level 1 as the early part of the brain, which we share with the animals, and Level 2 as the evolutionarily recent part of the brain that distinguishes us as human. But back in 1963, Ulric Neisser made the intriguing suggestion that it might be the sophistication of our unconscious processes that make us human:

> It is worth noting that, anatomically, the human cerebrum appears to be the sort of diffuse system in which multiple processes would be at home. In this respect it differs from the nervous system of lower animals. Our hypothesis leads us to the radical suggestion that the critical difference between the thinking of humans and of lower animals lies not in the existence of consciousness but in the capacity for complex processes outside of it.

Epistemological Modesty

Intuition and logic exist in partnership. The challenge is to organize this partnership, knowing when to rely on Level 1 and when to rely on Level 2, and how to organize the interchange between the two. The research doesn't yet provide clear answers about that, but it does point to an attitude—an attitude that acknowledges the weaknesses of the mind while prescribing strategies for action.

When Harold tried to use his research into the British Enlightenment to help Erica think about her problems, he emphasized a concept that was central to British Enlightenment thought: epistemological modesty. Epistemology is the study of how we know what we know. Epistemological modesty is the knowledge of how little we know and can know.

Epistemological modesty is an attitude toward life. This attitude is built on the awareness that we don't know ourselves. Most of what we

246 THE SOCIAL ANIMAL

think and believe is unavailable to conscious review. We are our own deepest mystery.

Not knowing ourselves, we also have trouble fully understanding others. In *Felix Holt*, George Eliot asked readers to imagine what a game of chess would be like if all the chessmen had their own passions and thoughts, if you were not only uncertain about your opponent's pieces but also about your own. You would have no chance if you had to rely upon mathematical stratagems in such a game, she wrote, and yet this imaginary game is far easier than the one we play in real life.

Not fully understanding others, we also cannot really get to the bottom of circumstances. No event can be understood in isolation from its place in the historical flow—the infinity of prior events, minute causes, and circumstances that touch it in visible and invisible ways.

And yet this humble attitude doesn't necessarily produce passivity. Epistemological modesty is a disposition for action. The people with this disposition believe that wisdom begins with an awareness of our own ignorance. We can design habits, arrangements, and procedures that partially compensate for the limits on our knowledge.

The modest disposition begins with the recognition that there is no one method for solving problems. It's important to rely on the quantitative and rational analysis. But that gives you part of the truth, not the whole.

For example, if you were asked what day in the spring you should plant corn, you could consult a scientist. You could calculate the weather patterns, consult the historical record, and find the optimal temperature range and date at each latitude and altitude. On the other hand, you could ask a farmer. Folk wisdom in North America decrees that corn should be planted when oak leaves are the size of a squirrel's ear. Whatever the weather in any particular year, this rule will guide the farmer to the right date.

This is a different sort of knowledge. It comes from integrating and synthesizing diverse dynamics. It is produced over time, by an intelligence that is associational—observing closely, imagining loosely, comparing like to unlike and like to like to find harmonies and rhythms in the unfolding of events.

The modest person uses both methods, and more besides. The modest person learns not to trust one paradigm. Most of what he knows accumulates through a long and arduous process of wandering.

The modest person is patient. His method is illustrated by the behavior of the little gobiid fish. This is a little fish that lives in shallow water. At low tide, its habitat is reduced to little pools and puddles. Yet the gobiid fish jump with great accuracy over rocks and dry ridges from pool to pool. How do they do it? They can't scope out the dry patches before they jump, or see where the next pool is. If you put a little gobiid fish in an unfamiliar habitat, it won't jump at all.

What happens is that during high tide the gobiid fish wander around absorbing the landscape and storing maps in their heads. Then when the tide is low, they have a mental map of the landscape, and they unconsciously know what ridges will be dry at low tide and what hollows will be full of water.

Human beings are good at accumulating this sort of wanderer's knowledge as well. For ninety thousand generations our race has been exploring landscapes, sensing dangers and opportunities. When you explore a new landscape or visit a new country, your attention is open to everything, like a baby's. One thing catches your eye. Then another.

This receptiveness can happen only when you are physically there. Not when you are reading about a place, but only when you are on the scene, immersed in it. If you don't actually visit a place, you don't really know it. If you just study the numbers, you don't know it. If you don't get used to the people, you don't know it. As the Japanese proverb puts it: Don't study something. Get used to it.

When you are out there on the scene, you are plunged into particulars. A thousand sensations wash over you. In ancient times a human wanderer would see a stream in a new landscape, and the sight would be coated with pleasure. He would see a dense forest or a craggy ravine, and a little marker of fear would lodge with the image in his brain.

The mind wants to make instant judgments about all the sensory details it receives, file new data away with some theory. People hate uncertainty and rush to judgment. Research by Colin Camerer has found that when people play card games in circumstances that don't allow them to calculate the odds of success, the fear-oriented centers of their brains light up. They try to end the fear by reaching a conclusion, any conclusion, about the pattern of the game, just to end the fear.

But the wanderer endures uncertainty. The wise wanderer holds off and restrains, possessing what John Keats called negative capability, the ability to be in "uncertainties, mysteries, doubts, without any irritable reaching after fact and reason."

The more complicated the landscape, the more the wanderer relies on patience. The more confusing the scene, the more tolerant his outlook becomes. He not only has an awareness of his own ignorance, but of his own weakness in the face of it. He knows that his mind will seize on the first bit of data it comes across and build a universal theory around it. This is the fallacy of anchoring. He knows that his mind will take his most recent experience and try to impose the lessons of that case onto this one. This is the fallacy of availability. He knows that he came onto this scene with certain stereotypes of how life works in his mind, and he will try to get what he sees here to conform to them. This is the fallacy of attribution.

He is on guard against his weaknesses. He pays attention to the sensations that come up from below. He makes tentative generalizations and analyses and focuses on sensations anew. He continues to wander and absorb, letting the information marinate deep inside. He is playing, picking up this and that. He sees a section of the landscape and slowly feels his way to another side. He meets people in this new landscape, and he reenacts pieces of their own behavior and thinking in his own mind. He begins to walk the way they walk, and laugh as they laugh. He sees the patterns of their daily existence, which they are no longer even aware of. His mind naturally oscillates between the outer texture of their lives—their jewelry, clothes and mementoes—and what he intuits of their inner hopes and goals.

Meanwhile, Level 1 is churning away, blending data, probing for similarities and rhythms in its own ceaseless way. It is working up a feel for this new landscape: How does the light fall? How do the people greet one another? What is the pace of life? It's not only the individuals the unconscious is trying to discern, but the patterns between them.

How closely do these people work together? What is the common un-spoken conception of authority and individuality? The point is not just to describe the fish in the river, but the nature of the water in which they swim.

At some point there is a moment of calm, and disparate observations integrate into a coherent whole. The wanderer can begin to predict how people will finish their sentences. He now possesses maps in his mind. The contours of his brainscape harmonize with the contours of reality in this new place. Sometimes this synchronicity will be achieved gradually. Sometimes there are bursts of inspiration, and the map comes into focus all at once. After these moments, the mind will rein-terpret every old piece of data in a radically new way. What seemed im-measurably complex will now seem beautifully simple.

Eventually—not soon, not until after many months or years of ardu-ous observation, with dry spells and frustrating longueurs—the wan-derer will achieve what the Greeks called *métis*. This is a state of wisdom that emerges from the conversation between Level 1 and Level 2.

Métis is very hard to put into words. A person with *métis* possesses a mental map of her particular reality. She possesses a collection of metaphors that arranges an activity or a situation. She has acquired a set of practical skills that enable her to anticipate change.

She understands the general properties of a situation but also the particulars. A mechanic may understand the general qualities of all cars, but is quick to get a feel for each particular car. A person with *métis* knows when to apply the standard operating procedure but also when to break the rules. A surgeon with *métis* has a feel or a knack for a cer-tain sort of procedure, and she senses what can be about to go wrong at what stage. In Asian cooking there are recipes that ask the chef to add ingredients when the oil is about to burn. A chef with *métis* knows the quality the oil takes on just before something else is about to happen.

During his discussion of Tolstoy in his famous essay "The Hedge-hog and the Fox," philosopher Isaiah Berlin comes close to describing a conception of *métis*. It is achieved, he writes, "not by a specific inquiry and discovery, but by an awareness, not necessarily explicit or con-scious, of certain characteristics of human life and experience."

We humans, he continues, live our lives in the midst of a specific flow of events, the medium in which we are. "We do not and cannot observe [this flow] as if from the outside; cannot identify, measure and seek to manipulate; cannot even be wholly aware of it, inasmuch as it enters too intimately into all our experience." It is "too closely interwoven with all that we are and do to be lifted out of the flow (it *is* the flow) and observed with scientific detachment, as an object. It—the medium in which we are—determines our most permanent categories, our standards of truth and falsehood, of reality and appearance, of the good and the bad, of the central and the peripheral, the subjective and the objective, of the beautiful and the ugly, of movement and rest, of past, present and future. . . .

"Nevertheless, though we cannot analyze the medium without some (impossible) vantage point outside it (for there is no 'outside'), yet some human beings are better aware—though they cannot describe it—of the texture and direction of these 'submerged' portions of their own and everyone else's lives; better aware of this than others, who either ignore the existence of the all-pervasive medium (the 'flow of life') and are rightly called superficial; or else try to apply to it instruments—scientific, metaphysical, etc.—adapted solely to objects above the surface, the relatively conscious, manipulable portion of our experience, and so achieve absurdities in their theories and humiliating failures in practice."

Wisdom, Berlin concludes, "is not scientific knowledge, but a special sensitiveness to the contours of the circumstances in which we happen to be placed; it is a capacity for living without falling foul of some permanent condition or factor which cannot either be altered or fully described and calculated; an ability to be guided by rules of thumb—the 'immemorial wisdom' said to reside in peasants and other 'simple folk'—where rules of science do not, in principle apply. This inexpressible sense of cosmic orientation is the 'sense of reality,' the 'knowledge' of how to live."

Harold actually read this passage from Berlin to Erica one night, even though the passage is abstract and she was tired, and he wasn't sure how much she really absorbed.

CHAPTER 16

THE INSURGENCY

RAYMOND AND ERICA STARTED EATING LUNCH TOGETHER AT the cafeteria at 11:45 (Raymond got up early but agreed to push back his normal lunch hour at least 45 minutes for Erica's sake). Soon, other like-minded people were lunching early so they could join them. Within a few weeks, there were twenty or thirty people having lunch together before noon in one corner of the cafeteria.

It was an odd mix of generations. There were a bunch of Erica's friends—people in their thirties—and there were a bunch of Raymond's old cronies, in their fifties and sixties. Most of the time they would just kibbitz about the latest Taggert stupidity. One day, the company announced a hiring freeze. "That'll never work," Raymond observed with a smile. "People will just hire temps and interns and keep them on. We used to have interns working with us who'd been here five or ten years. If you hire them as interns you can keep them on salary without having to send up another form, so the hiring freeze doesn't apply."

Raymond had been born on a ranch in northern Minnesota and had missed a lifetime of fashion trends. If they made a movie of his life, Gene Hackman would have been called in to play him.

He and Erica quickly formed a division of labor between them. Raymond would make observations about how Taggert and his team were screwing up, and she would plot revolution. Left to his own devices, Raymond would have been content to make sardonic comments about the passing scene, but Erica wanted to take action. Taggert was destroying everything others had built. She still had decades ahead of her and did not want to see her life blotted out both by her own business failure and the collapse of a major corporation she had been hired to help grow. And there was something else driving her. From girlhood, she knew what it was like to feel that, no matter what room she and her mom walked into, they would be deemed unworthy of whatever they found there. The thought of being condescended to by this team of overeducated nitwits produced a righteous anger that woke her up in the middle of the night.

Day after day, she would push Raymond: "We've got to do something! We can't just sit here talking." Finally he agreed, to a point.

Raymond was eating the tongue sandwich he brought every day, with a Dr. Brown's cream soda. He agreed they would put together a proposal, a different set of strategies the company might explore. But Raymond had a few stipulations: "First, no covert ops. We do everything aboveboard and out in the open. Second, no coup. We are not targeting personnel. We are offering suggestions about policy. Third, always helpful. We will never challenge anybody's ability. We will just try to provide them with constructive alternatives."

Erica thought he was making a distinction without a difference. It was inconceivable Taggert could turn into the sort of person who could adopt the sort of policies Raymond would come up with. Changing policy would mean changing personnel. But if Raymond had to have these stipulations so he could stay true to some ancient loyalty code, then that was fine with Erica.

They began putting together a group of proposals to save the company. They did it right there in the open, in the cafeteria, as members of what they came to call the Brunch Club, in honor of Raymond's early dining schedule.

They worked on their proposals for several weeks, and Erica was fascinated by how Raymond led the group. First, he seemed to spend most of his time talking about what he was not good at. "Sorry, I don't handle distraction very well," he would say as he turned off his cell phone before every discussion. The fact is, no human brain handles distraction very well, but Raymond was wise enough to know it. "Sorry, I'm not real good with generalizations," he interrupted one day. The fact is, most minds are more supple at handling visual images than abstract concepts, but Raymond was sensible enough to acknowledge it. "Could we lay out an agenda here?" he would say. "My mind is just wandering from subject to subject." The fact is, most people can hold a thought for only about ten seconds at a time, but Raymond was smart enough to see that he needed an external structure to keep himself on track. At the start of each lunch he'd write down a list of things to talk about, and he'd keep glancing down at the list.

Raymond's knowledge of his own shortcomings was encyclopedic. He knew he had trouble comparing more than two options at a time. If you gave him three, he got confused, so he would build brackets and move from one binary comparison to the next. He knew he liked hearing evidence that confirmed his own opinions, so he asked Erica and the others to give him the counterevidence first, and not bury it away. He knew he had a bias for the cautious course in any situation, so he would always force himself to summarize the case for the riskiest course before making the argument for the cautious one.

The Brunch Club's plan was to come up with eight or ten policy proposals that they could present to the board and the executive team. They worked on one proposal at a time. They'd sit around at lunch talking about it. Most of their time was not really spent coming up with new ideas. As Raymond explained to Erica one evening after a long day, most business meetings aren't about creating new plans, they are about maneuvering a group of managers so that they buy into a basic approach.

"Does this feel wrong to anyone?" Raymond asked once while they were talking about a new hiring procedure. The fact is, the mind is good at detecting its own errors. In the early 1990s Michael Falkenstein of the University of Dortmund in Germany noticed that when a test subject pressed the wrong key on a keyboard, the electrical potentials in his frontal lobe dropped by about ten microvolts. Patrick Rabbitt of the University of Manchester found that typing mistakes are made with slightly less pressure than correct strokes, as if the mind is trying to unconsciously hold back at the last second. In other words, through a complex of feedback mechanisms, the brain can recognize mistakes even as it is making them. This may be why it is generally a good idea to change your answers on a test if you have an inkling that the one you gave is wrong. A pile of research has found that people who go back and change doubtful answers improve their score. Raymond was asking people to be alert to these subtle warning signals that burble up inside them.

Sometimes Erica would get immensely frustrated with him. The group generally set themselves a timetable. Three days for each proposal. They'd be in the middle of the third day of discussion, hammering out one of the proposals, and suddenly Raymond would switch sides, and argue for an entirely different approach than the one they had just agreed upon. "You just made the exact opposite point," Erica would cry out in exasperation.

"I know. Part of me believes that. Part of me believes this. I just want all my schizo personalities to have a say," he would joke. In fact, researchers have found that people who engage in what they call "dialectical bootstrapping" often think better than people who don't. That means engaging in internal debates, pitting one impulse against another.

Finally, when every argument had been made, the Brunch Club would have a vote. When a proposal was approved, Raymond would invariably hold up the sheet of paper and announce with a big smile, "Well, this is a noble failure!"

The first time he said this, Erica didn't know what he meant, so Raymond explained: "The great business sage Peter Drucker said that about a third of the business decisions he observed turned out to have been right, another third turned out to be minimally effective, and another third were outright failures. In other words, there is at least a two-thirds chance that what we have done is wrong or largely wrong. We believe this is great, because we want to believe we are great. We want to preserve our own egos, so we're spinning ourselves. But the truth is life is about producing failure. We only progress through a series of regulated errors. Every move is a partial failure to be corrected by the next one. Think of it as walking. You shift your weight off balance with every step, and then you throw your other leg forward to compensate."

At night, Erica would come home and tell Harold about what Raymond had done that day. Harold had met him only a couple of times, at a barbecue and at a company party, but he thought Raymond reminded him of a guy he had once known who worked as a carpenter for a theater company downtown. The guy had always wanted to be in the theater, but he never really had any desire to be an actor. He'd tried it in high school, and being onstage just made him uncomfortable. So he'd become a stagehand. He enjoyed the esprit de corps of the theater troupe. He enjoyed contributing something to the whole production, and he enjoyed the knowledge that he often knew more about theater than the directors and the stars who were blinded by their own egos. Harold's theory was that Raymond was the kind of guy who just loved making things work. But Harold suspected that when the time came to make a move, he'd never actually want to challenge Taggert. He'd never actually want to get onstage and play a starring role in the drama of saving the company.

Erica wasn't so sure. Every day she saw how people gathered around him in the cafeteria. He was a weird mix of traits. He was extremely modest, but he could also be extremely willful. People assumed that humble people must also be pushovers, but sometimes there was a fierce stubbornness inside Raymond. He built his expertise upon an acute awareness of his own ignorance, but he was pretty self-confident.

The Meeting

The discussions around the Brunch Club were followed attentively by mid-level people around the company. Many employees looked at Raymond and Erica longingly, hoping these dissidents would save them from the downward slide. Taggert and his crew looked at them contemptuously when they considered them at all. They were just an unruly rabble of losers and flameouts.

Erica's main problem at this point was that she lacked an opening. The group had finished crafting their suggestions. They had composed a twenty-five-page memo encapsulating their collective wisdom. But there was no good way to present it. She could just send it up the decision chain, but it would get lost and buried. She could leak it to a trade journal, but that violated Raymond's "no covert ops" rule.

Fortunately, the Lord provided. One day, Jim Cramer, a CNBC talk-show host screamed out that Intercom was going down the toilet. He actually took one of their cable boxes, smashed it on the air and tried to flush it, piece by piece, down a toilet he had on the set.

These sorts of displays didn't always produce gigantic movements in the stock price. But this one touched a nerve. The next day, everybody was selling. The stock price, which had been as high as 73 a few years ago, dropped in one day from 23 to 14.

Taggert felt he had to get out in front of this storm, and concluded, naturally enough, that a public presentation of himself would be enough to restore confidence. He announced what he called an "Opportunity Summit." He invited the executive committee and members of the board and had it webcast so that Wall Street analysts could listen in. "We want to talk but also listen," Taggert said while announcing the meeting. "We want to present our plans, but also hear your concerns and ideas. This is a learning organization, and we will go forward together." This was all the invitation Erica needed. She told Raymond that he would stand up at this meeting and present their suggestions. Raymond, who was either scared or clever, said he would do it only if Erica stood up, too, and helped him.

The meeting took place in a theater downtown. Taggert and his team sat bathed in light onstage and everyone else sat in darkness down below. This was their idea of a listening campaign. "I want you to know that I am very excited about where this company is right now," Taggert began. "I've always had a very good sense of how growth happens, and I am confident that this company is on the verge of exponential growth. We have the best management team in the United States, the best workers, and the best product line! So I am bringing a lot of passion to my job every day.

"One of the things I set out to do when I took over is make this a top-tier growth company. I realized that the old methods would no longer work. We had to rip up the old rule book, pursue constant change and achieve game-changing breakthrough growth. That meant revolutionizing the value chain, and shaking up standard operating procedures. We no longer had the luxury of sitting back and learning from others.

"When we embarked on this daring course, we knew all along that from the outside it might be hard to understand the strategy. We knew there might be outside metrics that would be misleading to those who didn't understand the course we were undertaking. There might be well-intentioned critics who just couldn't see the long-term path from their vantage point. But we set up our own metrics, and I'm here to tell you today that we have met or surpassed every single metric we created. We are changing faster than we thought. We are innovating better. We have left no stone unturned. We have thrown everything we had at the problems facing this company. We have tried everything in an intense wave of activity. We are on the verge of explosive growth.

"I've always been good at reading what other people are thinking, and I know some of you are concerned. But I'm here to tell you that when this revolution is complete, you will see how careful the planning has been. Soon we will be taking another series of steps that will take us deeper into programming, deeper into growth markets and social networking. These acquisitions will revolutionize this company. We immediately double our contact with viewers and customers. We leapfrog over recent technology and put ourselves in a position to transform our industry. We will embark on a dramatic effort to restructure our company and reshape our identity."

He went on in this vein for a while, then a few members of his deference committee got up and presented some projections and growth numbers.

When the presentation was finished, nobody knew what to think. Everybody had heard these promises before. They had been taken to the mountaintop before. And yet good things had not come. And yet people wanted to believe. Taggert was charismatic. The members of his team were smart. The audience was not sold on the vision he had laid out, but it was not hostile either. It was uncertain.

Raymond stood up at one of the microphones in the aisles. "Excuse me, could we make some suggestions?"

"Of course, Ray," Taggert replied. Raymond never went by "Ray."

"Could I do it from up there?" Raymond pointed to the podium on stage.

"Of course."

Raymond gestured to Erica to join him onstage. Erica was seized by an awful wave of impostor syndrome, but walked up.

"As I think you know, Mr. Taggert, some of us old-timers and some of the young turks have been sitting around over the past few weeks trying to think of ways we might be helpful to your work. We don't have access to a lot of the information you have, so perhaps our ideas are unwise or unworkable. Probably, you've already considered each and every one of them.

"But one of the thoughts was that we wanted to get a clearer idea of what this company is about. It used to be a cable company. We laid cable. We put it in the ground and connected it to people's homes. We were a bunch of mechanical guys. We built new technologies and we made stuff work. That was our identity. It made us proud to work here and provided us with an unwritten code of conduct. I'm not sure that identity is so clear now. We seem to do a thousand different things, with a thousand different cultures. When I started here, the goal was to optimize our performance as cable providers, not maximize our growth, as measured on the revenue statement. I'm not sure that's the same either.

"I know I sound like an old duffer nostalgic for times gone by. But I started work here under John Koch. Many of you didn't know him, but I did, even though I was a junior guy at the time. He came out of the company instead of being appointed on top of it. The car he drove, the way he dressed and spoke—they were all similar to the cars we drove, the way we dressed and spoke. He made more than anybody else, sure, but he was part of the same pay scale the rest of us were on, not part of some CEO scale a galaxy removed from normal workers. You had the sense, talking with Koch, that he reacted to things the way you would react if you were in his job. He had a sense of the way the crews out in the streets worked and couldn't work.

"Koch was not one for grand plans. He just made constant adjustments. He always used the word 'stewardship' to describe his leadership style. He'd inherited something great and he was just taking care of it. He wanted to make sure he didn't screw it up. I remember he used to follow Peter Drucker's old advice. Every time he made a decision, he'd write himself a memo about what he expected to happen. Then nine months later he opened it up and read it to find out how wrong he'd been. He wanted to learn the most he could from each and every error."

Raymond went on in this reminiscent way for a few more minutes. Nothing he said was overtly critical toward Taggert and his team. He kept apologizing for being a backward-looking sentimentalist. He kept saying that of course you can't go home again, back to the old days, but the contrast between the spirit the company used to have and the denuded atmosphere that now prevailed—well, that was a difference too painful and searing to ignore.

Erica tried to continue the emotional atmosphere he had established. It was not her normal mode. Normally, she liked to be the spitfire in the tight white shirt. But Raymond had set a mellower tone.

She said that she and a bunch of her coworkers had been sitting around brainstorming, and she hoped that maybe a few of their ideas would be helpful to Taggert and his team. She started at the financial end. "One of the things we talked about a lot is the importance of cash," she said. "You pay your bills with cash. When you have cash in the bank you can withstand an unexpected jolt or two." But over the past few years, she observed, the company had drained its cash reserves. One sometimes got the impression that the current leaders thought cash was for cowards and that debt was a sign of daring. Over the past few years, the company had piled up debt to make one acquisition after another.

Then she talked about corporate structure. It was so complicated, it was hard to tell who was responsible for what. It was rare that somebody in the company could come in each morning and say, "I'm responsible for *x*" because in each case responsibility was spread around a multilayered decision chain. The Brunch Club, she said, had a few ideas for how to simplify that.

Then she talked about strategy. It's possible the company has been self-destructively hyperactive, she suggested. The people who make money at the horse track don't bet on every race. In fact, they seldom bet, and only when they think they have an insight that gives them an advantage. Warren Buffett used to say that most of the money he'd earned over his lifetime came from fewer than ten decisions. The lesson is that leaders can expect to have only a few good insights over the course of their careers, and they shouldn't be making moves when they don't have really good insights behind them.

Then she broke down the company's profit streams. She pointed out that the cable part of the business was still doing fine. It's just that there was all this other stuff piled on top of it. Maybe it was time to go back to the wonderful business still lying there at the core of the enterprise.

It might be a good idea to cut down on the teleconferences and work harder to get people face-to-face. Most communication is physical— through gestures not words. It's hard to understand others or share ideas and plans across a video screen. It might be a good idea, she added, to get more people working in what she called multiparadigm teams. Get different groups of people looking at the same problem from different perspectives. In the first place, human beings evolved to work in small bands. And in fact there's a great deal of evidence to suggest that much of the time groups think better than individuals. In one study 75 percent of groups successfully solved a complicated card game called the Wason selection task, compared to only 9 percent of individuals. In the second place, when you get people to look at the same problem they use different analytic modes. If you just rely on one model, you tend to amputate reality to make it fit your model.

"People in this company don't know each other," she added. She mentioned that when she'd first joined the company she'd gone to lunch with one of her fellow employees. She'd asked him if he knew a couple of the other people she knew at the company. He replied, "No, but I've only been here ten years. I don't know that many people yet."

Human beings do not leave their social selves at home when they come to work each day, she said. "It's going to seem stupid and cheesy, but a lot of people around here would like to have Fun Fridays with special activities. We could turn the cafeteria into a beach for beach-party bingo. We could have softball games and a volleyball court. They're the sorts of places where friendships are formed."

Erica went on in this way. She talked about company memos (executives should always mention why they want something done, not just what they want done). She talked about new hiring procedures the company could adopt (maybe people low on the totem pole could be involved in the interview process, too). She talked about mentoring programs, since the most important skills in any job are implicit ones, which cannot be taught but only imparted by sharing and modeling. She suggested that managers could be given slush funds for on-the-spot bonuses, so people could see the immediate results of a job well done. She described some ideas for rebranding the company. Over the past few years, the company had cast itself as a multinational conglomerate, like GE or Citigroup. But there'd been a decline in customer engagement. Maybe the company should again be the determinedly uncool company it had once been. The company used to give out fridge magnets. Now it sponsored golf tournaments. Something had changed.

Raymond and Erica didn't speak long—about fifteen minutes altogether. Then they handed Taggert the memo they had written, and sat down. Others spoke, too. Some were angry and critical. Some were sycophantic. The meeting didn't really even accomplish anything. The stock analysts listened only to Taggert's presentation, not anything that came after. They sent the price down a notch that afternoon. As for the employees and the board members, they didn't immediately embrace what Raymond and Erica had said. They didn't rush the stage and anoint them king and queen and ride Taggert out on a rail. But they did nod with approval. They did internalize the message that the company had once been something noble and it had squandered that core idea. And, as the months went by and the stock continued to go down and the debt continued to accumulate and the new acquisitions failed to deliver the company from decline, the atmosphere slowly changed.

The mass of employees and shareholders had once thought Taggert was a corporate star who had come in from the outside to turn everything around. Then they thought he was a well-meaning person who was having some trouble adapting to a new industry. But then, as time went on, key shareholders and members of the board concluded he was a self-admiring braggart who was more concerned with his own image than the company he was supposed to serve. As this conclusion hardened, another one formed alongside it—that this time the company should hire a leader from within, somebody who understood it in his bones and could bring back the excellence it had once possessed. What was needed was a restoration, not a revolution.

And so of course they turned to Raymond, who, when it came time to play the starring role, did not back down. He took the job, while never really expecting it. And more or less he succeeded. He was not the sort of CEO who makes the cover of *Forbes*. But he restored trust and faith. He shed the other divisions that didn't serve the core missions. He promoted a few of the mechanical guys—and it was no disgrace to be the sort of person who wears white short sleeve shirts and glasses a decade out of fashion. The company stabilized.

After a few years, Raymond retired. The board hired an outside CEO. He did fine and lasted six years in the job. After his tenure, the board decided to hire from inside the company, and after a somewhat Machiavellian process, decided to promote Erica. She was forty-seven when she took over. She had been at Raymond's side, as Raymond had been at Koch's side years before. She didn't revolutionize the company or make any daring breakthroughs. But it grew and adapted to new challenges during her years at the top. She loved the company and made it new in ways that were deeply consistent with the old.

CHAPTER 17

GETTING OLDER

OVER THE COURSE OF THEIR RELATIONSHIPS, MOST MAR-ried couples are compelled to navigate a transition between passionate love and companionate love. Passionate love is the kind that grips a couple in the first heady phase of their affair. Companionate love is the calmer state that comes after, filled more with quiet satisfaction, friendship, and a gentler happiness.

Some couples don't make the transition. UN data drawn from fifty-eight different societies between 1947 and 1989 suggests that divorce rates peak around the fourth year of marriage. But Harold and Erica seemed to do fine during those years. Erica succeeded Raymond as CEO of Intercom around their twelfth year of marriage, while Harold was living in centuries past, writing his books. For the next ten years they spent more time absorbed in their jobs than really being married to each other. They each spent a lot of time at work, they each had their philanthropic causes, and most other parts of their lives faded away, including their ability to communicate with each other.

After they had both established themselves, and could relax a bit, they found they no longer had as much in common as they had supposed. It wasn't that they fought. They just drifted into different interests and different spheres.

After years of ascent and struggle, they had grown weary of surrendering themselves to others. In her book *The Female Brain*, Louann

Brizendine writes that often a middle-aged woman "becomes less worried about pleasing others and now wants to please herself. . . . With her estrogen down, her oxytocin is down, too. She's less interested in the nuances of emotion; she's less concerned about keeping the peace; and she's getting less of a dopamine rush from the things she did before, even talking with her friends. She's not getting the calming oxytocin reward of tending and caring for her little children, so she's less inclined to be as attentive to others' personal needs." Men, needless to say, don't suddenly become more nurturing and communicative either when they and their wives hit fifty.

Erica had become a minor star in the business world. Intercom had rebounded and was registering steady gains. She traveled from conference to conference, gave her presentations to admiring audiences, and it was always something of a comedown to return home and find Harold dressed in shorts and a T-shirt, pecking away at his computer. Their lives had taken different shapes. Erica loved to be on the go, her days stuffed with meetings, lunches, and commitments. Harold liked to be alone, exploring an earlier historical age, with nothing on his calendar. Erica was absorbed with the challenges of leadership. Harold was more and more lost in his world of books, characters, and documents.

To Erica, his endearing traits now began to seem more like signs of deep character flaws. Wasn't his tendency to leave his socks in the hallway a sign of deep selfishness and narcissism? Wasn't his tendency to go unshaven a sign of deep laziness? Harold, for his part, was sometimes appalled by Erica's compulsive need to flatter anybody who might be able to help her company grow. When she dragged him out to receptions and parties, she'd invariably leave him within minutes. He'd be stuck in some pointless conversation, and when he looked around the room, she'd be yards away laughing with some CEO she probably privately detested. He was sometimes offended by the compromises she made to get ahead. She was sometimes offended by his essential passivity, which he coated with self-approving smugness.

William James once observed that "the art of being wise is the art of knowing what to overlook." In years past, they might have overlooked each other's flaws, but now Erica and Harold made silent and contemptuous notations.

As the years went by, they fell out of the habit of really talking, or even looking each other in the eye. In the evening, she'd be on the phone in one part of the house, and he'd be behind his laptop in another. Just as sharing everything had been a habit when they were first married, now not sharing had become a habit. Sometimes Erica would have some thought she wanted to express to him, but their relationship now had an unwritten constitution. It would now be inappropriate to rush into his office with some enthusiastic notion or curious fact.

Harold didn't even seem to listen when she spoke to him. About once a week, Erica would remind him of some party or task she'd committed them to. "You never told me about that," he would respond crossly.

"Yes, I did. We talked about it. You just don't listen to what I say," she'd answer.

"You must have imagined it. We never talked about this." They both acted as if they were sure they were right, but deep down they both wondered if they were losing their minds.

Marriage expert John Gottman argues that in a healthy relationship the partners make five positive comments to each other for every one negative one. Harold and Erica weren't near that bar. They weren't even in the game, since they didn't make many comments to each other, positive or negative. Both of them sort of wanted to return to the old days, when they were spontaneous and loving around each other, but they were afraid they would be rebuffed if they tried. So they just withdrew another step from each other. As their relationship withered, they both blamed it on the other person's character flaws. They both dreamed that they would someday go to a marriage counselor, and the counselor would utterly vindicate their view that the other partner was entirely to blame.

At work and at dinner parties, they were still cheerful, and they figured nobody could tell what was happening at home. But that wasn't true. Harold would tell a story and when he was done, Erica would blurt out "That's not what really happened," and everybody else could feel the harshness in her voice.

They both became profoundly sad. Erica would cry while blow-drying her hair. She wondered to herself if it would be worth trading all her career success in exchange for happiness at home. Harold would sometimes see couples his own age out for a walk, holding hands. That was unimaginable for him now. For Harold, as for Erica, the profoundest source of satisfaction was work, and it wasn't enough. Harold wasn't going to commit suicide, but if someone told him he had a fatal disease, he felt he could face the prospect with equanimity.

Loneliness

Harold and Erica's relationship was completely illogical. They both wanted to repair their marriage, and yet they were caught in a series of negative loops. There was the loneliness loop. People who feel lonely tend to be more critical of those around them, and so they judge others harshly, and thus become more lonely. Then there was the sadness loop. Both felt emotionally fragile and both sensed the other was no fun to be around, so both retreated further out of some emotional-survival instinct. Then there was the fatalism loop. People who think there is nothing to be done grow even more passive and more depressed.

Harold gained weight in this period, especially around the middle, where stress-related weight gain tends to appear. He drank too much. As was his wont, he turned his sadness into a philosophical problem. He lost himself in the Stoic philosophers. He concluded that people weren't put on this earth to be happy. Life is about suffering, he told himself, and except for his marriage, his life had turned out reasonably well. He tried to make himself impervious to what was going on at home, immune to his own feelings.

Erica saw her limping marriage through the prism of her worldly success. Maybe Harold was envious of her achievements. Maybe he felt humiliated and wanted to take it out on her. When they were first married, he was the more sophisticated of the two, but now she possessed more savoir faire. She was the one who got most of the attention. She was the shining star. It had been a mistake to marry someone so lacking in ambition, and now she was paying for her youthful indiscretion. She unconsciously aimed to free herself from this problem area in her life. She spent less time at home, and when she was there she grew more disengaged, so as not to feel hurt.

The stereotype is that men initiate most of the middle-aged divorces. They find trophy wives and run off. In fact, more than 65 percent of the divorces that strike couples after age fifty are initiated by women. Many simply find they no longer need their spouses—the chores, the duties, the taking care of them, when they get nothing in the way of affection and companionship in return. And so Erica, in her forward-looking strategic way, began to think about the future, about divorce and its consequences for her and for Harold. Could a separation be managed without too much blood on the floor?

Doldrums

One day, after a dustup over some minor thing, Erica told Harold that she'd been looking at apartments. Maybe it was time to divorce. She spoke to him analytically. They'd been heading for divorce for some time now, she observed. It had been a decade since the possibility of divorce first crossed her mind. She wished they'd never been married. There was no evidence to suggest they would ever turn this around.

As the words tumbled out of her mouth, she felt like she was taking a step off a cliff. Surely there'd be no going back now. Her mind was racing ahead: how to explain the divorce to her cousins and her coworkers. How to begin dating again. What would the official story be?

Harold wasn't shocked or surprised, but he didn't take the next logical step. He didn't start talking about what they should do. He didn't talk about getting divorce lawyers, or offer any ideas about how they would divide their property. He just absorbed her words, started talking about arrangements for a roofer they had engaged, and then went off to the kitchen for some scotch.

In the days and weeks to follow, it was as if nothing had been said. They fell back into their separate orbits. But Harold did feel the tectonic plates shifting inside him. A person's perspective can change on the inside even as life goes on without.

One day a few weeks after Erica's outburst, Harold was having lunch alone at a deep dish–pizza restaurant. He looked out the window across the street to a schoolyard. There were hundreds of elementary school-kids out on a blacktop for recess. They were scrambling, sprinting, climbing, wrestling, and kibitzing. It was amazing: You could just un-leash kids on a flat, empty space, and they would turn it into a carnival of joyful mayhem.

When they had married, Harold had assumed that of course he and Erica would have children. All families he knew did. But Erica was so busy in the first several years. The time was never right. Once, about five years into their marriage, he mentioned his desire to have kids, just in a normal, conversational way. "No, not now!" she screamed at him. "Don't you ever burst in on me with that!"

He was startled and stunned. She stormed off to her office.

Those words were the only ones they had ever exchanged on the subject. It was one of the most important subjects of their lives. It had been their most important disagreement, a cancer at the center of their relationship. And they never spoke about it again.

Harold had thought about kids every day, but he'd been afraid to raise the matter again. He shrunk from conflict with Erica, knowing he had no chance in any test of will with her. Somehow he'd thought by his very passivity he could bring her around. Surely she would see he wanted children and feel sympathy for him and do the thing that would make them both happy.

She had been aware of his passive-aggressive side, and it repelled her. He'd fumed privately about her gall in making the decision about kids without him. This had been one of the most important choices of their lives, and she hadn't even thought to consult him.

He often rehearsed their one brief exchange on the subject. He wondered what had sparked Erica's furious reaction. Maybe her own childhood had left some scar. Maybe she'd vowed never to bring chil-dren into the world. Maybe it was her devotion to work, or some lack of maternal instinct. Sometimes he wanted to force her to have kids, but you can't bring a child into the world on the basis of compulsion.

He still gazed at children, though. In these midlife doldrums, he watched little babies on airplanes, surreptitiously inspecting their little hands and feet. He noticed toddlers out with their grandfathers—the old guys ineptly trying to feed them and wheel them around. He watched packs of kids on the sidewalks, joking with one another, so joyfully self-absorbed they didn't even notice the heat or the cold or the bruises on their knees. In his angry moods, he saw his wife's barrenness as a sign of her ruthlessness, her inability to give, her selfish and shallow commitment to job and career. At these moments he despised her.

Squandered

For a few years, Harold was mildly depressed. He continued writing his books and organizing his exhibitions, but praise for his work began to strangely depress him. Public admiration put his secret loneliness into sharper relief.

His marriage was dormant. He had no kids. He wasn't active in some political or philanthropic cause. He had nothing to sacrifice for, nothing he could subjugate his own interests for. And of course Erica was always nearby, serving as his foil. He became contemptuous of her monomania and drive, and also sad that he seemed to lack that sort of energy and desire.

He'd always had a drink before bedtime. But in this period he began drinking earlier in the day. Scotch became his caffeine. His brain felt tired and inert much of the time. But if he had a tumbler of scotch, there'd be this moment of awakening, when ideas would surge and everything became sharp again. Then, of course everything would get blurry and he'd fall into one of those melodramatic moods, which were better than feeling nothing at all.

Most days, Harold downed a third of a bottle of scotch. He'd wake up in the morning vowing to change his life. But addiction weakens the learning mechanism in the brain. Alcoholics and other addicts understand what they are doing to themselves, but don't seem to be able to internalize the knowledge into a permanent life lesson. Some researchers believe they suffer from this disability because they have damaged the neural plasticity in their prefrontal cortex. They can no longer learn from mistakes.

One day, a day like many others, Harold had an insight. It was very much like the insight Erica had had the day she tried to get into the Academy years before. Harold realized that he could not change his drinking patterns on his own, but he could put himself in a context that might trigger changes. He decided to go to an AA meeting.

This was difficult for a loner like him. But one day he showed up at a kids' hockey rink, and in a side room, there was an AA group having their nightly meeting. He walked in and found himself in circumstances that went against every impulse in his body.

Harold had spent most of his life with the affluent and well educated, and here he was thrust in a room with clerks, salesmen, and bus drivers (a surprising number of bus drivers, actually). Harold had grown accustomed to living in his own world, but here, he was forced into deep fellowship with others. Harold had been raised in a culture of self-esteem and empowerment, but here, he was forced to surrender everything, to admit weakness and disempowerment. Harold had spent the last years not learning from his mistakes, but the 12-step methods threw his mistakes back at him. He had to wallow in them, time and time again. Harold had grown quite secular over the years, but a vague religiosity pervaded this group. The people there didn't just tell him to stop drinking. It wasn't a discrete and logical attempt to solve this one problem. They called on him to purify his soul, to rewire the deepest recesses of his heart and being. If he changed his whole life, abstinence from alcohol would be a happy byproduct.

Harold read the 12 steps. He kept the coins. But it was really the people in that group that saved him. Alcoholics Anonymous doesn't work for most people. Researchers have not been able to predict who will benefit from AA and who will not. They can't even agree on whether the program works better than the other programs that are out there, or at all.

That's because the fellowship of each group cannot be reduced to a formula, compared across groups, or captured in a social science experiment, and the quality of fellowship is what really matters. Harold's group had three people at its spiritual core. There was an enormously overweight lady who loved opera. There was a motorcycle mechanic. There was a banker. They'd been together for nearly a decade and set the tone. They accepted no bullshit. One teenager in the group had died when he covered his body with antidepressant patches. They helped everybody through the trauma. There were always a few people feuding with one another. The leaders enforced behavior guidelines. Harold came to admire them immensely, and model his behavior on theirs.

Harold went almost every day for a few months and then sporadically thereafter. It would be an exaggeration to say the group changed his life. It would be accurate to say that he found it very rewarding. Some of the people there were narcissistic. Many were incredibly immature. Many had seriously screwed up their lives. But the sessions forced him to talk about himself. He had to become more conscious of the gnawing needs inside him. He found himself looking up to people less sophisticated and less educated than he was. He awakened some emotional faculties that had lain dormant since high school. He became more aware of the shifting tides in his own psyche.

He didn't quit drinking, but now he never drank until after eleven p.m. What really changed was his shrivel instinct. Somehow over the course of his life he had become hypersensitive to emotional turmoil. He would recoil at the first sign of emotional pain. He avoided situations that might cause him inner suffering. He fled from confrontations that might arouse anger, hurt, and unpleasantness. Now he was a little less afraid. He could look at these hidden phantoms squarely. He didn't have to live in fear of sadness and hurt. He knew he could face it and survive.

Camp

His commitment to Incarnation Camp came about accidentally. A friend was going up to Connecticut to visit his daughter, a counselor there, and asked Harold if he'd like to come along for the ride. They pulled off a road in rural Connecticut and went over a long dirt driveway past tents and fields and ponds. Along the driveway, they came across a group of nine-year-old girls holding hands. Harold looked at them with soft fascination, the way he often looked at children these days. His friend parked near a cabin and he and Harold walked down the hill to a beach by a mile-long lake, surrounded by wooded hills. There was not a house or a road in sight. The camp was its own world, eight hundred acres of wilderness.

The camp served the rich and poor. Some of the kids were from Manhattan prep schools, and others were there on scholarship from Brooklyn and the Bronx. As time went by, Harold would come to see the camp as the only truly integrated institution he had ever known.

The first thing he noticed was that the physical equipment seemed worn and old. General-purpose camps like this faced grave challenges during the age of specialization, when most parents preferred resume-notching specialty setups—computer camp, music camp, baseball camp.

The zeitgeist seemed countercultural, too. There was almost a hippie spirit about the place. During that first day Harold saw counselors and children singing the old folk songs from the sixties—"Puff the Magic Dragon" and "One Tin Soldier." Harold also saw some amazingly good basketball games. Mostly he saw physical contact. The campers and the staff frolicked like bonobos. They lounged all over one another. They braided one another's hair and wrestled in playful piles. They played Marco Polo in the lake.

He met the camp director, who saw the gleam in Harold's eye and asked him if he'd ever have time to volunteer at the place. Twice more that summer, Harold visited the camp and helped do a few odd jobs, like supervising some teenagers during a square dance. Over the winter, he raised money for a swimming dock. The next summer, he visited on the weekends and helped repair the walking trails. One day, he saw a softball game. The kids were great at basketball, but absolutely terrible at softball. Some of them had never been taught to throw. Harold organized a softball program and even put together an instructional league for it.

In early August, the director asked if he could spare five days to help lead a canoe trip down the Connecticut River. There were fifteen teenagers; two counselors, who were college kids; and Harold. He was three decades older than anybody else on the trip, but he fit right in.

As they were paddling down the river, he'd organize trivia contests. He taught them songs, and learned about Katy Perry and Lady Gaga. At nights, they came to call him Daddyo, and in the earnest, heavy-but-open manner of teenagers, they told him about their problems—about their love lives, their parents' divorces, their confusion about what was expected from them. Harold was so touched that they trusted him. He listened with rapt attention. The kids seemed desperate for authority figures. He supposed the teachers and other professionals knew what to say when the kids told them about their problems and fears. He sure didn't.

The last full day of the canoe trip was arduous. They paddled all day, against a strong wind. Harold told the kids that, when they made it to their destination, they could take all the remaining supplies and have a food fight. When they made it to the final campground, the kids seized the supplies, and within minutes they began splattering them on one another. Great blobs of peanut butter were flying through the air. Everybody had jelly smeared across their shirts. Cake mix was gooped up into thick batter and rolled into sloppy warm snowballs. The kids, the counselors, and Harold hid behind trees, organized meatloaf ambushes, and warded off snow showers of powdered orange juice.

When the battle was over, they were all a mess, coated from head to shoes with gunk. They held hands and ran in a big line into the river to wash off. Then they came out, changed, and had their final campfire. Harold had brought no booze on the trip, and retired late that night to his tent sober and happy. He lay in his sleeping bag, feeling exhausted and lucky. It's interesting how fast a mood can change. In an instant something turned in him. Suddenly, he felt like weeping.

He had never cried in his entire adult life, except occasionally in the dark at the end of a sad movie. And he didn't actually cry this time. He felt tremors in his gut. He felt a pressure at the back of his eyes. But nothing actually came out. Instead, he had this weird sensation of imagining himself crying: He was floating above and got a glimpse of himself in a crouch heaving with sobs in his sleeping bag.

And then it passed. He thought about the life he had constructed and the life he would have constructed, if he had been a little more open and possessed a little more emotional courage. Eventually, he fell asleep.

CHAPTER 18

MORALITY

ERICA HAD NEVER SEEN A HOTEL CORRIDOR LINED WITH sleeve talkers before. She got to the top floor of the Parabola overlooking Central Park in New York, and as she left the elevator she saw bodyguards astride doorways up and down the hall, looking apathetically at one another and occasionally talking into their sleeves for scheduling updates. Inside the suites there were Saudi princes, Russian oligarchs, African despots, and Chinese billionaires, and each had a retinue of jar-headed muscle types waiting outside the room for prestige and protection.

A hotel concierge led Erica from the elevator to her own head-of-state suite, oddly called the India Suite. In the manner of a eunuch crouching before divinity, he ushered her into a complex of rooms four or five times the size of her childhood apartments. It was like Ralph Lauren's own personal heaven—a vast Anglophilic expanse with walnut paneling, various fireplaces with great stone hearths, English club chairs sprayed around alcoves, a large marble chess table in the corner, his-and-her showers in the bathroom suite in case you got the urge to shampoo in one and condition in the other. She wandered around the complex in a sort of wide-eyed disbelief, wondering things like "What? No trout stream?"

The concierge was on the wrong side of the service Laffer curve. At certain top-end facilities, the waiters and concierge types are at such a heightened state of attending to your every need that the more they do for you, the less convenient your life becomes. They refill your coffee cup after every sip so you have to remix sugar and cream just to keep it even. They brush down your jacket just as you're trying to put on your coat. In this case, the concierge insisted on trying to unpack Erica's suitcase and get her wireless service for her computer. Erica practically had to Taser the guy to get him to go away.

This was all the doing of her host, the man she called Mr. Make-Believe. She'd followed this guy's career for years on the covers of business magazines, and when they'd met at a charity event he'd asked her to join his board of directors.

Mr. Make-Believe took a special interest in Erica, summoning her frequently, consulting with her earnestly, and even putting her on his Christmas-box list. Every year he sent a giant box of goodies to his closest friends, including things like laptops, pretentious biographies, Moroccan duvet covers, antique Venetian prints, and whatever other lavish geegaws illuminated his eclectic good taste.

Mr. Make-Believe operated on a world-historical scale. He'd started out with nothing in a dysfunctional southern Illinois suburb, and he'd turned himself into the perfect master-of-the-universe, graying-at-the-temples, polo-playing, charity-hosting, six-foot-one-inch executive man.

His motto was Never Think Like An Employee, and from some phenomenally early age he had just assumed he would own and run whatever organization he was a part of. He started his business career in college, busing students to Fort Lauderdale for spring break. Decades later, capping a long series of acquisitions, he had bought a major airline and put himself at the head, but he seemed to spend a good deal of his time posing for Christmas cards atop the Matterhorn, negotiating to buy prominent European soccer teams, making the society pages while attending charity performances of Dante's *Inferno* on behalf of childhood-diabetes research, and attending Formula 1 races with his five perfect sons: Chip, Rip, Tip, Bip, and Lip.

Mr. Make-Believe was incapable of sitting still. He performed the slightest gesture in the manner of one who believes he is being watched admiringly by God. He studied photographs of JFK, and had spent hours in front of the mirror perfecting the one-thousand-yards-in-the-distance Man-of-Destiny stare. Yet every few minutes, a sort of wide-eyed laugh would break out of him, as if he couldn't quite believe the fantastic life he was leading. It was sort of like watching Dennis the Menace wake up every few minutes and discover that he's the pope.

He had a free day between meetings of the Aspen Strategy Group and the Trilateral Commission, so he'd invited Erica to come by for a consultation. Every year he put his goals for his airline on a single sheet of paper, and he wanted Erica to help him decide which priorities should make the list and which shouldn't—improve online check-in or revamp employee–health benefit options; replace the CFO or reduce air slots to the upper Midwest. Getting her installed in this suite was one of his characteristic acts of oppressive hospitality.

They lunched in her suite because Mr. Make-Believe thought he was too famous to dine uninterrupted in the restaurant downstairs. He ordered wine from the Russian River Valley and obscure crackers from Portugal, showing the kind of discernment that Erica found annoying—like a push-up bra of good taste. They talked about the corporate mission statement, but also Chinese currency values, wind energy, yoga, lacrosse, and his love for books about heroes who die at the end—the Robert Jordan canon, he called it.

Erica had left the bedroom door open even though this was a business lunch. She let her shoes fall off her feet and moved them about on the carpet with her stockinged feet. She was sort of entranced by the guy. They both tapped their fingers nervously as they talked. And it really wasn't the aridity of her own marriage at that point or her profound loneliness that made her sleep with him that day. It was mostly the novelty of having sex with a *Forbes*-cover boy and the excitement of having an experience she would always remember.

If there was any deeper longing she felt toward Mr. Make-Believe, it was her old fantasy of being part of some headline-grabbing power couple—part of some dynamic tycoon duo who would complement each other's skills—the F. Scott and Zelda of the corporate world.

Their lunch meeting went on for about two hours. He finally put the moves on her with his piety. She was his most-valued advisor, he told her as they stood close in the living room. His second most-valued advisor, he continued, was the priest who had been ministering him for thirty-five years. Through him, Mr. Make-Believe had become active in Catholic Charities, the Knights of Columbus, the Papal Foundation, and various other bigwig Catholic groups. It was characteristic of this fellow that he would talk about his service to the Vatican in order to get between a married woman's legs. He did not see himself as a guy who played by normal rules.

Erica let it be known by her body language that she was his for the taking, and as a matter of principle, Mr. Make-Believe could not let any opportunity for taking go unseized.

Shame

Years after, when she'd see his face on the cover of *Forbes* she'd allow herself a smile at her one episode of adultery. But on the night after it happened, her feelings were different.

The sex itself was nothing. Literally nothing. Just motions without any reverberations. But an hour or so after he left, she felt a strange sensation. It felt as though her insides were collapsing in on themselves. It came across her slowly at a business dinner as a background ache and then sliced sharpest, like being punctured by a blade, when she was alone back in the suite. She literally doubled over in pain, sitting there in a chair. She eventually realized it was self-hatred, shame, and revulsion. That night, she felt rancid in every way. Thoughts and images swarmed across her brain, not only of that afternoon's event, but also randomly associated terrible moments from her past. Her remorse seethed, and she could do nothing to will it away.

Brain-befogged, in the darkest hours of the night, she found herself thrashing in bed, punching the pillow, sitting up, and then throwing herself back down with a thump. She found herself groaning out loud in a sort of foggy-headed agony. She found herself on her feet, walking around the rooms, rushing over to the minibar in the kitchen and opening little bottles of scotch, which had no soothing effect, since they were so small. She wasn't really afraid of getting caught. She wasn't even afraid of any possible consequences. At this stage in her life, she didn't feel God's presence or God's judgment. She didn't even think the word "guilt" applied to this storm. It was just pain, which would be replaced the next day, after a few hours of sleep with a dull lassitude and a general feeling of vulnerability. For the next several days, her emotions were all on the surface. She listened to depressing Tom Waits music. She couldn't concentrate on work during the plane ride home but read a Faulkner novel instead. She was bruised and tender for weeks, and slightly different forever. She never committed adultery again, and the mere idea of it filled her with an intense and unthinking aversion.

Moral Sentiments

The traditional thing to say about this episode is that Erica had succumbed to selfish and shortsighted lust. In her passion, in her weakness, she betrayed the vow she had made to Harold on her wedding day.

This traditional understanding is based on a certain folk wisdom about the human mind. This folk wisdom presumes that there is a power struggle at the core of our moral decisions. On the one side there are the selfish and primitive passions. On the other side there is the enlightened force of reason. Reason uses logic to evaluate situations, apply relevant moral principles, resolve moral quandaries, and deduce a proper course of action. Reason then uses willpower to try to control the passions. When we act admirably, reason subdues passion and controls will. In Nancy Reagan's phrase, it just says no. When we act in selfish and shortsighted ways, then we either haven't applied reason, or passion has simply overwhelmed it.

In this approach, Level 2 consciousness is the hero. Level 1 instincts are the villains. The former is on the side of reason and morality; the other, on the side of passion, sin, and selfishness.

But this folk metaphor didn't really jibe with the way Erica experienced her escapade with Mr. Make-Believe. When Erica slid into sex with him and then suffered agony because of it, it wasn't because she had succumbed in a moment of passion and then realized calmly afterward that she had violated one of her principles. In fact, she was more passionate the night after, while in pain thrashing around in her bed, than she had been during the seduction and the sin. And it certainly wasn't because she later consciously reasoned her way through a quandary and then coolly came to rethink her decision. That's not how it felt at all. The regret had snuck up on her just as mysteriously as the original action.

Erica's experience didn't feel like a drama between reason and passion. Instead it seemed more accurate to say that Erica had felt her situation one way with Mr. Make-Believe, while he was in the room in front of her and she had acted in a certain way, and then later that night a different perception of the situation had swept over her. Somehow one emotional tide had replaced another.

She almost felt as if she were two different people: one of whom had seen the seduction in a mildly titillating way, and the other who had seen it as a disgrace. It was as it says in Genesis, after Adam and Eve were expelled from the Garden of Eden. Their eyes were opened up, and they saw that they were naked. Later, she looked at herself and was unable to explain her own actions: "What in God's name was I thinking?"

Furthermore, the mistake with Mr. Make-Believe had left some sort of psychic scar. When similar circumstances arose in the years that were to follow, she didn't even have to think about her response. There was no temptation to resist because the mere thought of committing adultery again produced an instant feeling of pain and aversion—the way a cat avoids a stove on which she has been burned. Erica didn't feel more virtuous because of what she had learned about herself, but she reacted differently to that specific sort of situation.

Erica's experience illustrates several of the problems with the rationalist folk theory of morality. In the first place, most of our moral judgments, like Erica thrashing about that night in agony, are not cool, reasoned judgments, they are deep and often hot responses. We go through our days making instant moral evaluations about behavior, without really having to think about why. We see injustice and we're furious. We see charity and we are warmed.

Jonathan Haidt of the University of Virginia provides example after example of this sort of instant moral intuition in action. Imagine a man who buys a chicken from the grocery store, manages to bring himself to orgasm by penetrating it, then cooks and eats the chicken. Imagine eating your dead pet dog. Imagine cleaning your toilet with your nation's flag. Imagine a brother and sister who are on a trip. One night they decide to have protected sex with each other. They enjoy it but decide never to do it again.

As Haidt has shown in a string of research, most people have strong intuitive (and negative) reactions to these scenarios, even though nobody is harmed in any of them. Usually, Haidt's research subjects cannot say why they found these things so repulsive or disturbing. They just do. The unconscious has made the call.

Furthermore, if the rationalist folk theory, with its emphasis on Level 2 moral reasoning, were correct, then you would expect people who do moral reasoning all day to be, in fact, more moral. Researchers have studied this, too. They've found there's relatively little relationship between moral theorizing and noble behavior. As Michael Gazzaniga wrote in his book *Human*, "It has been hard to find any correlation between moral reasoning and proactive moral behavior, such as helping people. In fact, in most studies, none has been found."

If moral reasoning led to more moral behavior, you would expect people who are less emotional to also be more moral. Yet at the extreme end, this is the opposite of the truth. As Jonah Lehrer has pointed out, when most people witness someone else suffering, or read about a murder or a rape, they experience a visceral emotional reaction. Their palms sweat and their blood pressure surges. But some people show no emotional reaction. These people are not hyper-rational moralists; they are psychopaths. Psychopaths do not seem to be able to process emotion about others' pain. You can show them horrific scenes of death and suffering and they are unmoved. They can cause the most horrific suffering in an attempt to get something they want, and they will feel no emotional pain or discomfort. Research on wife batterers finds that as these men become more aggressive their blood pressure and pulse actually drop.

Finally, if reasoning led to moral behavior, then those who could reach moral conclusions would be able to apply their knowledge across a range of circumstances, based on these universal moral laws. But in reality, it has been hard to find this sort of consistency.

A century's worth of experiments suggests that people's actual behavior is not driven by permanent character traits that apply from one context to another. Back in the 1920s, Yale psychologists Hugh Hartshorne and Mark May gave ten thousand schoolchildren opportunities to lie, cheat, and steal in a variety of situations. Most students cheated in some situations and not in others. Their rate of cheating did not correlate with any measurable personality traits or assessments of moral reasoning. More recent research has found the same general pattern. Students who are routinely dishonest at home are not routinely dishonest at school. People who are courageous at work can be cowardly at church. People who behave kindly on a sunny day may behave callously the next day, when it is cloudy and they are feeling glum. Behavior does not exhibit what the researchers call "cross-situational stability." Rather, it seems to be powerfully influenced by context.

The Intuitionist View

The rationalist assumptions about our moral architecture are now being challenged by a more intuitionist view. This intuitionist account puts emotion and unconscious intuition at the center of moral life, not reason; it stresses moral reflexes, alongside individual choice; it emphasizes the role perception plays in moral decision making, before logical deduction. In the intuitionist view, the primary struggle is not between reason and the passions. Instead, the crucial contest is within Level 1, the unconscious-mind sphere itself.

This view starts with the observation that we all are born with deep selfish drives—a drive to take what we can, to magnify our status, to appear superior to others, to exercise power over others, to satisfy lusts. These drives warp perception. It wasn't as if Mr. Make-Believe consciously set out to use Erica, or attack her marriage. He merely saw her as an object to be used in his life quest. Similarly, murderers don't kill people they regard as fully human like themselves. The unconscious has to first dehumanize the victim and change the way he is seen.

The French journalist Jean Hatzfeld interviewed participants in the Rwandan genocide for his book *Machete Season*. The participants were caught up in a tribal frenzy. They began to perceive their neighbors in radically perverse ways. One man Hatzfeld spoke with murdered a Tutsi who lived nearby: "I finished him off in a rush, not thinking anything of it, even though he was a neighbor, quite close on my hill. In truth, it came to me only afterward: I had taken the life of a neighbor. I mean, at the fatal instant I did not see in him what he had been before; I struck someone who was no longer either close or strange to me, who wasn't exactly ordinary anymore, I'm saying like the people you meet every day. His features were indeed similar to those of the person I knew, but nothing firmly reminded me that I had lived beside him for a long time."

These deep impulses treat conscious cognition as a plaything. They not only warp perception during sin; they invent justifications after it. We tell ourselves that the victim of our cruelty or our inaction had it coming; that the circumstances compelled us to act as we did; that someone else is to blame. The desire pre-consciously molds the shape of our thought.

But not all the deep drives are selfish ones, the intuitionists stress. We are all descended from successful cooperators. Our ancestors survived in families and groups.

Other animals and insects share this social tendency, and when we study them, we observe that nature has given them faculties that help them with bonding and commitment. In one study in the 1950s, rats were trained to press a lever for food. Then the experimenter adjusted the machine so that the lever sometimes provided food but sometimes delivered an electric shock to another rat in the next chamber. When the eating rats noticed the pain they were causing their neighbors, they adjusted their eating habits. They would not starve themselves. But they chose to eat less, to avoid causing undue pain to the other rats. Frans de Waal has spent his career describing the sophisticated empathy displays evident in primate behavior. Chimps console each other, nurse the injured, and seem to enjoy sharing. These are not signs that animals have morality, but they have the psychological building blocks for it.

Humans also possess a suite of emotions to help with bonding and commitment. We blush and feel embarrassed when we violate social norms. We feel instantaneous outrage when our dignity has been slighted. People yawn when they see others yawning, and those who are quicker to sympathetically yawn also rate higher on more complicated forms of sympathy.

Our natural empathy toward others is nicely captured by Adam Smith in *The Theory of Moral Sentiments*, in a passage that anticipates the theory of mirror neurons: "When we see a stroke aimed and just ready to fall upon the leg or arm of another person, we naturally shrink back our leg, our own arm; and when it does fall, we feel it in some measure and are hurt by it as well as the sufferer." We also feel a desire, Smith added, to be esteemed by our fellows. "Nature, when she formed man for society, endowed him with an original desire to please, and an original aversion to offend his brethren. She taught him to feel pleasure in their favorable, and pain in their unfavorable regard."

In humans, these social emotions have a moral component, even at a very early age. Yale professor Paul Bloom and others conducted an experiment in which they showed babies a scene featuring one figure struggling to climb a hill, another figure trying to help it, and a third trying to hinder it. At as early as six months, the babies showed a preference for the helper over the hinderer. In some plays, there was a second act. The hindering figure was either punished or rewarded. In this case, the eight-month-olds preferred a character who was punishing the hinderer over ones being nice to it. This reaction illustrates, Bloom says, that people have a rudimentary sense of justice from a very early age.

Nobody has to teach a child to demand fair treatment; children protest unfairness vigorously and as soon as they can communicate. Nobody has to teach us to admire a person who sacrifices for a group; the admiration for duty is universal. Nobody has to teach us to disdain someone who betrays a friend or is disloyal to a family or tribe. Nobody has to teach a child the difference between rules that are moral—"Don't hit"—and rules that are not—"Don't chew gum in school." These preferences also emerge from somewhere deep inside us. Just as we have a natural suite of emotions to help us love and be loved, so, too, we have a natural suite of moral emotions to make us disapprove of people who violate social commitments, and approve of people who reinforce them. There is no society on earth where people are praised for running away in battle.

It's true that parents and schools reinforce these moral understandings, but as James Q. Wilson argued in his book *The Moral Sense*, these teachings fall on prepared ground. Just as children come equipped to learn language, equipped to attach to Mom and Dad, so, too, they come equipped with a specific set of moral prejudices, which can be improved, shaped, developed, but never quite supplanted.

These sorts of moral judgments—admiration for someone who is loyal to a cause, contempt for someone who betrays a spouse—are instant and emotional. They contain subtle evaluations. If we see someone overcome by grief at the loss of a child, we register compassion and pity. If we see someone overcome by grief at the loss of a Maserati, we register disdain. Instant sympathy and complex judgment are all intertwined.

As we've seen so often in this story, the act of perception is a thick process. It is not just taking in a scene but, almost simultaneously, weighing its meaning, evaluating it, and generating an emotion about it. In fact, many scientists now believe that moral perceptions are akin to aesthetic or sensual perceptions, emanating from many of the same regions of the brain.

Think of what happens when you put a new food into your mouth. You don't have to decide if it's disgusting. You just know. Or when you observe a mountain scene. You don't have to decide if a landscape is beautiful. You just know. Moral judgments are in some ways like that. They are rapid intuitive evaluations. Researchers at the Max Planck Institute for Psycholinguistics in the Netherlands have found that evaluative feelings, even on complicated issues like euthanasia, can be detected within 200 to 250 milliseconds after a statement is read. You don't have to think about disgust, or shame, or embarrassment, or whether you should blush or not. It just happens.

In fact, if we had to rely on deliberative moral reasoning for our most elemental decisions, human societies would be pretty horrible places, since the carrying capacity of that reason is so low. Thomas Jefferson anticipated this point centuries ago:

> He who made us would have been a pitiful bungler, if He had made the rules of our moral conduct a matter of science. For one man of science, there are thousands who are not. What would have become of them? Man was destined for society. His morality, therefore, was to be formed to this object. He was endowed with a sense of right and wrong merely relative to this. This sense is as much a part of nature, as the sense of hearing, seeing, feeling; it is the true foundation of morality."

Thus, it is not merely reason that separates us from the other animals, but the advanced nature of our emotions, especially our social and moral emotions.

Moral Concerns

Some researchers believe we have a generalized empathetic sense, which in some flexible way inclines us to cooperate with others. But there is a great deal of evidence to suggest that people are actually born with more structured moral foundations, a collection of moral senses that are activated by different situations.

Jonathan Haidt, Jesse Graham, and Craig Joseph have compared these foundations to the taste buds. Just as the human tongue has different sorts of receptors to perceive sweetness, saltiness, and so on, the moral modules have distinct receptors to perceive certain classic situations. Just as different cultures have created different cuisines based on a few shared flavor senses, so, too, have different cultures created diverse understandings of virtue and vice, based on a few shared concerns.

Scholars disagree on the exact structure of these modules. Haidt, Graham, and Brian Nosek have defined five moral concerns. There is the fairness/reciprocity concern, involving issues of equal and unequal treatment. There is the harm/care concern, which includes things like empathy and concern for the suffering of others. There is an authority/ respect concern. Human societies have their own hierarchies, and react with moral outrage when that which they view with reverence (including themselves) is not treated with proper respect.

There is a purity/disgust concern. The disgust module may have first developed to repel us from noxious or unsafe food, but it evolved to have a moral component—to drive us away from contamination of all sorts. Students at the University of Pennsylvania were asked how it would feel to wear Hitler's sweater. They said it would feel disgusting, as if Hitler's moral qualities were a virus that could spread to them.

Finally, and most problematically, there is the in-group/loyalty concern. Humans segregate themselves into groups. They feel visceral loyalty to members of their group, no matter how arbitrary the basis for membership, and feel visceral disgust toward those who violate loyalty codes. People can distinguish between members of their own group and members of another group in as little as 170 milliseconds. These categorical differences trigger different activation patterns in the brain. The anterior cingulated cortices in Caucasian and Chinese brains activate when they see members of their own group endure pain; but much less than when they see members of another group enduring it.

The Moral Motivation

In the intuitionist view, the unconscious soulsphere is a coliseum of impulses vying for supremacy. There are deep selfish intuitions. There are deep social and moral intuitions. Social impulses compete with asocial impulses. Very often social impulses conflict with one another. Compassion and pity may emerge at the cost of fortitude, toughness, and strength. The virtue of courage and heroism may clash with the virtue of humility and acceptance. The cooperative virtues may clash with the competitive virtues. Our virtues do not fit neatly together into a complementary or logical system. We have many ways of seeing and thinking about a situation, and they are not ultimately compatible.

This means that the dilemma of being alive yields to no one true answer. In the heyday of the Enlightenment, philosophers tried to ground morality in logical rules, which could fit together like pieces of a logical puzzle. But that's not possible in the incompatible complexity of human existence. The brain is adapted to a fallen world, not a harmonious and perfectible one. Individuals contain a plurality of moral selves, which are aroused by different contexts. We contain multitudes.

But we do have a strong impulse to be as moral as possible, or to justify ourselves when our morality is in question. Having a universal moral sense does not mean that people always or even often act in good and virtuous ways. It's more about what we admire than what we do, more about the judgments we make than our ability to live up to them. But we are possessed by a deep motivation to be and be seen as a moral person.

Moral Development

The rationalist view advises us to philosophize in order to become more moral. The intuitionist view advises us to interact. It is hard or impossible to become more moral alone, but over the centuries, our ancestors devised habits and practices that help us reinforce our best intuitions, and inculcate moral habits.

For example, in healthy societies everyday life is structured by tiny rules of etiquette: Women generally leave the elevator first. The fork goes on the left. These politeness rules may seem trivial, but they nudge us to practice little acts of self-control. They rewire and strengthen networks in the brain.

Then there is conversation. Even during small talk, we talk warmly about those who live up to our moral intuitions and coldly about those who do not. We gossip about one another and lay down a million little markers about what behavior is to be sought and what behavior is to be avoided. We tell stories about those who violate the rules of our group, both to reinforce our connections with one another and to remind ourselves of the standards that bind us together.

Finally, there are the habits of mind transmitted by institutions. As we go through life, we travel through institutions—first family and school, then the institutions of a profession or a craft. Each of these comes with certain rules and obligations that tell us how to do what we're supposed to do. They are external scaffolds that penetrate deep inside us. Journalism imposes habits that help reporters keep a mental distance from those they cover. Scientists have obligations to the community of researchers. In the process of absorbing the rules of the institutions we inhabit, we become who we are.

The institutions are idea spaces that existed before we were born, and will last after we are gone. Human nature may remain the same, eon after eon, but institutions improve and progress, because they are the repositories of hard-won wisdom. The race progresses because institutions progress.

The member of an institution has a deep reverence for those who came before her and built up the rules that she has temporarily taken delivery of. "In taking delivery," the political theorist Hugh Heclo writes, "institutionalists see themselves as debtors who owe something, not creditors to whom something is owed."

A teacher's relationship to the craft of teaching, an athlete's relationship to her sport, a farmer's relationship to her land is not a choice that can be easily reversed when psychic losses exceed psychic profits. There will be many long periods when you put more into your institutions than you get out of them. Institutions are so valuable because they inescapably merge with who we are.

In 2005 Ryne Sandberg was inducted into the Baseball Hall of Fame. His speech is an example of how people talk when they are defined by their devotion to an institution: "I was in awe every time I walked onto the field. That's respect. I was taught you never, ever disrespect your opponent or your teammates or your organization or your manager and never, ever your uniform. Make a great play, act like you've done it before; get a big hit, look for the third base coach and get ready to run the bases."

Sandberg motioned to those inducted before him, "These guys sitting up here did not pave the way for the rest of us so that players could swing for the fences every time up and forget how to move a runner over to third. It's disrespectful to them, to you and to the game of baseball that we all played growing up.

"Respect. A lot of people say this honor validates my career, but I didn't work hard for validation. I didn't play the game right because I saw a reward at the end of the tunnel. I played it right because that's what you're supposed to do, play it right and with respect. . . . If this validates anything, it's that guys who taught me the game . . . did what they were supposed to do, and I did what I was supposed to do."

Responsibility

The intuitionist view emphasizes the moral action that takes place deep in the unconscious, but it is not a determinist view. Amid the tangled jostle of unconscious forces, the intuitionist still leaves room for reason and reflection. He still leaves room for individual responsibility.

It's true this new version of individual responsibility is not the same as it appeared in the old rationalist conceptions of morality, with their strong reliance on logic and will. Instead, responsibility in this view is best illustrated by two metaphors. The first is the muscle metaphor. We are born with certain muscles that we can develop by going to the gym every day. In a similar way, we are born with moral muscles that we can build with the steady exercise of good habits.

The second is the camera metaphor. Joshua Greene of Harvard notes that his camera has automatic settings ("portrait," "action," "landscape"), which adjust the shutter speed and the focus. These automatic settings are fast and efficient. But they are not very flexible. So sometimes, Greene overrides the automatic setting by switching to manual—setting the shutter speed and focusing himself. The manual mode is slower, but allows him to do things he might not be able to achieve automatically. In the same way as the camera, Greene argues, the mind has automatic moral concerns. But in crucial moments, they can be overridden by the slower process of conscious reflection.

In other words, even with automatic reactions playing such a large role, we have choices. We can choose to put ourselves in environments where the moral faculties will be strengthened. A person who chooses to spend time in the military or in church will react differently to the world than a person who spends his time in nightclubs or a street gang.

We can choose to practice those small acts of service that condition the mind for the moments when the big acts of sacrifice are required.

We can choose the narrative we tell about our lives. We're born into cultures, nations, and languages that we didn't choose. We're born with certain brain chemicals and genetic predispositions that we can't control. We're sometimes thrust into social conditions that we detest. But among all the things we don't control, we do have some control over our stories. We do have a conscious say in selecting the narrative we will use to organize perceptions.

We have the power to tell stories that deny another's full humanity, or stories that extend it. Renee Lindenberg was a little Jewish girl in Poland during World War II. One day a group of villagers grabbed her and set off to throw her down a well. But one peasant woman, who happened to overhear them, went up to them and said, "She's not a dog after all." The villagers immediately stopped what they were doing. Lindenberg's life was saved. This wasn't a moral argument about the virtue of killing or not killing a human being or a Jew. The woman simply got the villagers to see Lindenberg in a new way.

We have the power to choose narratives in which we absolve ourselves of guilt and blame everything on conspiracies or others. On the other hand, we have the power to choose narratives in which we use even the worst circumstances to achieve spiritual growth. "I am grateful that fate has hit me so hard," a young dying woman told Viktor Frankl during their confinement in a Nazi concentration camp. "In my former life I was spoiled and did not take spiritual accomplishments seriously," she said. She pointed to a branch of a tree, which she could see from her bunk window and described what it said to her in her misery. "It said to me, 'I am here—I am here—I am life, eternal life.'" This is a narrative of turning worldly defeat into spiritual victory. It's a different narrative than others might choose in that circumstance.

As Jonathan Haidt has put it, unconscious emotions have supremacy but not dictatorship. Reason cannot do the dance on its own, but it can nudge, with a steady and subtle influence. As some people joke, we may not possess free will, but we possess free won't. We can't generate moral reactions, but we can discourage some impulses and even overrule others. The intuitionist view starts with the optimistic belief that people have an innate drive to do good. It is balanced with the pessimistic belief that these moral sentiments are in conflict with one another and in competition with more selfish drives.

But the intuitionist view is completed by the sense that moral sentiments are subject to conscious review and improvement. The philosopher Jean Bethke Elshtain recalls that when she was a little girl in Sunday school she and her classmates sang a little hymn: "Jesus loves the little children/All the children of the world/Be they yellow, black or white/they are precious in his sight/Jesus loves the little children of the world." The song is not the sort of sophisticated philosophy that Elshtain now practices at the University of Chicago, but it is a lesson in seeing humanity, planted early and with reverberating force.

Redemption

Erica's family was not perfect. Her mother was haunted by demons. Her relatives were pains in the ass much of the time. But they had engraved upon her a sense that family was sacred, that country was sacred, that work was sacred. These ideas were crystallized by emotion.

But as Erica got older, she entered a different world. Some of her old ways of being went dormant—sometimes for good and sometimes for bad. Day by day, she became slightly different, often in superficial ways—how she dressed and talked—but also in profound ways.

If you had asked her about the old values, she would have told you that of course she still embraced them. But in fact, they had become less consecrated in her mind. A certain strategic and calculating mentality had weakened the sentiments that her relatives had tried in their messy way to instill in her.

By the time she found herself in that hotel room with Mr. Make-Believe, she had become a different person without realizing it. The decision to sleep with him was not the real moment of moral failing. That moment didn't even feel like a decision. It was just the culmination of a long unconscious shift. She had never consciously rejected her old values. She would have fiercely denied it if you'd asked. But those old ways of being had gained less prominence in the unconscious jockeying for supremacy inside. Erica had become a shallower person, disconnected from the deepest potential of her own nature.

In the weeks after, when she thought about the episode, she became newly aware that it really was possible to become a stranger to yourself, that you always have to be on the lookout, and to find some vantage point from which you can try to observe yourself from the outside.

She told herself a story about herself. It was the story of drift and redemption—of a woman who'd slid off her path inadvertently and who needed anchors to connect her to what was true and admirable. She needed to change her life, to find a church, to find some community group and a cause, and above all, to improve her marriage, to tether herself to a set of moral commitments.

She had always seen herself as a hustling young Horatio Alger girl. But she'd been through a period in which she was consumed by her quest. She would now right herself and sail on to better shores.

The redemption narrative helped Erica organize her view of herself. It helped her build integrity—integrating inner ideals with automatic action. It helped her attain maturity. Maturity means understanding, as much as possible, the different characters and modules that are active inside your own head. The mature person is like a river guide who goes over rapids and says, "Yes, I have been over these spots before."

In the following months, Erica rediscovered her love for Harold, and couldn't imagine what she'd been thinking before. He would never be an earthshaking titan like Mr. Make-Believe. But he was humble and good and curious. And with his disparate curiosities and research frenzies, he was engaged in the most important search, the search to find meaning in life. People like that are worth staying close to. In any case, he was hers. Over the course of many years they had become intertwined, and their relationship might not be inspiring or exciting and dynamic all the time, but it was her life, and the answer to any malaise consisted in going deeper into it and not trying to escape into some mythical land of make-believe.

CHAPTER 19

THE LEADER

THEY FIRST MET THE MAN WHO WOULD BE PRESIDENT BACK-stage before a campaign rally. He was still campaigning for the party nomination at that point and had been calling Erica for weeks to "bring her on the team." His staff had spent weeks looking for women, minorities, and people with business experience to bring into senior positions, and Erica was a trifecta. Grace called to talk for about forty-five seconds nearly every day—wooing, begging, laying it on thick with his instant intimacy and flattering persistence. "How's it going, sister? Have you made a decision?" And so she found herself in a high-school classroom next to a packed gym, with Harold in tow. They were supposed to meet him now, watch a rally, and then talk in the van on the way to the next event.

About thirty people milled about timidly in the classroom, none touching the cookies or cans of Coke. Suddenly there was a rhythm of rushing steps, and in he burst, somehow bathed in his own illumination. Erica was so used to seeing him on television that now she had the disorienting sensation that she was watching him on some super HDTV, not actually seeing him in the flesh.

Richard Grace was the projection of a great national fantasy—tall, flat stomach, gleaming white shirt, perfectly creased slacks, historically important hair, Gregory Peck face. He was followed by his famously wild daughter—the promiscuous beauty whose behavior was the product of a childhood marked mostly by paternal neglect. Behind them, there was a bevy of ugly-duckling aides. The aides had the same interests as Grace, the same secret ambitions as he, but they had paunches, thinning hair, a slouch, so they were destined to play the role of whispering tacticians, while he was Political Adonis. Because of these minor genetic differences, they'd spent their lives as hall monitors and he'd spent his life getting away with things.

Grace swept the room with a glance and saw immediately it was used to teach health class, with anatomical posters of the male and female reproductive systems on one wall. There wasn't even a conscious disturbance across his mind; just the vaguest ripple of knowledge that he couldn't allow himself to get photographed with a uterus and a dick splayed out behind his shoulders. He slid to the other side of the room.

He hadn't been alone in six months. He'd been the center of attention in every room he entered for the past six years. He had cast off from normal reality and lived now only off the fumes of the campaign, feeding off human contact the way other people survive on food and sleep.

He was all energy and adrenaline as he moved around the classroom. In rapid succession, he gave his Man-of-Destiny smile to a quartet of World War II vets, to two overawed honor students, six local donors, and a county commissioner. Like a running back, he knew how to keep his legs moving. Talk, laugh, hug, but never stop moving. A thousand intimate encounters a day.

People told him the most amazing things. "I love you." ... "I love you, too." ... "Hit him harder!" ... "I'd trust you with my son's life." ... "Can I have just five minutes?" ... "Can I have a job?" They told him about the most awful health-care tragedies. They wanted to give him things—books, artwork, letters. Some just grabbed his arm and melted.

He surrendered himself to fifteen-second bursts of contact, detecting and reflecting, with that razor sense of his, the play of movement around each person's lips and the expression in their eyes. Everyone got sympathy and everyone got a touch; he'd touch arms, shoulders, and hips. He'd send out these momentary pulsar beams of bonhomie or compassion, and he never showed impatience with the celebrity drill. A camera would appear. He'd drape his arm around each person as they posed with him. Over the years, he'd developed a mastery of every instant camera manufactured on earth, and if the photographer stumbled, he could throw out patient advice on which button to push and how long to hold it down, and he could do it like a ventriloquist without altering his smile. He could take attention and turn it into energy.

Finally, he came over to where Erica and Harold were standing. He gave her a hug, offered Harold the sly conspiratorial grin he reserved for trailing spouses, and then brought them into the envelope of his greatness. With the others in the room he'd been ebullient and loud. With them, he was insiderish, quiet, and confidential. "We'll visit later," he whispered in Erica's ear. "I'm so glad you could come . . . so glad." He gave her a serious, knowing look, then clapped his hand behind Harold's head while staring into his eyes as if they were partners in some conspiracy. Then he was gone.

They heard a rapturous roar from the gym and hustled over to watch the show. It was a thousand people smiling at their hero, waving at him, bouncing on their sneakers, screaming their heads off, and pointing their camera phones. He flung off his jacket and basked there in the rush of support.

The stump speech had a simple structure: twelve minutes of "you" and twelve minutes of "me." For the first half, he talked about his audience's common sense, about their fine values, about the wonderful way they had united to build this great cause. He wasn't there to teach them anything, or argue for something. He was there to give voice to their feelings, to express back to them their hopes, fears, and desires, to show them that he was just like them, could possibly be a friend or a family member, even though he was so much prettier.

So for twelve minutes he told them about their lives. He'd said all this hundreds of times, but he still paused at crucial moments, as if a sentiment had just popped into mind. He gave them a chance to applaud their own ideas. "This movement is about you and what you are doing for this country."

Grace, like most first-class minds in his business, tried to find a compromise between what his voters wanted to hear and what he felt they needed to hear. They were normal people who paid only sporadic attention to policy, and he tried to respect their views and passions. At the same time he thought of himself as a real policy wonk, who loved nothing more than to dive down into an issue with a crowd of experts. He tried to keep these two conversations within shouting distance of each other in his head. Occasionally he'd give himself permission to flat out pander, and say the crude half-truth that got the big applause. He was a mass-market brand, after all, and had to win the votes of millions. But he also tried to keep his own real views in his head, too, for the sake of his self-respect. Fed by adulation, the former was always threatening to smother the latter.

In the final half of the speech, Grace turned to the "Me" section. He tried to show his audience that he possessed the traits the country needed at that moment in history. He talked about his parents—he was the son of a truck driver and a librarian. He talked about his dad's membership in the union. He made it clear, as all candidates must, that his character was formed before he ever thought about politics—in his case by his military service and the death of his sister. He told all the facts of his life, and they were all sort of true but he had repeated them so many times he'd lost contact with the actual reality of the events. His childhood and early manhood was just the script he had been campaigning on all his life.

Self-definition is the essence of every campaign, and Grace stuck to his narrative, which, as one consultant had put it, was "Tom Sawyer grows up." He described his small-town Midwestern upbringing, his charming pranks, the lessons he learned about the wider world and the injustice contained in it. He showed his wholesome manners, which came from a simpler time, his innocent virtue and his common sense.

The final passage of the speech was "You and I Together." He told an anecdote about a meeting with a wise old lady who told him stories that just happened to confirm every plank in his campaign platform. He told them about the acres of diamonds they would seize together, the garden of plenty they would find at the end of the road, the place where inner conflict would be replaced by peace and joy. Nobody in the audience really thought a political campaign could produce such utopia, but for the moment the vision of it swept them away and erased all tension from their lives. They loved Grace for giving them that. As he finished his speech, shouting over their cheers and applause, the gym went wild.

The Private Campaign Speech

An aide appeared and swept Erica and Harold into the van—Erica in the middle row and Harold in the rear. Grace appeared cool and matter-of-fact, as if he had just come from a dull meeting on quarterly-earnings reports. He made a few scheduling consultations with an aide, did a three-minute cell-phone interview with a radio station, and then turned his laser beam on Erica, who was sitting next to him.

"First I want to make my offer," he said. "I have political people and I have policy people, but I don't have anybody first-rate who will make this organization run. That's what I'm hoping you'll do, be the chief operating officer of the campaign and then do the same thing in the White House after I win."

Erica wouldn't have been in the van unless she was prepared to say yes to his offer, which she did.

"That's fantastic. Now that you've committed, I want to tell you both about the world you two are about to enter. I especially want to tell you, Harold, because I've read your work, and I think you're going to find yourself in a strange new place.

"The first thing to say is that nobody who is in this business has any right to complain. We choose it and it has its pleasures and rewards. But between us, there is no arena in which the character challenges are so large. You don't get to serve unless you win. To win you have to turn yourself into a product. You have to do things you never thought you would do. You have to put your sense of reserve on the back burner and beg for money and favors. You have to talk endlessly. Walk into a room and talk, walk into a rally and talk, meet with supporters and talk. I call it logorrhea dementia—talking so much you drive yourself insane.

"And what do you talk about? You have to talk endlessly about yourself. Every speech is about me. Every meeting I have is about me. Every article that's shoved under my nose is about me. When they start writing about you, it'll happen to you, too.

"At the same time, this is a team sport. You can't do anything alone, which means you sometimes have to suppress your individual ideas and say and believe the things that are good for the party and the team. You have to be brothers in arms with people you probably wouldn't like if you gave yourself a minute to think about it. You can't get too far out in front of your party or the people you serve. You can't be right too early or interesting too often. You have to support measures you really oppose and sometimes object to things you think are for the good. You have to pretend that when you're elected you'll be able to control everything and change everything. You have to pretend that the team myths are true. You have to pretend that the other team is uniquely evil, and would be the ruin of America. Saying otherwise is seen as a threat to party solidarity, and that's just the way it is.

"You live in a cocoon. I once read a beautiful essay on the life of a tick. A tick can apparently respond to only three types of stimulus. It knows skin. It knows temperature. It knows hair. Those three things constitute the entire *umwelt* for a tick. '*Umwelt*' is a word for the relevant environment of any creature. When you're in this business your umwelt will shrink and be crazy. You will be asked to pay furious attention to minute-by-minute breaking-news stories of no consequence, which you will completely forget by the next day. You will find yourself monitoring the blogs of the twenty-two-year-old kids with their webcams who have been sent out to cover this campaign—kids who have never seen an election before, who have no sense of history and the attention span of a ferret. Because of their presence you can never utter an unrehearsed thought. You can never try out a notion in public.

"All of these things threaten your ability to be honest with yourself, to see the world clearly, to have some basic integrity as a person. And yet we endure this theater of the absurd because there is no other life so filled with consequence. When you are in the White House with me, you will be busier than ever and every decision will be an important decision. Once we're in the White House, we won't have to pander to the nation so much. We'll be able to lead and educate it. When we're there, you will never want to take time off, and you won't.

"Once we're in the White House, we're not going to swing for singles. We're going to hit home runs. I refuse to be a timid president. I'm going to be a great president. I have the gifts. I know more about more policy areas than anybody else in this country. I have more political courage than anybody in politics. My attitude is going to be, 'I've got game. Give me the ball.' "

Other people, viewing Grace from beyond the reach of his charisma, might have mixed reactions to this little speech. But Erica and Harold were deep in the gravitational pull of the aura. At that moment, they thought it was the most impressive speech they'd ever heard. They thought it showed his amazing self-awareness, his astonishing wisdom, and his remarkable commitment to service. They'd been with him just minutes, but they'd already been caught up in the starstruck love affair that would consume them, especially Erica, for the next eight years.

Political Psychology

Harold had never really paid close attention to an election before. He'd never had access to the internal polling and the inside-strategy memos. After a few days, Erica was more or less submerged within the organization, but Harold got to float around the fringes, with not all that much to do but observe and think. He was struck by the fundamental divide amongst Grace's advisors. Some thought that campaigning was primarily about delivering goods to voters. Give voters policies that will make their lives better, and they will pay you for services rendered with their votes. Good policies at good prices.

Others thought campaigns were primarily about arousing emotions—forging an elemental bond with groups and voters; inspiring hope with a vision of the future; sending the message "I am just like you. I will react to events as you would react. I will be what you would be." Politics isn't primarily about defending interests. It's primarily about affirming emotions.

Harold, given his background and life's work, sided with the latter group. Grace was in a tough primary with a flinty New England governor named Thomas Galving. Their policies were basically the same, and so the race had become a battle of social symbols. Grace was the son of a truck driver, and yet he campaigned with a poetic, lyrical style, so he became the candidate of the idealistic educated class. In primary after primary, he won college-educated voters by twenty-five percentage points or more. For the first ten primaries, he seemed to hold every rally within fifty yards of a provost's office. He didn't just offer lists of programs. He offered experiences. He offered hope instead of fear, unity instead of discord, intelligence instead of rashness. The message was: "Life is beautiful. Our possibilities are endless. We just have to throw off the shackles of the past and enter a golden tomorrow."

Galving's family had been in the United States for three hundred years, and yet he was a pugnacious, combative sort. He positioned himself as a warrior, fighting for your interests. His campaign played up clan loyalty, sticking together, fighting together and defending one another to the death. As the weeks went on, Galving had himself photographed in a bar or on a factory floor every single day. He'd be seen throwing back a shot of whiskey, wearing a flannel shirt, riding shotgun in a pickup truck. The message was: "It's a rotten world out there. Regular folks are getting the shaft. They need someone who puts toughness and loyalty over independence and ideals."

The candidates' methods weren't subtle, but each approach worked to some degree. In primary after primary Galving won working-class voters by gigantic margins. Grace won the cities, the affluent suburbs, and the university towns. Nationally, Grace won the coasts. Galving won the wide swathe of farming and former manufacturing centers in the South and Midwest, especially where the Scots-Irish had settled centuries before. In Connecticut, Grace won most of the towns that had been settled by the English in the seventeenth century. Galving won most of the towns that had been settled by immigrant groups two centuries after. These were century-old patterns, but they still shaped voting. As weeks went by, campaigning didn't seem to matter. Demography was destiny. In states with large working-class populations,

Galving won. In states with large educated-class populations, Grace won.

Harold was fascinated by these deep tribal cultural currents. His theory was that the political party, like many institutions, had segmented into different subcultures. There was no great hostility between the cultures; they would come together once a nominee was selected. Nonetheless, people in different social classes, defined largely by education level, had developed different unconscious maps of reality. They had developed different communal understandings of what constitutes a good leader, of what sort of world they live in. They had developed different definitions of justice and fairness, liberty, security, and opportunity, without even realizing it.

Voters form infinitely complex mental maps, which are poorly understood even by those who adopt them. They pick up millions of subtle signals from the candidates—from body language, word choice, facial expressions, policy priorities, and biographical details. Somehow voters form emotional affiliations on that basis.

What Harold saw during the campaign certainly didn't fit the rationalist model of politics, in which voters carefully weigh programs and pick the candidate with the policies that serve their interests. Instead, it fit the social-identity model. People favor the party that seems to be filled with the sort of people they like and admire.

As political scientists Donald Green, Bradley Palmquist, and Eric Schickler argue in their book *Partisan Hearts and Minds*, most people either inherit their party affiliations from their parents, or they form an attachment to one party or another early in adulthood. Few people switch parties once they hit middle age. Even major historic events such as the world wars and the Watergate scandal do not cause large numbers of people to switch.

Moreover, Green, Palmquist, and Schickler continue, when people do select their own party affiliations, they do not choose parties by comparing platforms and then figuring out where the nation's interests lie. Drawing on a vast range of data, the authors argue that party attachment is more like attachment to a religious denomination or a social club. People have stereotypes in their heads about what Democrats are like and what Republicans are like, and they gravitate toward the party made up of people like themselves.

Once they have formed an affiliation, people bend their philosophies and their perceptions of reality so they become more and more aligned with members of their political tribe. Paul Goren of the University of Minnesota has used survey data to track the same voters over time. Under the classic model, you'd expect to find that people who valued equal opportunity would become Democrats and that people who valued limited government would become Republicans. In fact, you're more likely to find that people become Democrats first, then place increasing value on equal opportunity, or they become Republicans first, then place increasing value on limited government. Party affiliation often shapes values, not the other way around.

Party affiliation even shapes people's perceptions of reality. In 1960 Angus Campbell and others published a classic text, *The American Voter,* in which they argued that partisanship serves as a filter. A partisan filters out facts that are inconsistent with the party's approved worldview and exaggerates facts that confirm it. Over the years, some political scientists have criticized that observation. But many researchers are coming back to Campbell's conclusion: People's perceptions are blatantly biased by partisanship.

For example, the Princeton political scientist Larry Bartels has pointed to survey data collected after the Reagan and Clinton presidencies. In 1988 voters were asked if they thought the nation's inflation rate had fallen during the Reagan presidency. In fact, it had. The inflation rate fell from 13.5 percent to 4.1 percent. But only 8 percent of strong Democrats said the rate had fallen. More than 50 percent of partisan Democrats believed that inflation had risen under Reagan. Strong Republicans had a much sunnier and more accurate impression of economic trends. Forty-seven percent said inflation had declined.

Then, at the end of the Clinton presidency, voters were asked similar questions about how the country had fared in the previous eight years. This time, it was Republicans who were inaccurate and negative. Democrats were much more positive. Bartels concludes that partisan loyalties have a pervasive influence on how people see the world. They reinforce and exaggerate differences of opinion between Republicans and Democrats.

Some people believe that these cognitive flaws can be eradicated with more education, but that doesn't seem to be true, either. According to research by Charles Taber and Milton Lodge of Stony Brook University, educated voters may be more factually right most of the time, but they are still factually wrong a significant amount of the time. They are actually less willing to correct their false opinions than less-informed voters because they are so confident that they are correct about everything.

The overall impression one gets from this work is that the search for a candidate is an aesthetic search—a search for a candidate who clicks. Some of the things that influence a voter's decisions can be instantaneous and seemingly unimportant. As noted earlier, Alex Todorov and others at Princeton showed their research subjects black-and-white photographs of the faces of rival political candidates. The subjects were asked which of the candidates looked more competent. (The subjects were not familiar with either of the candidates).

The candidate who was perceived as the more competent by the people looking at the photographs won 72 percent of the actual Senate races in which they were involved, and 67 percent of the actual House races. The research subjects could impressively predict the actual winners even if they were given just one second to look at the candidates' faces. This result has been replicated internationally as well. In one study called "Looking Like a Winner," Chappell Lawson, Gabriel Lenz, and others gave people in the U.S. and India quick glimpses of people running for office in Mexico and Brazil. Despite ethnic and cultural differences, the Americans and the Indians agreed about which candidate would be more effective. The American and Indian preferences also predicted the Mexican and Brazilian election results with surprising accuracy.

A study by Daniel Benjamin of Cornell University and Jesse Shapiro of the University of Chicago found that research subjects could predict the outcome of gubernatorial races with some accuracy just by looking at ten-second silent video clips of the candidates talking. Their accuracy dropped if the sound was turned up. A study by Jonah Berger and others at Stanford found that the location of a voting booth can also influence voter decisions. Voters who went to polling stations in schools are more likely to support tax increases to fund education than voters who went to other polling stations. Voters who were shown a photograph of a school were also more likely to support a tax increase than voters not shown such a photograph.

Some of these are experiments conducted in a lab. In real campaigns, the races go on and on, month after month. The voters make snap judgments by the minute, hour, day, week, and month, and their instant perceptions accrete to form a thick and complex web of valuation.

To say that voter decisions are emotional does not mean that voters are stupid and irrational. Since unconscious processes are faster and more complicated than conscious ones, this intuitional search can be quite sophisticated. While following a political campaign, voters are both rational and intuitive. The two modes of cognition inform and shape each other.

The Underdebate

At the end of the day, Grace just ground down Galving. There were more of his kind of people than there were of Galving's kind of people. He won the party nomination, and within months all was forgiven as members of the two wings of the party went into battle with the other party. They were united by a new us-them distinction.

The general election was bigger and, at least on the surface, stupider. In the primary fight, everybody knew everybody on all sides. It was a fight within the family. But the general election was a combat against a different party, and almost nobody knew anybody on the other side. The "others" were like creatures from a different solar system, and it was convenient to believe the worst.

The general view on Grace's campaign was that the people running the other campaign were uniquely evil and devilishly clever. The people in Grace's camp believed that their side was riven with internal disputes (because of their superior intellects and independence of mind), whereas the other side marched with totalitarian unity and precision (because of their clonelike conformity). Their side was thoughtful but fractious, while the other side was mindless but disciplined.

By the fall, the campaign was just a series of jet hops. Grace would hold rallies at one airport hangar after another, in an effort to hit as many TV markets in a day as possible. Most of the internal campaign debates seemed to be about where to put the risers for the TV cameras and how high they should be.

The candidates traded insults relayed at BlackBerry speed. The media kept track of who won each week, day, and hour, though it's not clear that these victories meant anything to the actual electorate. Grace's supporters turned bipolar. A senator would come on the campaign plane one day, exultant over certain victory. The next day the same senator would be back, in despair over the prospect of certain defeat.

There were consultants all around honing the message. "Never say 'families'; say, 'working families.' Never say 'spend'; say 'invest.' " These subtle word alterations were used to provoke entirely different associations in voters' minds.

The most important part of the campaign was taking place away from the candidate, among the consultants who designed the TV commercials. They were pitching them toward voters who didn't normally pay attention to politics and who were woefully misinformed about where each candidate stood on the issues.

Weird issues popped up and became the subject of furious insults between the two campaigns. Grace and his opponent spent a week furiously accusing the other of causing childhood obesity, though it was not clear that either of them had caused it or could do anything about it. A minor crisis in Lebanon turned into a major campaign showdown, with each side demonstrating toughness and resolve and accusing the other of treason. Mini-scandals erupted. People in Grace's camp were genuinely outraged by a leaked memo from the other side that included the phrase "How to fuck them over." They were genuinely unmoved by the memos produced by their own campaign with the exact same wording.

The process seemed stupid and superficial. But Harold couldn't get over the crowds. There was real passion at each event—thousands of people, and sometime tens of thousands, roaring their support for Grace with some sort of orgiastic hope.

Given what he had learned so far about life, Harold concluded that all the campaign trivialities were really triggers. They served to trigger deep chains of associations in people's minds. Grace would spend an hour getting photographed at a flag factory. The event was stupid on its face, but somehow the sight of him holding all those American flags triggered some set of unconscious associations. Another day, they put him on a stool and he held a rally in Monument Valley, where all those John Wayne westerns were set. It was a tacky device, but it triggered another set of associations.

The campaign managers had no clue what they were doing. They lived in a blizzard of meaningless data. They'd try various gimmicks to see what clicked with voters. They'd try a new sentence in the stump speech and then look to see if people at the rallies nodded unconsciously as Grace said it. If they nodded, the sentence stayed. If not, it went.

Somehow the electorate possessed a hidden G-spot. The consultants were like clumsy lovers trying to touch it. The two campaigns would spar over some detail in a tax plan, but the argument wasn't really about tax regulations; it was about some deeper set of values that were being stoked indirectly. The candidates argued about material things, which were easy to talk about and understand, but the real subject of their debate was spiritual and emotional: Who we are and who we should be.

One day on a plane ride, Harold tried to explain his theory of the campaign to Grace and Erica—how each position about, say, energy policy was really a way of illuminating values of nature and community and human development. Positions were simply triggers for virtues. Grace was tired and couldn't really follow what Harold was saying. Between rallies he sort of shut down, and put his brain on pause. Erica was sitting nearby pounding on her BlackBerry. There was a silence, after which Grace said with an air of exhaustion: "This shit would be really interesting if we weren't in the middle of it."

But Harold kept watching. He was, as we know, mostly a watcher. And what he saw beneath the normal thrust and counterthrust of the opposing teams was a bunch of underdebates, arguments about things that were addressed only implicitly. These arguments went deep into the nation's soul and divided voters in important ways.

One underdebate was about the nature of leadership. Grace's opponent bragged that he made his decisions quickly, by trusting his gut and then moving on. He claimed (dishonestly) that he didn't bother reading the pundits and the papers. He portrayed himself as a straightforward man of action and faith, who prized the vigorous virtues: loyalty to friends, toughness against foes, strong and quick decisiveness.

Grace, on the other hand, conspicuously embodied a set of reflective leadership traits. He came across as the sort of person who read widely, discussed problems thoroughly, understood nuances and shades of gray. He came across as cautious, cerebral, thoughtful, and calm. Sometimes, he gave interviews in which he left the impression that he read more than he really did. Thus, there were two definitions of the leadership virtues, vying in the frenzy of a campaign.

Another underdebate concerned the basic morality of the country. The easiest way to predict who was going to vote for and against Grace was by asking about church attendance. People who went once a week or more were very likely to vote against him. People who never went were very likely to vote for him. This was despite the fact that Grace was himself a religious person, who attended regularly.

And yet somehow the contest between the two men and the two parties had put each on the side of some semi-articulated moral divide. People on one side were more likely to emphasize that God plays an active role in human affairs. People on the other were less likely to believe that. People on one side were more likely to talk about submission to God's will and divinely inspired moral rules. People on the other were less likely to talk about these things.

Yet another underdebate concerned geography, lifestyle, and social groupings. People who lived in densely populated parts of the country tended to support Grace. People who voted in sparsely populated parts supported his opponent. The two groups seemed to have different no-tions about personal space, individual liberty, and communal responsibility.

Every day Grace's pollsters came in with new ways to slice the electorate. People who enjoyed sports involving engines—motorcycling, powerboating, snowmobiling—opposed Grace, while people who enjoyed nonengine leisure activities—hiking, cycling, and surfing—supported him. People with neat desks opposed Grace, people with messy ones supported him.

The interesting thing was that everything was connected to everything else. Lifestyle choices correlated with political choices, which correlated with philosophical choices, which connected to religious and moral choices, and so on and so on. The campaigns never engaged the neural chains directly, but they did send off little cues that triggered the mental networks.

One day Grace's opponent went hunting. Acts like these activated networks in voters' minds, too. Hunting meant guns, which meant personal freedom, which meant traditional communities, which meant conservative social values, which meant reverence for family and reverence for God. The next day Grace ladled soup in a soup kitchen. The soup kitchen visit meant charity, which meant compassion, which meant a craving for social justice, which meant understanding the losers in the great game of life, which meant an activist government that would spend more to promote equality. The candidates needed only to set off the first step in these networks of meanings. Voters did the rest. Message received.

Some days Harold watched the campaign and thought about how meaningful it really was. Despite all the triviality and show, it really did highlight, if only subliminally, the fundamental choices in life. Politics, he would conclude some days, is a noble undertaking. On other days, of course, he just wanted to throw up.

Teamism

The thing that disturbed Harold was this: Most voters held centrist views and were moderate in disposition. But political values are not expressed in the abstract. They are expressed in the context of a campaign, and the campaign structures how political views get expressed.

The campaign was structured to take a moderate nation and to make it polarized. The parties were organized into teams. The pundits were organized into teams. There were two giant idea spaces, a Democratic idea space and a Republican idea space. The contest was over what mental model would get to dominate the country for the next four years. It was an either/or decision, and voters who didn't share either of the dominant idea spaces simply had to hold their nose and choose. The campaign itself took a moderate nation and turned it into a bitterly divided one.

Harold watched week by week as Grace got swallowed up by his party's idea space. Deep down he held quirky and idiosyncratic views. But in the frenzy of the final push he was swallowed up by the crowds, by the party apparatus, by the donors. If in the final weeks of the race you had judged Grace by the things he said, you'd have concluded that he wasn't really a person, just the living and breathing embodiment of the party positions, which emerged from history and transcended individual thought.

The only thing that remained distinct about Grace, through it all, was his equipoise. He never lost his cool. He never snapped at his aides. He never panicked. He'd always been the coolest person in any room, and drew people to him by force of his coolness, and that never changed. Harold used to watch him in the most trying circumstances and think, "Graceful is as Graceful does."

Even on election day, Grace was calm. He projected order and predictability. He aroused trust. And that, along with economic news that helped his campaign and a few other historical accidents, pushed him over the top. Harold saw Grace smile on election night, but he did not see him elated. After all, he knew he was going to win. He had known it since fourth grade. He had never doubted his destiny.

What really startled Harold that night was Erica. In the final few weeks she had become utterly absorbed by campaign work, to the point of exhaustion. Late at night, back in one of the hotel bedrooms, away from the party, he came upon her in an armchair heaving with sobs. He came up to her, sat on the armrest, and put his hand on the back of her neck.

In moments like this, Erica thought about her journey. Erica thought about the grandfather sneaking across the Mexican border, the other grandfather arriving by ship from China. She thought about the apartments she had lived in with her mother, where the doors didn't shut because they'd been painted and repainted so many times that they had grown too wide for the frame. She thought about the hopes and dreams that her mother had, the small nothing she had sometimes felt like. And then she thought with some pride but with more astonishment of the White House, where she would soon work, the amazing intensity of the campaign, and her love for the people who had put her boss in the office where Lincoln had once sat. There were hundreds of years of history behind her, many generations of ancestors and workers and parents, and none of those people had had a chance to enjoy the privileges that had now fallen into her lap.

CHAPTER 20

THE SOFT SIDE

T HERE'S A CROSS STREET IN WASHINGTON, D.C., WITH A THINK tank on each corner. There's a foreign-policy think tank, a domestic-policy think tank, an international-economics think tank, and one specializing in regulatory affairs. Many people consider this the most boring spot on the face of the earth.

The research assistants gather at coffee shops, scheming about how to get C-SPAN to cover their boss's "Whither NATO?" conference next spring. The junior fellows share cabs to Capitol Hill and generously agree to sit on each other's panel discussions. The senior fellows, the former deputy secretaries of this or that department, engage in a Washington institution called the Powerless Lunch, in which two previously influential people dine and have portentous conversations of no importance whatsoever. Meanwhile, they all have to deal with the emotional consequences of their Sublimated Liquidity Rage, which is the anger felt by Upper–Middle Class Americans who make decent salaries but have to spend 60 percent of their disposable incomes on private-school tuitions. They have nothing left to spend on themselves, which causes deep and unacknowledged self-pity.

When Erica disappeared into the administration as deputy chief of staff, Harold joined these happy symposiasts by taking a job as the Robert J. Kolman Senior Research Fellow for Public Policy Studies. Kolman was a four-foot-ten-inch investment banker on his fifth six-foot wife (that's thirty feet of combined womanhood) who thought most of America's problems would be solved if he got invited to the White House more often.

Harold thus found himself in the land of policy johnnies. He found them emotionally avoidant overall, people who had established their credentials as university grinds, built their authority on analytic rigor, and then had congregated, like swallows to Capistrano, at a place where sexuality was rigorously suppressed, pleasure was a low priority, and where if you attended four entitlement-reform conferences you found that your virginity had been magically restored. Harold noticed that his new colleagues were very nice and incredibly smart, but they suffered from the status rivalries endemic to the upper middle class. As law-school grads, they resent B-school grads. As Washingtonians, they resent New Yorkers. As policy wonks, they resent people with good bone structure. They all had NordicTrack machines crammed into their kids' play areas downstairs, but no matter how hard they labored they were careful never to become beautiful, because if they did they would never be taken seriously at the Congressional Budget Office.

Harold's office was directly next to a guy whose political career had blown up because of rank-link imbalance. He'd spent the first part of his life defining himself by his career rank. He'd developed the social skills useful on the climb up the greasy pole: the capacity to imply false intimacy; the ability to remember first names; the subtle skills of effective deference. He got elected to the Senate and had come to master the patois of globaloney—the ability to declaim for portentous hours about the revolution in world affairs brought about by technological change/environmental degradation/the fundamental decline in moral values—had achieved fame and a spot as chairman of the Senate Foreign Relations Committee, and was often talked about as a presidential hopeful.

But then, gradually, some cruel cosmic joke got played on him. He realized in middle age that his Senate grandeur was not enough and that he was lonely. Some Senators manage to build friendships once they are in Congress. In fact, a study by Katherine Faust and John Skvoretz found that the friendship networks within the U.S. Senate were remarkably similar in structure to the social licking networks among cows. But this poor fellow never built those friendships. He had spent his entire life building vertical relationships with people above him; he had not spent time building horizontal relationships with people who might be peers and true companions. The ordinariness of his intimate life was made more painful by the exhilaration of his public success.

And so the crisis came. Perhaps alpha-male gorillas don't wake up in the middle of the night feeling sorry for themselves because "nobody knows the real me." But Harold's neighbor went off to heal the hurt as best as he knew how. After years of repression he had the friendship skills of a six-year-old. When he tried to bond, it was like watching a Saint Bernard try to French-kiss. It was overbearing, slobbery, and desperately wanting. Some perfectly normal young woman would be sitting at a dinner party and suddenly she'd find a senator's tongue in her ear. Having decided in midlife that in fact he did have an inner soul, he took it out for a romp and discovered he had just bought a ticket on the self-immolation express.

Embarrassing revelations surfaced. Call girls appeared in the press with interesting stories to tell. The Ethics Committee met. Late-night comics made jokes. Resignations were handed in and the former presidential aspirant found himself at a think tank sitting around in the afternoons shooting the breeze with Harold.

The Hard Side

Harold also noticed that certain ideas in the wider scientific culture had scarcely penetrated the policy-making world. He found that whether on the right or the left, people in this world shared certain assumptions. They both had individualistic worldviews, tending to assume that society is a contract between autonomous individuals. Both promoted policies designed to expand individual choice. Neither paid much attention to social and communal bonds, to local associations, or invisible norms.

Conservative activists embraced the individualism of the market. They reacted furiously against any effort by the state to impinge upon individual economic choice. They adopted policy prescriptions designed to maximize economic freedom: lower tax rates so people could keep and use more of their money, privatized Social Security so people could control more of their own pensions, voucher programs so parents could choose schools for their children.

Liberals embraced the individualism of the moral sphere. They reacted furiously against any effort by the state to impinge upon choices about marriage, family structure, the role of women, and matters of birth and death. They embraced policies designed to maximize social freedom. Individuals should be free to make their own choices about abortion, euthanasia, and other matters. Activist groups stood up for the rights of individuals accused of crimes. Religion, in the form of crèches and menorahs, was rigorously separated from the public square so as not to impinge on individual conscience.

The individualism of the left and right produced two successful political movements—one in the 1960s and one in the 1980s. For a generation, no matter who was in power, the prevailing winds had been blowing in the direction of autonomy, individualism, and personal freedom, not in the directions of society, social obligations, and communal bonds.

Harold also found that his new colleagues shared a materialistic mind-set. Both liberals and conservatives gravitated toward economic explanations for any social problem and generally came up with solutions to this problem that involved money. Some conservatives argued for child–tax credits to restore marriage, low-tax enterprise zones to combat urban poverty, and school vouchers to improve the education system. Liberals emphasized the other side of the fiscal ledger, spending programs. They tried to direct more dollars to fix broken schools. They expanded student-aid subsidies to increase college-completion rates. Both sides assumed there was a direct relationship between improving material conditions and solving problems. Both sides neglected matters of character, culture, and morality.

In other words, they split Adam Smith down the middle. Smith wrote one book, *The Wealth of Nations*, in which he described economic activity and the invisible hand. But he wrote another book, *The Theory of Moral Sentiments*, in which he described how sympathy and the unconscious desire for esteem molded individuals. Smith believed that the economic activity described in *The Wealth of Nations* rested upon the bedrock described in *The Theory of Moral Sentiments*. But in recent decades, the former book became famous, while the latter was cited but never applied. The prevailing mentality treasured the first but didn't know what to make of the second.

Harold found that in Washington the highest status went to those who studied things involving guns and banks. People who wrote about war, budgets, and global finance strode around like titans, but people who wrote about family policy, early-childhood education, and community relationships were treated like pudgy geeks at a frat party. You could pull a senator aside and try to talk about the importance of maternal bonds to future human development and the senator would look at you indulgently, as if you were raising money for a group-therapy farm for lonely puppies. Then he'd go off to talk about something serious— a tax bill or a defense contract.

Politicians themselves were intensely social creatures. They'd made their way in the world with these brilliant emotional antennae, but when it came to thinking about policy, they ignored those faculties entirely. They thought mechanistically, and took seriously only those factors that could be rigorously quantified and toted up in an appropriations bill.

The Shallow View

Harold believed that, over the course of his lifetime, this mentality had led to a series of disastrous policies. These policies had produced bad effects for a common reason. They rearranged the material conditions in positive ways, but they undermined social relationships in ways that were unintended and destructive.

Some of the mistakes had emanated from the left. In the 1950s and 1960s, well-intentioned reformers saw run-down neighborhoods with decaying tenement houses, and vowed to replace them with shiny new housing projects. Those old neighborhoods may have been decrepit, but they contained mutual support systems and community bonds.

When they were destroyed and replaced with the new projects, people's lives were materially better but spiritually worse. The projects turned into atomized wastelands, ultimately unfit for human habitation.

Welfare policies in the 1970s undermined families. Government checks lifted the material conditions of the recipients but in the midst of a period of cultural disruption, they enabled lonely young girls to give birth out of wedlock, thus decimating the habits and rituals that led to intact families.

Other policy failures came from the right. In the age of deregulation, giant chains like Walmart decimated local shop owners, and the networks of friendship and community they helped create. Global financial markets took over small banks, so that the local knowledge of a town banker was replaced by a manic herd of traders thousands of miles away.

Abroad, free-market experts flooded into Russia after the collapse of the Soviet Union. They offered mountains of advice on privatization but almost none on how to rebuild communal trust and law and order, which are the real seedbeds of prosperity. The United States invaded Iraq, believing that merely by replacing the nation's dictator and political institutions they could easily remake a nation. The invaders were oblivious to the psychological effects a generation of tyranny had wrought on Iraqi culture, the vicious hatreds that lurked just below its surface—circumstances that quickly produced an ethnic bloodbath.

Harold's list of failed policies went on and on: financial deregulation that assumed global traders needed no protection from their own emotional contagions; enterprise zones based on the suppositions that, if you merely reduced tax rates in inner cities, then local economies would thrive; scholarship programs designed to reduce college-dropout rates, which pretended the main problem was lack of financial aid, when in fact only about 8 percent of students are unable to complete college for purely financial reasons. The more important problems have to do with emotional disengagement from college and lack of academic preparedness, intangible factors the prevailing mind-set found it hard to factor and acknowledge.

In short, government had tried to fortify material development, but had ended up weakening the social and emotional development that underpins it. Government was not the only factor in the thinning of society. A cultural revolution had decimated old habits and traditional family structures. An economic revolution had replaced downtowns with big isolated malls with chain stores. The information revolution had replaced community organizations that held weekly face-to-face meetings with specialized online social networking where like found like. But government policy had unwittingly played a role in all these changes.

The result was the diminution of social capital that Robert Putnam described in *Bowling Alone* and other books. People became more loosely affiliated. The webs of relationship that habituate self-restraint, respect for others, and social sympathy lost their power. The effects were sometimes liberating for educated people, who possessed the social capital to explore the new loosely knit world, but they were devastating for those without that sort of human capital. Family structures began to disintegrate, especially for the less educated. Out-of-wedlock births skyrocketed. Crime rose. Trust in institutions collapsed.

The state had to step in in an attempt to restore order. As British philosopher Phillip Blond has written, the individualist revolutions did not end up creating loose, free societies. They produced atomized societies in which the state grows in an attempt to fill the gaps created by social disintegration. The fewer informal social constraints there are in any society, the more formal state power there has to be. In Britain you wound up with skyrocketing crime rates, and, as a result, four million security cameras. Neighborhoods disintegrated and the welfare state stepped in, further absorbing or displacing the remaining social-support networks. A careening market, unconstrained by the traditions or informal standards, required intrusive prosecutors to police them. As Blond observed, "Look at the society we have become: We are a bipolar nation, a bureaucratic centralized state that presides over an increasingly fragmented, disempowered and isolated citizenry."

Without a healthy social fabric, politics became polarized. One party came to represent the state. The other came to represent the market. One party tried to shift power and money to government; the other tried to shift those things to vouchers and other market mechanisms. Both of them neglected and ignored the intermediary institutions of civil life.

In socially depleted nations, many people began to form their personal identities around their political faction. They had nothing else to latch on to. Politicians and media polemicists took advantage of the psychic vacuum and turned parties into cults, demanding and rewarding complete loyalty to the tribe.

Once politics became a contest pitting one identity group against another, it was no longer possible to compromise. Everything became a status war between my kind of people and your kind of people. Even a small concession came to seem like moral capitulation. Those who tried to build relationships across party lines were ostracized. Among politicians, loyalty to the party overshadowed loyalty to institutions like the Senate or the House. Politics was no longer about trade-offs, it was a contest for honor and group supremacy. Amidst this partisan ugliness, public trust in government and political institutions collapsed.

In a densely connected society, people can see the gradual chain of institutions that connect family to neighborhood, neighborhood to town, town to regional association, regional associations to national associations, and national associations to the federal government. In a stripped-down society, that chain has been broken and the sense of connection gets broken with it. The state seems at once alien and intrusive. People lose faith in the government's ability to do the right thing most of the time and come to have cynical and corrosive attitudes about their national leaders.

Instead of being bound by fraternal bonds, and occasionally responding to a call for joint sacrifice, a cynical "grab what you can before the other guys steal it" mentality prevails. The result is skyrocketing public debt and a public unwilling to accept the sacrifice of either tax increases or spending cuts required for fiscal responsibility. Neither side trusts the other to hold up their end of any deal. Neither party believes the other would honestly participate in truly shared sacrifice. Without social trust, the political system devolves into a brutal shoving match.

The Soft Side

Harold believed that the cognitive revolution had the potential to upend these individualistic political philosophies, and the policy approaches that grew from them. The cognitive revolution demonstrated that human beings emerge out of relationships. The health of a society is determined by the health of those relationships, not by the extent to which it maximizes individual choice.

Therefore, freedom should not be the ultimate end of politics. The ultimate focus of political activity is the character of the society. Political, religious, and social institutions influence the unconscious choice architecture undergirding behavior. They can either create settings that nurture virtuous choices or they can create settings that undermine them. While the rationalist era put the utility-maximizing individual at the center of political thought, the next era, Harold believed, would put the health of social networks at the center of thought. One era was economo-centric. The next would be socio-centric.

The socio-centric intellectual currents, he hoped, would restore character talk and virtue talk to the center of political life. You can pump money into poor areas, but without cultures that foster self-control, you won't get social mobility. You can raise or lower tax rates, but without trust and confidence, companies won't form and people will not invest in one another. You can establish elections but without responsible citizens, democracy won't flourish. After a lifetime spent designing and writing about public policy, the criminologist James Q. Wilson arrived at this core truth: "At root, in almost every area of public concern, we are seeking to induce persons to act virtuously, whether as schoolchildren, applicants for public assistance, would-be lawbreakers or voters and public officials."

On his wall, Harold had tacked another quotation, from Benjamin Disraeli: "The spiritual nature of man is stronger than codes or constitutions. No government can endure which does not recognize that for its foundation, and no legislation last which does not flow from this foundation."

Everything came down to character, and that meant everything came down to the quality of relationships, because relationships are the seedbeds of character. The reason life and politics are so hard is that relationships are the most important, but also the most difficult, things to understand.

In short, Harold entered a public-policy world in which people were used to thinking in hard, mechanistic terms. He thought he could do some good if he threw emotional and social perspectives into the mix.

Socialism

As Harold worked his way through the process of discovering how his basic suppositions applied to the world of politics and policy, he came to lament the fact that the word "socialism" was already taken. The nineteenth- and twentieth-century thinkers who had called themselves socialists weren't really socialists. They were statists. They valued the state over society.

But true socialism would put social life first. He imagined that the cognitive revolution could foster more communitarian styles of politics. There would be a focus on the economic community. Did people in different classes have a sense they were joined in a common enterprise, or were the gaps between classes too wide? There would be a focus on the common culture. Were the core values of the society expressed and self-confidently reinforced? Were they reflected in the nation's institutions? Did new immigrants successfully assimilate? In the political sphere Harold imagined, conservatives would emphasize that it is hard for the state to change culture and character. Liberals would argue that we still, in pragmatic ways, have to try. Both would speak the language of fraternity, and inspire with a sense that we are all in this together.

Harold didn't really know whether he should call himself a liberal or a conservative at this point. One of his guiding principles was drawn from a famous quotation from Daniel Patrick Moynihan: "The central conservative truth is that it is culture, not politics, that determines the success of a society. The central liberal truth is that politics can change a culture and save it from itself."

He did know that his job in Washington was to show the locals that character and culture really shape behavior, and that government could, in limited ways, shape culture and character. State power is like fire—warming when contained, fatal when it grows too large. In his view, government should not run people's lives. That only weakens the responsibility and virtue of the citizens. But government could influence the setting in which lives are lived. Government could, to some extent, nurture settings that serve as nurseries for fraternal relationships. It could influence the spirit of the citizenry.

Part of that is done simply by performing the elemental tasks of the state, establishing a basic framework of order and security—defending against external attack, regulating economic activity to punish predators, protecting property rights, punishing crime, upholding rule of law, providing a basic level of social insurance and civic order.

Some of this is done by reducing the programs that weaken culture and character. The social fabric is based on the idea that effort leads to reward. But very often, government rewards people who have not put in the effort. It does this with good intentions (the old welfare programs that discouraged work) and it does it with venal intentions (lobbyists secure earmarks, tax breaks, and subsidies so their companies can secure revenue without having to earn it in the marketplace). These programs weaken social trust and public confidence. By separating effort from reward, they pollute the atmosphere. They send the message that the system is rigged and society is corrupt.

But Harold thought government, properly led, could also play a more constructive role. Just as remote and centralized power creates a servile citizenry, decentralized power and community self-government creates an active and cooperative citizenry. Infrastructure projects that create downtown hubs strengthen relationships and spur development. Charter schools bring parents together. Universities that are active beyond campus become civic and entrepreneurial hot spots. National service programs bring people together across class lines. Publicly funded, locally administered social-entrepreneurship funds encourage civic activism and community-service programs. Simple and fair tax policies rouse energies, increase dynamism, lift the animal spirits, and encourage creative destruction.

Aristotle wrote that legislators habituate citizens. Whether they mean to or not, legislators encourage certain ways of living and discourage other ways. Statecraft is inevitably soulcraft.

Experiments in Thinking

Harold began writing a series of essays for policy journals on what his soft side approach might mean in the real world. All his essays had a common theme: How the fracturing of unconscious bonds was at the root of many social problems and how government could act to repair this tear in the social fabric.

He began in areas as far removed as possible from the gushy world of emotion and relationships. His first essay was about global terrorism. Many commentators had originally assumed that terrorism was a product of poverty and a lack of economic opportunity. It was a problem with material roots. But research into the backgrounds of terrorists established that, according to one database, 75 percent of the anti-Western terrorists come from middle-class homes and an amazing 63 percent had attended some college. The problem is not material but social. The terrorists are, as Olivier Roy argues, detached from any specific country and culture. They are often caught in the no-man's-land between the ancient and modern. They invent a make-believe ancient purity to give their lives meaning. They take up violent jihad because it attaches them to something. They are generally not politically active before they join terror groups, but are looking for some larger creed to give their existence shape and purpose. That choice can only be prevented if there are other causes to give them a different route to fulfillment.

Then Harold wrote about military strategy, the essence of guns-and-mayhem machismo. Harold described how military officers in Iraq and Afghanistan had found that it was impossible to defeat an insurgency on the battlefield by simply killing as many of the bad guys as possible. The only route to victory, they had learned, was through a counterinsurgency strategy called COIN, which started with winning the trust of the population. The soldiers and marines discovered that it was not enough to secure a village; they had to hold it so that people could feel safe; they had to build schools, medical facilities, courts, and irrigation ditches; they had to reconvene town councils and give power to village elders. It was only when this nation-building activity was well along that the local societies would be strong enough and cohesive enough to help them provide intelligence about and repel the enemy. Harold pointed out that the hardest political activity—warfare— depended on the softest social skills—listening, understanding, and building trust. Victory in this kind of war is not about piling up dead bodies; it is about building communities.

His next essay was about global AIDS policy. The West had thrown great technical knowledge at this problem and produced drugs that could help treat this plague. But the effectiveness of these drugs was limited if people continued to engage in the behaviors that lead to the disease.

Harold pointed out that technical knowledge alone would not change behavior. Raising awareness is necessary but insufficient. Surveys show that vast majorities in the most severely afflicted countries understand the dangers of HIV, but they behave in risky ways anyway. Providing condoms is necessary but insufficient. Most people in these countries have access to condoms. But that doesn't mean they actually use them, as rising or stable infection rates demonstrate. Economic development, too, is necessary but insufficient. The people who most aggressively spread the disease—often miners or truck drivers—are relatively well off. Providing health-care facilities is also necessary but insufficient. Harold described a hospital in Namibia where 858 women were receiving treatments. After a year of effort, they could get only five of their male partners to come in for testing. Though it meant a death sentence, the men would not come to the hospital. In their culture, men did not go near hospitals.

Harold visited a village in Namibia where all the middle-aged people were dead from AIDS. The children had nursed their parents into their graves. And yet, against all the most primal incentives of survival, the children were replicating the exact same behaviors that had led to their parents' deaths. He pointed out that the cause of this behavior defied all logic, as well as the principle of rational self-interest as commonly understood. The programs that actually changed behavior did not focus primarily upon logic and self-interest. The programs that worked best tried to change an entire pattern of life. They didn't merely try to change decisions about safe sex. They tried to create virtuous people, who would not put themselves in the path of temptation. These programs were often led by religious leaders. These men and women spoke in the language of right and wrong, of vice and virtue. The people leading these programs spoke the language of "ought." They talked about salvation and biblical truth, and safer sexual activity was a byproduct of a much larger change in outlook.

This is a language unaddressed by technical knowledge. It's a language that has to be spoken by an elder, a neighbor, by people who know one another's names. Harold pointed out that the West has thrown a tremendous amount of medical and technical knowledge at the HIV/AIDS problem, but not enough moral and cultural knowledge, the kind of knowledge that changes lives, viewpoints, and morality, and through those larger patterns alters the unconscious basis of behavior.

Then Harold got closer to home. He described how suburbia had strained community bonds across modern America. He pointed out that, in the 1990s, developers built vast, exurban housing developments. In those days if you asked home buyers what they wanted in their development, they said a golf course—the sign of status. But if a decade later you asked people what they wanted, they said a community center, a coffee shop, a hiking trail, and a health club. These folks had overshot the mark. They moved out to far-flung suburbs to get their piece of the American dream, which they equated with big property, but they missed the social connections that come from living in more densely populated areas. So the market had partially responded, with pseudo-urban streetscapes in the middle of the sprawl—dense downtown areas where people could stroll and eat at sidewalk cafés.

Social Mobility

Harold's biggest research project was about social mobility. His basic premise was that over the past few decades scholars had spent too much time thinking about globalization, the movement of goods and ideas across borders. Globalization, he thought, was not the central process driving change. For example, according to the U.S. Bureau of Labor Statistics, offshore outsourcing was responsible for only 1.9 percent of layoffs in the first decade of the twenty-first century, despite all the talk and attention. According to Pankaj Ghemawat of Harvard Business School, 90 percent of fixed investment around the world is domestic.

The real engine of change, Harold believed, was a change in the cognitive load. Over the past few decades, technological and social revolution had put greater and greater demands on human cognition. People are now compelled to absorb and process a much more complicated array of information streams. They are compelled to navigate much more complicated social environments. This is happening in both localized and globalized sectors, and it would be happening if you tore up every free-trade deal ever inked.

The globalization paradigm emphasizes the fact that information can travel 15,000 miles in an instant. But the cognitive-load paradigm holds that the most important part of the journey is the last few inches—the space between a person's eyes or ears and the various regions of the brain. Through what sort of lens does the individual perceive the information? Does the individual have the capacity to understand the information? Does he or she have the training to exploit it? What emotions and ideas does the information set off? Are there cultural assumptions that distort or enhance the way it is understood?

This change in the cognitive load has had many broad effects. It has changed the role of women, who are able to compete equally in the arena of mental skill. It has changed the nature of marriage, as men and women look for partners who can match and complement each other's mental abilities. It has led to assortative mating, as highly educated people marry each other and less-educated people marry each other. It has also produced widening inequality, so that societies divide into two nations—a nation of those who possess the unconscious skills to navigate this terrain and a nation of those who have not had the opportunity to acquire those skills.

Over the past decades there has been a steady rise in the education premium, the economic rewards that go to people with more education. In the 1970s it barely made economic sense to go to college, some argued. There wasn't a big difference in the income levels of college grads and non–college grads. But starting in the early 1980s, the education premium started to grow and it hasn't stopped. Today, money follows ideas. The median American with a graduate degree is part of a family making $93,000 a year. The median person with a college degree is in a family making $75,000. The median person with a high-school degree is in a family making $42,000 and the average high school dropout is in a family making $28,000.

Moreover, there is a superstar effect, even at the top. People who possess unique mental abilities become prized; their salaries soar. People with decent education but fungible mental traits become commodities. Their salaries trudge slowly upward or even stagnate.

These mental abilities tend to get passed down in families, and so you get an inherited meritocracy. It doesn't matter as much as it did in the 1950s whether you were born into an old Protestant family whose ancestors came over on the *Mayflower*. But it still matters a great deal what family you were born into, maybe more than ever. A child born into a family making $90,000 has a 50 percent chance of graduation from college by age twenty-four. A child born into a family making $70,000, has a one-in-four chance. A child born into a family making $45,000 has a one-in-ten chance. A child born into a family making $30,000 has a one-in-seventeen chance.

Elite universities become bastions of privilege. Anthony Carnevale and Stephen Rose surveyed the top 146 U.S. colleges and found that only 3 percent of the students there came from families in the bottom economic quartile. Seventy-four percent of students came from families in the top quartile.

A healthy society is a mobile society, one in which everybody has a shot at the good life, in which everybody has reason to strive, in which people rise and fall according to their deserts. But societies in the cognitive age produce their own form of inequality, lodged deep in the brains of the citizenry, which is more subtle than ancient class distinctions under feudalism, but nearly as stark and unfair.

Harold pointed out that most nations have tried to battle this problem, spending a lot of money in the process. The United States has spent over a trillion dollars to try to reduce the achievement gap between white and black students. Public-education spending per pupil increased by 240 percent in real terms between 1960 and 2000. Major universities offer lavish aid packages and some of the richest, like Harvard, waive tuition entirely for those from families making less than $60,000 a year. The United States spends enough money on antipoverty programs to hand every person in poverty a check for $15,000 a year. A mother with two kids would get a $45,000 check every year if the programs were converted into a simple transfer.

But money can't solve the problem of inequality because money is not the crucial source of the problem. The problem is in the realm of conscious and unconscious development. Harold needed only to compare his upbringing to Erica's to see this. Some children are bathed in an atmosphere that encourages human-capital development—books, discussion, reading, questions, conversations about what they want to do in the future—and some children are bathed in a disrupted atmosphere. If you read part of a story to kindergarten children in an affluent neighborhood, about half of them will be able to predict what will happen next in the story. If you read the same fragment to children in poor neighborhoods, only about 10 percent will be able to anticipate the flow of events. The ability to construct templates about the future is vitally important to future success.

In 1964, before the cognitive age had truly kicked in, rich families and poor families were demographically similar, which meant that children up and down the income scale began adulthood with similar outlooks and capacities. But as more and more demands were put on mental processing, gaps opened up and more-educated children grow up in different landscapes than less-educated children. More-educated children live amidst virtuous feedback loops. High skills and stable families lead to economic success, which makes stable family life easier, which makes skill acquisition and future economic success easier. Less-educated children live amidst vicious feedback loops. Low skills and family breakdown leads to economic stress, which makes family breakdown even more likely, which makes skill acquisition and economic security even harder to achieve.

Today college-educated and non–college-educated people inhabit different landscapes. Over two-thirds of middle-class children are raised in intact two-parent families, while less than a third of poor children are raised in them. About half the students in community colleges have either been pregnant or gotten somebody pregnant. Isabel Sawhill has calculated that if family structures were the same today as they were in 1970, then the poverty rate would be roughly one-quarter lower than it is today.

Vast attitudinal gaps have opened up as well. As Robert Putnam has shown, college-educated people are much more likely to trust the people around them. They are much more likely to believe they can control their own destinies and to take actions in order to achieve their goals.

People on both sides of the divide tend to want the same things. The highly educated and the less-educated tend to want to live in stable two-parent homes. They tend to want to earn college degrees and have their children surpass them. It's just that the more-educated have more emotional resources to actually execute these visions. If you get married before having children, graduate from high school, and work full-time, there is a 98 percent chance that you will not live in poverty. But many people are unable to achieve these things.

As Harold conducted his research on poverty, family disruption, and other issues related to social mobility, he sometimes wanted to just shake people and tell them to get their act together. Show up for the job interview. Take the SAT test you registered for. Study for the final so you can graduate from college. Don't quit your job just because it's boring or because you've got a minor crisis at home. He knew that at some level there is no substitute for individual responsibility and no prospect for success unless people are held accountable for their decisions and work relentlessly to achieve their goals.

On the other hand, he knew it was no good to just give bootstrap sermons. Flourishing depends on unconscious skills that serve as a prerequisite for conscious accomplishments. People who haven't acquired those unconscious skills find it much harder to fall into a workday routine and trudge off to a job each morning even if they don't really feel like it. It will be harder for them to be polite toward a boss who drives them crazy, to smile openly when they meet a new person, to present a consistent face to the world, even as they go through different moods and personal crises. They'll find it hard to develop a fundamental faith in self-efficacy—a belief that they can shape the course of their life. They'll be less likely to have confidence in the proposition that cause leads to effect, that if they sacrifice now, something good will result.

Then there are the psychic effects of inequality itself. In their book *The Spirit Level*, Richard Wilkinson and Kate Pickett argue that the mere fact of being low on the status totem pole brings its own deep stress and imposes its own psychic costs. Inequality and a feeling of exclusion causes social pain, which leads to more obesity, worse health outcomes, fewer social connections, more depression and anxiety. Wilkinson and Pickett point, for example, to a study of British civil servants. Some of the civil servants had high-status, high-pressure jobs. Others had low-status, low-pressure jobs. You'd think the people in the high-pressure jobs would have higher rates of heart disease, gastrointestinal disease, and general sickness. In fact, it was the people in the low-pressure jobs. Low status imposes its own costs.

With his soft-side approach, Harold put his faith in programs that reshaped the internal models in people's minds. If you felt, as Harold did, that in some low-income communities achievement values were not being transmitted from one generation to another, then you had no choice but to try to instill them. That meant you had to be somewhat paternalistic. If parents were not instilling these achievement values, then churches and charity groups should try. If those institutions were overwhelmed, then government should try to step in to help people achieve the three things they need to enter the middle class: marriage, a high-school degree, and a job.

"All of us need to be prodded to do things that will improve our long-term well-being, whether it is eating the right foods or setting aside funds for retirement," Ron Haskins and Isabel Sawhill write in their book *Creating an Opportunity Society*. "Low-income families are no different." There was no single policy that could build these unconscious skills. Human-capital policies are like nutrition. You have to instill them constantly. But Harold did see a sequence of policies that could help those who are cut off from the social-mobility ladder.

The biggest impact comes from focusing on the young. As James Heckman argues, learners learn and skill begets skill, so investments in children have much bigger payoffs than investments in people who are older. Parenting classes teach teenage moms how to care for their children. Nurse home visits help provide structure for disorganized families and provide on-the-job pointers for young mothers. Quality early-education programs have lasting effects on childhood development. Sometimes the IQ gains fade away as children from quality preschools enter the regular school population. But social and emotional skills do not seem to fade away, and those produce lasting gains—higher graduation rates and better career outcomes.

Integrated neighborhood approaches like the Harlem Children's Zone produce the most impressive results. These programs offer a deluge of different programs, all designed to put young people into a high-achieving counterculture. KIPP academies and other "no-nonsense" schools significantly improve their students' prospects. These schools, like the one Erica attended, give students a whole new way of living, much more disciplined and rigorous than they are used to.

The most important thing about any classroom is the relationship between a teacher and a student. Small classes may be better, but it's better to have a good teacher in a big class than a bad teacher in a small class. Merit pay for teachers should help keep talented teachers in the classroom. Students learn best from someone they love. Mentoring programs also create relationships. Students are much less likely to drop out of high school or college if they have an important person in their life, guiding them and encouraging them day by day. The City University of New York has a program called ASAP, which has an intensive mentoring component and seems to increase graduation rates.

The first generation of human-capital policies gave people access to schools, colleges, and training facilities. Second-generation policies would have to help them develop the habits, knowledge, and mental traits they needed to succeed there. It's not enough to give a student the chance to go to a community college if, once she gets there, she finds the requirements confusing, the guidance counselors rude and unavailable, the registration process baffling, the important courses already full, and the graduation requirements mysterious. These obstacles defeat students lacking social capital. Second-generation human-capital policies have to pay attention to the hidden curriculum of life as much as to the overt one.

A Nation of Grinders

The more time Harold spent thinking about politics and trying to form a governing philosophy, the more he realized that personal development and social mobility were at the heart of his vision of a great society. Social mobility opens up horizons because people can see wider opportunities and transformed lives. Social mobility reduces class conflict because no one is sentenced to spend their days in the caste into which they were born. Social mobility unleashes creative energies. It mitigates inequality, because no station need be permanent.

Harold found himself in a nation with two dominant political movements. There was a liberal movement that believed in using government to enhance equality. There was a conservative movement that believed in limited government to enhance freedom. But historically, there once had been another movement that believed in limited but energetic government to enhance social mobility. This movement had its start on a small Caribbean island a few hundred years ago.

In the eighteenth century, there was a little boy who lived on the island of St. Croix in the Caribbean. His father abandoned him when he was ten. His mother died in the bed next to him when he was twelve. He was adopted by a cousin, who promptly committed suicide. His remaining family consisted of an aunt, an uncle, and a grandmother. They all died within a few years. A probate court came in and confiscated the small bit of property he had inherited from his mother. He and his brother were left destitute, orphaned, and alone.

By seventeen, Alexander Hamilton was managing a trading firm. By twenty-four, he was George Washington's chief of staff and a war hero. By thirty-four, he had written fifty-one essays of *The Federalist Papers* and was New York's most successful lawyer. By forty, he was stepping down as the most successful treasury secretary in American history.

Hamilton created a political tradition designed to help young strivers like himself. He hoped to create a nation where young ambitious people could make full use of their talents, and where their labor would build a great nation. "Every new scene, which is opened to the busy nature of man to rouse and exert itself, is the addition of a new energy to the general stock of effort."

"Rouse" . . . "exert" . . . "energy." These are Hamiltonian words. He promoted policies designed to nurture this dynamism. At a time when many people were suspicious of manufacturing and believed that only agriculture produced virtue and wealth, Hamilton championed industry and technological change. At a time when traders and financial markets were disdained by the plantation oligarchy, Hamilton promoted vibrant capital markets to stir the nation. At a time when the economy was broken into local fiefdoms, run by big landowners, Hamilton sought to smash local monopolies and open opportunity. He nationalized the Revolutionary War debt, creating capital markets, and binding the nation's economy into one more competitive exchange. He believed in using government to enhance market dynamism by fostering competition.

The Hamiltonian tradition was carried on in the early nineteenth century by Henry Clay and the Whig Party, which championed canals and railroads and other internal improvements to open up opportunity and bind the nation. That cause was taken up by a young Whig, Abraham Lincoln. Like Hamilton, Lincoln had grown up in a poor family and was fired by an ambition that knew no rest. But Lincoln gave more speeches about labor and economics than he did about slavery, and sought to create a nation that would welcome self-transformation and embrace the gospel of work.

"I hold the value of life is to improve one's condition," he told an audience of immigrants in 1861. Under his leadership, the Civil War–era government unified the currency, passed the Homestead Act, the Land Grant College Act, and railroad legislation. These policies were designed to give Americans an open field and a fair chance to spread the spirit of enterprise, enhance social mobility, and so build the nation.

The next great figure in this tradition was Theodore Roosevelt. He, too, believed in the character-building force of competition, its ability to produce people who possessed the vigorous virtues he lauded in his 1905 inaugural address—energy, self-reliance, and initiative.

Roosevelt, too, believed that government must sometimes play an active role in encouraging the strenuous life and giving everyone a fair chance in the race. "The true function of the state, as it interferes in social life," he wrote, "should be to make the chances of competition more even, not to abolish them."

This Hamiltonian tradition dominated American politics for many decades. But in the twentieth century, it faded. The big debate of the twentieth century was over the size of government. The Hamiltonian tradition sat crosswise to that debate.

But Harold came to believe it was time to revive that limited but energetic government tradition—with two updates. Hamiltonians of the past lived before the dawning of the cognitive age, when the mental demands on young strivers were relatively low. That situation had changed, and so a movement that sought to enhance social mobility would have to handle the more complicated social and information environments. Furthermore, Hamilton, Lincoln, and Roosevelt had been able to assume a level of social and moral capital. They took it for granted that citizens lived in tight communities defined by well-understood norms, a moral consensus, and restrictive customs. Today's leaders could not make that assumption. The moral and social capital present during those years had eroded, and needed to be rebuilt.

Harold spent his years in Washington championing a Hamiltonian approach that offered second-generation human capital policies. He never developed what you might call an ideology, an all-explaining system of good government. The world was too complex an organism for that, too filled with a hidden tangle of latent functions for some hyper-confident government to come in and reshape according to some pre-fab plan.

Nor did he have a heroic vision of political leadership. Harold had a more constrained image of what government can and should do. The British philosopher Michael Oakeshott was issuing a useful warning against hubris when he wrote, "In political activity, then, men sail a boundless and bottomless sea; there is neither harbor for shelter nor floor for anchorage, neither starting place nor appointed destination. The enterprise is to keep afloat on an even keel; the sea is both friend and enemy; and the seamanship consists in using the resources of a traditional manner of behavior in order to make a friend of every hostile occasion."

When thinking about government Harold tried to remind himself how little we know and can know, how much our own desire for power and to do good blinds us to our own limitations.

But he did, like most Americans, believe in progress. Thus, while he had an instinctive aversion to change that alters the fundamental character of society, he had an affection for reform that repairs it.

He spent those years writing his essays, peppering the world with his policy proposals. Not many people seemed to agree with him. There was a *New York Times* columnist whose views were remarkably similar to his own, and a few others. Still, he plugged away, feeling that he was mostly right about things and that someday others would reach the conclusions he had reached. Karl Marx once said that Milton wrote *Paradise Lost* the way a silkworm produces silk, as the unfolding of his very nature. Harold felt fulfilled during his think-tank years. He wasn't always happy when Erica would disappear for weeks at a time, but he felt he was making some contribution to the world. He was confident that his "socialist" approach, in one guise or another, would someday have a large impact on the world.

CHAPTER 21

THE OTHER EDUCATION

EVERY WINTER THE GREAT AND THE GOOD MEET IN DAVOS, Switzerland, for the World Economic Forum. And every night during that week at Davos, there are constellations of parties. The people in the outer-ring parties envy the people in the mid-ring parties, and the people in the mid ring wish they were invited to the ones in the inner ring. Each ring features a slightly more elevated guest list than the last—with economists and knowledgeable people on the outside and ascending levels of power, fame, and lack of expertise toward the center.

At the molten core of the party constellation, there is always one party that forms the social Holy of the Holies—where former presidents, cabinet secretaries, central bankers, global tycoons, and Angelina Jolie gather to mingle and schmooze. And this party is without question the dullest in the whole constellation. The Davos social universe, like social universes everywhere, consists of rings of interesting and insecure people desperately seeking entry into the realm of the placid and self-satisfied.

After a few decades of business success and eight years of ever more prominent public service—as deputy chief of staff during the first Grace term and commerce secretary in the second—Erica had gained entry to the Davos epicenter. She was the sort who got invited to all the most exclusive and boring parties.

In retirement, she now served on worthy commissions on intractable problems—deficit spending, nuclear proliferation, the trans-Atlantic alliance, and the future of global trade agreements. She was not one of those people whose face lights up at the sound of the words "plenary session," but she had become a battle-hardened summiteer—able to withstand barrages of eminent tedium. She had become friends or acquaintances with the former world leaders who also sat on these commissions and who traveled during the year from Davos to Jackson Hole to Tokyo and beyond to express grave concern about the looming crises that people still in power were too shortsighted to solve.

At first, Erica had been anxious and self-conscious when chatting with former presidents and global celebrities. But the awe fell away pretty quickly, and now it was just like the same old knitting circle gathered once again at a different world resort. One former minister had resigned in disgrace, a president had been a complete flop in office, a former secretary of state had been gracelessly pushed from power. Everybody's sore spots were avoided, and all was forgiven in the rough-and-tumble world they had endured.

And as for their conversation . . . well, it was a conspiracy buff's worst nightmare. It transpires that when the people in charge of the world's great institutions get together, what they really want to talk about is golf, jet-lag remedies, and gallstones. The days were consumed with portentous concern over the threat of rising protectionism, and the nights by intense stories about prostates. The meetings operated on what was called the Chatham House Rule, which meant that nobody was permitted to say anything interesting. The highlight of the nightly conversations was the occasional tale of backroom idiocy.

Former world leaders inevitably have a repertoire of backroom stories that they use to entertain people at dinner parties. One former president told the story of the time he made the mistake of bragging about his dog to Russian leader Vladimir Putin. During the next Moscow summit, Putin entered at lunch with four Rottweilers, and bragged, "Bigger, faster, and stronger than yours." That led a former National Security Advisor to tell the story of the time Putin stole his ring. He'd been wearing his West Point graduation ring at a meeting. Putin asked to see it and put it on his own finger, and then deftly slipped it into his pocket while they were talking. The State Department raised a ruckus trying to get it back, but Putin wouldn't give. Another prime minister told of the time he snuck out of a cocktail party at Buckingham Palace to snoop around the private quarters and got caught and screamed at by the queen. Stories like those were always delicious and left the impression that world affairs are controlled by third graders.

Erica nonetheless enjoyed this whirl. She thought the commissions did some good, despite their insipidness. And she enjoyed her continued glimpses into the inner workings of world affairs. She often would sit back in the middle of some long meeting and wonder how it was that these men and women had risen to the top of the global elite. They weren't marked by exceptional genius. They did not have extraordinarily deep knowledge or creative opinions. If there was one trait the best of them possessed, it was a talent for simplification. They had the ability to take a complex situation and capture the heart of the matter in simple terms. A second after they located the core fact of any problem, their observation seemed blindingly obvious, but somehow nobody had simplified the issue in quite those terms beforehand. They took reality and made it manageable for busy people.

As for herself, Erica had reached a status plateau. She had reached a certain eminence. She was treated as a significant person wherever she went. Strangers would approach and say they were honored to meet her. This didn't make her feel happy by itself, but it did mean that she was no longer gnawed by the sort of ambition anxiety that had driven her through much of her life. Recognition and wealth, she had learned, do not produce happiness, but they do liberate you from the worries that plague people who lack but desire these things.

In outer appearance, Erica still thought of herself as the pushy young girl. She experienced those moments of shock, when she came upon her own face unexpectedly in the mirror and was stunned to find it was not the face of a twenty-two-year-old woman. It was the face of an older woman.

Now, she had trouble hearing women with high voices, and she had trouble hearing anyone at loud parties. She sometimes could not get out of low chairs without pushing herself up with her arms. Her teeth were darker than before and her gums had shrunk, leaving more of her teeth exposed. She had shifted to softer foods (the muscles around the jaw lose 40 percent of their mass over the course of a normal life).

In addition, she had begun holding the handrails when she descended a staircase. She heard stories of more elderly friends who had fallen and broken hips (of those who do, 40 percent end up in a nursing home and 20 percent never walk again). She had also begun taking an array of pills each day, and had broken down and bought one of those pill organizers.

Culturally, Erica felt mildly out of it. There were now a couple of generations of young movie starlets who she could not tell apart. Pop music trends had come and gone without really attracting her notice.

On the other hand, Erica felt that in her later years she had arrived at a more realistic appraisal of herself. It was as if she had achieved such a level of worldly security that she now could look realistically at her shortcomings. In this way, success had brought a humility that she had never felt before.

She had read the books and plays that treated old age as a remorseless slide into decrepitude. In *As You Like It*, Shakespeare's morose character, Jaques, calls old age "second childishness and mere oblivion." In the middle of the twentieth century developmental psychologists, when they treated old age at all, often regarded it as a period of withdrawal. The elderly slowly separate themselves from the world, it was believed, in preparation for death. They cannot be expected to achieve new transformations. "About the age of fifty," Freud wrote, "the elasticity of the mental processes on which treatment depends is, as a rule, lacking. Old people are no longer educable."

But Erica did not feel any of that, and indeed more-recent research has shown that seniors are completely capable of learning and growth. The brain is capable of creating new connections, and even new neurons, all through life. While some mental processes—like working memory, the ability to ignore distractions, and the ability to quickly solve math problems—clearly deteriorate, others do not. While many neurons die and many connections between different regions of the brain wither, older people's brains reorganize to help compensate for the effects of aging. Older brains might take longer to produce the same results, but they do tend to get the problems solved. One study of air traffic controllers found that thirty-year-olds had better memories than their older colleagues, but sixty-year-olds did just as well in emergency situations.

A series of longitudinal studies, begun decades ago, are producing a rosier portrait of life after retirement. These studies don't portray old age as surrender or even serenity. They portray it as a period of development—and they are not even talking about über-oldsters who take their coming mortality as a sign they should start parachuting out of airplanes.

Most people report being happier as they get older. This could be because as people age they pay less attention to negative emotional stimuli. Laura Carstensen of Stanford has found that older people are better able to keep their emotions in balance, and bounce back more quickly from negative events. John Gabrieli of MIT has found that in older people's brains the amygdala remains active when people are viewing positive images but is not active when people are viewing negative images. They've unconsciously learned the power of positive perception.

Gender roles begin to merge as people age. Many women get more assertive while many men get more emotionally attuned. Personalities often become more vivid, as people become more of what they already are. Norma Haan of Berkeley conducted a fifty-year follow-up of people who had been studied while young, and concluded that the subjects had become more outgoing, self-confident, and warm with age.

There's no evidence to suggest that people get automatically wiser as they get older. The tests, such as they are, that try to assess "wisdom" (a combination of social, emotional, and informational knowledge) suggest a kind of plateau. People achieve a level of competence on these tests in middle age, which holds steady until about age seventy-five.

But wisdom is the sort of quality that eludes paper-and-pencil tests, and Erica felt that she possessed skills in pseudo-retirement that she did not possess even in middle age. She felt she had a better ability to look at problems from different perspectives. She felt she was better at observing a situation without leaping to conclusions. She felt she was better at being able to distinguish between tentative beliefs and firm conclusions. That is to say, she was better able to accurately see the ocean of her own mind.

There was one thing she didn't experience much—a sense of being vividly alive. In the early days of her career, she'd be flown out to some Los Angeles hotel, put up in a suite by the client, and walk around the rooms giggling at the grandeur of it all. In those days, she would book an extra day in nearly every city she visited to experience the museums and the historic sights. She could remember those solitary walks around the Getty or the Frick, and the feeling of being transported by art. She remembered the special energy of her exalted moods—a night spent getting lost in Venice with a novel under her arm, or touring the old mansions in Charleston. Somehow that didn't happen anymore. She no longer booked the extra sightseeing days at the end of her trips—there was no time.

As her career got more demanding, her cultural activities got less so. Her poetic, artistic, and theatrical tastes had dropped from highbrow to middlebrow and below. "By the time we reach age fifty," University of Pennsylvania neuroscientist Andrew B. Newburg has written, "we are less likely to elicit the kinds of peak or transcendent experiences that can occur when we are young. Instead, we are more inclined to have subtle spiritual experiences, and refinements of our basic belief."

In addition, Erica's work had dragged her in a prosaic direction. She had a great talent for organization and execution. This had pulled her, over the course of her life, to become a CEO and a government official. It had pulled her into the world of process.

The number of her acquaintances multiplied over the years as the number of her true friendships diminished. The Grant Longitudinal Study found that people who were neglected in childhood are much more likely to be friendless in old age (in this way the working models submerge and then surface through life). Erica was not solitary. But sometimes she felt she lived in crowded solitude. She was around a shifting mass of semi-friends, but was without a small circle of intimates.

Over the years, in other words, she had become more superficial. She had been publicly active but privately neglectful. She had, over the course of her career, reorganized her own brain in ways that were perhaps necessary to professional achievement, but which were not satisfying now that her drive for worldly achievement had been fulfilled.

She entered retirement beset by a feeling of general numbness. It was as if there was a great battle she had never noticed before, a battle between the forces of shallowness and the forces of profundity. Over the years the forces of shallowness had staged a steady advance.

And then of course the river Styx was coming into view—death, pegging out, the final frontier. Erica did not think this would happen to her or Harold anytime soon. (Surely not. They were too healthy. They each could point to relatives who had lived into their nineties, though of course in reality such comforting correlations mean almost nothing.)

Nonetheless, her older acquaintances were dying at a regular rate. She could, if she chose, go on the Internet and find her morbidity odds—one in five women her age gets cancer; one in six gets heart disease; one in seven diabetes. It was a little like living in wartime; every few weeks another member of her social platoon was gone.

The effect was both terrorizing and energizing. (She seemed to live permanently in a state of mixed emotions.) The rushing presence of death changed her perception of time. Slowly a challenge formed in Erica's mind. Retirement would liberate her from the forces of shallowness. She could design her own neural diet, the influences and things that would flow into her brain. She could turn to deeper things. Now she could embark on a glorious lark.

Being Erica, she had to write out a business plan for herself. In the final chapter of her life, she wanted to live more vividly. She took out a legal pad and wrote a list of different spheres of her life: reflection, creativity, community, intimacy, and service. Under each category she wrote down a list of activities she could pursue.

She would like to write a short memoir. She'd like to master some new art form, to do something difficult and achieve some competence. She'd like to be a member of a circle of girlfriends who could come together every year to laugh and drink and share. She would like to find some way to teach the young. She'd like to learn the names of the trees so that when she walked through a forest she would know what she was seeing. She'd like to strip away the bullshit and find out whether or not she believed in God.

Mindfulness

In the first months of retirement, she had an urge to reconnect with old friends. She had not kept in touch with anyone from the Academy, and almost all of her friends from college had fallen away as well. But Facebook allowed her to remedy all that, and within weeks she was happily exchanging e-mails with friends from decades gone by.

Renewing these old friendships gave her pleasure beyond all reckoning. These contacts aroused parts of her own nature that had lain dormant. She discovered that one of her old college roommates, a southern woman named Missy, lived not twenty-five miles away from her, and one day they arranged to have lunch. Erica and Missy had lived together in their junior year, and though they shared a room, they had not grown particularly close. Erica was frantically busy in those days, and Missy, a premed student, had spent all her time in the library.

Missy was still thin and tiny. Her hair had gone gray, but her skin was still smooth. She'd become an eye surgeon, had a family, recovered from a double mastectomy, and had retired a few years ahead of Erica.

During lunch Missy excitedly described the passion that had transformed her life over the past few years: mindfulness meditation. Erica felt her stomach drop, expecting to hear stories of yogis, spiritual retreats at ashrams in India, and Missy resplendently getting in touch with her inner core—the normal New Age rigmarole. Missy had been the hardened scientist at school, and now she'd apparently gone to mush. But Missy talked about her meditations the way she used to talk about her homework assignments, with the same cool rigor.

"I sit cross-legged and upright on the floor," Missy was saying. "At first I concentrate on my breathing, anticipating the exhaling and inhaling, and then feeling my body fulfilling my anticipations. I feel my nostrils open and close, and my chest rise and fall. Then I center my thoughts on a word or phrase. I don't repeat it over and over again, I just keep it in the front of my mind, and if I find my thoughts wandering, I bring them back. Some people pick 'Jesus' or 'God' or 'Buddha' or 'Adonai,' but I just picked 'Diving within.'

"Then I watch to see what feelings and perceptions and images flow into my brain, letting the experience unfold naturally. It's like sitting still as various thoughts emerge into consciousness. Often in the beginning, I lose focus. I find myself thinking about my chores or the e-mails I have to answer. That's when I repeat my phrase. After a little while, most of the time, the outside world begins to fade back into the shadows. I don't even have to repeat the phrase anymore. I don't know how to describe it. I begin to be aware of awareness.

"My identity, my 'I-ness' fades away and I enter the sensations and feelings that are bubbling up from down below. The object is to welcome them nonjudgmentally, without interpreting them. Just welcome them as friends. Welcome them with a smile. One of my teachers compares it to watching clouds drift into a valley. These puffs of awareness float by, and they are replaced by other puffs and other mental states. It's like having access to processes that are there all along, but are usually unseen.

"I'm not doing a good job of putting it into words, because the whole point is that it is beneath words. When I try to describe it, it seems so stale and conceptual. But when I'm in that state there is no narrator. There's no interpreter. There are no words. I'm not really aware of time. I'm not telling myself a story about myself—the play-by-play announcer is gone. It's all sensations happening. Does that make any sense?"

Apparently Missy had found a way to directly perceive Level 1.

"When I come out of the state, I'm changed. I see the world differently. Daniel Siegel says it's like you've been walking through a forest at night, shining a flashlight to light your way. Suddenly you turn off the flashlight. You lose the bright beam of light on the narrow spot. But gradually your eyes start to adjust to the darkness, and you can suddenly see the whole scene.

"I used to assume that my emotions were me. But now I sort of observe them rising and floating through me. You realize that things you thought were your identity are really just experiences. They are sensations that flow through you. You begin to see that your ordinary ways of perceiving are only a few vantage points among many. There are other ways of seeing. You develop what the Buddhists call 'beginner's mind.' You see the world as a baby sees it, aware of everything all at once, without conscious selection and interpretation."

Missy said all this briskly over a salad, spearing her asparagus. Her description of mindfulness meditation suggested that in fact it is possible, with the right training, to peer beneath the waterline of consciousness, into the hidden kingdom. The normal conscious mind might see only colors in a small slice of the electromagnetic spectrum, but perhaps it was possible to widen the view and suddenly be able to see the rest of the actual world.

In fact, neuroscientists—who are generally a hardheaded lot—have profound respect for these sorts of meditative practices. They've hosted the Dalai Lama at their conferences, and some of them make their way to monasteries in Tibet precisely because there is an overlap between the findings of the science and the practices of the monks.

It's now clear that the visions and transcendent experiences that religious ecstatics have long described are not just fantasies. They are not just the misfirings caused by an epileptic seizure. Instead, humans seem to be equipped to experience the sacred, to have elevated moments when they transcend the normal boundaries of perceptions.

Andrew Newberg found that when Tibetan monks or Catholic nuns enter a period of deep meditation or prayer, their parietal lobes, the region of the brain that helps define the boundaries of our bodies, becomes less active. They experience a sensation of infinite space. Subsequent research found that Pentecostal worshipers undergo a different, though no less remarkable, brain transformation when they are speaking in tongues. Pentecostals do not have a sense of losing themselves in the universe. Their parietal lobes do not go dark. On the other hand, they do experience a decrease in memory functions and an increase in emotional and sensory activation. As Newberg writes, "In the

Pentecostal tradition, the goal is to be transformed by the experience. Rather than making old beliefs stronger, the individual is opening the mind in order to make new experiences more real." The different religious practices produce different brain states, each of which are consistent with the different theologies.

Brain scans don't settle whether God exists or not, because they don't tell you who designed these structures. They don't solve the great mystery, which is the mystery of consciousness—how emotion reshapes the matter in the brain and how the matter in the brain creates spirit and emotion. But they do show that people who become expert at meditation and prayer rewire their brains. It is possible, by shifting attention inward, to peer deep into the traffic of the unconscious, achieving an integration of conscious and unconscious processes, which some people call wisdom.

Missy glanced up from her salad from time to time, just to make sure Erica wasn't looking at her as if she were nuts. She was matter-of-fact, but also made clear how much these experiences meant to her. She kept apologizing for the inadequacies of her descriptions, her inability to really put into words what it felt like to perceive things holistically instead of deductively, and the feeling of expanded awareness. She wasn't sipping on some organic carrot shake while she was talking about all this. She hadn't gone all Yoko Ono. She was a surgeon, who still practiced part-time, who drove a gas-guzzling SUV and drank white wine with lunch. It's just that she had found a scientifically plausible way to access a deeper level of cognition.

Toward the end of lunch she asked Erica if she would like to come to her next session and try out this mindfulness-meditation stuff. Erica heard her mouth saying, "No thanks, it's not really for me." She didn't know why she answered this way. The idea of peering directly inside herself filled her with a deep aversion. All her life she had been looking outward and trying to observe the world. Hers had been a life of motion, not tranquility. The fact is she was afraid of looking directly inside. It was a pool of dark water she did not want to plunge into. If she was going to live more vividly, she'd have to find another way.

The Second Education

Over the next several months, Erica became something of a culture vulture—diving into the world of the arts with a voracious hunger and her characteristic drive. She read some books on the history of Western painting. She bought some poetry anthologies and found herself reading them in bed before she drifted off to sleep. She bought a CD course in classical music and listened to it while driving in her car. She began going to museums again with friends.

Like most people, life had given her one sort of education. She had gone to school. She had taken such and such management courses, worked her way through various jobs, and learned such and such skills. She had come to possess a certain professional expertise.

But now she was beginning her second education. This education was an emotional one, about how and what to feel. This second education did not work like the first one. In the first education, the information to be mastered walked through the front door and announced itself by light of day. It was direct. There were teachers to describe the material to be covered, and then everybody worked through it.

In the second education, there was no set curriculum or set of skills to be covered. Erica just wandered around looking for things she enjoyed. Learning was a by-product of her search for pleasure. The information came to her indirectly, seeping through the cracks of the windowpanes, from under the floorboards, and through the vents of her mind.

Erica read *Sense and Sensibility, The Good Soldier,* or *Anna Karenina* and she would find herself moving with the characters, imitating their states of mind, and discovering new emotional flavors. The novels, poems, paintings, and symphonies she consumed never applied directly to her life. Nobody was writing poems about retired CEOs. But what mattered most were the emotional sensations portrayed in them.

In his book *Culture Counts,* the philosopher Roger Scruton writes that "the reader of Wordsworth's 'Prelude' learns how to animate the natural world with pure hopes of his own; the spectator of Rembrandt's 'Night Watch' learns of the pride of corporations, and the benign sadness of civic life; the listener to Mozart's 'Jupiter' symphony is presented with the open floodgates of human joy and creativity; the reader of Proust is led through the enchanted world of childhood and made to understand the uncanny prophecy of our later griefs which those days of joy contain."

Even at her age, Erica was learning to perceive in new ways. Just as living in New York or China or Africa gives you a perspective from which to see the world, so, too, spending time in the world of a novelist inculcates its own preconscious viewpoint.

Through trial and error, Erica discovered her tastes. She thought she loved the Impressionists, but now they left her strangely unmoved. Maybe their stuff was too familiar. On the other hand, she became enraptured by the color schemes of the Florentine Renaissance and Rembrandt's homely, knowing faces. Each of them tuned her mind, the instrument with a million strings. She had some moments of pure pleasure, when she could feel her heart beating faster and a quiver in her stomach—standing in front of a painting, or discovering a new installation or poem. There was a time, reading Anthony Trollope of all people, when she could feel the emotions of the story in her own body, and was alive to the sensations produced there. "Mine is no callous shell," Walt Whitman wrote about his body, and Erica was beginning to appreciate what he meant.

The Dancing Scouts

Erica's experience with art is a microcosm of all the different kinds of perception we have seen in this story. Seeing and hearing were thick, creative processes, not just a passive taking in.

When you listen to a piece of music, for example, sound waves travel through the air at 1,100 feet per second and collide with your eardrums, setting off a chain of vibrations through the tiny bones of the ear, against the membrane of the cochlea; producing tiny electrical charges that reverberate all across the brain. Maybe you don't know anything about music in the formal sense, but all your life—from the time when you were nursing in rhythm with your mother—you have been unconsciously constructing working models of how music works. You have been learning how to detect timed patterns and anticipate what will come next.

Listening to music involves making a series of sophisticated calculations about the future. If the last few notes have had pattern Y, then the next few notes will probably have pattern Z. As Jonah Lehrer writes in his book *Proust Was a Neuroscientist*, "While human nature largely determines how we hear the *notes*, it is nurture that lets us hear the *music*. From the three-minute pop song to the five-hour Wagner opera, the creations of our culture teach us to expect certain musical patterns, which over time are wired into our brain."

When the music conforms to our anticipations, we feel a soothing drip of pleasure. Some scientists believe that the more fluently a person can process a piece of information, the more pleasure it produces. When a song or a story or an argument achieves limerence with the internal models of the brain, then that synchronicity produces a warm swelling of happiness.

But the mind also exists in a state of tension between familiarity and novelty. The brain has evolved to detect constant change, and delights in comprehending the unexpected. So we're drawn to music that flirts with our expectations and then gently plays jokes on them. As Daniel Levitin observes in *This Is Your Brain on Music*, the first two notes of "Over the Rainbow" arrest our attention with the jarring octave-gap between them, then the rest of the song eases us into a more conventional, soothing groove. In his book *Emotion and Meaning in Music*, Leonard Meyer showed how Beethoven would establish a clear rhythmic and harmonic pattern and then manipulate it, never quite repeating it. Life is change, and the happy life is a series of gentle, stimulating, melodic changes.

Perceiving a painting follows a similar process. First the mind creates the painting. That is to say, each eye makes a series of fast, complex saccades across the surface of the picture, which then get blended and re-created inside the cortex, producing a single image. There are parts of each view the mind cannot see, because of the blindspot in the middle of each eye where the optic nerve connects to the retina. The brain fills in the holes based on its own predictions. Simultaneously, the mind imposes its concepts upon the painting. For example, it imposes color. Depending on lighting and other factors, there are huge fluctuations in the wavelength energy of light bouncing off a painting, and yet the mind uses internal models to give the impression that the color on the surface is remaining constant. If the mind couldn't assign constant color to things, the world would be in chaotic flux and it would be hard to deduce any useful information from the environment.

How it creates this illusion of constant color is not well understood, but it seems to involve ratios. Imagine a green surface surrounded by yellows and blues and purples. The brain understands there is a constant ratio between the wavelengths bouncing off green and the wavelengths bouncing off yellow. It can assign constant qualities to each even amidst changing conditions. As Chris Frith of the University College, London, has written, "Our perception of the world is a fantasy that coincides with reality."

As it is creating the painting, the mind is also evaluating it. A wide body of research has found that there are certain tastes that most people share. As Denis Dutton argues in *The Art Instinct*, people everywhere gravitate to a similar sort of painting—landscapes with open spaces, water, roads, animals, and a few people. A cottage industry has grown up to investigate this preference. Evolutionary psychologists argue that people everywhere prefer paintings of landscapes that correspond to the African savanna, where humanity emerged. People generally don't like looking at dense vegetation, which is forbidding, or spare desert, which has no food. They like lush open grasses, with thickets of trees and bushes, a water source, diversity of vegetation including flowering and fruiting plants and an unimpeded view of the horizon in at least one direction. Some critics have noted that Kenyans prefer pictures of the Hudson River School to pictures of their own native landscape. That's because, the critics argue, the landscape near the Hudson River in New York state more closely resembles the African savanna back in the Pleistocene era than does the present, and much drier, Kenya.

More broadly, people like fractals, patterns that recur at greater levels of magnification. Nature is full of fractals: mountain ranges with peaks that gently echo one another, the leaves and branches on trees, a copse of aspens, rivers with their tributaries. People like the fractals that are gently flowing but not too complicated. Scientists even have a way to measure fractal density. Michael Gazzaniga illustrates the process in this example: Imagine that you were asked to draw a tree on a piece of paper. If you left the paper entirely blank, that would have a D (fractal density) of 1. If you drew a tree with so many branches the paper was entirely black, that would have a D of 2. Humans generally prefer patterns with a fractal density of 1.3—some complexity, but not too much.

Erica didn't have to think about fractals as she was looking at Vermeers or van Eycks or Botticellis. That's the point; her action was unconscious. She just stood there savoring the pleasure.

Creativity

After a while, Erica decided to create her own art. She tried photography and watercolors, but she found that she was unengaged and untalented. Then one day she found a beautiful piece of wood, and she fashioned it into a small cutting board. Having it around the house and using it every day gave her immense satisfaction, and for the next few years, as long as her hands could perform the tasks, she made simple household items out of wood.

She'd exercise in the pool in the morning and go for a walk, and then in the afternoons she would return to the little workshop she had built. Gene Cohen, founding chief of the Center on Aging at the National Institute of Mental Health has argued that the duration of an activity is more important than the activity itself: "In other words, a book club that meets on a regular basis over a course of months or years contributes a great deal more to a person's well-being than the same number of one-shot activities, such as movies, lectures or outings."

As she continued to carve, Erica found that she was building a repertoire of knowledge and skills. She had to observe the wood she had in
front of her—not the generic concept of wood, but the specific piece.
She had to divine what household item—napkin holder, a bookstand, or
even a piece of a table—lay in its grain.

At first she moved forward clumsily. But she'd walk through stores
and crafts fairs, observing how craftsmen worked. She didn't like the
whole "authenticity" atmosphere of the crafts movement. But she liked
the objects themselves and how they fit together. As she observed and
worked, she got better. She developed a set of hunches that guided her
along, a repertoire of feels and gestures. She was astonished to find that
she had her own style. She didn't know how she got it. She just fiddled
around with things until they seemed right.

Over and over again, Erica tried to do too much. This late in life she
still underestimated how long any project was likely to take her. But she
found herself enjoyably dissatisfied by her work. She got a glimpse of
some ideal thing she would want to create, and then she'd tinker and
tinker with it, never quite eliminating the tension between the reality
and the perfection she felt inside. But still she chased it. She understood
what Marcel Proust might have been feeling when he dictated new passages of a novel from his deathbed. He wanted to change a section in
which a character was dying, because now he knew how it really felt.

The muses came and went. After working for a few hours, she felt
her brain running dry, as if little carbonated bubbles in her brain had
been used up and everything had gone flat. She became clumsy, lazy and
stale. Then other times she would awake in the middle of the night, absolutely sure of what she should do to solve a problem. The mathematician Henri Poincaré solved one of the most difficult problems of his life
while stepping onto a bus. The answer just came to him. "I went on
with the conversation already commenced, but I felt a perfect certainty," he later wrote. Erica sometimes had little revelations like that,
too, while she was parking the car or making a cup of tea.

Like all artists and craftsmen, she was a plaything of the muses. Creativity seemed to happen in a hidden world beyond her control. The
poet Amy Lowell wrote, "An idea will come into my head for no appar-

ent reason; 'The Bronze Horses,' for instance. I register the horses as a good subject for a poem; and, having so registered them, I consciously thought no more about the matter. But what I had really done was to drop my subject into the subconscious, much as one drops a letter into the mailbox. Six months later, the words of the poem began to come into my head, the poem—to use my private vocabulary—was 'there.' "

Erica learned little tricks to stoke the unreachable furnace. Art, as Wordsworth put it, is emotion recollected in tranquility. Erica had to put herself in a state in which her emotions bubbled to the surface. She had to go see a thrilling play, or climb a mountain, or read a tragedy. Then, her heart a-tingle, she had to be relaxed enough to express the feelings welling up inside.

As she had gotten older, she found she needed long periods of uninterrupted solitude for her conscious mind to slowly relax and surrender itself to the pulses generated inside. One interruption could ruin her mind-set for an entire day.

She found that this creative mind-set was most likely to come late in the morning or early in the evening. She would work with her headphones on, playing soft classical music to loosen her thoughts. She needed to be near windows, with a view of distant horizons. For some reason she worked best in her dining room, which faced south, not in her studio.

She also learned that when you are trying something new, it is best to do it quickly and wrong, and then go back and do it over and over again. And at rare and precious moments, she even got a sense of what athletes and artists must have meant when they talked about being in the flow. The narrative voice in her head went silent. She lost track of time. The tool seemed to guide her. She integrated with her task.

What did she get out of all this? Did it improve her brain? Well, there is some evidence that children who participate in arts education experience a small IQ boost, just as there is some evidence that participating in music and drama classes seems to improve social skills. But these results are sketchy, and it is not true that just listening to Mozart or going to a museum will make you smarter.

Did Erica's creativity help her live longer? A bit. There is substantial evidence to suggest that mental stimulation improves longevity. People with college degrees live longer than people without, even after controlling for other factors. Nuns with college degrees live longer, even though their lifestyles through adulthood are the same as nuns without them. People with larger vocabularies in adolescence are less likely to suffer dementia in old age. According to one California study, seniors who participate in arts programs require fewer doctor visits, use fewer medications, and generally experience better health than seniors who don't.

But the real rewards were spiritual. It's said that people who go into therapy do it either because they need tightening (their behavior is too erratic) or because they need loosening (they are too repressed). Erica needed loosening. Reading poetry, visiting museums, and carving seemed to help her do it.

As she relaxed she became more patient, more of a wandering explorer. Summarizing a body of recent research, Malcolm Gladwell wrote that artists who succeed in their youth tend to be conceptual. Like Picasso, they start with a concept of what they want to achieve and then execute it. Those that thrive near the end of life tend to be exploratory. Like Cezanne, they don't start with clear conceptions, but go through a process of trial and error that eventually leads them to a destination.

This is not always a passive, gentle process. In 1972 the great art historian Kenneth Clark wrote an essay on what he called the "old-age style." Looking across the arts, and especially at Michelangelo, Titian, Rembrandt, Donatello, Turner, and Cezanne, he believed he could detect a common pattern that many great elderly artists shared: "A sense of isolation, a feeling of holy rage, developing into what I have called transcendental pessimism; a mistrust of reason, a belief in instinct. . . . If we consider old-age art from a more narrowly stylistic point of view, we find a retreat from realism, an impatience with established technique and a craving for complete unity of treatment, as if the picture were an organism in which every member shared in the life of the whole."

Erica obviously did not have these masters' genius, nor their inner turbulence. But she did have a desire to push hard through her final years and create surprises for herself. Erica found that the arts gave her access to her deeper regions. Artists take the sentiments that are buried in inchoate form across many minds and bring them to the surface for all to see. They express the collective emotional wisdom of the race. They keep alive and transmit states of mind from one generation to the next. "We pass on culture, therefore," Roger Scruton has written, "as we pass on science and skill: not to benefit the individual, but to benefit our kind, by conserving a form of knowledge that would otherwise vanish from the world."

You Are There

One summer, a couple of years after retirement, Harold and Erica took the best vacation of their lives. They traveled around France looking at cathedrals. Harold prepared for the trip for a few months, reading up on cathedral construction and medieval history, just as he had back at school. He put different passages of the books he was reading on his computer tablet, to take with him, and he planned an itinerary and outlined a narration for their entire voyage. His narration would be just like the old presentations he used to give at work, except this time he'd be talking about architecture and chivalry, and they'd be walking through towns and churches as he spoke.

Harold didn't spend a lot of time memorizing the names of the kings and the processions of battles. He operated under the assumption that each group and each age inadvertently produce their own symbolic system—buildings, organizations, teachings, practices, and stories—and then people live within the moral and intellectual structure of those symbols, without really thinking about it. So when Harold talked about medieval life, he was just trying to capture what it felt like to be the sort of person who lived at that time. As he put it, he wasn't describing the fish; he was describing the water they swam in.

Harold loved this sort of educational travel. He could touch and feel the past—the darkness of an old building in daytime, the mildew of a castle keep, the glimpse of a forest through the slit of a castle lookout. With these prompts flooding his mind, he could imaginatively enter into other ages.

They traveled through Caen and Reims and Chartres. They'd walk side by side, Harold whispering information from the books he had read, speaking as much for his own pleasure as for hers. "Life was more extreme then," he said at one point. "There were extremes of summer heat and winter cold, with few conveniences to temper them. There were extremes of light and darkness, health and sickness. Political boundaries were arbitrary and changed with the death of a king or lord. Government was hodgepodge with different mixtures of custom and Roman and Church law. One year could produce plenty and the next, famine, and it was possible to walk from one town where times were good to another where people were starving. One in three people were under fourteen and the life expectancy was forty, so there was no great throng of people in their forties, fifties, or sixties to sort of calm things down.

"As a result, their life was more emotionally intense than ours is today. On festival days, they celebrated with a drunken joy that we scarcely seem to know. On the other hand, they could succumb to mind-grabbing terror that we only remember from childhood. They were capable of enjoying tender love stories one moment and then cheering as a beggar was dismembered the next. Their perception of tears and suffering and color itself seems to have been more vivid. There were certain modulating ideas that we take for granted that they did not have in their mental toolbox. They didn't have a concept for diminished capacity, the idea that a mentally disabled person might not be fully responsible for his actions. They didn't have a concept for judicial fallibility, or for the idea that criminals should be rehabilitated instead of simply being made to suffer. For them it was all extremes—guilt or innocence, salvation or damnation."

Harold and Erica were walking through the village of Chartres as he said this, and crossing toward the cathedral. They walked across a square with coffee shops, and Harold described how the medieval Frenchmen of the twelfth century lived in squalor and filth, and yet yearned for an ideal world. They constructed elaborate codes of chivalry and courtly love. He described the intricate rules of courtesy that governed everyday court life, the profusion of rituals, the many organizations that required oaths and other sacred rites, the stately procession in which each participant in the social order had his or her own socially approved fabric, color scheme, and place.

"It was almost as if they were putting on a play for themselves. It was almost as if they were turning their short, squalid lives into a dream," Harold continued. He said that tournaments were supposed to be stylized, though in reality they were often shambolic brawls. Love was supposed to be stylized, though often it was just brutal rape. In imagination everything was turned into a mythical ideal version of itself, though in reality there was degradation and stench all around.

"They had a great yearning for beauty and a great faith in God and the ideal world. And somehow that great faith produced this," Harold said, gesturing up at the Chartres cathedral. He described how nobles and peasants would volunteer their labor to build the great church, how whole villages would move close to the cathedral town so they could help create these great edifices soaring above the normal hovels of wood and grass.

He described the intricate recurring patterns of tracery, the recursive rhythm of arches, the countless replicating folds of stone, each reflecting and magnifying the last. They spent an hour before the west front, tracing the symbols of the Trinity carved into the central door, the way Christ's body is connected to the signs of the zodiac and the labors of the month on the ascension door. As much as he could, Harold described the great bombardment of symbols and meaning that would have rained down on the illiterate pilgrims, setting off strings of associations and awe in their minds.

Inside, he described the revolutionary splendor of the design. Through most of history until the twelfth century, men had constructed buildings to be heavy and formidable. Now here they constructed buildings to be light and weightless. They used stones to create a feeling for the spiritual. "Man may rise to the contemplation of the divine through the senses," Abbot Suger wrote.

Harold loved teaching. He loved being a tour guide more than anything he had ever done. On odd occasions, talking about this or that historical scene, he'd find himself strangely moved. People in centuries past, he came to believe, devoted more energy to the sacred. They spent more time building sacred spaces, and practicing sacred rituals. They built gateways to a purer mode of existence. Harold was drawn to these ancient places and gateways—to ruins, cathedrals, palaces, and holy grounds—more than to any modern place or living city. In Europe especially, he divided cities between those that were living, like Frankfurt, and those that were dead, like Bruges and Venice. He liked the dead cities best.

After an hour or so inside the cathedral, Harold and Erica left and began walking back to dinner. As they did, they passed the west portals, and saw a range of statues arrayed about the doorways. Harold knew nothing about them. They were church elders of some sort. Or maybe donors, or scholars or heroes from the ancient past. Erica paused unexpectedly to look at them. Their bodies were elongated cylinders, with gracefully carved draping robes. Their gestures mimicked one another, one hand down around the waist and the other clutching something by the neck. But it was the faces that caught Harold's attention.

Some of the statues they had seen on the trip were generic and impersonal. The artists had tried to symbolize a person's face rather than represent a particular one. But these sculptures depicted real people, idiosyncratic and ensouled. Their faces held different expressions of selflessness, detachment, patience, and acquiescence. They were the product of a specific set of personal experiences and reflected a unique set of hopes and ideals. Though he was tired after a long day, Harold actually experienced a chill looking into those faces and eyes. He had the sensation that they saw him; that they sympathized with him and gazed at him gazing at them. Historians sometimes speak of moments of historical ecstasy, the feeling that magically comes over them when the distance of the centuries disappears, and they have the astonishing sensation of direct contact with the past. Harold felt something like that now, and Erica could see a glow on his cheeks.

It was a wonderful day, and an exhausting one. At nightfall they went to a restaurant and had a long, happy meal. Erica was struck by how enchanted the world seemed to people in the Middle Ages. For us, the night sky is filled with distant balls of fire and vast empty space. But for them, it was alive with creatures and magic. The stones of the church and the trees in the woods resonated with spirits, ghosts, and divine presences. The cathedrals were not just buildings—they were like spiritual powerhouses, places where heaven and earth met. People back then seemed voracious for mythology, she observed. They blended Greek, Roman, Christian, and pagan myths together, regardless of internal logic, and made everything alive. Even the bones of saints had magical powers. It was as if every material thing was crystallized with a spiritual presence; every aesthetic thing was also a sacred thing. Our world seems disenchanted in comparison, she thought with a sigh.

Harold mentioned how much fun he was having. Somehow knowledge only came alive to him when he was teaching it to somebody, and at the end he mused that maybe he'd missed his calling as a tour guide. Erica gave him an energized look. "Would you like to be?"

That night they hatched a plan. Harold would lead tours for small groups of cultivated travelers. Maybe they'd conduct three a year. He'd study a period for a few months, just as he had with the Middle Ages, and then take a group to France or Turkey or the Holy Land. They'd contract with a tour company so they wouldn't have to worry too much about the travel arrangements. Erica could run the rest of the operation. It would be their postretirement small business. Erica figured they could compete with the alumni groups that run these sort of tours, because theirs would be more intimate. They'd rely mostly on friends, so the travelers would pretty much know one another before they signed up.

And that's pretty much what happened for the next eight years. They created a company called You Are There Tours, which was like a traveling course in human civilization, with nice hotels and wine. They'd be at home for a few months and Harold would bury himself in his books, preparing. And then they'd take two weeks off with a group, getting an all-expenses-paid educational vacation in Greece or some other spot on the itinerary of human accomplishment. Harold loved it. For Harold, the preparation for the trips was actually better than the trips themselves. Three times a year, Erica got to experience intense bursts of learning. When she was on those trips, time would slow down. She'd notice a thousand novel things. It was like feeling the pores of her skin open.

Erica never got to the point in her life when she could really relax. She always had to be moving and doing and achieving. But this was a delicious sort of exertion. For someone who'd spent her life struggling and climbing, these trips were pure joy.

CHAPTER 22

MEANING

I T'S HARD TO KNOW WHEN THE IMMORTALS STARTED APPEARING on the mountains. You'd be hiking or biking or cross-country skiing outside of Aspen, Colorado, and from behind you'd hear this whoosh that sounded like an incoming F-18. You'd turn around and see this little nugget of Spandex. It was one of those superfit old guys who'd decided to go on a fitness jihad in retirement. He'd shrunk as he crossed age seventy, so he'd be four ten and ninety-five pounds of hard gristle wrapped in Spandex action gear. He'd be coming at you at ferocious speed, wearing weights on his wrists and ankles and a look of fierce determination on his small wrinkled face. You'd be huffing and puffing on the mountainside, and this superbuff Spandex senior would whiz by like a little iron Raisinette.

These old guys had succeeded at everything else they had ever tried, so they had simply decided to say a big Fuck You to death. Earlier in life, they had been the sort of ambitious young strivers who had started their first paper route at six, made their first million by twenty-two, and they'd married a string of beauties so that they had achieved this weird genetic phenomenon in which their grandmothers looked like Gertrude Stein but their granddaughters looked like Uma Thurman.

In their postretirement quest for eternal youth, they'd hired personal trainers, graduated from fitness boot camps, and spent much of their time at their resort homes strategizing about energy shakes, veggie-centric cuisine, and bone-marrow preservation. They could be counted upon to take up windsurfing at seventy, and K2 expeditions at seventy-five, and by ninety they'd be popping Cialis like breath mints and working out so furiously their fitness trainers would be dropping with coronaries just trying to keep up.

They had the time and means and focus to do all this because they'd entered their pluto-adolescence. When highly ambitious men make a lot of money and then retire to high-end vacation communities, they enter a phase of life in which they have the money, the time, and the mentality to make a profession out of all the puerile stuff they enjoyed at age eighteen. They don't actually have the energy levels they used to, but for brief bursts they are raging libidos with platinum Amex cards. They hang out with resort-town celebrities—George Hamilton, Kevin Costner, and Jimmy Buffett. They unsuccessfully flirt with young waitresses, then go home to the event planners they married as trophy wives a few decades ago and who have now in their fifties turned into modern American centaurs. Because cosmetic surgeons are apparently more proficient the lower down the body you get, these women have legs like Serena Williams but overstretched g-force cheeks and the stuffed-pillow lips.

It's become fashionable to be interested in education, so many of these guys have three homes, six cars, four mistresses, and five charter schools. They also spend a lot of time bonding with one another. If you go to a resort community, from Bridgehampton to Aspen to Malibu, you can see packs of these overly fit oldsters meeting on the sidewalk in the early evening on their way to a tapas restaurant.

None of them really wants to go to the tapas restaurant, which is filled with dishes they don't understand. But they are in the grip of some primordial New Urbanist force, and as modern cosmopolitan sophisticates, they are sentenced to endless tapas ordeals. They and everybody in their party will be condemned to spend ninety minutes wrestling with traditional date fritters, squid with aioli, saffron rice with cuttlefish and grilled peppers straight from the Canary Islands, which they neither look forward to nor savor but which they must simply endure as one of the mysteries of their civilization.

As they walk that long gray mile to the tapas of doom the group will radiate a certain sort of male giddiness, and a strange transformation will take place. For it is a law of human nature that the more men you concentrate in one happy pack, the more each of them will come to resemble Donald Trump. They possess a sort of masculine photosynthesis to start with—the ability to turn sunlight into self-admiration. By the law of compound egotism, they create this self-reinforcing vortex of smugness, which brings out the most pleased-with-themselves aspects of their own personalities.

These men are, in other circumstances, loving grandfathers, eager to talk about their offspring at Stanford, who are in year-abroad programs in Cambodia. But when sucked into the psychodynamics of a haute-bourgeois boy gang, striding around sockless in their performance sandals, they become immature versions of themselves. Their decibels rise. Their chests puff. Their laughs explode. They become temporary geriatric gangstas, and brag and swagger in a spirit of rising male hysteria. They get a form of millionaire titan Alzheimer's; they forget everything but their erections.

The Contemplative Life

After they retired, Erica and Harold bought a second home in Aspen, where they lived during the summer and for a few weeks around Christmas. They saw the Immortals swooshing by and carousing when they went downtown, but their own lives had taken a different path. They had also achieved what is called success, but theirs was a different kind of success. Without really thinking about it, they had created a counterculture. They didn't consciously reject the lifestyle of the affluent mainstream; they just sort of ignored it. They lived and thought differently, and their lives had taken on a different and deeper shape. They had a greater awareness of the wellsprings of the human heart, and when you met them you were impressed by their substance and depth.

On summer afternoons, they'd sit in Adirondack chairs on the front porch and look out over the Roaring Fork River and wave at the occasional raft trip going by. Harold would read his serious nonfiction books, and Erica would read novels and nap. Harold would look over at her as she slept. Her Chinese features had become more pronounced as she had gotten older, and she was thinner and smaller. Harold would remember a story he had once read, by Mark Saltzman. It was about a man in China who was learning English. One day, his teacher asked him what had been the happiest moment of his life. The Chinese man paused for a long time. And then he smiled with embarrassment and said that once his wife had gone to Beijing and eaten duck, and she often told him about the delicious duck. And so, the story concluded, "He would have to say the happiest moment in his life was her trip, and the eating of the duck."

Harold would think back on his own life and then try to squeeze it into the shape of that story. And he would remember a blue shirt Erica had earned in high school for making the honor roll, which had made her so proud, and which she would talk about when she welcomed young interns to their firm, or when she was invited to speak at a company or college commencement. He had heard her tell the story of the shirt hundreds of times over the years, first when she was young and starting out in life, when she told it to him over dinner; then when she was confident and middle-aged and being interviewed and feted; and now when she was older and smaller and wrinkled. He reflected that it wouldn't be totally inaccurate for him to say that the happiest moment of his life had been her making the honor roll before she knew him, and the earning of the shirt.

On those afternoons, they would talk about things, sometimes over a glass of wine—or two or three for Harold. In the late afternoons, Erica would rise and get Harold a sweater, and then she'd go in to cook them an early dinner. Harold would sit there watching the shadows of the evening sun.

They had run their tour company for about eight years, but eventually they had to give it up. Harold's knees had begun to go, then his hips and his ankles, which had been prone to tendonitis all his life. He was largely immobile now, walking awkwardly and slowly with two canes. He would never play tennis again, never golf again, never carelessly get up and walk across the room again.

His body was breaking down. He'd been in the hospital nearly once a year for the past few years, for one thing or another. Some men grow thin and frail as they age, but he, immobile, grew heavy and round. For the first few years of his old, old age, he found, he needed more and more help, for little chores he'd never given a second thought to all his life—sometimes to even get out of bed or a chair. Erica would grab his hands and then lean back, like a sailor leaning against the pull of the sail, and leverage him up.

Then, as the decay worsened, he needed help all the time. Harold was imprisoned in his chair. He endured three bouts of depression as he realized he would no longer be a participant in the life of the planet, but just a decaying observer of it. For several months he lay awake at night in a sort of madness, imagining the horrors to come—surgeons opening his chest, his throat gorging with blood and choking off his air supply, losing speech and pieces of his mind, losing limbs, sight, and hearing.

He could no longer participate in parties and social occasions. He just sat against the wall. On the other hand, his wife and his nurses served him with a care, patience, and devotion that surpassed all expectation. Their efforts were more dear to him because he knew that he could never repay them. He had to surrender his male pride, his egoism, his sense of self-mastery and depend utterly upon their service and affection. It was hard at first to simply fall backward into their love. At first their attention made him cranky and cross. But their patient love soothed him. Eventually his physical condition stabilized and his moods lifted.

He'd sit on his porch and he could look out at the elementals of nature: sky, mountains, trees, water, and sun. Researchers have found, not surprisingly, that sunlight and natural scenes can have a profound effect on mind and mood. People in northern latitudes, where the sunlight is less bright, have higher rates of depression than people in lower latitudes. So do people on the western edges of time zones, where the sun rises later in the mornings. People who have spent much of their lives working the night shift have higher chances of suffering breast cancer than those who work in the day. Researchers have found that hospital patients in rooms with natural views seem to recover slightly faster than patients in rooms without them. In a study done in Milan, patients with bipolar depression who stayed in east-facing hospital rooms were discharged three and a half days sooner than patients housed in west-facing ones.

Harold found he could play a little game with himself. He'd sit on the porch looking at a little flower in the grass down below. He'd concentrate on the petals and their fragile beauty. Then, by lifting his head, he'd gaze out at the icy mountain peaks miles and miles away. Suddenly, he was swept up in an entirely different set of sensations, feelings of awe, veneration, submission, and greatness. Just sitting there, he could move from the beautiful to the sublime and back again.

He loved these grand views. They gave him a feeling of elevation, of being connected to a sacred and all-encompassing order, a part of some stupendous whole. People who are out in nature do better on tests of working memory and attention than people who are in urban settings. Their moods are better. As the philosopher Charles Taylor writes, "Nature draws us because it is in some way attuned to our feelings, so that it can reflect and intensify those we already feel or else awaken those which are dormant. Nature is like a great keyboard on which our highest sentiments are played out. We turn to it, as we might turn to music, to evoke and strengthen the best in us."

The views of the mountains and trees soothed him and enlivened him. But they didn't really satisfy him. As others have noted, nature is a preparation for religion, but it is not religion.

Harold was still in pain much of the time. During those horrendous hours, pain filled his mind the way a gas fills the available space in a container. He could barely remember what it was like to not be in pain. Yet when it was gone, he couldn't remember the pain itself. He just had a cold intellectual concept of it.

Most of the time, Harold thought about people. He'd remember quick visual images—a playmate and her toy car sitting in the snow; his parents taking him to look at a new house; an office mate on a terrible day, washing his red face over a sink in the restroom—but there were mysterious gaps in his memory too. He found he could not recall ever sitting around the dinner table with his parents, though it must have happened all the time.

Harold found that his memories came in strings. He remembered a catch he made playing dodge ball in fourth grade. This set him thinking about his teacher that year, who he had a crush on. He felt her presence but couldn't really make out her face. She had long dark hair. She was tall, or seemed so. Nothing else was distinct but the aura of her beauty and sweetness and his feelings for her at the time.

Harold would ask Erica to bring him boxes of their old stuff—photographs, papers, and documents that they kept hodgepodge from decades past. Then he'd rummage around in the boxes. Even while younger he'd had the presence of mind to save only the happy reminders, and so the bad times faded away.

He was slightly deranged while rummaging through these old things. Or drunk, for he was back to drinking during the day. Emotions and feelings streamed through him. He found he could remember old poems in their entirety. He had images of Olympics and elections and national events coursing through his head. He could relive the atmosphere of a decade—the way people wore their hair, the kinds of jokes they told.

He would sit there, giddily playing with time. Psychologists have a term for seniors who have trouble inhibiting their thoughts, and whose conversations veer off in random directions. They call it "off-topic verbosity." Harold suffered from that sort of malady, except it was going on inside. One second, he'd remember bodysurfing in the waves as a boy, and the next, a drive he took last week.

There's an old fable about a monk who went for a walk in the woods, and paused to listen to the lovely trilling of a small bird. When he returned to his monastery, he found nothing but strangers there. He had been gone fifty years. Some afternoons Harold felt that his personal time scale had slipped its gears.

Harold felt rejuvenated by his memories. In 1979 the psychologist Ellen Langer conducted an experiment in which she equipped an old monastery in Peterborough, New Hampshire, with props from the

1950s. She invited men in their seventies and eighties to stay for a week. They watched old Ed Sullivan shows, listened to Nat King Cole on the radio, and talked about the 1959 championship game between the Baltimore Colts and the New York Giants. At the end of the week, the men had gained an average of three pounds and looked younger. They tested better on hearing and memory. Their joints were more flexible and 63 percent did better on an intelligence test. Experiments like that are more suggestive than scientific, but Harold felt better when he was living back in the past. The pains diminished. The joys increased.

Search for Meaning

Harold spent a lot of time thinking about his teenage years, when he was about sixteen. This is the period researchers call the "reminiscence bump," because memories from late adolescence to early adulthood tend to be more vivid than those from any other time of life. He wondered how accurate his memories could possibly be.

When George Vaillant from the Grant Longitudinal Study sent an elderly subject reports on his early life for fact-checking purposes, he sent back the reports insisting, "You must have sent these to the wrong person." He simply could not remember any of the events from his own life that had been recorded at the time. The subject of another longitudinal study had suffered a brutal childhood at the hands of abusive parents, well documented at the time. But at age seventy, he remembered his father as a "good family man" and his mother as "the kindest woman in the world."

Harold also experienced a sort of negative enjoyment. After a lifetime spent preparing for things and building for things, he was finally free from the burden of the future. "How pleasant is the day," William James once observed, "when we give up striving to be young—or slender."

Even though old and dying, Harold was plagued by an intellectual discontent. Without even thinking about it, he, like most of us, regarded life not only as a set of events to be experienced, but as a question to be answered. What is it all for? Sitting there on that porch with his canes propped against the chair, Harold set out, in the twilight of his life, to understand the meaning of his existence, to bring it all to a point.

In his famous book *Man's Search for Meaning*, Viktor Frankl writes, "Man's search for meaning is the primary motivation in his life." He quotes Nietzsche's words, "He who has a *why* to live for can bear with almost any *how*." But then Frankl made a crucial, helpful point: It's fruitless to try to think in the abstract about what life in general means. The meaning of one's life is only discernible within the specific circumstances of one's own specific life. In the concentration camp, he writes, "We had to learn ourselves and, furthermore, we had to teach the despairing men, that *it did not really matter what we expected from life, but rather what life expected from us.* We needed to stop asking the meaning of life, and instead to think of ourselves as those who were being questioned by life—daily and hourly. Our answer must consist, not in talk and meditation, but in right action and right conduct."

Harold thought back on his life as a son, a husband, a business consultant, and a historian and wondered what question life had asked of him. He looked for something that could be defined as his life's calling or mission. He thought the project would be easy, but the more he looked for a key to his life, the harder it was to find. When studied honestly and accurately, his life had been a series of fragmented events. Sometimes he had been very money oriented, but other times he was oblivious to money. Sometimes he had been ambitious, but in other phases he was not. During some years he wore the mask of a scholar, while at others he wore the mask of a businessman, and who was the true self beneath the masks? In *The Presentation of Self in Everyday Life*, Erving Goffman argues that it's masks all the way down.

Scientists and writers have tried to impose certain schema to describe how life evolves. Abraham Maslow defined his hierarchy of needs—from the physical to safety, love, esteem, and self-actualization. But much recent research has cast doubt on the idea that human lives fall into such neat schemas—there are no simple progressions of the sort Maslow described. Some days Harold felt defeated, and concluded that life is unknowable. Take something as simple as buying a car. Did he choose his last car because of the shape of the body, the write-up in

Consumer Reports, some vague image he had of the brand personality, how it felt in the test drive, some sense of the status it would give him, or maybe because of the dealer discount? All of those things must have played a role, but he couldn't really define the proportions. There was a murky twilight zone between the factors that must have gone into his choice, and the actual choice as it had emerged at the dealership.

"We can never, even by the strictest examination, get completely behind the secret springs of action," Immanuel Kant had written. And if that is true of buying a car, how much more true must it be about pursuing the grand goals of a life. If Harold had a true understanding of himself, he would be able to predict what he would want from life in a year, but he had no confidence he could do that, or even in a month. If Harold had a true understanding of himself, he would be able to describe certain qualities he possessed, but he had no confidence he could do that reliably either. People vastly overrate and misapprehend their abilities. Numerous studies have shown that there is low correlation between how people rate their own personality and how people around them rate it.

Harold would sit there trying to think about himself, but in seconds he found he was thinking about people he had known or things he had experienced. Sometimes he'd think about some project he'd done at work, or a fight he had had with a coworker. He had a sense of himself as a coherent presence in these dramas. But when he tried to think of himself in isolation—what he was and what he lived for—he could conjure up no clear concept in his mind. It was as if he were an optical illusion, visible when you weren't looking straight at it, but invisible when you made it the object of your attention.

Some of his friends had off-the-shelf narratives to tell about themselves. One was a poor boy who had risen from rags to riches. Another was a sinner who had been saved in an instant by God. Another had changed his mind about everything in the course of his life—he had started in the forest of error and emerged into the light of truth.

In his book *The Redemptive Self*, Dan McAdams writes that Americans are especially prone to organize their lives into stories of redemption. Once upon a time, they had strayed on the path of tribulation, but

then they met a mentor or found a wife, or went to work at a foundation, or did some other thing, and they were redeemed. They were delivered from error and put onto a proper path. Their life had purpose
from that moment forth.

As he reviewed his own life, Harold couldn't see how his life fit into
any of those narrative molds. And as this process of self-analysis went
on, Harold grew intensely sad—plagued by the sense that there was an
ultimate deadline he would not meet. Some psychologists urge patients
to sit in a chair and look inside themselves. But there's a great deal of evidence to suggest that this sort of rumination is often harmful. When
people are depressed, they pick out the negative events and emotions of
their lives, and, by fixing attention upon them, they make those neural
networks stronger and more dominant. In his book *Strangers to Ourselves*, Timothy Wilson of the University of Virginia summarizes several
experiments in which rumination made depressed people more depressed while distraction made them less depressed. Ruminators fell
into self-defeating, negative patterns of thought, did worse in problem-
solving tasks, and had much gloomier predictions about their own future.

At times, the whole self-examination exercise seemed futile to
Harold. "How pathetically scanty my self-knowledge is compared with,
say, my knowledge of my room," Franz Kafka once observed. "There is
no such thing as observation of the inner world, as there is of the outer
world."

The Final Day

One afternoon in late summer, Harold was out on the porch of the
Aspen house, watching the river go by. He could hear Erica in her office
upstairs, tapping away at her keyboard. He had a scratched metal box on
his lap, and he was leafing through some papers and photographs.

He came across a picture of himself from long ago. He was about six
when the photo was taken. He was wearing a navy-style peacoat, and he
was atop a metal playground slide, about to come down, looking with
intense concentration on the chute below.

"What do I have in common with that boy?" Harold asked himself. Nothing, except that it was himself. The knowledge, the circumstances, the experience, and the appearance were all different, but there was something alive in that boy that was still alive within him now. There was a certain essence that had changed as he had aged, but without fundamentally becoming something other than itself, and that essence Harold chose to call his soul.

He supposed that this essence was manifested in neurons and synapses. He had been born with certain connections, and since the brain is the record of the feelings of a life, he had slowly accreted new neural connections in his head. And yet Harold couldn't help but think how enchanted it all was. The connections had been formed by emotion. The brain was physical meat, but out of the billions of energy pulses emerged spirit and soul. There must be some supreme creative energy, he thought, that can take love and turn it into synapses and then take a population of synapses and turn it into love. The hand of God must be there.

Harold looked at the little boy's hands clutching the railing of the slide and at the expression on the little boy's face. Harold didn't have to imagine what the boy's affections and fears were, because at some level he could still experience them directly. He didn't have to reconstruct the manner in which that boy saw the world because it was still, at some level, his own manner. That little boy was afraid of heights. That little boy felt light-headed at the sight of blood. That little boy was in love but often felt alone. That little boy already possessed a hidden kingdom, a cast of characters and responses that would grow, mature, assert themselves, recede, and regress at different times of his life. That hidden kingdom was he, then as now.

Part of that kingdom grew out of his relationships with his parents. They weren't the most profound people ever. They spent too much time in the world of commerce, focusing on appearances and vanities. They could never really answer his deepest needs, but they had been good people, who loved him. One of them had probably taken him to this playground, and stood behind the camera to take this picture, and had filed it away somewhere so Harold could see it now. There'd been an emotion when the picture was taken and an emotion when it was filed away, and there was an emotion when Harold looked at it now and imagined his mom or dad behind the camera pushing the button. The loops still reverberated across the decades, from generation to generation.

The soul emerged from these loops of affection. The loops were momentary and fragile, also permanent and enduring. Even today, there were little sleeper cells lodged in his mind—affections and fears planted long ago which could lie dormant for decades and then suddenly spring to life in the right circumstances. The way his parents reacted to his small accomplishments—that delicious feeling motivated him his whole life. The way his working-class grandparents never felt truly accepted in middle-class America, as if their presence was contingent and peripheral—that insecurity lingered in him his whole life. The way his friends in school draped their arms around his shoulder and leaned against him in the cafeteria—that feeling of comradeship that strengthened him until his dying day. Social connections early in life predict longevity and good health at the end.

Harold tried and failed to see into the tangle of connections, the unconscious region, which he came to think of as the Big Shaggy. The only proper attitude toward this region was wonder, gratitude, awe, and humility. Some people think they are the dictators of their own life. Some believe the self is an inert wooden ship to be steered by a captain at the helm. But Harold had come to see that his conscious self—the voice in his head—was more a servant than a master. It emerged from the hidden kingdom and existed to nourish, edit, restrain, attend, refine, and deepen the soul within.

For all his life until this period, he had wondered how his life would turn out. But now the story was complete. He knew his fate. He was relieved from the burden of the future. The cold fear of death was there in his mind, but so was the knowledge that he'd been extraordinarily lucky.

He stepped back and asked some questions of himself, assessments of the life he had lived. And each question generated its own instant feeling, so he didn't even have to put the answer into words. Had he deepened himself? In a culture of instant communication, in which it was so easy to live superficially, had he spent time on the important things, developing his most consequential talents? This question felt good to ask, because while he had never become a prophet or sage, he had read the serious books, engaged the serious questions, and had tried, as best he could, to cultivate a luxuriant inner realm.

Had he contributed to the river of knowledge, left a legacy for future generations? This question he could not feel so good about. He had tried to discover new things. He had written essays and delivered lectures. But he had been an observer more than an actor. For too many years he had drifted, flitting from one interest to another. At other times, he had held back, unwilling to take the risks and suffer the blows that come from living in the arena. He had not done all that he might have to offer gifts to those who would live on.

Had he transcended this earthly realm? No. He always had a sense there was something beyond life as science understands it. He had always somehow believed in a God who existed beyond time and space. But he had never fallen in with religion. He had lived a worldly life and, regretfully, had never tasted Divine transcendence.

Had he loved? Yes. The one constant in his adult life had been his admiration and love for the good woman who was his wife. He knew that she did not reciprocate his love with the same strength and devotion. He knew that she had overshadowed him, and their life paths had followed her achievements. He knew that she had sometimes lost interest in him and there had been lonely years in the middle of their marriage. But that didn't matter to him now. In the end, his ability to be with her and to sacrifice himself for her had been another of life's gifts. And now, in his vulnerable final years, she was offering back everything that he had given. Even if they had been married only this month, with him immobile and her caring for him in a thousand ways, life would still have been worth living. As the hours ahead had shortened, his love for her had only grown.

Just then, Erica came out onto the porch and asked him if he wanted some dinner brought out. "Oh, is it dinnertime already?" he asked.

She said it was and there was some cold chicken in the fridge she could bring out, with some potato chips. She went back inside, and Harold was left to go back to his reverie. And as he reviewed different scenes from his life, the questions life asked of him—and his assessments of them—dissolved, and he was left with just sensations. It was like being in a concert or a movie. His sense of self faded away. It was like the way he had been in his room as a boy, moving trucks around while lost in some great adventure.

Erica came back out onto the porch and dropped the tray she was carrying and screamed and rushed over to Harold and grabbed his hand. His body had sagged and was inert. His head was on his chin and drool was coming out of his mouth. She looked into his eyes, the eyes she had grown accustomed to looking into all these decades, and she could see no reaction there, though he was breathing. She made a move to run to the phone, but Harold's hand tightened around hers. She sat back down looking him in the face and weeping.

Harold had lost consciousness but not life. Images flowed into his head the way they do in the seconds before one falls asleep. They came in a chaotic succession. In his unselfconsciousness, he didn't regard them the way he would have at an earlier time. He regarded them in a way that was beyond words. We would say he regarded them holistically, somehow feeling everything at once. We would say he participated in them impressionistically, rather than analytically. He felt presences.

As I put them down on this page I have to put them in one sentence after another, but this is not how Harold experienced them. There were images of the paths he used to ride his bike on as a boy and the mountains he looked out upon that day. There he was doing homework with his mother, and also tackling a running back in high school. There were speeches he had made, compliments he had received, sex he had had, books he had read and moments when some new idea had broken over him like a wave.

For a few moments, consciousness seemed about to flicker back. He could sense Erica weeping out there and compassion enveloped him. Inside, the swirls in his mind were still interlooping with hers. They were shared swirls that leaped across from her conscious world to his unconscious one. Categories fell away. Tenderness was out of control. His ability to focus attention ended and at the same time his ability to interpenetrate the souls of others increased. His relation to her at this moment was direct. There were no analytics, no reservations, no ambitions, no future desires or past difficulties. It was just I and Thou. A unity of being. A higher state of knowledge. A merger of souls. At this point his questions about the meaning of life were no longer asked, but were answered.

Harold entered the hidden kingdom entirely and then lost consciousness forever. In his last moments there were neither boundaries nor features. He was unable to wield the power of self-consciousness but also freed from its shackles. He had been blessed with consciousness so that he might help direct his own life and nurture his inner life, but the cost of that consciousness was an awareness that he would die. Now he lost that awareness. He was past noticing anything now, and had entered the realm of the unutterable.

It would be interesting to know if this meant he had also entered a kingdom of heaven, God's kingdom. But that was not communicated back to Erica. His heart continued to beat for a few minutes, and his lungs filled and emptied with air and electrochemical impulses still surged through his brain. He made some gestures and twitches, which the doctors would call involuntary but which in this case were more deeply felt than any other gesture could be. And one of them was a long squeeze of the hand, which Erica took to mean good-bye.

What had been there at the start was there at the end, the tangle of sensations, perceptions, drives, and needs that we call, antiseptically, the unconscious. This tangle was not the lower part of Harold. It was not some secondary feature to be surpassed. It was the core of him—hard to see, impossible to understand—but supreme. Harold had achieved an important thing in his life. He had constructed a viewpoint. Other people see life primarily as a chess match played by reasoning machines. Harold saw life as a neverending interpenetration of souls.

POSTSCRIPT

THE RESEARCH DESCRIBED IN THIS BOOK ATTESTS TO A SIMPLE point: Our experience of ourselves is misleading. We have a sense that there is a central spot in our brains where information is processed, options are considered, and decisions are made. We have a voice in our head, which seems to be responsible for what we do. We have a sense that as we look out onto the world we are aware of what we are seeing.

But these propositions are not quite right. There is no central homunculus—no simple self—making decisions. The voice in the head may think it is in control, but in fact it is a mere supporting actor, unaware of the main protagonists down below. We are not aware of most of what we see and sense around us, or even of how we are responding to it.

We are not who we think we are.

People have always known that there are hidden forces that propel us, of course, but over the last thirty years researchers have begun to appreciate just how dominant these unconscious processes are. This is one of the big intellectual stories of our time.

When historians of ideas look back to this new understanding of ourselves, I suspect they will give great prominence to the work of Daniel Kahneman and Amos Tversky. For much of the nineteenth and twentieth centuries, a systematizing ethos prevailed, which held that people are rational, utility-maximizing, self-aware, consistent, and predictable. But, starting in the early 1970s, Kahneman and Tversky started poking holes in all this. They detected all sorts of hidden processes involved in the way people perceive and process the world.

In one experiment, Kahneman directed a camera at people's eyes and then asked them to do math problems. As soon as people began to concentrate on the problems, their pupils dilated. Kahneman and his colleagues could track people's concentration levels by the size of their pupils. When their pupils would contract Kahneman would ask, "Why did you stop working just now?" The subjects would cry out, "How did you know?" To which Kahneman would reply, "We have a window into your soul."

Soon Kahneman and Tversky were systematizing people's unconscious biases. One of the powerful ones is loss aversion. We work harder to avoid losses than to achieve gains. Two economists, Devin Pope and Maurice Schweitzer, came up with an elegant illustration of this. They looked at 2.5 million putts by professional golfers. They discovered that from every distance, golfers are more successful when putting for par than when putting for birdie. They fear making a bogey more than they hunger for the birdie, and as a result, their motivation to sink the putt is a bit higher.

In the ensuing years, Kahneman, Tversky, and others demonstrated hundreds of ways unconscious processes influence our thinking. Some of these are quite disturbing. For example, researchers studied a parole board in Israel, where judges spend an average of six minutes to decide whether to grant parole to individual prisoners. The board grants parole in about 35 percent of all cases—except in those cases that have been presented to the board shortly after breakfast and lunch. Just after meals, the board grants 65 percent of the parole requests. People think differently depending on how satiated or depleted they are.

Kahneman and Tversky also established—and a mountain of subsequent research has confirmed this—that the unconscious mind wants stories. When we see two phenomena, we are quick to make up stories to link and explain them. Story making—you might call it model building—is a large part of what the mind does. Kahneman has pointed out much of the pleasure we get from a vacation comes in anticipating it before it happens and in remembering it after it was over. We would enjoy the moments we are on vacation much less if we knew that some amnesiac pill would make us forget it when it was done. We have an experiencing self and a remembering self, and the remembering self is more powerful.

Michael Gazzaniga is another person who will probably figure prominently in intellectual histories of this era. Gazzaniga discovered that when split-brain patients are given unconscious prompts to do certain things, like walk across the room to grab a soda, they are not particularly troubled by their own strange behavior. They just invent a bogus story to explain themselves to themselves. That is, in some cases, your conscious mind doesn't tell you what to do; it observes what you do and then confabulates a story to account for it.

That's because the brain is a vastly complicated collection of parallel and distributed thinking systems, gazillions of which are churning at any one time. The conscious mind generally can't follow what's really going on, so it just looks at the results and forms an interpretation. It makes up a story. (Some researchers believe this is all the conscious mind does. We have no free will, just a bunch of post-hoc rationalizations.)

We've learned a lot about these hidden processes over the past few decades. Still, it's hard to wrap your head around these truths, because the evidence our conscious minds are feeding us every second of every day is trying to lead us astray.

It is hard to continually remind yourself that you are not what you appear to be. It is also very hard to get a fair and comprehensive view of how much we should trust the unconscious. Much of the early research pointed out ways unconscious processes lead us to deviate from the economic model of perfectly rational man. We will agree to undergo surgery if we are told the procedure has an 85 percent success rate but we will decline if we are told it has a 15 percent failure rate. The early researchers emphasized these sorts of unconscious deficiencies because they were pushing against the social science model of perfectly rational men and women.

On the other hand, if you hang around experienced athletes, artists, firemen, or soldiers, you will find they perform amazing feats through intuition. Experience has given them phenomenal pattern-recognition skills and creative abilities. If you watch two people fall in love, you are amazed by the vast number of brilliant unconscious valuations the lovers are making about each other.

Some researchers take a dim view of the unconscious. Others take a very rosy view. It is hard to tell why different experts make these very different generalizations, except that some of them seem temperamentally inclined to trust emotion and intuition and some are temperamentally distrustful.

It's even hard to properly describe what's going on. At the moment, we still have to rely upon old, misleading words like "emotion" and "reason" to try to describe these processes. These words probably obscure more than they reveal.

We are stuck with obsolete metaphors. For example, we seem stuck with the idea that emotion and reason are on a seesaw—if emotion is up, then reason is down—when we know this isn't always the case. If you improve your emotional sensitivity, you will improve your powers of rational deduction because you'll be able to make more subtle valuations.

We mix up emotion with arousal. We imagine that to be emotional is to be screaming and crying all the time. This isn't true. We would all say that Emily Dickinson was emotionally astute. That doesn't mean she was perpetually flying off the handle.

In short, it takes a constant effort to understand and apply the implications of this research. It is still hard to see ourselves as we really are.

One thing we know is that we need both systems to thrive—the conscious and unconscious, the rational and the emotional. When learning, we need to consciously labor to master facts. We need to write essays or perform analytic reasoning in order to organize and propel our knowledge. But we also need to stir and excite the unconscious networks, to allow them to do their magic—producing "eureka moments" or combining adjacent idea systems in new and creative ways.

When we make a decision, we have to use our unconscious mapmaking powers to survey the field and detect the minuscule gradations of a given situation. On the other hand, we need to check our unreliable intuitions with data.

One of the constant implications of this research is that we have to be completely modest about what we know or can know. We don't even know ourselves, let alone other people. We don't really know any situation, even as much as our own brain does. We can't trust our own evaluations of how much we know. We have a constant tendency to be overconfident.

Entire industries are based on overconfidence. There are large numbers of fund managers who think they can beat the market when picking stocks. The vast majority are wrong. Every few months a business book like *Built to Last* gets published, celebrating certain companies for their enduring excellence. In an astonishing number of cases, the celebrated companies falter or go bankrupt in the years after publication. Philip E. Tetlock publishes studies exposing the hubris of experts. In many spheres, experts predict the future only slightly better than regular civilians, if they can do it at all. One study analyzed the judgment of doctors who were "completely certain" they had correctly diagnosed the disease of an ailing patient. After the patients died, autopsies were performed. The clinicians who were "completely certain" were wrong 40 percent of the time.

Fortunately the new research gives us a sense of the ways we are likely to be wrong, and it gives us ways to anticipate our most common errors and guard against them. For example, there is "path dependence." Things that seemed normal today began with a choice that made sense at a particular time, and survived even though it might no longer make sense at all.

There is the focusing illusion. As Kahneman puts it: "Nothing in life is as important as you think it is while you are thinking about it." For example, education is one of the most important determinants of income. But if everyone had the same education level, income inequality would be reduced by less than 10 percent. There are a zillion other factors that help shape income levels, and cumulatively their influence is much greater.

There is the Pareto Principle. We have in our heads the idea that most distributions fall along a bell curve (most people are in the middle). But this is not how the world is often organized. The top two percent of Twitter users send 60 percent of the messages. The top

20 percent of workers will contribute a giant share of any company's actual productivity.

Cognitive tools like this are helpful in overcoming the mind's natural biases, but the most important thing is to develop an attitude of epistemological humility, an awareness of how little you are likely to know and how little you will understand the things you do know. Much of life is about failure, whether we acknowledge it or not, and your destiny is profoundly shaped by how effectively you learn from and adapt to failure.

The journalist Tim Harford points out that 2,000 car companies sprang into being at the dawn of the automobile era. Less than 1 percent survived. Even if you do succeed, you are probably not going to stay at the top. None of the ten largest American companies in 1912 ranked among the top 100 American companies by 1990.

It's important to fail productively. First, as Harford puts it, you should seek out new ideas and new projects. Then you should try new things on a small scale so that their failure is survivable. You should make sure each of your projects is insulated from the others so the failure of one doesn't pull down the whole lot. Then you have to find a feedback mechanism so you can tell which new thing is failing and which is succeeding. Fight your natural tendency to loss aversion and kill the failing projects.

The encouraging part of all this research is that we have deep in ourselves all these wondrous unconscious powers. The discouraging thing is that we aren't aware of many of these powers, and they generally come with downsides—biases and distortions that can lead us astray in the wrong circumstances.

There's an ancient Jewish tale of a rabbi who came to synagogue with two slips of paper, one in each of his front pockets. In one pocket, the slip read, "You are nothing but dust and ashes." In the other, the slip read, "The world was created for you."

This wonderful new research suggests that, when taken together, those statements are true.

ACKNOWLEDGMENTS

YOU NEVER KNOW HOW THINGS ARE GOING TO COME TOGETHER. Ever since college I've been interested in research about the mind and the brain. But this had been a sidelight as I went about my normal work—writing about politics and policy, sociology and culture. But as the years went by, the same thought kept recurring. The people studying the mind and brain are producing amazing insights about who we are, and yet these insights aren't having a sufficient impact on the wider culture.

This book is an attempt to do that. It's an attempt to integrate science and psychology with sociology, politics, cultural commentary, and the literature of success.

No one needs to remind me that this is a perilous enterprise. The study of the mind is still in its early stages, and many findings are under dispute. When a journalist tries to apply the findings from a complicated discipline to the wider world, it is easy to miss nuance, and the distinctions that the specialists hold dear. Moreover, there is a natural resentment of people like me, who have platforms like *The New York Times*, PBS, and Random House, and who often try to capture the gist of a lifetime's worth of research in a paragraph or a page.

Nonetheless, I thought this enterprise was worth undertaking, because the insights gained over the past thirty years really are important. They really should reshape the way we think about policy, sociology, economics, and life in general. I've tried to describe these findings while playing it safe scientifically. I've tried to describe the findings that are reasonably well established, even if there is still some disagreement about them (there always will be). I'm aware that I am not a science writer. I have not tried to describe how the brain works. I almost never venture into the complexities of which brain region is producing which behavior. I have merely set out to describe the broad implications of this work.

There is no way to do this in a manner that satisfies all the researchers all the time. I have at least tried to give credit to the original scientists as often as possible. I have tried to direct readers to sources where they can read about the original work and draw their own conclusions about its implications. I have also incurred debts to many people who helped me with substance and style.

Jesse Graham of the University of Southern California policed the book for scientific errors. His wife, Sarah Graham, provided a sensitive literary reading. The psychologist Mindy Greenstein, author of *The House on Crash Corner*, read most of the manuscript, and Walter Mischel of Columbia read a part. Both offered crucial suggestions. Cheryl Miller, formerly of *The New York Times* and now of the American Enterprise Institute, did a superlative job of research, copyediting, and fact checking. Her intelligence and competence are legendary among those who have been fortunate enough to work with her. My parents, Lois and Michael Brooks, read the book, offering large thoughts and careful editing suggestions. They applied their usual high standards. My *Times* colleague David Leonhardt also offered invaluable feedback.

I benefited from conversations with many researchers. But I should at least thank Jonathan Haidt of the University of Virginia, Antonio Damasio of USC, Michael Gazzaniga of the University of California at Santa Barbara, Martha Farah of the University of Pennsylvania, Timothy Wilson of the University of Virginia, and others who steered me in the direction of relevant research. I should also thank the leaders of the Social and Affective Neuroscience Society, Edge, the Templeton Foundation, the Center of Neuroscience and Society, and other organizations who let me participate in conferences and panels with people in the field.

My editor, Will Murphy, was an unfailingly wise and encouraging presence. My agents, Glen Hartley and Lynn Chu, have been ardent champions. My speaking agent Bill Leigh read the manuscript and offered sage counsel. My associates at the *Times*—Reihan Salam, Rita Koganzon, Ari Schulman, and Anne Snyder—have earned my undying gratitude. I consulted roughly twenty-four million people in my search for an acceptable title, of whom I would certainly like to thank Lynda Resnick and Yossi Siegel.

Of course, I need to thank my kids, Joshua, Naomi, and Aaron. And it is a pleasure to thank my wife, Sarah. As she can attest, I may write about emotion and feelings, but that's not because I'm naturally good at expressing them. It's because I'm naturally bad at it.

NOTES

INTRODUCTION

x **The most generous estimate** Timothy D. White, *Strangers to Ourselves: Discovering the Adaptive Unconscious* (Cambridge, MA: Belknap Press, 2002), 24.

x **"Some researchers"** White, 5.

xi **"removed the earth"** John A. Bargh, "The Automaticity of Everyday Life," in *The Automaticity of Everyday Life*, ed. Robert S. Wyer (Mahwah, NJ: Lawrence Erlbaum Associates, Inc., 1997), 52.

xvii **"I looked at her face"** Douglas R. Hofstadter, *I Am a Strange Loop* (New York: Basic Books, 2007), 228.

CHAPTER 1: DECISION MAKING

6 ***Playboy* bunnies tend** David M. Buss, *The Evolution of Desire: Strategies of Human Mating* (New York: Basic Books, 2003), 47–58.

6 **Even the famously thin** Daniel Akst, "Looks Do Matter," *The Wilson Quarterly*, Summer 2005, http://www.wilsonquarterly.com/article.cfm?AID=648&AT=0.

6 **The orbicularis oculi muscle** Steven Johnson, *Mind Wide Open: Your Brain and the Neuroscience of Everyday Life* (New York: Scribner, 2004), 25–26.

7 **Men consistently rate** Ayala Malakh Pines, *Falling In Love: Why We Choose the Lovers We Choose* (New York: Routledge, 2005), 33.

7 **Women are sexually attracted** Peter G. Caryl et al., "Women's Preference for Male Pupil-Size: Effects of Conception Risk, Sociosexuality and Relationship Status," *Personality and Individual Differences* 46, no. 4 (March 2009): 503–508, http://www.sciencedirect.com/science?_ob=ArticleURL&_udi=B6V9F-4VC73V2-2&_user=10&_coverDate=03/31/2009&_rdoc=1&_fmt=high&_orig=search&_origin=search&_sort=d&_docanchor=&view=c&_acct=C000050221&_version=1&_urlVersion=0&_userid=10&md5=3f12f3106917cee6e3fbfdc27ba9386&searchtype=a.

8 **Zero percent say yes** David M. Buss, "Strategies of Human Mating," *Psychological Topics* 15 (2006): 250.

8 **Marion Eals and Irwin Silverman** Matt Ridley, *The Red Queen: Sex and the Evolution of Human Nature* (New York: Penguin Books, 1995), 251.

9 **People rarely revise** Janine Willis and Alexander Todorov, "First Impressions," *Psychological Science* 17, no. 7 (2006): 592.

9 **His research subjects could predict** Charles C. Ballew II and Alexander Todorov, "Predicting Political Elections from Rapid and Unreflective Face Judgments," *Proceedings of*

the National Academy of Sciences of the United States of America 104, no. 46 (November 13, 2007): 17948–53.

9   **He was tall** Ridley, 298.

10   **A woman may be partner** John Tierney, "The Big City: Picky, Picky, Picky," *New York Times*, February 12, 1995, http://www.nytimes.com/1995/02/12/magazine/the-big-city -picky-picky-picky.html.

10   **They imagine there is** Martie G. Haselton and David M. Buss, "Error Management Theory: A New Perspective on Biases in Cross-Sex Mind Reading," *Journal of Personality and Social Psychology* 78, no. 1 (2000): 81–91.

10   **As Helen Fisher wrote** Helen Fisher, "The Drive to Love: The Neural Mechanism for Mate Selection," in *The New Psychology of Love*, eds. Robert J. Sternberg and Karin Weis (Binghampton, NY: Yale University Press, 2006), 102.

10   **There's even some evidence** Judith Rich Harris, *The Nurture Assumption: Why Children Turn Out the Way They Do* (New York: Touchstone, 1999), 140.

11   **In college, people are** Malakh Pines, 5.

11   **As Geoffrey Miller notes** Geoffrey Miller, *The Mating Mind: How Sexual Choice Shaped Human Nature* (New York: Anchor Books, 2000), 373–74.

12   **Ninety percent of emotional** Iain McGilchrist, *The Master and His Emissary: The Divided Brain and the Making of the Western World* (New Haven, CT: Yale University Press, 2009), 257.

13   **He calculates that** Miller, 369–75.

13   **there's plenty of evidence** Helen Fisher, *Why We Love: The Nature and Chemistry of Romantic Love* (New York: Owl Books, 2004), 110–12.

14   **Though men normally spend** Michael S. Gazzaniga, *Human: The Science Behind What Makes Us Human* (New York: Harper Perennial, 2008), 95.

14   **David Buss's surveys suggest** Buss, 44–45.

14   **A woman's attractiveness** Buss, 63–64.

14   **Women resist dating outside** Guenter J. Hitsch, Ali Hortacsu, and Dan Ariely, "What Makes You Click?—Mate Preferences and Matching Outcomes in Online Dating," MIT Sloan Research Paper No. 4603-06, http://papers.ssrn.com/sol3/Papers.cfm?abstract_id =895442.

15   **"The greatest happiness love"** Stendhal, *Love*, trans. Gilbert Sale and Suzanne Sale (New York: Penguin Books, 2004), 104.

16   **People who lose their sense** Rachel Herz, *The Scent of Desire: Discovering Our Enigmatic Sense of Smell* (New York: HarperCollins, 2008), 4–5.

16   **They could somehow tell** Esther M. Sternberg, *Healing Spaces: The Science of Place and Well-Being* (Cambridge, MA: Belknap Press, 2009), 83–84.

16   **According to famous research by Claus Wedekind** Claus Wedekind et al., "MHC-Dependent Mate Preferences in Humans," *Proceedings: Biological Sciences* 260, no. 1359 (June 22, 1995): 245–49, http://links.jstor.org/sici?sici=0962-8452%2819950622%29260 %3A1359%3C245%3AMMPIH%3E2.0.CO%3B2-Y.

18   **As Damasio put it** Antonio R. Damasio, *Descartes' Error: Emotion, Reason, and the Human Brain* (New York: Penguin Books, 2005), 51.

18   **Another of Damasio's research subjects** Damasio, 193–94.

19   **"This behavior is a good example"** Damasio, 194.

19   **"Somatic markers do not deliberate"** Damasio, 174.

21   **As LeDoux writes** Joseph E. LeDoux, *The Emotional Brain: The Mysterious Underpinnings of Emotional Life* (New York: Simon & Schuster, 1996), 302.

21   **Nobel Laureate Gerald Edelman** Gerald Edelman, *Bright Air, Brilliant Fire: On the Matter of the Mind* (New York: Basic Books, 1992), 69.

22   **"All information processing"** Kenneth A. Dodge, "Emotion and Social Information

Processing," in *The Development of Emotion Regulation and Dysregulation*, eds. Judy Garber and Kenneth A. Dodge (Cambridge: University of Cambridge Press, 1991), 159.

CHAPTER 2: THE MAP MELD

26 **Marital satisfaction generally follows** Daniel Gilbert, *Stumbling on Happiness* (New York: Alfred A. Knopf, 2006), 221.

27 **People used to argue** Roy F. Baumeister, *The Cultural Animal: Human Nature, Meaning, and Social Life* (Oxford: Oxford University Press, 2005), 116.

27 **Studies in strip clubs** Joseph T. Hallinan, *Why We Make Mistakes: How We Look Without Seeing, Forget Things in Seconds, and Are All Pretty Sure We Are Way Above Average* (New York: Broadway Books, 2009), 47.

28 **she got lubricated even** Natalie Angier, "Birds Do It. Bees Do It. People Seek the Keys to It," *New York Times*, April 10, 2007, http://www.nytimes.com/2007/04/10/science/10desi.html?pagewanted=1&_r=1&adxnnl=1&adxnnlx=1277571934-Wb1eIWRnCZrsHvyLoHJExg.

28 **Julia's sexual tastes** Baumeister, 115–16.

28 **An orgasm is not** Barry R. Komisaruk, Carlos Beyer-Flores, and Beverly Whipple, *The Science of the Orgasm* (Baltimore, MD: Johns Hopkins University Press, 2006), 72.

28 **Touches and sensations release** Regina Nuzzo, "Science of the Orgasm," *Los Angeles Times*, February 11, 2008, http://www.latimes.com/features/health/la-he-orgasm11feb11,0,7227478.story.

28 **A woman in Taiwan** Mary Roach, *Bonk: The Curious Coupling of Science and Sex* (New York: W.W. Norton & Co., 2008), 237.

28 **A man studied by V. S. Ramachandran** Regina Nuzzo, "Science of the Orgasm."

29 **Julia had the mental traits** Melvin Konner, *The Tangled Wing: Biological Constraints on the Human Spirit* (New York: Henry Holt & Co., 2002), 291.

CHAPTER 3: MINDSIGHT

30 **Harold grew 250,000** Joseph LeDoux, *The Synaptic Self: How Our Brains Become Who We Are* (New York: Viking, 2002), 67.

30 **he had well over 20 billion** Jeffrey M. Schwartz and Sharon Begley, *The Mind and the Brain: Neuroplasticity and the Power of Mental Force* (New York: HarperCollins, 2002), 111.

30 **Fetuses swallow more** Kim Y. Masibay, "Secrets of the Womb: Life's Most Mind-Blowing Journey: From Single Cell to Baby in Just 266 Days," *Science World*, September 13, 2002.

31 **He began touching his umbilical** Betsy Bates, "Grimaces, Grins, Yawns, Cries: 3D/4D Ultrasound Captures Fetal Behavior," *Ob.Gyn. News*, April 15, 2004, http://www.obgynnews.com/article/S0029-7437(04)70032-4/fulltext.

31 **By the third trimester** Janet L. Hopson, "Fetal Psychology," *Psychology Today*, September 1, 1998, http://www.psychologytoday.com/articles/199809/fetal-psychology.

31 **After birth, babies will suck** Bruce E. Wexler, *Brain and Culture: Neurobiology, Ideology, and Social Change* (Cambridge, MA: MIT Press, 2006), 97.

31 **French babies cry differently** Bruce Bower, "Newborn Babies May Cry in Their Mother Tongues," *Science News*, December 5, 2009, http://www.sciencenews.org/view/generic/id/49195/title/Newborn_babies_may_cry_in_their_mother_tongues.

31 **Anthony J. DeCasper** Janet L. Hopson, "Fetal Psychology."

31 **In 1981 Andrew Meltzoff** Otto Friedrich, Melissa Ludtke, and Ruth Mehrtens Calvin, "What Do Babies Know?" *Time*, August 15, 1983, http://www.time.com/time/magazine/article/0,9171,949745-1,00.html.

33   **At an amazingly early age** Frederick Wirth, *Prenatal Parenting: The Complete Psychological and Spiritual Guide to Loving Your Unborn Child* (New York: HarperCollins, 2001), 14.

33   **He could tell the difference** Alison Gopnik, *The Philosophical Baby: What Children's Minds Tell Us About Truth, Love, and the Meaning of Life* (New York: Farrar, Straus, & Giroux, 2009), 205.

33   **six-month-old babies can spot** Hillary Mayell, "Babies Recognize Faces Better Than Adults, Study Says," *National Geographic*, May 22, 2005, http://news.nationalgeographic.com/news/2005/03/0321_050321_babies.html.

33   **It's a form of body-to-body communication** Louis Cozolino, *The Neuroscience of Human Relationships: Attachment and the Developing Social Brain* (New York: W.W. Norton & Co., Inc., 2006), 103.

34   **Soon, he could copy hand gestures** Edward O. Wilson, *Consilience: The Unity of Knowledge* (New York: Alfred A. Knopf, 1998), 145.

35   **The average baby demands** John Medina, *Brain Rules: 12 Principles for Surviving and Thriving at Work, Home, and School* (Seattle, WA: Pear Press, 2008), 197.

35   **New mothers lose** Katherine Ellison, *The Mommy Brain: How Motherhood Makes You Smarter* (New York: Basic Books, 2005), 21.

35   **Marital satisfaction plummets** Medina, 197.

36   **as Jill Lepore once noted** Jill Lepore, "Baby Talk," *The New Yorker*, June 29, 2009, http://www.newyorker.com/arts/critics/books/2009/06/29/090629crbo_books_lepore.

36   **testosterone can compromise** David Biello, "The Trouble with Men," *Scientific American*, September 16, 2007, http://www.scientificamerican.com/article.cfm?id-the-trouble-with-men.

36   **Kenneth Kaye has suggested** Wexler, 111.

37   **"still-face" research** Alva Noë, *Out of Our Heads: Why You Are Not Your Brain and Other Lessons from the Biology of Consciousness* (New York: Hill & Wang, 2009), 30–31.

37   **Rat pups who are licked** Wexler, 90.

37   **Rats raised in interesting environments** Robin Karr-Morse and Meredith S. Wiley, *Ghosts from the Nursery: Tracing the Roots of Violence* (New York: Atlantic Monthly Press, 1997), 27.

37   **Back in the 1930s** H. M. Skeels and H. B. Dye, "A Study of the Effects of Different Stimulation on Mentally Retarded Children," *Proceedings and Addresses of the American Association of Mental Deficiency*, 44 (1939), 114–36.

39   **As Marco Iacoboni has observed** Gordy Slack, "I Feel Your Pain," *Salon*, November 5, 2007, http://www.salon.com/news/feature/2007/11/05/mirror_neurons.

40   **The monkey's brains would not fire** Marco Iacoboni, *Mirroring People: The New Science of How We Connect with Others* (New York: Farrar, Straus & Giroux, 2008), 26.

40   **Their neurons fired** Iacoboni, 35–36.

40   **They share the same** Richard Restak, *The Naked Brain: How the Emerging Neurosociety Is Changing How We Live, Work, and Love* (New York: Three Rivers Press, 2006), 58.

40   **Human mirror neurons** Michael S. Gazzaniga, *Human: The Science Behind What Makes Us Human* (New York: Harper Perennial, 2008), 178.

40   **Carol Eckerman** Iacoboni, 50.

41   **Tanya Chartrand and John Bargh** Iacoboni, 112–14.

42   **Robert Provine of the University of Maryland** Steven Johnson, *Mind Wide Open: Your Brain and the Neuroscience of Everyday Life* (New York: Scribner, 2004), 120.

42   **Only 15 percent** Johnson, 119.

42   **As Steven Johnson has written** Johnson, 120–21.

43   **Coleridge described how** Raymond Martin and John Barresi, *The Rise and Fall of Soul and Self: An Intellectual History of Personal Identity* (New York: Columbia University Press, 2006), 184.

CHAPTER 4: MAPMAKING

44 **"explanatory drive"** Alison Gopnik, Andrew N. Meltzoff, and Patricia K. Kuhl, *The Scientist in the Crib: What Early Learning Tells Us About the Mind* (New York: Harper Perennial, 1999), 85.

45 **Young children don't seem** Alison Gopnik, *The Philosophical Baby: What Children's Minds Tell Us About Truth, Love, and the Meaning of Life* (New York: Farrar, Straus, & Giroux, 2009), 17.

45 **He couldn't remember earlier thoughts** Gopnik, Meltzoff, and Kuhl, 46.

45 **If you put a sticker** Gopnik, 145.

45 **When you ask preschoolers** Gopnik, 124.

45 **As Alison Gopnik writes** Gopnik, 152.

45 **"lantern consciousness"** Gopnik, 129.

46 **As John Bowlby wrote** John Bowlby, *Loss: Sadness and Depression* (New York: Basic Books, 1980), 229.

46 **Elizabeth Spelke believes** Margaret Talbot, "The Baby Lab," *The New Yorker,* September 5, 2006, http://www.newyorker.com/archive/2006/09/04/060904fa_fact_talbot.

46 **Meltzoff and Kuhl showed** Gopnik, Meltzoff, and Kuhl, 69.

47 **But young children are able** Gopnik, 82–83.

47 **Some scientists calculate** Jeffrey M. Schwartz and Sharon Begley, *The Mind and the Brain: Neuroplasticity and the Power of Mental Force* (New York: HarperCollins, 2002), 117.

47 **Harold could end up** Schwartz and Begley, 111.

47 **A mere 60 neurons** Thomas Carlyle Dalton and Victor W. Bergenn, *Early Experience, the Brain, and Consciousness: An Historical and Interdisciplinary Synthesis* (New York: Lawrence Erlbaum Associates, 2007), 91.

47 **Imagine a football stadium** Jeff Hawkins and Sandra Blakeslee, *On Intelligence* (New York: Times Books, 2004), 34.

47 **"It's as if"** Gopnik, Meltzoff, and Kuhl, 185.

48 **a cat was taught** Bruce E. Wexler, *Brain and Culture: Neurobiology, Ideology, and Social Change* (Cambridge, MA: MIT Press, 2006), 23.

48 **In another experiment** James Le Fanu, *Why Us?: How Science Rediscovered the Mystery of Ourselves* (New York: Pantheon Books, 2009), 54.

48 **Violinists have dense connections** Schwartz and Begley, 214–15.

50 **We store in our heads** Gilles Fauconnier and Mark Turner, *The Way We Think: Conceptual Blending and the Mind's Hidden Complexities* (New York: Basic Books, 2002), 12.

50 **"Building an integration network"** Fauconnier and Turner, 44.

54 **But the game Harold** Jerome Bruner, *Actual Minds, Possible Worlds* (Cambridge, MA: Harvard University Press, 1986).

55 **Dan P. McAdams argues** Dan P. McAdams, *The Stories We Live By: Personal Myths and the Making of the Self* (New York: Guilford Press, 1993), 48.

CHAPTER 5: ATTACHMENT

57 **Julia dimly suspected** Claudia Wells, "The Myth About Homework," *Time,* August 29, 2006, http://www.time.com/time/magazine/article/0,9171,1376208,00.html.

61 **"She left because I'm no good"** Ann B. Barnet and Richard J. Barnet, *The Youngest Minds: Parenting and Genetic Inheritance in the Development of Intellect and Emotion* (New York: Touchstone, 1998), 197.

61 **"All of us, from cradle"** Louis Cozolino, *The Neuroscience of Human Relationships: Attachment and the Developing Social Brain* (New York: W.W. Norton & Co., Inc., 2006), 139.

63 **Over the subsequent decades** L. Alan Sroufe, Byron Egeland, Elizabeth A. Carlson, and W. Andrew Collins, *The Development of the Person: The Minnesota Study of Risk and Adaptation from Birth to Adulthood* (New York: Guilford Press, 2005), 59–60.

64 **Insecurely attached children** Barnet and Barnet, 130.

64 **Neither do they hold** Sroufe et al., 133–34.

64 **They also tend to be** Sroufe et al., 154.

64 **In the Strange Situation Tests** Sroufe et al., 60.

65 **"He walked in a series"** Sroufe et al., 138.

65 **Adults who are avoidantly** Daniel J. Siegel, *The Developing Mind: How Relationships and the Brain Interact to Shape Who We Are* (New York: Guilford Press, 1999), 94.

65 **Pascal Vrticka of the University of Geneva** Kayt Sukel, "Brain Responds Quickly to Faces," *BrainWork*, Dana Foundation Newsletter, November 1, 2008, http://www.dana.org/news/brainwork/detail.aspx?id=13664.

65 **They are three times** George Vaillant, *Aging Well: Surprising Guideposts to a Happier Life from the Landmark Harvard Study of Adult Development* (New York: Little, Brown & Co., 2002), 99.

65 **Children with ambivalent** Ayala Malakh Pines, *Falling in Love: Why We Choose the Lovers We Choose* (New York: Routledge, 2005), 110.

65 **They feel a simultaneous urge** Cozolino, 230.

65 **They look away from** Alison Gopnik, *The Philosophical Baby: What Children's Minds Tell Us About Truth, Love, and the Meaning of Life* (New York: Farrar, Straus, & Giroux, 2009), 184.

65 **more fearful than other children** Susan D. Calkins, "Early Attachment Processes and the Development of Emotional Self-Regulation," in *Handbook of Self-Regulation: Research, Theory, and Applications*, eds. Roy F. Baumeister and Kathleen D. Vohs (New York: Guilford Press, 2004), 332.

66 **more promiscuous in adolescence** David M. Buss, *The Evolution of Desire: Strategies of Human Mating* (New York: Basic Books, 2003), 93.

66 **higher rates of psychopathology** Mary Main, Erik Hesse, and Nancy Kaplan, "Predictability of Attachment Behavior and Representational Processes at 1, 6, and 19 Years of Age: The Berkeley Longitudinal Study" in *Attachment from Infancy to Adulthood: The Major Longitudinal Studies*, eds. Klaus E. Grossmann, Karin Grossmann, and Everett Waters (New York: Guilford Press, 2005), 280.

66 **retarded synaptic development** Thomas Lewis, Fari Amini, and Richard Lannon, *A General Theory of Love* (New York: Vintage, 2001), 199.

66 **That's in part because** Kathleen Kendall-Tackett, Linda Meyer Williams, and David Finkelhor, "Impact of Sexual Abuse on Children: A Review and Synthesis of Recent Empirical Studies," *Psychological Bulletin* 113, no. 1 (1993): 173, http://www.unh.edu/ccrc/pdf/VS69.pdf.

66 **They've found, for example** Gopnik, 182.

67 **"predictive power of childhood experience"** Sroufe et al., 268.

67 **Attachment-security and caregiver-sensitivity** Sroufe et al., 164.

67 **Kids who had dominating, intrusive** Sroufe et al., 167.

67 **By observing quality of care** Sroufe et al., 210.

67 **Most reported having no** Sroufe et al., 211.

68 **Forty percent of the parents** Sroufe et al., 95.

68 **"When Ellis seeks help"** Sroufe et al., 287.

CHAPTER 6: LEARNING

74 **In 1954 Muzafer Sherif conducted** Muzafer Sherif et al., *The Robbers Cave Experiment: Intergroup Conflict and Cooperation* (Middletown, CT: Wesleyan University Press, 1988).

74   **Gossip is the way** Roy F. Baumeister, *The Cultural Animal: Human Nature, Meaning, and Social Life* (Cambridge: Oxford University Press, 2005), 286–87.

76   **big eyes and puffy cheeks** Gordon B. Moskowitz, *Social Cognition: Understanding Self and Others* (New York: Guilford Press, 2005), 78.

76   **Most people automatically assume** Ayala Malach Pines, *Falling in Love: Why We Choose the Lovers We Choose* (New York: Routledge, 2005), 93.

77   **As the novelist Frank Portman** Frank Portman, *King Dork* (New York: Delacorte Press, 2006), 123.

77   **And in fact** Steven W. Anderson et al., "Impairment of Social and Moral Behavior Related to Early Damage in Human Prefrontal Cortex," in *Social Neuroscience: Key Readings in Social Psychology*, eds. John T. Cacioppo and Gary G. Berntson (New York: Psychology Press, 2005), 29.

77   **Work by David Van Rooy** Anderson et al., 34.

80   **In some studies, fourteen-year-olds** John D. Bransford, Ann L. Brown, and Rodney R. Cocking, eds., *How People Learn: Brain, Mind, Experience, and School* (Washington, DC: National Academies Press), 119.

80   **The pituitary glands** Louann Brizendine, *The Female Brain* (New York: Broadway Books, 2006), 33.

80   **In the first two weeks** Brizendine, 45.

81   **As a result of hormonal surges** Brizendine, 34.

81   **As John Medina writes** John Medina, *Brain Rules: 12 Principles for Surviving and Thriving at Work, Home, and School* (Seattle, WA: Pear Press, 2008), 110.

81   *Fish Is Fish* Bransford, Brown, and Cocking, eds., 11.

82   **She didn't so much teach** Peter Carruthers, "An Architecture for Dual Reasoning," in *In Two Minds: Dual Processes and Beyond*, eds. Jonathan Evans and Keith Frankish (Cambridge: Oxford University Press, 2009), 121.

83   **Edith Hamilton's book** Edith Hamilton, *The Greek Way* (New York: W.W. Norton & Co., Inc., 1993), 156.

85   **Benjamin Bloom has found** Daniel Coyle, *The Talent Code: Greatness Isn't Born. It's Grown. Here's How.* (New York: Bantam Books, 2009), 175.

86   **Again, the younger** Bransford, Brown, and Cocking, eds., 97.

86   **Researcher Carol Dweck has found** Carol S. Dweck "The Secret to Raising Smart Kids," *Scientific American Mind*, December 2007, http://www.scientificamerican.com/article.cfm?id-the-secret-to-raising-smart-kids.

87   **Alfred North Whitehead saw** David G. Myers, *Intuition: Its Powers and Perils* (New Haven, CT: Yale University Press, 2004), 17.

87   **reach and reciprocity** Richard Ogle, *Smart World: Breakthrough Creativity and the New Science of Ideas* (Boston, MA: Harvard Business School Press, 2007).

88   **The grandmasters could remember** Geoff Colvin, *Talent Is Overrated: What Really Separates World-Class Performers from Everybody Else* (New York: Portfolio, 2008), 46–47.

88   **IQ is, surprisingly** Colvin, 44.

88   **When the same exercise** Colvin, 46–47.

89   **A telephone transmits only** Robert E. Ornstein, *Multimind: A New Way of Looking at Human Behavior* (New York: Houghton Mifflin, 1986), 105.

90   **"You know more than you know"** Jonah Lehrer, *How We Decide* (New York: Houghton Mifflin Co., 2009), 248.

90   **"Life for him was an adventure"** Hamilton, 147.

90   **"All arrogance will reap"** Hamilton, 108.

91   **"The mind wheels"** Ornstein, 23.

92   **A person who is interrupted** Medina, 92.

92   **researchers showed Shereshevskii** Medina, 147.

93 **"We cultivate refinement"** Thucydides, *The History of the Peloponnesian War* (Middlesex: Echo Library, 2006), 77–80.

94 **German scientist Jan Born** Nell Boyce and Susan Brink, "The Secrets of Sleep," *U.S. News & World Report*, May 17, 2004, http://health.usnews.com/usnews/health/articles/040517/17sleep.htm.

95 **Research by Robert Stickgold** Emma Young, "Sleep Tight: You spend around a third of your life doing it, so surely there must be a vital reason for sleep, or is there?" *New Scientist*, March 15, 2008, 30–34.

95 **In these sorts of early-morning** Jonah Lehrer, "The Eureka Hunt," *The New Yorker*, July 28, 2008, http://www.newyorker.com/reporting/2008/07/28/080728fa_fact_lehrer.

95 **A second before an insight** Lehrer, "The Eureka Hunt."

95 **It was a sensation** Robert Burton, *On Being Certain: Believing You Are Right Even When You're Not* (New York: St. Martin's Press, 2008), 23.

95 **As Robert Burton wrote** Burton, 218.

97 **"an unsuspected kinship"** Diane Ackerman, *An Alchemy of Mind: The Marvel and Mystery of the Brain* (New York: Scribner, 2004), 168.

CHAPTER 7: NORMS

102 **According to the Fragile Families** "The Retreat From Marriage by Low-Income Families," Fragile Families Research Brief No. 17, June 2003, http://www.fragilefamilies.princeton.edu/briefs/ResearchBrief17.pdf.

105 **"Whining, which was pervasive"** Annette Lareau, *Unequal Childhoods: Class, Race, and Family Life* (Berkeley, CA: University of California Press, 2003), 107.

106 **Language, as Alva Noë** Alva Noë, *Out of Our Heads: Why You Are Not Your Brain, and Other Lessons from the Biology of Consciousness* (New York: Hill & Wang, 2009), 52.

106 **"The amount of talking"** Lareau, 146.

106 **Betty Hart and Todd Risley** David L. Kirp, "After the Bell Curve," *New York Times Magazine*, July 23, 2006, http://www.nytimes.com/2006/07/23/magazine/23wwln_idealab.html.

106 **On an hourly basis** Paul Tough, "What It Takes to Make a Student," *New York Times Magazine*, November 26, 2006, http://www.nytimes.com/2006/11/26/magazine/26tough.html?pagewanted=all.

107 **This affects a variety** Martha Farah et al., "Childhood Poverty: Specific Associations with Neurocognitive Development," *Brain Research* 1110, no. 1 (September 19, 2006): 166–174, http://cogpsy.skku.ac.kr/cwb-bin/CrazyWWWBoard.exe?db-newarticle&mode=download&num=3139&file=farah_2006.pdf.

107 **Research with small mammals** Shirley S. Wang, "This Is Your Brain Without Dad," *Wall Street Journal*, October 27, 2009, http://online.wsj.com/article/SB10001424052748704754804574491811861197926.html.

107 **Students from the poorest** David Brooks, "The Education Gap," *New York Times*, September 25, 2005, http://select.nytimes.com/2005/09/25/opinion/25brooks.html?ref=davidbrooks.

107 **economist James J. Heckman** Flavio Cunha and James J. Heckman, "The Economics and Psychology of Inequality and Human Development," *Journal of the European Economic Association*, 7, nos. 2–3 (April 2009): 320–64, http://www.mitpressjournals.org/doi/abs/10.1162/JEEA.2009.7.2-3.320?journalCode=jeea.

108 **As Albert-László Barabási wrote** Albert-László Barabási, *Linked: How Everything Is Connected to Everything Else and What It Means* (New York: Plume, 2003), 6.

109 **"Local information can lead"** Steven Johnson, *Emergence: The Connected Lives of Ants, Brains, Cities, and Software* (New York: Touchstone, 2001), 79.

109 **As Deborah Gordon of Stanford** Johnson, 32–33.

110   **"The honest answer to"** Turkheimer, "Mobiles: A Gloomy View of Research into Complex Human Traits," in *Wrestling with Behavioral Genetics: Science, Ethics, and Public Conversation*, eds. Erik Parens, Audrey R. Chapman, Nancy Press (Baltimore, MD: Johns Hopkins University Press, 2006), 100–101.

111   **"No complex behaviors"** Turkheimer, 104.

CHAPTER 8: SELF-CONTROL

117   **Another big shock** Daniel Coyle, *The Talent Code: Greatness Isn't Born. It's Grown. Here's How*. (New York: Bantam Books, 2009), 148.

118   **Walter Lippmann once wrote** Walter Lippman, "Men and Citizens," in *The Essential Lippmann: A Political Philosophy for Liberal Democracy*, eds. Clinton Rossiter and James Lare (Cambridge, MA: Harvard University Press, 1963), 168.

121   **Some newborns startle more** Daniel J. Siegel, *The Developing Mind: How Relationships and the Brain Interact to Shape Who We Are* (New York: Guilford Press, 1999), 20.

121   **psychologist Jerome Kagan** John T. Cacioppo and William Patrick, *Loneliness: Human Nature and the Need for Social Connection* (New York: W.W. Norton & Co., Inc., 2008), 133.

122   **dandelion children and orchid children** David Dobbs, "The Science of Success," *The Atlantic*, December 2009, http://www.theatlantic.com/magazine/archive/2009/12/the-science-of-success/7761/.

122   **A study of engineers** Blair Justice, "The Will to Stay Well," *New York Times*, April 17, 1988, http://www.nytimes.com/1988/04/17/magazine/the-will-to-stay-well.html.

123   **Angela Duckworth and Martin Seligman** Angela L. Duckworth and Martin E. P. Seligman, "Self-Discipline Outdoes IQ in Predicting Academic Performance of Adolescents," *Psychological Science* 16, no. 12 (2005): 939–44, http://www.citeulike.org/user/kericson/article/408060.

124   **The marshmallow test turned** Jonah Lehrer, *How We Decide* (New York: Houghton Mifflin Co., 2009), 112.

124   **The kids who possessed** Jonah Lehrer, "Don't! The Secret of Self-Control," *The New Yorker*, May 18, 2009, http://www.newyorker.com/reporting/2009/05/18/090518fa_fact_lehrer?currentPage=all.

124   **These children could wait** Walter Mischel and Ozlem Ayduk, "Willpower in a Cognitive-Affective Processing System: The Dynamics of Delay of Gratification," in *Handbook of Self-Regulation: Research, Theory, and Applications*, eds. Roy F. Baumeister and Kathleen D. Vohs (New York: Guilford Press, 2004), 113.

126   **a 2001 survey** Douglas Kirby, "Understanding What Works and What Doesn't in Reducing Adolescent Sexual Risk-Taking," *Family Planning Perspectives* 33, no. 6 (November/December 2001): http://www.guttmacher.org/pubs/journals/3327601.html.

128   **It's very hard to build** Clive Thompson, "Are Your Friends Making You Fat?" *New York Times*, September 13, 2009, http://www.nytimes.com/2009/09/13/magazine/13contagion-t.html?pagewanted=all.

129   **"One of the most enduring"** Timothy D. Wilson, *Strangers to Ourselves: Discovering the Adaptive Unconscious* (Cambridge, MA: Belknap Press, 2002), 212.

131   **expert players experience sports** Carl Zimmer, "Why Athletes Are Geniuses," *Discover Magazine*, April 16, 2010, http://discovermagazine.com/2010/apr/16-the-brain-athletes-are-geniuses.

131   **Daniel J. Siegel calls "mindsight"** Daniel J. Siegel, *Mindsight: The New Science of Personal Transformation* (New York: Bantam Books, 2010).

131   **"[T]he whole drama of voluntary life"** Jeffrey M. Schwartz and Sharon Begley, *The Mind and the Brain: Neuroplasticity and the Power of Mental Force* (New York: HarperCollins, 2002), 262–64.

CHAPTER 9: CULTURE

133 **Geoff Cohen and Greg Walton** Daniel Coyle, *The Talent Code: Greatness Isn't Born. It's Grown. Here's How.* (New York: Bantam Books, 2009), 110–11.

135 **The sense of identity** Coyle, 102–104.

136 **top performers devote five** David Dobbs, "How to Be a Genius," *New Scientist*, September 15, 2008, http://www.newscientist.com/article/mg19125691.300-how-to-be-a-genius.html.

136 **John Hayes of Carnegie Mellon** Geoff Colvin, *Talent Is Overrated: What Really Separates World-Class Performers from Everybody Else* (New York: Portfolio, 2008), 152.

136 **If somebody nearby can hear** Coyle, 85.

136 **At the Spartak Tennis Club** Coyle, 82.

136 **Benjamin Franklin taught himself** Colvin, 106.

137 **"Which CEO Characteristics"** Steven N. Kaplan, Mark M. Klebanov, and Morten Sorensen, "Which CEO Characteristics and Abilities Matter?" Swedish Institute for Financial Research Conference on the Economics of the Private Equity Market, July 2008, faculty.chicagobooth.edu/steven.kaplan/research/kks.pdf.

138 *Good to Great* Jim Collins, *Good to Great: Why Some Companies Make the Leap . . . and Others Don't* (New York: HarperCollins, 2001).

138 **Murray Barrick, Michael Mount, and Timothy Judge** Murray R. Barrick, Michael K. Mount, and Timothy A. Judge, "Personality and Performance at the Beginning of the New Millennium: What Do We Know and Where Do We Go Next?" *International Journal of Selection and Assessment* 9, nos. 1–2 (March/June 2001): 9–30, http://www.uni-graz.at/psy5www/lehre/kaernbach/doko/artikel/bergner_Barrick_Mount_Judge_2001.pdf.

138 **Ulrike Malmendier and Geoffrey Tate** Ulrike Malmendier and Geoffrey Tate, "Superstar CEOs," *Quarterly Journal of Economics*, 124, no. 4 (November 2009): 1593–1638, http://citeseerx.ist.psu.edu/viewdoc/download?doi=10.1.1.146.1059&rep=rep1&type=pdf.

139 **When people around the world** Tyler Cowen, "In which countries do kids respect their parents the most?" *Marginal Revolution*, December 5, 2007, http://www.marginalrevolution.com/marginalrevolution/2007/12/in-which-countr.html.

140 **"A man has as many social"** Judith Rich Harris, *The Nurture Assumption: Why Children Turn Out the Way They Do* (New York: Touchstone, 1998), 56.

140 **By the third generation** David Brooks, "The Americano Dream," *New York Times*, February 24, 2004, http://www.nytimes.com/2004/02/24/opinion/the-americano-dream.html?ref=davidbrooks.

141 **The core lesson** Richard Nisbett, *The Geography of Thought: How Asians and Westerners Think Differently . . . and Why* (New York: Free Press, 2003), 90.

141 **"Thus, to the Asian"** Nisbett, 100.

141 **Korean parents emphasize** Alison Gopnik, Andrew N. Meltzoff, and Patricia Kuhl, *The Scientist in the Crib: What Early Learning Tells Us About the Mind* (New York: Perennial, 2001), 89.

141 **Asked to describe video** Nisbett, 95.

142 **Chinese students are more** Nisbett, 140.

142 **American six-year-olds make** Nisbett, 87–88.

142 **Chinese subjects were more** Bruce E. Wexler, *Brain and Culture: Neurobiology, Ideology, and Social Change* (Cambridge, MA: MIT Press, 2006), 149.

142 **Americans tend to exaggerate** Timothy D. Wilson, *Strangers to Ourselves: Discovering the Adaptive Unconscious* (Cambridge, MA: Belknap Press, 2002), 38.

142 **choose between three computers** Nisbett, 185.

142 **The Chinese eyes perform** John Roach, "Chinese, Americans, Truly See Differently,

Study Says," *National Geographic News*, August 22, 2005, http://news.nationalgeographic.com/news/2005/08/0822_050822_chinese.html.

142 **East Asians have a tougher time** Rachel E. Jack et al., "Cultural Confusions Show that Facial Expressions Are Not Universal," *Current Biology* 19, no. 18 (August 13, 2009), 1543–48, http://www.cell.com/current-biology/retrieve/pii/S0960982209014778.

145 **"The country of my childhood"** Wexler, 175.

148 **As Michael Tomasello** Roy F. Baumeister, *The Cultural Animal: Human Nature, Meaing, and Social Life* (Oxford: Oxford University Press, 2005), 31.

148 **You can teach a chimpanzee** Baumeister, 131.

148 **"What sets him off most graphically"** Clifford Geertz, *The Interpretation of Cultures* (New York: Basic Books, 1973), 46.

149 **"We build 'designer environments' "** Andy Clark, *Being There: Putting Brain, Body, and World Together Again* (Cambridge, MA: MIT Press, 1998), 191.

149 **Human brains, Clark believes** Clark, 180.

150 **If the culture adds** Baumeister, 53.

150 **Children born without sight** Wexler, 33.

150 **Donald E. Brown lists traits** Donald E. Brown, *Human Universals* (New York: McGraw-Hill, 1991).

150 **Plays written and produced** Wexler,187–88.

150 **Half of all people in India** David P. Schmitt, "Evolutionary and Cross-Cultural Perspectives on Love: The Influence of Gender, Personality, and Local Ecology on Emotional Investment in Romantic Relationships," in *The New Psychology of Love*, eds. Robert J. Sternberg and Karin Sternberg (New Haven, CT: Yale University Press, 2006), 252.

150 **Nearly a quarter of Americans** Helen Fisher, *Why We Love: The Nature and Chemistry of Romantic Love* (New York: Henry Holt & Co., 2004), 5.

151 **Craig MacAndrew and Robert B. Edgerton** Craig MacAndrew and Robert B. Edgerton, *Drunken Comportment: A Social Explanation* (Clinton Corners, NY: Percheron Press, 2003).

151 **couples having coffee** Dacher Keltner, *Born to Be Good: The Science of a Meaningful Life* (New York: W.W. Norton & Co., Inc., 2009), 195.

151 **But if you bump** Steven Pinker, *The Blank Slate: The Modern Denial of Human Nature* (New York: Penguin Books, 2002), 328.

151 **Cities in the South** Marc D. Hauser, *Moral Minds: The Nature of Right and Wrong* (New York: Harper Perennial, 2006), 134.

151 **A cultural construct** Guy Deutscher, "You Are What You Speak," *The New York Times Magazine*, August 26, 2010, 44.

152 **Her head was filled** Douglas Hofstadter, *I Am a Strange Loop* (New York: Basic Books, 2007), 177.

152 **They seem to be growing** David Halpern, *The Hidden Wealth of Nations* (Cambridge: Polity Press, 2010), 76.

152 **"Cultures do not exist"** Thomas Sowell, *Migrations and Cultures: A World View* (New York: Basic Books, 1996), 378.

152 **Haitians and Dominicans share** Lawrence E. Harrison, *The Central Liberal Truth: How Politics Can Change a Culture and Save It from Itself* (Cambridge: Oxford University Press, 2006), 26.

153 **In Ceylon in 1969** Thomas Sowell, *Race and Culture: A World View* (New York: Basic Books, 1994), 67.

153 **In Chile, three-quarters** Sowell, *Race and Culture*, 25.

153 **By the time they enter kindergarten** Margaret Bridges, Bruce Fuller, Russell Rumberger, and Loan Tran, "Preschool for California's Children: Unequal Access, Promising Benefits," PACE Child Development Projects, University of California Linguistic Minority Research Institute (September 2004): 7, http://gse.berkeley.edu/research/pace/reports/PB.04-3.pdf.

153   **Roughly 54 percent of Asian Americans** Abigail Thernstrom and Stephan Thernstrom, *No Excuses: Closing the Racial Gap in Learning* (New York: Simon & Schuster, 2003), 85.

153   **The average Asian American in New Jersey** David Brooks, "The Limits of Policy," *New York Times*, May 3, 2010, http://www.nytimes.com/2010/05/04/opinion/04brooks.html.

153   **"Cultures of Corruption"** Fisman, Raymond, and Edward Miguel, "Corruption, Norms and Legal Enforcement: Evidence from Diplomatic Parking Tickets," *Journal of Political Economy* 115, no. 6 (2007): 1020–48, http://www2.gsb.columbia.edu/faculty/rfisman/parking_20july06_RF.pdf.

154   **People in progress-prone** Harrison, 53.

156   **People in trusting cultures** Francis Fukuyama, *Trust: The Social Virtues and the Creation of Prosperity* (New York: Free Press, 1996), 338.

156   **Germany and Japan have high** Edward Banfield, *The Moral Basis of a Backward Society* (New York: Free Press, 1967).

156   **The merging of these two idea spaces** Richard Ogle, *Smart World: Breakthrough Creativity and the New Science of Ideas* (Boston, MA: Harvard Business School Press, 2007), 8–10.

156   **Ronald Burt** Ronald Burt, *Structural Holes: The Social Structure of Competition* (Cambridge, MA: Harvard University Press, 1992).

CHAPTER 10: INTELLIGENCE

160   **"The Dunsinane Reforestation"** Christopher Hitchens, *Hitch 22* (New York: Twelve, 2010), 266. This exchange is based on a conversation the author witnessed between Hitchens and Salman Rushdie, two masters of these kinds of games.

160   **Male babies make less** Matt Ridley, *The Agile Gene: How Nature Turns on Nurture* (New York: Perennial, 2004), 59.

160   **a person's emotional state** Daniel Goleman, *Social Intelligence: The New Science of Human Relationships* (New York: Bantam Dell, 2006) 139.

160   **verbal memory and verbal fluency** John Medina, *Brain Rules: 12 Principles for Surviving and Thriving at Work, Home, and School* (Seattle, WA: Pear Press, 2008), 262.

160   **They don't necessarily talk more** Michael S. Gazzaniga, *Human: The Science Behind What Makes Us Human* (New York: Harper Perennial, 2008), 96.

162   *Varieties of Capitalism* Peter A. Hall and David W. Soskice, "An Introduction to the Varieties of Capitalism," in *Varieties of Capitalism: The Institutional Foundations of Comparative Advantage*, eds. Peter A. Hall and David W. Soskice (Oxford: Oxford University Press, 2004), 1–70.

163   **People who are really good** Arthur Robert Jensen, *The G Factor: The Science of Mental Ability* (Westport, CT: Praeger Publishers, 1998), 34–35.

163   **The single strongest predictor** Robin Karr-Morse and Meredith S. Wiley, *Ghosts from the Nursery: Tracing the Roots of Violence* (New York: Atlantic Monthly Press, 1997), 28.

163   **Dean Hamer and Peter Copeland** Dean H. Hamer and Peter Copeland, *Living with Our Genes: Why They Matter More Than You Think* (New York: Anchor Books, 1999), 217.

164   **black children in Prince Edward County** Richard W. Nisbett, *Intelligence and How to Get It: Why Schools and Cultures Count* (New York: W.W. Norton & Co., Inc., 2009), 41.

164   **They have to divide their** Bruce E. Wexler, *Brain and Culture: Neurobiology, Ideology, and Social Change* (Cambridge, MA: MIT Press, 2006), 68.

164   **Between 1947 and 2002** Nisbett, 44.

164   **"Today's children"** James R. Flynn, *What Is Intelligence?: Beyond the Flynn Effect* (Cambridge: Cambridge University Press, 2007), 19.

165   **They are not better** David G. Myers, *Intuition: Its Powers and Perils* (New Haven, CT: Yale University Press, 2002), 35.

165   **"IQ predicts only about 4 percent"** Richard K. Wagner, "Practical Intelligence," in *Handbook of Intelligence*, ed. Robert J. Sternberg (Cambridge: Cambridge University Press, 2000), 382.

165   **There is great uncertainty** John D. Mayer, Peter Salovey and David Caruso, "Models of Emotional Intelligence," in *Handbook of Intelligence*, ed. Robert J. Sternberg (Cambridge: Cambridge University Press, 2000), 403.

165   **"What nature hath joined together"** Nisbett, 18.

165   **They were the ones who** Daniel Goleman, "75 Years Later, Study Still Tracking Geniuses," *New York Times*, March 7, 1995, http://www.nytimes.com/1995/03/07/science/75-years-later-study-still-tracking-geniuses.html?pagewanted=all and Richard C. Paddock, "The Secret IQ Diaries," *Los Angeles Times*, July 30, 1995, http://articles.latimes.com/1995-07-30/magazine/tm-29325_1_lewis-terman.

165   **As Malcolm Gladwell demonstrated** Malcolm Gladwell, *Outliers: The Story of Success* (New York: Little, Brown & Co., 2008) 81–83.

165   **National Longitudinal Survey of Youth** John Tierney, "Smart Doesn't Equal Rich," *New York Times*, April 25, 2007, http://tierneylab.blogs.nytimes.com/2007/04/25/smart-doesnt-equal-rich/.

166   **"The tendency to collect information"** Keith E. Stanovich, *What Intelligence Tests Miss: The Psychology of Rational Thought* (New Haven, CT: Yale University Press, 2009), 31–32.

166   **distinctions between clocks and clouds** Jonah Lehrer, "Breaking Things Down to Particles Blinds Scientists to Big Picture," *Wired*, April 19, 2010, http://www.wired.com/magazine/2010/04/st_essay_particles/.

167   **"Many different studies involving"** Stanovich, 34–35.

167   **Firsthand Technology Value mutual fund** Stanovich, 60.

168   **GED recipients are much** James J. Heckman and Yona Rubinstein, "The Importance of Noncognitive Skills: Lessons from the GED Testing Program," *American Economic Review* 91, no. 2 (May 2001): 145–49, http://www.econ-pol.unisi.it/bowles/Institutions%20of%20capitalism/heckman%20on%20ged.pdf.

168   **"The words of the language"** Robert Scott Root-Bernstein and Michèle Root-Bernstein, *Sparks of Genius: The Thirteen Thinking Tools of the World's Most Creative People* (New York: First Mariner Books, 2001), 3.

168   **Others proceed acoustically** Root-Bernstein and Root-Bernstein, 53–54.

168   **Others do so emotionally** Root-Bernstein and Root-Bernstein, 196.

CHAPTER 11: CHOICE ARCHITECTURE

171   **Grocers know that shoppers** "6 Ways Supermarkets Trick You to Spend More Money," *Shine*, March 1, 2010, http://shine.yahoo.com/event/financiallyfit/6-ways-supermarkets-trick-you-to-spend-more-money-974209/?pg=2.

171   **the smell of baked goods** Martin Lindstrom and Paco Underhill, *Buyology: Truth and Lies About Why We Buy* (New York: Doubleday, 2008), 148–49.

171   **Researchers in Britain found** Joseph T. Hallinan, *Why We Make Mistakes: How We Look Without Seeing, Forget Things in Seconds, and Are All Pretty Sure We Are Way Above Average* (New York: Broadway Books, 2009), 92–93.

171   **In department stores** Paco Underhill, *Call of the Mall: The Geography of Shopping by the Author of Why We Buy* (New York: Simon & Schuster, 2004), 49–50.

172   **pairs of panty hose** Timothy D. Wilson, *Strangers to Ourselves* (Cambridge, MA: Belknap Press, 2002), 103.

172   **At restaurants, people eat more** Richard H. Thaler and Cass R. Sunstein, *Nudge: Improving Decisions About Health, Wealth, and Happiness* (Ann Arbor, MI: Caravan Books, 2008), 64.

172   Marketing people also realize Hallinan, 99.

172   Capital Pacific Homes David Brooks, "Castle in a Box," *The New Yorker*, March 26, 2001, http://www.newyorker.com/archive/2001/03/26/010326fa_fact_brooks.

173   For all of human history Steven E. Landsburg, "The Theory of the Leisure Class," *Slate*, March 9, 2007, http://www.slate.com/id/2161309.

173   the owls John Medina, *Brain Rules: 12 Principles for Surviving and Thriving at Work, Home, and School* (Seattle, WA: Pear Press, 2008), 163.

177   As Angela Duckworth Jonah Lehrer, "The Truth about Grit," *Boston Globe*, August 2, 2009, http://www.boston.com/bostonglobe/ideas/articles/2009/08/02/the_truth_about _grit/.

178   M. Mitchell Waldrop Richard Bronk, *The Romantic Economist: Imagination in Economics* (Cambridge: Cambridge University Press, 2009), 17.

178   "If I were to distill one" Dan Ariely, *Predictably Irrational: The Hidden Forces That Shape Our Decisions* (New York: HarperCollins, 2008) 243.

179   Health officials in New York Anemona Hartocollis, "Calorie Postings Don't Change Habits, Study Finds," *New York Times*, October 6, 2009, http://www.nytimes.com/2009/ 10/06/nyregion/06calories.html.

180   a series of words Ariely, 170–71.

180   If you merely use the words John A. Bargh, "Bypassing the Will: Toward Demystifying the Nonconcious Control of Social Behavior," in *The New Unconscious*, eds. Ran R. Hassin, James S. Uleman, and John A. Bargh (Oxford: Oxford University Press), 40.

181   If you remind African American students Claude M. Steele, "Thin Ice: Stereotype Threat and Black College Students," *The Atlantic*, August 1999, http://www.theatlantic .com/magazine/archive/1999/08/thin-ice-stereotype-threat-and-black-college-students/ 4663/1/.

181   Asian American women Margaret Shih, Todd L. Pittinsky, and Nalini Ambady, "Stereotype Susceptibility: Identity Salience and Shifts in Quantitative Performance," *Psychological Science* 10, no. 1 (January 1999): 80–83.

181   Genghis Khan's death Hallinan, 102.

181   The manager of a Brunswick pool-table Robert E. Ornstein, *Multimind: A New Way of Looking at Human Behavior* (New York: Houghton Mifflin, 1996), 86.

181   high Social Security numbers Dan Ariely, "The Fallacy of Supply and Demand," *Huffington Post*, March 20, 2008, http://www.huffingtonpost.com/dan-ariely/the-fallacy-of -supply-and_b_92590.html.

182   People who are given Hallinan, 50.

182   "Their predictions became" Jonah Lehrer, *How We Decide* (New York: Houghton Mifflin Co., 2009), 146.

182   They just stick with Thaler and Sunstein, 34.

182   The picture of the smiling Hallinan, 101.

182   In the aroused state Ariely, 96 and 106.

183   Daniel Kahneman and Amos Tversky Jonah Lehrer, "Loss Aversion," *The Frontal Cortex*, February 10, 2010, http://scienceblogs.com/cortex/2010/02/loss_aversion.php.

CHAPTER 12: FREEDOM AND COMMITMENT

187   In Guess culture Oliver Burkerman, "This Column Will Change Your Life," *The Guardian*, May 8, 2010, http://www.guardian.co.uk/lifeandstyle/2010/may/08/change- life-asker-guesser.

189   Thirty-eight percent of young Americans "Pew Report on Community Satisfaction," Pew Research Center (January 29, 2009): 10, http://pewsocialtrends.org/assets/pdf/ Community-Satisfaction.pdf.

190   In Western Europe William A. Galston, "The Odyssey Years: The Changing 20s,"

Brookings Institution, November 7, 2007, http://www.brookings.edu/interviews/2007/1107_childrenandfamilies_galston.aspx.

190 **postponing marriage** William Galston, "The Changing 20s," Brookings Institution, October 4, 2007, http://www.brookings.edu/speeches/2007/1004useconomics_galston.aspx.

190 **finish their education** Galston, "The Changing 20s."

191 **In 1970 only 26 percent** Robert Wuthnow, *After the Baby Boomers: How Twenty- and Thirty-Somethings Are Shaping the Future of American Religion* (Princeton, NJ: Princeton University Press, 2007), 29.

191 **"I am certain that someday"** Jeffrey Jensen Arnett, *Emerging Adulthood: The Winding Road from the Late Teens through the Twenties* (Oxford: Oxford University Press, 2004), 16.

191 **In 1950 a personality test** Jean Twenge, *Generation Me: Why Today's Young Americans Are More Confident, Assertive, Entitled—and More Miserable Than Ever Before* (New York: Free Press, 2006), 69.

192 **young people today** Wuthnow, 62.

192 **subsidies from Mom and Dad** Wuthnow, 32.

192 **Michael Barone argues** Michael Barone, "A Tale of Two Nations," *US News & World Report*, May 4, 2003, http://www.usnews.com/usnews/opinion/articles/030512/12pol.htm.

196 **This inequality doesn't seem** Elizabeth Kolbert, "Everybody Have Fun," *The New Yorker*, March 22, 2010, http://www.newyorker.com/arts/critics/books/2010/03/22/100322crbo_books_kolbert.

196 **Winning the lottery produces** Elizabeth Kolbert, "Everybody Have Fun."

196 **"fulfill all their dreams"** Derek Bok, *The Politics of Happiness: What Government Can Learn from the New Research on Well-Being* (Princeton, NJ: Princeton University Press, 2010), 13.

196 **People in long-term marriages** Bok, 17–18.

196 **being married produces** David Blanchflower and Andrew Oswald, "Well-Being Over Time in Britain and the USA," *Journal of Public Economics* 88 (July 2004): 1359–86, http://www2.warwick.ac.uk/fac/soc/economics/staff/faculty/oswald/wellbeingnew.pdf.

196 **joining a group** Robert D. Putnam, *Bowling Alone: The Collapse and Revival of American Community* (New York: Simon & Schuster, 2000), 333.

196 **People who have one recurrent** David Halpern, *The Hidden Wealth of Nations* (Cambridge: Polity Press, 2010), 26.

196 **People who have more friends** Tara Parker-Pope, "What Are Friends For? A Longer Life," *New York Times*, April 21, 2009, http://www.nytimes.com/2009/04/21/health/21well.html.

197 **the daily activities** Bok, 28.

197 **professions that correlate** Halpern, 28–29.

197 **"Whether someone has"** Roy F. Baumeister, *The Cultural Animal: Human Nature, Meaning, and Social Life* (Oxford: Oxford University Press, 2005), 109.

CHAPTER 13: LIMERENCE

203 **Adrian Furnham of University College, London** Joan Raymond, "He's Not as Smart as He Thinks," *Newsweek*, January 23, 2008, http://www.newsweek.com/2008/01/22/he-s-not-as-smart-as-he-thinks.html.

203 **Women underestimate their IQ** Joan Raymond, "He's Not as Smart as He Thinks."

204 **"Below the surface-stream"** Lionel Trilling, *Sincerity and Authenticity* (Cambridge, MA: University of Harvard Press, 1972), 5.

205 **"Fires run through my body"** Helen Fisher, *Why We Love: The Nature and Chemistry of Romantic Love* (New York: Henry Holt & Co., 2004), 1.

205 **Faby Gagné and John Lydon** Kaja Perina, "Love's Loopy Logic," *Psychology Today*, January 1, 2007, http://www.psychologytoday.com/articles/200612/loves-loopy-logic.

205 **"What I have called crystalization"** Stendhal, *Love*, trans. Gilbert Sale and Suzanne Sale (New York: Penguin Books, 2004), 45.

206 **Norepinephrine** Fisher, 53.

206 **Phenylethylamine** Ayala Malakh Pines, *Falling in Love: Why We Choose the Lovers We Choose* (New York: Routledge, 2005), 154.

206 **"The caudate is also"** Fisher, 69.

206 **Arthur Aron** Sadie F. Dingfelder, "More Than a Feeling," *Monitor on Psychology* 38, no. 2 (February 2007): 40, http://www.apa.org/monitor/feb07/morethan.aspx.

206 **Neuroscientist Jaak Panksepp** Daniel Goleman, *Social Intelligence: The New Science of Human Relationships* (New York: Bantam Dell, 2006) 192.

207 **A person in love** Helen Fisher, "The Drive to Love: The Neural Mechanism for Mate Selection," in *The New Psychology of Love*, eds. Robert J. Sternberg and Karin Weis (New Haven, CT: Yale University Press, 2006), 92–93.

207 **A crucial answer came** P. Read Montague, Peter Dayan, and Terrence J. Sejnowski, "A Framework for Mesencephalic Domanine Systems Based on Predictive Hebbian Learning," *Journal of Neuroscience* 16, no. 5 (March 1, 1996): 1936–47, http://www.jneurosci.org/cgi/reprint/16/5/1936.pdf.

207 **The main business** Read Montague, *Your Brain Is (Almost) Perfect: How We Make Decisions* (New York: Plume, 2007), 117.

208 **Dennis and Denise** Brett W. Pelham, Matthew C. Mirenberg, and John T. Jones, "Why Susie Sells Seashells by the Seashore: Implicit Egotism and Major Life Decisions," *Journal of Personality and Social Psychology* 82, no. 4 (2002): 469–87, http://futurama.tistory.com/attachment/ck10.pdf.

209 **As Bruce Wexler argues** Bruce E. Wexler, *Brain and Culture: Neurobiology, Ideology, and Social Change* (Cambridge, MA: MIT Press, 2006), 143.

209 **"The child will love a crusty"** C. S. Lewis, *The Four Loves* (Orlando, FL: Harcourt Brace & Co., 1988), 33.

209 **Within two weeks** James Q. Wilson, *The Moral Sense* (New York: Free Press, 1997), 124.

210 **Austrian physician René Spitz** Bruce D. Perry, *Born For Love: Why Empathy Is Essential—and Endangered* (New York: HarperCollins, 2010), 51.

210 **It takes the average college student** Elaine Hatfield, Richard L. Rapson, and Yen-Chi L. Le, "Emotional Contagion and Empathy," in *The Social Neuroscience of Empathy*, eds. Jean Decety and William John Ickes (Cambridge, MA: MIT Press, 2009), 21.

210 **neuroscientist Marco Iacoboni notes** Marco Iacoboni, *Mirroring People: The New Science of How We Connect with Others* (New York: Farrar, Straus & Giroux, 2008), 4.

210 **"When your friend has become"** Lewis, 34.

210 **"free from all duties"** Lewis, 77.

211 **Solomon Asch conducted** Andrew Newburg and Mark Robert Waldman, *Why We Believe What We Believe: Uncovering Our Biological Need for Meaning, Spirituality, and Truth* (New York: Free Press, 2006), 143–44.

211 **Dean Ornish surveyed** Thomas Lewis, Fari Amini, and Richard Lannon, *A General Theory of Love* (New York: Vintage, 2001), 80.

211 **"Words are inadequate"** Jonathan Haidt, *The Happiness Hypothesis: Finding Modern Truth in Ancient Wisdom* (New York: Basic Books, 2006), 237.

212 **"Animals have sex"** Allan Bloom, *Love and Friendship* (New York: Simon & Schuster, 1993), 19.

213 **"Love you? I *am* you."** Lewis, 95.

213 **"We are one"** John Milton, *Paradise Lost*, book 9, lines 958–59.

CHAPTER 14: THE GRAND NARRATIVE

216 **"There is no craving"** David Hume, "Of Interest," in *Selected Essays*, eds. Stephen Copley and Andrew Edgar (Oxford: Oxford University Press, 2008), 182.

217 **Long-term unemployment** Don Peck, "How a New Jobless Era Will Transform America," *The Atlantic*, March 2010, http://www.theatlantic.com/magazine/archive/2010/03/how-a-new-jobless-era-will-transform-america/7919/.

218 **Ninety percent of drivers** Robert H. Frank, *The Economic Naturalist: In Search of Explanations for Everyday Enigmas* (New York: Basic Books, 2007), 129.

218 **Ninety-four percent of college professors** Andrew Newburg and Mark Robert Waldman, *Why We Believe What We Believe: Uncovering Our Biological Need for Meaning, Spirituality, and Truth* (New York: Free Press, 2006), 73.

218 **Ninety percent of entrepreneurs** Richard H. Thaler and Cass R. Sunstein, *Nudge: Improving Decisions About Health, Wealth, and Happiness* (Ann Arbor, MI: Caravan Books, 2008), 32.

218 **Ninety-eight percent of students** Keith E. Stanovich, *What Intelligence Tests Miss: The Psychology of Rational Thought* (New Haven, CT: Yale University Press, 2009), 109.

218 **College students vastly overestimate** Daniel Gilbert, *Stumbling on Happiness* (New York: Vintage, 2007), 18.

219 **Golfers on the PGA tour** Joseph T. Hallinan, *Why We Make Mistakes: How We Look Without Seeing, Forget Things in Seconds, and Are All Pretty Sure We Are Way Above Average* (New York: Broadway Books, 2009), 170.

219 **Half of all students** David G. Myers, *Intuition: Its Powers and Perils* (New Haven, CT: Yale University Press, 2004), 83.

219 **Russo and Schoemaker** Hallinan, 167.

219 **Brad Barber and Terrance Odean** Myers, 159.

219 **Andrew Lo of MIT** Stephen J. Dubner, "This Is Your Brain on Prosperity," *New York Times*, January 9, 2009, http://freakonomics.blogs.nytimes.com/2009/01/09/this-is-your-brain-on-prosperity-andrew-lo-on-fear-greed-and-crisis-management/.

220 **Daniel Gilbert of Harvard** Gilbert, 180.

220 **incompetent people exaggerate** Erica Goode, "Among the Inept, Researchers Discover, Ignorance Is Bliss," *New York Times*, January 18, 2000, http://www.nytimes.com/2000/01/18/health/among-the-inept-researchers-discover-ignorance-is-bliss.html.

221 **the more sectors they entered** Jerry Z. Muller, "Our Epistemological Depression," *The American*, February 29, 2009, http://www.american.com/archive/2009/february-2009/our-epistemological-depression.

222 **BPR "escalates the efforts"** "Business Processing Reengineering," *Wikipedia*, http://en.wikipedia.org/wiki/Business_process_reengineering.

223 **John Maynard Keynes** John Maynard Keyes, *The General Theory of Employment, Interest and Money* (New York: Classic Books America, 2009), 331.

223 **"If the better elements"** Plato, *Phaedrus*, trans. Alexander Nehamas and Paul Woodruff (New York: Hackett, 1995), 44.

224 **In this scientific age** Francis Bacon, "Preface to the *Novum Organum*," in *Prefaces and Prologues*, vol. 34, ed. Charles William Eliot (New York: P.F. Collier & Son, 1909–14; Bartleby.com, 2001), http://www.bartleby.com/39/22.html.

224 **"Reason is to the philosopher"** Cesar Chesneau Dumarsais, "Philosophe," in *Encyclopédie*, vol. 22, ed. Denis Diderot.

225 **This mode, as Guy Claxton** Guy Claxton, *The Wayward Mind: An Intimate History of the Unconscious* (New York: Little, Brown Book Group, 2006).

227 **Lionel Trilling diagnosed** Lionel Trilling, *The Liberal Imagination: Essays on Literature and Society* (New York: New York Review of Books, 2008), ix–xx.

227 **"deals with introspection"** Robert Skidelsky, *Keynes: The Return of the Master* (New York: PublicAffairs, 2009), 81.

228 **Paul Samuelson applied** Clive Cookson, Gillian Tett, and Chris Cook, "Organic Mechanics," *Financial Times*, November 26, 2009, http://www.ft.com/cms/s/0/doe6abde-dacb-11de-933d-00144feabdco.html.

228 **George A. Akerlof and Robert Shiller** George A. Akerlof and Robert J. Shiller, *Animal Spirits: How Human Psychology Drives the Economy, and Why It Matters* (Princeton, NJ: Princeton University Press, 2010), 1.

229 **Jim Collins argues** Jim Collins, "How the Mighty Fall: A Primer on the Warning Signs," *Businessweek*, May 14, 2009, http://www.businessweek.com/magazine/content/09_21/b4132026786379.htm.

CHAPTER 15: *MÉTIS*

232 **historian Johan Huizinga** John Lukacs, *Confessions of an Original Sinner* (South Bend, IN: St. Augustine's Press, 2000), 39.

234 **"Reason is and ought only"** David Hume, *A Treatise of Human Nature*, bk. 2, sect. 3 (Ithaca, NY: Cornell University Press, 2009), 286.

234 **"We are generally"** Edmund Burke, *Reflections on the Revolution in France* (Oxford: Oxford University Press, 1999), 87.

234 **"senses and imagination captivate"** Gertrude Himmelfarb, *The Roads to Modernity: The British, French, and American Enlightenments* (New York: Vintage, 2005), 76.

236 **Level 2 is like Mr. Spock** Richard H. Thaler and Cass R. Sunstein, *Nudge: Improving Decisions About Health, Wealth, and Happiness* (Ann Arbor, MI: Caravan Books, 2008), 22.

236 **The recall process** James Le Fanu, *Why Us?: How Science Rediscovered the Mystery of Ourselves* (New York: Vintage, 2010), 213.

236 **Half had significant errors** Robert A. Burton, *On Being Certain: Believing You Are Right Even When You're Not* (New York: St. Martin's Press, 2008), 10.

237 **201 prisoners in the United States** Joseph T. Hallinan, *Why We Make Mistakes: How We Look Without Seeing, Forget Things in Seconds, and Are All Pretty Sure We Are Way Above Average* (New York: Broadway Books, 2009), 41

237 **Research by Taylor Schmitz** Taylor W. Schmitz, Eve De Rosa, and Adam K. Anderson, "Opposing Influences of Affective State Valence on Visual Cortical Encoding," *Journal of Neuroscience* 29, no. 22 (June 3, 2009): 7199–7207, http://www.jneurosci.org/cgi/content/short/29/22/7199.

237 **doctors who got the candy** Hallinan, 219.

237 **sunny days** Norbert Schwarz and Gerald L. Clore, "Mood, Misattribution, and Judgments of Well-Being: Informative and Directive Functions of Affective States," *Journal of Personality and Social Psychology* 45, no. 3 (1983): 513–23, http://sitemaker.umich.edu/norbert.schwarz/files/83_jpsp_schwarz___clore_mood.pdf.

237 **The bridge guys** Timothy D. Wilson, *Strangers to Ourselves: Discovering the Adaptive Unconscious* (Cambridge, MA: Belknap Press, 2002), 101–102.

238 **"We hear and apprehend"** Henry David Thoreau, *I To Myself: An Annotated Selection from the Journal of Henry D. Thoreau*, ed. Jeffrey S. Kramer (New Haven, CT: Yale University Press, 2007), 420.

238 **A shooter who has made** John Huizinga and Sandy Weil, "Hot Hand or Hot Head: The Truth About Heat Checks in the NBA," MIT Sloan Sports Analytics Conference, March 7, 2009, http://web.me.com/sandy1729/sportsmetricians_consulting/Hot_Hand_files/HotHandMITConf03.pdf.

238 **When told he was a dancer** Robert E. Christiaansen, James D. Sweeney, and Kathy Ochalek, "Influencing Eyewitness Descriptions," *Law and Human Behavior* 7, no. 1 (March 1983), 59–65, http://www.springerlink.com/content/xm1lm15u08w1q1oh/.

238 **This project's work** "Roots of Unconscious Prejudice Affect 90 to 95 percent of Peo-

ple," *ScienceDaily*, September 30, 1998, http://www.sciencedaily.com/releases/1998/09/980930082237.htm.

238 **The prejudices against the elderly** Carey Goldberg, "Even Elders Reflect Broad Bias Against the Old, Study Finds," *Boston Globe*, October 28, 2002, http://pqasb.pqarchiver.com/boston/access/225621771.html?FMT=ABS&date=Oct%2028,%202002.

239 **They fear chain saws** David G. Myers, *Intuition: Its Powers and Perils* (New Haven, CT: Yale University Press, 2004), 205.

239 **Measured at its highest** Ap Dijksterhuis, Henk Aarts, and Pamela K. Smith, "The Power of the Subliminal: On Subliminal Persuasion and Other Potential Applications," in *The New Unconscious*, eds. Ran R. Hassim, James S. Uleman, and John A. Bargh (Oxford: Oxford University Press, 2005), 82.

240 **Ian Waterman** Wilson, 19.

241 **"choking on thought"** Jonah Lehrer, *How We Decide* (New York: Houghton Mifflin Co., 2009), 136.

241 **Beatrice de Gelder** Benedict Carey, "Blind, Yet Seeing: The Brain's Subconscious Visual Sense," *New York Times*, December 23, 2008, http://www.nytimes.com/2008/12/23/health/23blin.html.

241 **When scientists flash cards** Jonah Lehrer, *Proust Was a Neuroscientist* (New York: Houghton Mifflin Co., 2007), 184.

241 **professional chicken sexers** Myers, 55.

241 **movement of the** *X* Wilson, 26–27.

242 **"My body suddenly got cooler"** Benedict Carey, "In Battle, Hunches Prove to Be Valuable," *New York Times*, July 28, 2009, http://www.nytimes.com/2009/07/28/health/research/28brain.html.

242 **Antonio and Hanna Damasio** Antoine Bechara, Hanna Damasio, Daniel Tranel, and Antonio R. Damasio, "Deciding Advantageously Before Knowing the Advantageous Strategy," *Science* 28, no. 5304 (February 1997): 1293–95, http://www.sciencemag.org/cgi/content/short/275/5304/1293.

242 **Swiss doctor Édouard Claparède** Wilson, 25.

242 **That one implicit rule** Gerd Gigerenzer, *Gut Feelings: The Intelligence of the Unconscious* (New York: Penguin Books, 2007), 9–11.

243 **fuzzy-trace theory** Paul A. Klaczynski, "Cognitive and Social Cognitive Development: Dual-Process Research and Theory," in *In Two Minds: Dual Processes and Beyond*, eds. Jonathan Evans and Keith Frankish (Oxford: Oxford University Press, 2009), 270.

244 **The immediate choosers** Ap Dijksterhuis and Loran F. Nordgren, "A Theory of Unconscious Thought," *Perspectives on Psychological Science* 1, no. 2 (June 2006): 95–109, http://www.unconsciouslab.nl/publications/Dijksterhuis%20Nordgren%20-%20A%20Theory%20of%20Unconscious%20Thought.pdf.

244 **five different art posters** Dijksterhuis and Nordgren, 100.

244 **a study set in IKEA** Dijksterhuis and Nordgren, 104.

244 **"dark and dusty nooks"** Dijksterhuis and Nordgren, 102.

245 **"It is worth noting"** John A. Bargh, "Bypassing the Will: Toward Demystifying the Nonconscious Control of Social Behavior," in *The New Unconscious*, eds. Ran R. Hassim, James S. Uleman, and John A. Bargh (Oxford: Oxford University Press, 2005), 53.

246 **You would have no chance** George Eliot, *Felix Holt, the Radical* (New York: Penguin Books, 1995), 279.

246 **Folk wisdom in North America** James C. Scott, *Seeing Like a State: How Certain Schemes to Improve the Human Condition Have Failed* (New Haven, CT: Yale University Press, 1998), 311.

247 **gobiid fish** Guy Claxton, *Hare Brain, Tortoise Mind: How Intelligence Increases When You Think Less* (New York: Harper Perennial, 2000), 18.

247 **Research by Colin Camerer** Colin Camerer et al., "Neural Systems Responding to Degrees of Uncertainty in Human Decision-Making," *Science* 310, no. 5754 (December 9, 2005): 1680–83, http://www.sciencemag.org/cgi/content/abstract/310/5754/1680.

249 **During his discussion of Tolstoy** Isaiah Berlin, "The Hedgehog and the Fox," in *Russian Thinkers*, eds. Henry Hardy and Aileen Kelly (New York: Penguin Books, 1978), 71–72.

CHAPTER 16: THE INSURGENCY

252 **Raymond led the group** David Rock, *Your Brain at Work: Strategies for Overcoming Distraction, Regaining Focus, and Working Smarter All Day Long* (New York: HarperCollins, 2009), 49.

253 **Michael Falkenstein** Gerald Traufetter, "Have Scientists Discovered Intuition?" *Der Spiegel*, September 21, 2007, http://www.spiegel.de/international/world/0,1518,507176,00.html.

253 **Patrick Rabbitt** Patrick Rabbitt, "Detection of Errors by Skilled Typists," *Ergonomics* 21, no. 11 (November 1978): 945–58, http://www.informaworld.com/smpp/content~db=all~content=a777698565.

254 **change doubtful answers** Joseph T. Hallinan, *Why We Make Mistakes: How We Look Without Seeing, Forget Things in Seconds, and Are All Pretty Sure We Are Way Above Average* (New York: Broadway Books, 2009), 53.

254 **"Peter Drucker said"** Peter F. Drucker, *The Essential Drucker: In One Volume the Best of Sixty Years of Peter Drucker's Essential Writings on Management* (New York: HarperCollins, 2001), 127.

259 **"Koch was not one"** Drucker, 218.

260 **Wason selection task** David Moshman and Molly Geil, "Collaborative Reasoning, Evidence for Collective Rationality," *Thinking and Reasoning* 4, no. 3 (July 1998): 231–48, http://digitalcommons.unl.edu/cgi/viewcontent.cgi?article=1053&context=edpsychpapers.

CHAPTER 17: GETTING OLDER

263 **UN data drawn** Helen Fisher, "The Drive to Love: The Neural Mechanism for Mate Selection," in *The New Psychology of Love*, eds. Robert J. Sternberg and Karin Sternberg (New Haven, CT: Yale University Press, 2006), 105.

263 **Louann Brizendine** Louann Brizendine, *The Female Brain* (New York: Broadway Books, 2006), 136–37.

264 **"the art of being wise"** William James, *The Principles of Psychology*, vol. 2, Chap. 22.

265 **Marriage expert John Gottman** John Gottman, *Why Marriages Succeed or Fail: And How You Can Make Yours Last* (New York: Fireside, 1995), 57.

266 **loneliness loop** John Cacioppo and William Patrick, *Loneliness: Human Nature and the Need for Social Connection* (New York: W.W. Norton & Company, 2008), 170.

267 **more than 65 percent** Brizendine, 147.

270 **Alcoholics Anonymous doesn't work** Brendan L. Koerner, "Secret of AA: After 75 Years, We Don't Know How It Works," *Wired*, June 23, 2010, http://www.wired.com/magazine/2010/06/ff_alcoholics_anonymous/.

CHAPTER 18: MORALITY

281 **Jonathan Haidt** Jonathan Haidt, "What Makes People Vote Republican," *Edge*, September 9, 2008, http://www.edge.org/3rd_culture/haidt08/haidt08_index.html.

281 **As Haidt has shown** Jonathan Haidt, *The Happiness Hypothesis: Finding Modern Truth in Ancient Wisdom* (New York: Basic Books, 2006), 20–21.

281 **"It has been hard to find"** Michael S. Gazzaniga, *Human: The Science Behind What Makes Us Unique* (New York: Harper Perennial, 2008), 148.

281 **Psychopaths do not seem** Jonah Lehrer, *How We Decide* (New York: Houghton Mifflin Co., 2009), 15.

281 **Research on wife batterers** Lehrer, 170.

282 **Behavior does not exhibit** Kwame Anthony Appiah, *Experiments in Ethics* (Cambridge, MA: Harvard University Press, 2008), 40–41.

283 **"I finished him off"** Jean Hatzfield, *Machete Season: The Killers in Rwanda Speak*, trans. Linda Coverdale (New York: Farrar, Straus & Giroux, 2003), 24.

283 **rats were trained to press** Paul Bloom, *Descartes' Baby: How the Science of Child Development Explains What Makes Us Human* (New York: Basic Books, 2004), 114.

283 **Chimps console each other** Bloom, 122.

284 **People yawn when they see** Liz Seward, "Contagious Yawn 'Sign of Empathy,' " BBC, September 10, 2007, http://news.bbc.co.uk/2/hi/science/nature/6988155.stm.

284 **"When we see a stroke"** Adam Smith, *The Theory of Moral Sentiments* (New York: Cosimo, 2007), 2.

284 **"Nature, when she formed"** Smith, 118.

284 **rudimentary sense of justice** J. Kiley Hamlin, Karen Wynn, and Paul Bloom, "Social Evaluation by Preverbal Infants," *Nature* 450 (November 22, 2007): 557–59, http://www.nature.com/nature/journal/v450/n7169/abs/nature06288.html.

285 **James Q. Wilson argued** James Q. Wilson, *The Moral Sense* (New York: Free Press, 1997), 142.

285 **Max Planck Institute for Psycholinguistics** J. J. A. Van Berkum et al., "Right or Wrong? The Brain's Fast Response to Morally Objectional Statements," *Psychological Science* 20 (2009): 1092–99, http://coreservice.mpdl.mpg.de/ir/item/escidoc:57437/components/component/escidoc:95157/content.

286 **"He who made us"** Marc D. Hauser, *Moral Minds: The Nature of Right and Wrong* (New York: Harper Perennial, 2006), 60–61.

286 **Just as different cultures** Jonathan Haidt and Craig Joseph, "The Moral Mind: How 5 Sets of Innate Moral Intuitions Guide the Development of Many Culture-Specific Virtues, and Perhaps Even Modules," in *The Innate Mind*, eds. P. Carruthers, S. Laurence, and S. Stich (New York: Oxford, 2007), 367–91, and Jonathan Haidt and Jesse Graham, "When Morality Opposes Justice: Conservatives Have Moral Intuitions That Liberals May Not Recognize," *Social Science Research* 20, no. 1 (March 2007): 98–116.

287 **Human societies have their** Jesse Graham, Jonathan Haidt, and Brian Nosek, "Liberals and Conservatives Use Different Sets of Moral Foundations," *Journal of Personality and Social Psychology* 96, no. 5 (May 2009): 1029–46, http://www.ncbi.nlm.nih.gov/pubmed/19379034.

287 **Hitler's sweater** Hauser, 199.

287 **People can distinguish between** Kyle G. Ratner and David M. Amodio, "N170 Responses to Faces Predict Implicit In-Group Favoritism: Evidence from a Minimal Group Study," Social & Affective Neuroscience Society Annual Meeting, October 10, 2009, http://www.wjh.harvard.edu/~scanlab/SANS/docs/SANS_program_2009.pdf.

287 **The anterior cingulated cortices** Xiaojing Xu, Xiangyu Zuo, Xiaoying Wang, and Shihui Han, "Do You Feel My Pain? Racial Group Membership Modulates Empathic Neural Responses," *Journal of Neuroscience* 29, no. 26 (July 1, 2009): 8525–29, http://www.jneurosci.org/cgi/content/short/29/26/8525.

289 **"In taking delivery"** Hugh Helco, *On Thinking Institutionally* (Boulder, CO: Paradigm Publishers, 2008), 98.

289 **"I was in awe every time"** Ryne Sandberg, Induction Speech, National Baseball Hall of Fame and Museum, July 31, 2005, http://baseballhall.org/node/11299.

290 **But in crucial moments** Joshua D. Greene, "Does Moral Action Depend on Reason-

ing?" *Big Questions Essay Series*, John Templeton Foundation, April 2010, http://www
.templeton.org/reason/Essays/greene.pdf.

291 **"She's not a dog"** Appiah, 160.

291 **"I am grateful that fate"** Viktor Emil Frankl, *Man's Search for Meaning* (Boston, MA:
Beacon Press, 1992), 78.

292 **philosopher Jean Bethke Elshtain** Jean B. Elshtain, "Neither Victims Nor Heroes: Reflections from a Polio Person," in *Philosophical Reflections on Disability*, eds. Christopher
D. Ralston and Justin Ho (New York: Springer, 2009), 241–50.

CHAPTER 19: THE LEADER

302 **Few people switch parties** Donald Green, Bradley Palmquist, and Eric Schickler, *Partisan Hearts and Minds: Political Parties and the Social Identity of Voters* (New Haven, CT:
Yale University Press, 2002), 12.

302 **People have stereotypes** Green, Palmquist, and Schickler, 4.

303 **Party affiliation often shapes** Paul Goren, Christopher M. Federico, and Miki Caul
Kittilson, "Source Cues, Partisan Identities, and Political Value Expression," *American
Journal of Political Science* 53, no. 4 (2009): 805–820, http://www3.interscience.wiley
.com/journal/122602945/abstract?CRETRY=1&SRETRY=0.

303 **A partisan filters out** Angus Campbell, Philip E. Converse, Warren E. Miller, and Donald E. Stokes, *The American Voter* (Chicago, IL: University of Chicago Press, 1980).

303 **Bartels concludes that** Larry M. Bartels, "Beyond the Running Tally: Partisan Bias in
Political Perceptions," *Political Behavior* 24, no. 2 (June 2002): 117–150, http://
www.uvm.edu/~dguber/POLS234/articles/bartels.pdf.

304 **Charles Taber and Milton Lodge** Joseph T. Hallinan, *Why We Make Mistakes: How We
Look Without Seeing, Forget Things in Seconds, and Are All Pretty Sure We Are Way Above
Average* (New York: Broadway Books, 2009), 44–45.

304 **The candidate who was perceived** Joe Keohane, "How Facts Backfire," *Boston Globe*,
July 11, 2010, http://www.boston.com/bostonglobe/ideas/articles/2010/07/11/how_facts
_backfire/.

304 **ten-second silent video clips** Daniel Benjamin and Jesse Shapiro, "Thin-Slice Forecasts
of Gubernatorial Elections, *Review of Economics and Statistics* 91, no. 3 (2009): 523–26,
http://www.arts.cornell.edu/econ/dbenjamin/thinslice022908.pdf.

305 **location of a voting booth** Jonah Berger, Marc Meredith, and S. Christian Wheeler,
"Contextual Priming: Where People Vote Affects How They Vote," *Proceedings of the
National Academy of Sciences* 105, no. 26 (July 1, 2008): 8846–49, http://www.sas
.upenn.edu/~marcmere/workingpapers/ContextualPriming.pdf.

307 **The event was stupid** Ran R. Hassin, Melissa J. Ferguson, Daniella Shidlovski, and
Tamar Gross, "Subliminal Exposure to National Flags Affects Political Thought and Behavior," *Proceedings of the National Academy of the Sciences* 104, no. 50 (December 2007):
19757–61, http://www.pnas.org/content/104/50/19757.abstract.

CHAPTER 20: THE SOFT SIDE

315 **The individualism of the left** Mark Lilla, "A Tale of Two Reactions," *New York Review
of Books*, May 1998, http://www.nybooks.com/articles/archives/1998/may/14/a-tale-of
-two-reactions/.

317 **8 percent of students** William G. Bowen, Martin Kurzweil, and Eugene Tobin, *Equity
and Excellence in American Higher Education* (Charlottesville, VA: University of Virginia
Press, 2005), 91.

318 **In Britain you wound up** "Britain is 'surveillance society,' " BBC, November 2, 2006,
http://news.bbc.co.uk/2/hi/uk_news/6108496.stm.

318   **"Look at the society"** Phillip Blond, "Rise of the Red Tories," *Prospect*, February 28, 2009, http://www.prospectmagazine.co.uk/2009/02/riseoftheredtories/.

320   **"At root, in almost every"** James Q. Wilson, "The Rediscovery of Character: Private Virtue and Public Policy," *The Public Interest* 81 (Fall 1985): 3–16, http://www.nationalaffairs.com/public_interest/detail/the-rediscovery-of-character-private-virtue-and-public-policy.

320   **"The spiritual nature of man"** Clinton Rossiter, *Conservatism in America* (Cambridge, MA: Harvard University Press, 1982), 43.

321   **"The central conservative truth"** Lawrence E. Harrison, *The Central Liberal Truth: How Politics Can Change a Culture and Save It from Itself* (Cambridge: Oxford University Press, 2006), xvi.

323   **75 percent of the anti-Western** Marc Sageman, *Understanding Terror Networks* (Philadelphia, PA: University of Pennsylvania Press, 2004), 73–75.

323   **Olivier Roy argues** Olivier Roy, *Globalized Islam: The Search for a New Ummah* (New York: Columbia University Press, 2004).

324   **Harold pointed out** David Brooks, "The Wisdom We Need to Fight AIDS," *New York Times*, June 12, 2005, http://www.nytimes.com/2005/06/12/opinion/12brooks.html.

324   **a hospital in Namibia** David Brooks, "In Africa, Life After AIDS," *New York Times*, June 9, 2005, http://www.nytimes.com/2005/06/09/opinion/09brooks.html.

325   **So the market had partially** David Brooks, "This Old House," *New York Times*, December 9, 2008, http://www.nytimes.com/2008/12/09/opinion/09brooks.html.

326   **U.S. Bureau of Labor Statistics** Daniel Drezner, "The BLS Weighs in on Outsourcing," DanielDrezner.com, June 10, 2004, http://www.danieldrezner.com/archives/001365.html and "Extended Mass Layoffs Associated with Domestic and Overseas Relocations, First Quarter 2004 Summary," Bureau of Labor Statistics Press Release, June 10, 2004, http://www.bls.gov/news.release/reloc.nro.htm.

326   **Pankaj Ghemawat** Pankaj Ghemawat, "Why the World Isn't Flat," *Foreign Policy*, February 14, 2007, http://www.foreignpolicy.com/articles/2007/02/14/why_the_world_isnt_flat?page=full.

327   **The median person** Ron Haskins and Isabel Sawhill, *Creating an Opportunity Society* (Washington, DC: Brookings Institution Press, 2009), 127.

327   **A child born into** Ross Douthat, "Does Meritocracy Work?" *The Atlantic*, November 2005, http://www.theatlantic.com/magazine/archive/2005/11/does-meritocracy-work/4305/.

327   **Anthony Carnevale and Stephen Rose** Douthat, "Does Meritocracy Work?"

328   **Public-education spending** Eric Hanushek, "Milton Friedman's Unfinished Business," *Hoover Digest*, Winter 2007, http://edpro.stanford.edu/hanushek/admin/pages/files/uploads/friedmanhoover_digest.pdf.

328   **A mother with two kids** Haskins and Sawhill, 46.

328   **If you read part** Margaret Bridges, Bruce Fuller, Russell Rumberger, and Loan Tran, "Preschool for California's Children: Unequal Access, Promising Benefits," PACE Child Development Projects, University of California Linguistic Minority Research Institute (September 2004): 9, http://gse.berkeley.edu/research/pace/reports/PB.04-3.pdf.

329   **About half the students** Haskins and Sawhill, 223.

329   **Isabel Sawhill has calculated** Haskins and Sawhill, 42.

329   **If you get married before** Haskins and Sawhill, 70.

330   **Wilkinson and Pickett point** Richard Wilkinson and Kate Pickett, *The Spirit Level: Why Greater Equality Makes Societies Stronger* (London: Bloomsbury Press, 2009), 75

331   **"Low-income families"** Haskins and Sawhill, 101.

331   **As James Heckman argues** James Heckman and Dimitriy V. Masterov, "The Productivity Argument for Investing in Young Children," Invest in Kids Working Group, Com-

mittee for Economic Development, Working Paper 5 (October 4, 2004): 3, http://jenni.uchicago.edu/Invest/FILES/dugger_2004-12-02_dvm.pdf.

331 **But social and emotional skills** Heckman and Masterov, 28–35.

331 **Small classes may be better** Malcolm Gladwell, "Most Likely to Succeed," *The New Yorker*, December 15, 2008, http://www.newyorker.com/reporting/2008/12/15/081215 fa_fact_gladwell.

332 **The City University of New York** Marc Santora, "CUNY Plans New Approach to Community College," *New York Times*, January 26, 2009, http://www.nytimes .com/2009/01/26/education/26college.html?fta=y.

333 **"Every new scene"** Alexander Hamilton, "Report on Manufactures," December 5, 1791, University of Chicago Press, *The Founders' Constitution*, http://press-pubs.uchicago.edu/founders/documents/v1ch4s31.html.

333 **He believed in using government** Ron Chernow, *Alexander Hamilton* (New York: Penguin Press, 2004).

334 **"I hold the value of life"** Abraham Lincoln, Speech to Germans in Cincinnati, Ohio, February 12, 1861, *Collected Works of Abraham Lincoln*, vol. 4 (Piscataway, NJ: Rutgers University Press, 1990), 203.

334 **"The true function of the state"** Theodore Roosevelt, "Social Evolution," in *American Ideals, and Other Essays, Social and Political*, vol. 2 (New York: G.P. Putnam's Sons, 1907), 154.

335 **"In political activity"** Michael Oakeshott, "Political Education," in *Rationalism in Politics and Other Essays* (London: Methuen, 1977), 127.

335 **Milton wrote *Paradise Lost*** Thomas Sowell, *Marxism: Philosophy and Economics* (London: George Allen & Unwin, Ltd., 1985), 14.

CHAPTER 21: THE OTHER EDUCATION

339 **the muscles around the jaw** Atul Gawande, "The Way We Age Now," *The New Yorker*, April 30, 2007, http://www.newyorker.com/reporting/2007/04/30/070430fa_fact _gawande.

339 **40 percent end up** Gawande, "The Way We Age Now."

339 **While many neurons die** Patricia A. Reuter-Lorenz and Cindy Lustig, "Brain Aging: Reorganizing Discoveries About the Aging Mind," *Current Opinion in Neurobiology* 15 (2005): 245–51, http://www.bus.umich.edu/neuroacrp/Yoon/ReuterLorenzLustig2005 .pdf.

340 **air traffic controllers** Louis Cozolino, *The Healthy Aging Brain: Sustaining Attachment, Attaining Wisdom* (New York: W.W. Norton & Co., 2008), 172.

340 **Laura Carstensen** Stephen S. Hall, "The Older-and-Wiser Hypothesis," *New York Times*, May 6, 2007, http://www.nytimes.com/2007/05/06/magazine/06Wisdom-t.html.

340 **John Gabrieli of MIT** Hall, "The Older-and-Wiser Hypothesis."

340 **Norma Haan of Berkeley** Norma Haan, Elizabeth Hartka, and Roger Millsap, "As Time Goes By: Change and Stability in Personality Over Fifty Years," *Psychology and Aging* 1, no. 3 (1986): 220–32, http://www.psych.illinois.edu/~broberts/Haan%20et %20al,%201986.pdf.

340 **People achieve a level** George Vaillant, *Aging Well: Surprising Guideposts to a Happier Life from the Landmark Harvard Study of Adult Development* (New York: Little, Brown & Co., 2002), 254.

341 **"By the time we reach"** Andrew Newberg and Mark Robert Waldman, *Why We Believe What We Believe: Uncovering Our Biological Need for Meaning, Spirituality, and Truth* (New York: Free Press, 2006), 211–212.

341 **The Grant Longitudinal Study** Vaillant, 99–100.

344 "One of my teachers compares" Daniel J. Siegel, *The Mindful Brain: Reflection and Attunement in the Cultivation of Well-Being* (New York: W.W. Norton & Co., Inc., 2007), 62.

344 "But gradually your eyes" Siegel, 159.

345 Tibetan monks or Catholic nuns Andrew Newberg and Mark Robert Waldman, *Born to Believe: God, Science, and the Origin of Ordinary and Extraordinary Beliefs* (New York: Free Press, 2006), 175.

345 "In the Pentecostal tradition" Newberg and Waldman, *Why We Believe What We Believe*, 203–205.

347 philosopher Roger Scruton Roger Scruton, *Culture Counts: Faith and Feeling in a Besieged World* (New York: Encounter Books, 2007), 41.

348 "Mine is no callous shell" Walt Whitman, *Leaves of Grass* (New York: Penguin Books, 1986), 53.

349 "While human nature largely" Jonah Lehrer, *Proust Was a Neuroscientist* (New York: Houghton Mifflin Co., 2007), 140.

349 Some scientists believe that Michael S. Gazzaniga, *Human: The Science Behind What Makes Us Unique* (New York: Harper Perennial, 2008), 210.

349 As Daniel Levitin observes Daniel J. Levitin, *This Is Your Brain on Music: The Science of a Human Obsession* (New York: Dutton, 2006), 116.

349 Leonard Meyer showed Leonard Meyer, *Emotion and Meaning in Music* (Chicago, IL: University of Chicago Press, 1961).

350 Depending on lighting Semir Zeki, *Splendors and Miseries of the Brain: Love, Creativity, and the Quest for Human Happiness* (Malden, MA: Wiley-Blackwell, 2009), 29.

350 "Our perception of the world" Chris Frith, *Making Up the Mind: How the Brain Creates Our Mental World* (Malden, MA: Blackwell Publishing, 2007), 111.

350 They like lush open grasses Denis Dutton, *The Art Instinct: Beauty, Pleasure, and Human Evolution* (New York: Bloomsbury Press, 2009), 17–19.

351 people like fractals Gazzaniga, 229.

351 Humans generally prefer patterns Gazzaniga, 230.

351 "a book club that meets" Gene D. Cohen, *The Mature Mind: The Positive Power of the Aging Brain* (New York: Basic Books, 2005), 148.

352 He wanted to change Lehrer, 87.

352 "I went on with the conversation" Nancy C. Andreasen, *The Creative Brain: The Science of Genius* (New York: Plume, 2006), 44.

352 "An idea will come" Guy Claxton, *Hare Brain, Tortoise Mind: How Intelligence Increases When You Think Less* (New York: Harper Perennial, 2000), 60.

354 People with college degrees Cozolino, 28.

354 People with larger vocabularies Cozolino, 29–30.

354 seniors who participate in arts Cohen, 178.

354 Malcolm Gladwell wrote Malcolm Gladwell, "Late Bloomers," *The New Yorker*, October 20, 2008, http://www.newyorker.com/reporting/2008/10/20/081020fa_fact_gladwell.

354 "A sense of isolation" Kenneth Clark, "The Artist Grows Old," *Daedalus* 135, no. 1 (Winter 2006): 87, http://mitpress.mit.edu/journals/pdf/Clark_77_90.pdf.

355 "We pass on culture" Scruton, 44.

357 "Man may rise" Kenneth S. Clark, *Civilization: A Personal View* (New York: Harper & Row, 1969), 60.

359 The cathedrals were not Michael Ward, "C. S. Lewis and the Star of Bethlehem," *Books & Culture*, January–February 2008, http://www.booksandculture.com/articles/2008/janfeb/15.30.html.

CHAPTER 22: MEANING

364   **"He would have to say"** Lydia Davis, "Happiest Moment," in *Samuel Johnson Is Indignant* (New York: Picador, 2002), 50.

365   **sunlight and natural scenes** Esther M. Sternberg, *Healing Spaces: The Science of Place and Well-Being* (Cambridge, MA: Belknap Press, 2009), 49.

366   **a study done in Milan** Sternberg, 50.

366   **"Nature draws us because"** Charles Taylor, *Sources of the Self: The Making of the Modern Identity* (Cambridge: University of Cambridge Press, 2006), 297.

367   **psychologist Ellen Langer** Jennifer Ruark, "The Art of Living Mindfully," *The Chronicle of Higher Education*, January 3, 2010, http://chronicle.com/article/The-Art-of-Living-Mindfully/63292/.

368   **"reminiscence bump"** Daniel L. Schacter, *Searching For Memory: The Brain, The Mind, and the Past* (New York: Basic Books, 1996), 298.

368   **He simply could not remember** George E. Vaillant, *Aging Well: Surprising Guideposts to a Happier Life from the Landmark Harvard Study of Adult Development* (New York: Little, Brown & Co., 2002), 31.

368   **But at age seventy** Vaillant, 10–11.

368   **"How pleasant is the day"** Louis Cozolino, *The Healthy Aging Brain: Sustaining Attachment, Attaining Wisdom* (New York: W.W. Norton & Co., 2008), 188.

369   **"Man's search for meaning"** Viktor Emil Frankl, *Man's Search for Meaning* (Boston, MA: Beacon Press, 1992), 105.

369   **"He who has a *why*"** Frankl, 84.

369   **"We had to learn ourselves"** Frankl, 85.

369   **Erving Goffman argues** Erving Goffman, *The Presentation of Self in Everyday Life* (New York: Anchor Books, 1962).

369   **there are no simple progressions** Roy F. Baumeister, *The Cultural Animal: Human Nature, Meaning, and Social Life* (Oxford: Oxford University Press, 2005), 167.

370   **"We can never"** Immanuel Kant, "Fundamental Principles of the Metaphysics of Morals," *Basic Writings of Kant*, ed. Allan Wood (New York: Random House, 2001), 165.

370   **Numerous studies have shown** Timothy D. Wilson, *Strangers to Ourselves* (Cambridge, MA: Belknap Press, 2002), 84.

370   **Dan McAdams writes** Dan P. McAdams, *The Redemptive Self: Stories Americans Live By* (Oxford: Oxford University Press, 2006).

371   **rumination made depressed people** Wilson, 175–76.

371   **"How pathetically scanty"** Steven Johnson, *Mind Wide Open: Your Brain and the Neuroscience of Everyday Life* (New York: Simon & Schuster, 2004), 1.

INDEX

DAVID BROOKS is one of the nation's leading writers and commentators. He is an op-ed column for *The New York Times* and appears regularly on *PBS NewsHour* and *Meet the Press*. He is the bestselling author of *The Second Mountain: The Quest for a Moral Life*; *The Road to Character*; *The Social Animal: The Hidden Sources of Love, Character, and Achievement*; *Bobos in Paradise: The New Upper Class and How They Got There*; and *On Paradise Drive: How We Live Now (And Always Have) in the Future Tense*.